D0079287

Public Affairs Reporting

Covering the News in the Information Age

PUBLIC AFFAIRS
REPORTING

Covering the News
in the
Information Age

George M. Killenberg
University of South Florida—St. Petersburg

ST. MARTIN'S PRESS
New York

Editor: Cathy Pusateri
Managing editor: Patricia Mansfield
Project editor: Cheryl Friedman
Production supervisor: Katherine Battiste
Text design: Leon Bolognese & Associates, Inc.
Photo researcher: Inge King
Cover design: John Jeheber

Library of Congress Catalog Card Number: 90-71637
Copyright © 1992 by St. Martin's Press, Inc.
All rights reserved. No part of this book may be reproduced,
stored in a retrieval system, or transmitted by any form or
by any means, electronic, mechanical, photocopying, recording,
or otherwise, except as may be expressly permitted by the applicable
copyright statutes or in writing by the Publisher.
Manufactured in the United States of America.
65432
fedcba

For information, write:
St. Martin's Press, Inc.
175 Fifth Avenue
New York, NY 10010

ISBN: 0-312-03637-X

 The text of this book has been printed on recycled paper.

TO GEORGE A. KILLENBERG

my father and
my first editor

AND TO THERESE M. KILLENBERG

my mother and
my first teacher

Preface

At the core of nearly all accredited journalism programs is a course in public affairs reporting. Students may aspire to write for *Sports Illustrated* or to direct corporate communications for AT&T, but they must first learn about covering city hall, the courthouse and the police beat, among other areas of public affairs. Some students find public affairs reporting exceedingly dull and unglamorous, assuming the job mainly entails spending evenings at school board or city council meetings. It is not what they seek as a career. So they sleepwalk through the course only to be awakened the first day on the job—at a newspaper of all places—when the city editor says, "Greg, go down to the federal building and check into the Plaza Hotel's Chapter 11 filing."

Public affairs reporting *is* the staple of American journalism, and stories that qualify as public affairs often dominate the news. The headlines reflect the scope and importance of the field:

Court Ruling Allows Death with Dignity

Banker Accused of Laundering Drug Money

Health Officials Issue Warning on Radon Gas Readings

Senate Kills Bill for Catastrophic-Illness Insurance

This is hardly dull stuff, and a reporter a few months out of journalism school may be called upon to cover comparable stories—to make sense of a world that is becoming increasingly difficult to understand.

More than ever before, people rely on the news media for warnings, explanations and insights. The profession—and society—

cannot afford lazy, inept, uncommitted journalists. Today's reporters must learn how to cover public affairs intelligently and thoroughly. First they must learn about the institutions and people who influence the news; understanding how a legislative conference committee functions or how a trial is conducted remain important prerequisites. But it is not enough merely to know how to report. Journalists must also understand how they see, define and *influence* the news.

Public Affairs Reporting: Covering the News in the Information Age is intended to help prepare women and men for the challenges of journalism in the 21st century. On one level, the book is a practical, example-laden guide to the traditional beats of public affairs. On another level, it examines how public affairs reporters go about their work, with attention given to the implications and consequences of their behavior. As a result, emphasis is placed on multicultural perspectives, interpersonal competence and ethical issues. Students, however, should view the book as a departure point, not a comprehensive set of instructions. The best reporters never stop learning and discovering new things about themselves and others.

Public Affairs Reporting is based, in part, on what I have learned in 15 years of teaching students about courts, politics, law enforcement, education, business and government. My students have gone into the cellblock to interview inmates at the county jail; watched F. Lee Bailey argue a motion in a murder-for-insurance case; participated in a press briefing held a few hours after a major drug bust; questioned the state attorney general in his conference room; and listened to a police chief tell them how to be "good" reporters.

Few books are solitary efforts; in this instance, dozens of people helped with ideas, criticism and editing. A longtime colleague and collaborator on writing projects, Rob Anderson, professor of speech communication at Southern Illinois University at Edwardsville, read and edited every chapter. His comments and suggestions enabled me to recognize missing ingredients and find solutions to organizational or writing problems. His contributions were substantial.

My father, George A. Killenberg, former executive editor of the *St. Louis Globe–Democrat,* taught me about humanistic reporting long before that term became popular. His philosophy of news has guided me as a journalist and a teacher of journalism. His contributions to this book began when I was old enough to appreciate his wisdom. More directly and immediately, he carefully critiqued each chapter, offering concrete examples and pointing out flabby prose or faulty reasoning. Most of all he encouraged me to believe that *Public Affairs Reporting* had something important to say to both students and working professionals.

My colleagues at the University of South Florida and associates in journalism and law also read and commented on various chapters. I thank Tim Reilly and Cecil Greek, professors of criminology; Darryl Paulson, professor of political science; Donna L. Dickerson, professor of mass communications; Judge Anthony Rondolino of the Pinellas County circuit court; Kyle Parks, business news editor of the *St. Petersburg Times*; Jo A. Cates, chief librarian at the Poynter Institute for Media Studies; and Lauretta Johnston, who furnished the student perspective along with dozens of useful tips.

Cathy Pusateri, communication editor at St. Martin's Press, provided support, encouragement and thoughtful analysis of the manuscript as it evolved into a book. Her editing touch is light, but adroit. Cheryl Friedman, the project editor, transformed a plain manuscript into a well-edited, attractively designed book and provided well-timed words of encouragement along the way. The reviewers enlisted by St. Martin's offered suggestions that improved the flow, content and format. Those reviewers are Michael E. Abrams, Florida A&M University; Mary Painter Bohlen, Sangamon State University; Robert K. Daly, Kansas State University; Mike Masterson, Director, Kiplinger Public Affairs Reporting Program, Ohio State University; William McCorkle, Baylor University; and Roger V. Wetherington, California State University, Long Beach.

Finally, I thank my family—Penny, my wife, and our children, Andrew, Kristen, Anne and Mark. They put up with my long hours at the office, weekend writing binges and mood swings as the book and I grappled. I know I missed much of what was going on in our household over the past two years; I am grateful that they continued to give of themselves, allowing me to be self-indulgent in putting my needs before theirs.

GEORGE M. KILLENBERG

Contents

Public Affairs Reporting

Covering the News in the Information Age

Chapter One

A news reporter conducts an interview in New York City. (Mike Kagan/Monkmeyer)

The Roles
and Realities
of Reporting

On a raw winter night in 1899, an 18-year-old reporter named H.L. Mencken struggled to compose what was to be his first published news story—a minor item from police records. "I wrote and tore up, wrote and tore up," Mencken later recounted in *Newspaper Days*. "Finally there emerged the following:"

> A horse, buggy and several sets of harnesses, valued in all at about $250, were stolen last night from the stable of Howard Quinlan, near Kingsville. The county police are at work on the case, but so far no trace of either thieves or booty has been found.[1]

Following a path familiar to generations of journalists, Mencken apprenticed on the police beat, eventually moving on to other areas of public affairs reporting. He also wrote more than 30 books and collections of essays and reported on the American political scene for nearly a half century. Despite recent criticism focusing on Mencken's anti-Semitic statements, journalists in the 1990s still admire his style and craftsmanship.

Mencken, no doubt, would admire their work, too, recognizing that the world reporters now cover is vastly more dangerous, complex and ambiguous than the one he knew. The realities of reporting have changed, and so have the reporter's roles. In a few short decades, gang violence displaced stickball on city streets. Silicon Valley supplanted the factory town. And technicians, wearing protective suits against dangerous wastes, took over jobs the garbage collectors once handled. The reporter's working knowledge came to include "crack," microcircuitry and Agent Orange, as the problems and the complexities of urban life spilled over into suburban and small-town America.

Today most Americans, seldom by preference, lead an existence characterized by Big Macs served at the drive-through window instead of leisurely meals enjoyed around the dining-room table. "Haven't got time for the pain" says an advertisement, appealing to those so bent on success they cannot allow a headache to slow them down. Life rushes on, but who can budget an hour or two for the week's grocery shopping, much less fit in a meeting of the school board or the city council? In an increasingly confusing, troubling world, people depend on journalists to discover and report news of import in their lives. While Bob and Sue Jenkins run errands, the school board is debating whether a 9-year-old carrying the AIDS virus will attend class with 25 other third-graders, among them the Jenkins' daughter, Mary. Across town, lawyers for a huge waste-hauling corporation pressure the city council to double the size of the municipal landfill. Beyond reporting these stories—and stories on water rates, revenue bonds and purse snatchings—journalists are expected to scan the horizon, alert for signs of tomorrow's emerging news. It is a challenging, serious calling that requires astute, sensitive and, above all, responsible practitioners.

A REPORTER'S REALITY

Skill at the mechanics of reporting is not enough to do the job well. Journalists must also understand the processes by which they see, define, convey and, indeed, influence that churning mass of information known as "news." By understanding these processes, reporters can recognize their own limitations and weaknesses. Journalists enjoy no special ability to discover the truth or achieve objectivity, says professor James Carey. "The press," he says, "should not present itself as seer, but simply as doing the best it can to figure out today what is going on."[2] As Carey suggests, reporters must resist being lulled into a false sense of security or smugness over their powers to detect and verify news.

To come to grips with the implications of their work, reporters should begin with a careful examination of their own attitudes, values and experiences. Reporters who take time to understand themselves can better observe and analyze events and people. In an enduring passage written more than 60 years ago, journalist and commentator Walter Lippmann described how people generally perceive the world: "For the most part we do not first see and then define; we define first and then see. In the great blooming, buzzing confusion of the outer world we pick out what our culture has already defined for us."[3] Lippmann's words refer to a process known as *socialization*—the way people come to accept the prevailing standards and attitudes of their culture. Socialization starts in childhood, and in its wake can be blind spots, biases and misconceptions.

By adulthood, fixed habits of association, lifestyle and belief combine to further influence what reporters see—or fail to see. Psychologist Mauricio Gaborit says people tend to attribute a higher probability to what they believe is typical, disregarding evidence that challenges their assumptions. "In general, we seek information that conforms to our prior knowledge, and often ignore outright any information that contradicts it."[4] The implications for journalists are clear. Although editors and reporters bring varied experiences and perspectives to their work, they tend to lead lives that are different and removed from those of many Americans. Occasional visits to places like a refinery, a veterans' hospital or a housing project might be necessary for reporters to expand—or renew—their views of "reality."

Jack Newfield of the *Village Voice* reminds journalists that socialization is a double-edged process of both seeing and being seen: "We all carry a variety of identities in our heads. I'm an only child and a poor kid from Bed-Stuy. I'm a graduate of a mostly black high school and of the City University—when it was still tuition-free. I'm a civil rights and antiwar activist from the 1960s, and a friend and biographer of Robert Kennedy. I'm a father and a husband; a democrat and a Jew; a muckraker and an empiricist. I cherish both Martin Luther King and Sugar Ray Robinson, so, please don't understand me too quickly."[5] On one hand, Newfield acknowledges his own socialization. But he also underscores how others might misread him if they fail to take the time and care necessary to see him clearly and fully. Reporters must try to understand others as well as understand themselves.

Journalists who recognize that news can be their—or someone else's—prejudiced, subjective, imperfect perceptions of reality will make efforts to compensate. A reporter who once marched with civil rights protesters will attempt to listen with an open mind to a Ku Klux Klan organizer; a reporter who golfs and reads John Le Carré mysteries will strive to understand the world as seen by the cab driver who bowls and buys the *National Enquirer* at the supermarket checkout lane; and a reporter whose news judgment sometimes is twisted by overconfidence or zeal will remember this admonition from a reader of the *Los Angeles Times:* "Get a grip on yourselves, guys, and do the best job you can, but don't suffer an identity crisis while doing it. Just try to spell the names right, get your facts straight and never forget that today's big story is tomorrow's birdcage carpet."[6]

A journalist's sense of "reality" may also be influenced by the patterned, predictable methods news organizations often employ to gather information. Sociologist Gaye Tuchman sees news as a "construction of reality"—a product of reporters' work routines and contact with sources.[7] When a government reporter, for example, relies heavily for stories and information from a handful of public officials, all within the physical and attitudinal confines of the city hall, news can become a narrow, slanted construction of reality. If "news" frequently is what sources *say,* and if those sources are predominantly people in authority positions—such as police officers and city council members—stories are not likely to reflect divergent opinions and present different, perhaps conflicting, accounts of reality.[8]

Building on Tuchman's theory, another sociologist, Mark Fishman, uses coverage of a "crime wave" against New York City's elderly to illustrate the concept of news as a self-fulfilling prophecy. Once legitimized as "news," the crime wave begat even more news, such as the mayor's vow to make the streets safe for the elderly. Crime-wave coverage dominated the news for weeks, despite police statistics revealing a decrease in crimes against the city's elderly compared with the previous year.[9]

The work of Tuchman and Fishman raises a question confronting all journalists: Does the press only report the news or does it sometimes manufacture it? While the term *construction of reality* hints of fabrication or fiction, reporters in New York City did not invent stories about rapes, murders or muggings of the elderly. But they did *selectively* concentrate on a particular variety of crime, and, in turn, "confirmed" the existence of a crime wave in the minds of politicians, police and the public. Certain stories—usually "happenings" like a hurricane or plane crash—are less subject to journalistic selectivity. But with many other stories, reporters, editors and news directors are free to define and prioritize the news. Of course, the press is expected to help set society's agenda. So when journalists target particular problems for attention, such as crime against the elderly, they perform a vital role of mobilizing public interest and action. In the process, however, journalists must regularly remind themselves of their power to determine what is "news"—and their duty to exercise that power responsibly.

Journalists also need to acknowledge that their power to learn and report the "truth" is limited. Truth is elusive, subjective and intangible; it is affected by many variables, among them the perspective, distance, emotional state and motives of those purporting to know the truth. A young man witnesses a police officer making an arrest. The witness passionately tells a reporter that the police officer, without provocation, grabbed the suspect and shoved him roughly into the patrol car. The account is the truth as he believes it. But consider the variables. The young man came around a corner to see the end of the arrest. He watched from 20 feet away, his view partially blocked by the officer's back. What he sees angers him, further impairing his view of the truth, because a few days before a traffic cop hassled him over a broken tail light. The young man believes cops enjoy hassling civilians. He is not lying, but his version is distorted and incomplete. The 1981 film *Absence of Malice* unfairly portrays the work of journalists, but it does contain a memorable line delivered by Paul Newman as he scolds a reporter: "You don't come across the truth that easily. Maybe it's just what you think. What you feel. Things aren't always what they seem."[10]

Truth can be hard to detect for other reasons. As *Newsday*'s Adrian Peracchio points out, "The facts are not necessarily truth." Reporters in stenographic fashion can collect detail after detail, figure after figure and quotation after quotation—all accurate—and still miss the truth, which remains hidden beneath a pile of "obvious" facts.[11] Had Carl Bernstein and Bob Woodward merely reported the obvious facts of the Watergate break-in, the story would have ended with a minor police-blotter report and not revealed a scandal that resulted in a president's resignation.

Sometimes, even the journalistic ideal of "objectivity" keeps reporters from the truth. "Objectivity may become the mere presentation of two sides of an issue in a way that distorts the proportionate importance of each," says Wesley G. Pippert, whose 30-year career with United Press International included coverage of the Watergate scandal. Pippert urges reporters to go beyond the obligatory "two-sides formula" and determine whose account suggests the "greater grasp of truth."[12]

While journalists should always pursue the truth, at times they must reluctantly and realistically settle on the best *obtainable* version of the truth. But truth seeking is what journalists are supposed to do, even if their best efforts sometimes fall short. British journalist Gerald Priestland offers these encouraging words: "Although we may never arrive at the central core of the truth, we must never foreclose on it or assume that the little progress we can make towards it is not worthwhile."[13]

A realistic understanding of journalism is at once humbling and reassuring. Rather than approach their work with certitude and bravado, realistic reporters try hard to analyze events, conduct research and detect biases—their own and those of their news subjects. They know the reward will not be perfection, but their efforts will bring them closer to the journalistic ideal of accurate, truthful, fair and meaningful news coverage.

THE EDUCATED REPORTER

Unlike lawyers or doctors, journalists are not required to demonstrate a level of competence or knowledge to gain a license to practice. Early in the history of American journalism, typical qualifications for the job of reporter were a high school diploma, street smarts and a gift for writing. In the 1870s Horace Greeley, founder and editor of the *New York Tribune,* told a bright-eyed college graduate hoping to be hired as a reporter, "I'd a damned sight rather you had graduated at a printer's case."[14] Greeley put more stock in a practical, informal education than in a degree. At the turn of the century, H.L. Mencken shunned college and "the balderdash of chalky pedagogues" to learn about life and journalism through self-education.

Modern journalists are not necessarily better educated than past generations, but they are largely college graduates—and many are products of journalism schools. Today most editors and educators would say a key prerequisite for a career in journalism is a sound, broadly based education. Professor Melvin Mencher says reporters need a full, regularly restocked storehouse of knowledge. "The good reporter," he observes, "is aware of the past and its relation to the present. . . . When a speaker refers to the New Deal, the reporter knows what he means."[15] The contents and size of each reporter's storehouse inevitably will vary. Above all, the educated reporter is a literate person, and, for the 1990s and beyond, that literacy spans knowledge of communication, culture and technology.

Communication Literacy

Literacy in the use and understanding of language is an obvious requirement for reporters. But communication literacy encompasses far more than the ability to craft graceful prose. It includes knowledge of the intricacies of human communication. Reporters spend much greater time talking and listening than they do writing. Yet, as one veteran educator says, the journalism student "strangely . . . gets little or no theory and practice in interviewing—probably the most important 'technique' which a journalist can have."[16] Deborah Tannen, author of *That's Not What I Meant!*, says an understanding of how language works "restores a sense of control over our lives, making it possible to improve communications and relationships in all the settings in which people talk to each other: at work, in interviews, in public affairs."[17]

Putting Tannen's observation in practical terms, the literate reporter is competent in the nonverbal, symbolic and psychological facets of language. Such competency is crucial if reporters are to comprehend fully and understand correctly. Grasping the "message" of a news subject's trembling voice, set jaw or raised eyebrow might be as important as recognizing a quotable comment. Proficiency in communication is not simply intuitive; communication between people is more complicated than most reporters realize. Journalists must develop a sensitivity to the needs and feelings of others and an understanding of the power of words, questions and other means of communication, including what anthropologist Edward T. Hall calls the "silent language" of behavior and cultural differences.[18] A reporter's ignorance of or indifference to verbal and nonverbal cues may well result in an unsatisfactory interview and a botched story.

Reporter Mary Jo Melone of the *St. Petersburg Times* encountered such subtleties in an interview with a gay activist who launched a 1988 recall movement that forced the resignation of Arizona's governor, Evan Mecham. Melone found herself preoccupied with the activist's homosexuality instead of concentrating on the recall movement and the subsequent smear campaign Mecham waged against the man: "Before I got to it (the recall experience), I asked him about AIDS. I even asked him about how the phenomenon of AIDS had changed his sex life. I'm not sure why I asked him these things. I did it all without thinking. Put another way, I did it by thinking like Evan Mecham. The rules are different for judging gay people, aren't they?"[19] The man answered her questions without outward signs of displeasure, but Melone recognized the flaws in her interviewing approach, admitting that she asked some "stupid" questions. How many reporters, though, never recognize the potency of language in their day-to-day communication? How many never recognize the damage done and opportunities lost? Reporters who appreciate and understand how language works can anticipate better interviews, keener perceptual power and ultimately more complete, more accurate stories.

Cultural Literacy

E.D. Hirsch Jr. created a stir when he suggested in his 1987 best seller, *Cultural Literacy*, that most Americans lack fundamental knowledge of history, politics, geography and the arts. Hirsch worried in particular about today's students. "They know a great deal," he said. "The trouble is that, from the standpoint of their literacy and ability to communicate with others in our culture, what they know is ephemeral and narrowly confined to their own generation."[20]

Presumably, young reporters, too, are deficient in intergenerational knowledge. In some instances, the gaps are painfully apparent, as journalism instructors know from grading stories riddled with gaffes like "Joan of Ark" and "Porky and Bess." The consequences of intergenerational ignorance, of course, are more serious than an occasional malaprop. A reporter, for example, cannot intelligently cover—much less analyze—a school integration case without knowing the significance of *Brown v. Board of Education.* And all reporters, male and female, should know about suffragists and Susan B. Anthony if they hope to interpret contemporary women's issues.

Although Hirsch deserves credit for illuminating a serious problem, some critics found his list of 5,000 essential names, dates, phrases and concepts too ethnocentric, too outdated, too mainstream or too short. In response, critics Rick Simonson and Scott Walker proposed a "multicultural literacy" to account for diversity in gender, race, age and nationality. As Simonson and Walker colorfully put it, "Though Hirsch's list does include 'penis envy,' 'macho,' and 'vasectomy,' he fails to find significant 'mastectomy,' 'gynecology,' or

'Georgia O'Keeffe.' Nor does he deem it important for culturally literate Americans to know about 'alcoholism,' 'internment camps,' 'Bhagavad Gita,' 'Pele,' 'rhythm and blues,' 'computer crash,' 'El Salvador,' or 'One Hundred Years of Solitude.' " The concept of America as a "melting pot" no longer applies, if it ever did. Differences and diversity in our society reflect a colorful, complex mosaic. "None of us," Simonson and Walker say, "can afford to remain ignorant of the heritage and culture of any part of our population."[21]

Cultural illiteracy sometimes leads to cultural insensitivity. Betty Friedan, a leader of the women's movement of the 1960s, admitted that at the age of 57 she failed to relate to a vast segment of society—the elderly. "I had the same view of aging as everyone else in America. You know: Poor things, dreary. Not me." Now she is an advocate for older citizens.[22] With reporting increasingly becoming the work of young people, sensitivity by the press to the problems and issues of aging is especially needed. Otherwise, reporters will continue to write stories peppered with patronizing stereotypes. Journalism teacher Carole Rich cites this feature lead from the *Arizona Daily Star:*

> This place hops. The food's tame, the dance steps slower than they used to be, the stiffest drink comes from the water fountain. Still, the Gray Crowd jams the Armory Park Senior Citizens Center. Typically, 1,200 men and women gather daily for gossip, games, and yes—even to cast some plain old-fashioned goo-goo eyes.

"The reporter who wrote that was 26 years old," Rich says. "Certainly, he was not going to help me feel positive about getting old."[23]

Cultural illiteracy can go beyond age, gender or ethnic insensitivities to result in serious deficiencies in news coverage. In her book *Cities on a Hill*, Pulitzer Prize–winning writer Frances FitzGerald examined four enclaves that reflect America's continuing cultural transformation—Rajneeshpuram, Ore., a town taken over by an Indian guru; Jerry Falwell's Liberty Baptist Church in Lynchburg, Va.; the Castro in San Francisco, one of the country's first gay neighborhoods; and Sun City, Fla., a retirement community whose residents, she says, are "pioneers on the frontier of age." FitzGerald believes each community heralded important societal changes that many journalists failed to detect immediately. The emergence of the Christian fundamentalist movement of the early 1980s illustrates her point. "That most journalists (myself included) knew nothing about fundamentalist theology even though Falwell and many others had been preaching it for a decade on national television suggested a blind spot. It suggested a gap in our education and a gap that had developed relatively recently."[24]

Problems compound when communication and cultural illiteracy intersect, as journalist Joan Didion recounts in her book, *Miami.* She describes how the *Miami Herald* clumsily marked the failed 1961 Bay of Pigs invasion. The Cuban exiles who fought and died to oust Fidel Castro and reclaim their homeland are remembered in Miami with pride and pain. According to Didion, "That the *Herald* should have run, on the 1985 anniversary of the Bay of Pigs, a story about Canadian and Italian tourists vacationing on what had been the invasion beaches (RESORT SELLS SUN, FUN—IN CUBA: TOPLESS BATHERS FROLIC AS HAVANA TRIES HAND AT TOURISM) was . . . not just a minor historical irony, not just an arguably insensitive attempt to find a news peg for a twenty-four-year-old story, but a calculated affront to the Cuban community."[25]

Calculated affront or not, the episode demonstrates the potential for harm to be inflicted by journalists who are insensitive to the feelings—and the heritage—of others. With technology, jet travel and immigration reducing the planet to what Marshall McLuhan called a "Global Village," journalism needs reporters who are fluent in the culture, language and history of other peoples, particularly blacks and two growing segments of the American population—Hispanics and Asians. U.S. Census Bureau figures put America's black population at 30 million in 1990, which amounted to 12 percent of the nation's total population of 249.6 million. The Hispanic population stood at 22.4 million (9 percent of the national total), a figure that marks an increase of 53 percent from the 1980 census. The Asian population grew even more dramatically, reaching 7.3 million in 1990—a 107 percent increase in a decade's time. At this rate of growth, whites from European backgrounds could become a minority in New Mexico and California by the year 2000.[26] As the nation becomes more ethnically diverse, reporters who are bilingual and multicultural will gain greater access to stories and news subjects; moreover, they will be less apt to misjudge or misinterpret.

Technological Literacy

With much information now stored in data banks, reporters who have not mastered the computer as a newsgathering tool face a serious disadvantage. Records and data that reporters once laboriously scoured now are available at a keystroke. Using modems to link computers, reporters can examine public documents, such as court rulings, without making a trip to the courthouse or county building.

The computer does more than speed and extend access to information; it enables reporters to analyze records more efficiently for meaning and patterns. Technology invites the press to monitor public affairs systematically through what is known as *precision reporting*. Instead of relying on anecdotal, impressionistic evidence, reporters can use census data, crime reports and court records to produce in-depth stories that are proactive—not merely reactive—accounts of events and issues. With precision-reporting methods, the validity of stories based on assumptions and theories, such as the crime wave described in Mark Fishman's study, are put to tougher, more valid tests of accuracy and completeness.

Computer-assisted reporting requires a degree of expectancy tempered by patience, but for reporters willing and able to pore over data, the reward can be substantial. When a federal agency sent the *Atlanta Journal* and *Constitution* seven computer tapes listing real estate loans made by the city's lending institutions, arrival of the data generated little excitement. But subjected to computer analysis, the tapes revealed that whites were five times as likely to be granted home loans in Atlanta as blacks in the same income bracket. Based on its analysis, the newspaper published a four-part series, "The Color of Money," that surprised Atlanta, a city that previously had touted its advances in race relations. The newsgathering potential of computers, says media consultant Tim Miller, is producing a new breed of "technoscribes" who are using information technology to extend and reinforce their reporting abilities.[27]

Computer skill, however, is just one aspect of technical literacy. A basic, up-to-date knowledge of science and technology is also needed. Without scientific-technical literacy people cannot make sound judgments about broad issues of human endeavor. If nothing else, technical illiteracy poses the risk that reporters may either dismiss or exaggerate the significance of developments. Journalism lore includes the apocryphal story of the big-city editor who decided that the 1957 launch of Sputnik, mankind's first artificial satellite, warranted no more than placement on page 10A. Technical developments played out over a period of time are much harder to spot and explain. Despite a brilliant career as foreign correspondent, A.M. Rosenthal was faulted by *New York Times* colleagues for missing the importance of Japan's technological revolution and its implications for the American economy.[28] With science and technology influencing modern life in so many ways—energy, environment and economics—reporters cannot afford to be technically illiterate or insensitive.

Reporters do not acquire *communication, cultural* and *technical literacy* through happenstance or casual encounters; it takes a determined, enthusiastic effort to grow in both knowledge and experience. Journalists of all ages and backgrounds who take their work seriously constantly *read* and *discover*. They relish a trip to a book store for browsing and buying. They enroll for courses in other disciplines, not simply to earn electives but to gain new perspectives. They travel for enjoyment and education, uninhibited and curious about sampling other cultures. They venture into the community to learn about others and themselves. Melvin Mencher, renowned for his teaching at Columbia University's School of Journalism, used two techniques to help his students grow—reading assignments from an array of publications and live-in experiences, such as working in a homeless shelter or tutoring children. "Good reporters have their own databases," he says. "They work their own retrieval systems. They consider themselves morally obligated to be informed, and they never stop learning."[29]

MODELS FOR JOURNALISM AND JOURNALISTS

Traditionally, news has been event-centered. Even in the 1990s, coverage tends to focus on the standard menu of news—disasters, human confrontations and assorted acts of violence, drama or aberration. By such criteria, news rarely rises above the level of journalism reflected in coffee-shop conversation: "Hey, Fred. Did you see the story about the guy who killed his six kids? Can you believe it?" A paradox of our complex, turbulent society is that reporters, overwhelmed at times by waves of information and daily occurrences, resort to superficial coverage when people most need something of substance. Of course, straight "process" news, such as covering a fire or a city council meeting, remains important. But other models of reporting are needed to elevate journalism to a more important role. Three models, in particular, address the demands placed on journalists who will be covering news in the 21st century.

Humanistic Reporting

News becomes meaningful when it is related in ways ordinary people can understand. Twenty years ago, Alex Edelstein and William

Ames said, "Humanistic reporting is not human interest reporting. The latter stresses unusual or unique qualities of individuals. The former tells how one person is like another, how he shares special human qualities with the reader."[30] Humanistic reporting stresses the human condition; it is personal and involving, not abstract. Journalists engaged in humanistic reporting know the difference between the river and its banks, says journalist Christopher Scanlan, who borrows a quotation from philosopher Will Durant to make a point: "Civilization is a stream with banks. The stream is sometimes filled with blood from people killing, stealing, shouting and doing the things that historians [and journalists] usually record; while on the banks, unnoticed, people build homes, make love, raise children, sing songs, write poetry and even whittle statues. The story of civilization is the story of what happened on the banks."[31]

Humanistic reporters walk along the banks. One of them is Michael Winerip of the *New York Times,* whose work Nat Hentoff of the *Village Voice* compared to Dickens'. "Charles Dickens seldom covered breaking news," says Hentoff. "He was more interested in what could be called chronic news—litigants covered with spider webs in the courts, children barely surviving and barely knowing why it was worth the effort, and the ballooning hypocrisy of those in charge of 'saving' these children. Michael Winerip's . . . stories hardly ever make the front page of the A section, but are sometimes of a more lasting importance than the thunderclap news of the day. Winerip, for example, has made child abuse and neglect a haunting concern."[32]

Humanistic reporting also calls for respect and caring in the gathering of news. A common public misperception of reporters is that they are callous, manipulative and untrustworthy. Actually, most reporters show great regard for the feelings and needs of news subjects. But journalists who believe they need to approach assignments with business-like detachment may leave interviewees feeling unappreciated and may never reach the level of dialogue necessary for full communication. Humanistic reporting begins well before journalists sit down to write.

Anticipatory Reporting

Preoccupation with hard news may prevent reporters from seeing past the moment and beyond the obvious. At its best, journalism should serve as society's early warning system. In 1962, Morton Mintz of the *Washington Post* alerted American women to the dangers of Thalidomide, a tranquilizer then widely prescribed in pregnancy.[33] Thalidomide caused thousands of babies to be born without arms or legs. More recently, Randy Shilts of the *San Francisco Chronicle* fought a lonely battle in the early 1980s to focus national attention on AIDS. Why did it take the death of movie star Rock Hudson for AIDS to become a news story deserving thorough coverage?[34] One answer is that the press often waits until a hard news "peg" or "angle" provides the justification to pursue a story. What's more, the reporting effort necessary to tell the full story of Thalidomide or AIDS is complicated and time-consuming; it is not done by spending an afternoon covering a speech, protest march or press conference.

In the 1960s, the press failed to anticipate the racial and poverty ills that later exploded into violence, as flames and rioting swept through city after city. When reporters get absorbed in covering the obvious news, they may fail to see larger problems beneath the surface. Educator Sandy Moore explains how the turmoil of the 1960s ended any notion that reporting the news simply meant covering events or strings of events: "Too often, event-oriented journalists didn't have a clue as to where the civil rights revolution came from, or how it differed from the black-power movement. Women's liberation came as something of a surprise to many journalists, as did the free-speech, free-sex ferment on college campuses (in the 1960s). To understand any of these required a lively and deep sense of American history and culture that transcended simple coverage of sit-ins, bra burnings, and love fests."[35]

When a social problem finally appears for all to see, the press usually does a thorough job of catch-up journalism. By then, though, major damage may already have been done. The savings and loan scandal of the late 1980s is a classic example of the press arriving on the scene too late. Media policy expert Ellen Hume, offering one explanation for the press's failure to sound an alarm, notes that it was a "numbers" story, too complicated and boring to interest many mainstream journalists. "If the press had seen and reported earlier the savings and loan industry's eight-year suicidal spree," Hume says, "the subsequent political pressure might have saved taxpayers tens or even hundreds of billions of dollars."[36]

Anticipatory reporting is decidedly more difficult than event-centered, episodic reporting. Reporters must occasionally pause—indeed, be given the time—to brainstorm, research and explore. In his book *Behind the Front Page*, David Broder urges newspapers and television stations to free reporters from regular assignments periodically so they can roam. "We need journalistic scout parties out there on the fringes of society," he says, "where the ideas that may ultimately change our politics and government often first appear."[37]

In most cases, those best positioned to anticipate significant developments are specialists in areas like law, medicine, human behavior, environment and economics. Journalism needs its generalists as well, but all reporters are capable of fine tuning their antennae, no matter where they work or what they do. A *Philadelphia Inquirer* labor reporter might break a medical story about carcinogenic dangers in the American workplace; a courthouse reporter in Beloit, Wis., might alert the public to chemical hazards in the local cement plant.

Explanatory Reporting

Explanatory reporting differs from anticipatory reporting in that it often looks *back* instead of *ahead*. Reporter William Greider, noted for his controversial, provocative 1983 interview with David Stockman, President Reagan's chief economic aide, advises the press, "Instead of being preoccupied with what's going to happen next, papers should ask more frequently and more coherently what really did happen."[38] When the press stops to explain and interpret, the results are impressive. After publishing dozens of spot news stories on dioxin contamination at Times Beach, Mo., now a ghost town, the *St. Louis Post-Dispatch* produced a 48-page supplement entitled "Dioxin: Quandary for the '80s." A researcher calls it a "*tour de force* in interpretive reporting"—the most comprehensive newspaper piece on the subject and widely used by scientists, public officials and journalists.[39]

James Reston of the *New York Times* once criticized the press for concentrating on dramatic, splashy spot news. "We are fascinated with events, but not by the things that cause events. We will send 500 correspondents to Viet Nam after the war breaks and fill the front pages with their reports, meanwhile ignoring the remainder of the world, but we will not send one or two reporters there when the danger of war is developing."[40]

Perhaps Reston overstates the problem. Public affairs reporters are on the job from Pottsville to the Pentagon, covering meetings, press conferences and pronouncements. But his central point is valid. Pressured to stay abreast of the day's news, few reporters for local newspapers or television or radio stations enjoy the luxury of time and resources needed to practice explanatory journalism of the caliber most often found in network documentaries, monthly magazines or elite newspapers. But on a smaller scale in everyday coverage, explanatory reporting can be accomplished by stressing *how* and *why* something happened as opposed to *what* happened. If an honor roll student takes her life, why? If a black candidate for mayor ousts the established white incumbent, how?

Explanatory reporting does not focus exclusively on the big story. Ordinary subjects, when explained well and thoroughly, offer great insight and meaning. Columnist Bob Greene, who above all is a reporter, frequently pursues ordinary subjects, such as "two 15-year-old boys growing up in a sprawling suburban shopping mall" or "a father begging someone to help his wayward son before it became too late." In Greene's view, "Those are the kinds of things that don't really qualify as 'news,' but that seem to me to have as much to do with the way we live as most of the events that warrant bold banner headlines."[41] Explanatory reporting helps people more clearly understand their lives, which is no small accomplishment.

American journalists are entering a period of great challenge and great opportunity. A highly skilled, educated and motivated cadre of public affairs reporters is needed to produce stories that cannot be based on a handful of questions or told in a few paragraphs. Print journalists face a special test of their abilities. With television, cable and radio dramatically and instantaneously covering society's events and occurrences, newspapers, in particular, cannot afford to remain headline services. If newspapers fail to emphasize stories other than "happenings," they can expect further loss of readership. But print journalists must be mindful that readers will not tackle long, involved stories unless they are exceptionally well reported, written and presented.

Reporters in the 21st century, covering a world as diverse and confusing as ours, must operate with great sensitivity and insight. How else can journalists report and write about what commentator Roger Rosenblatt called our surreal existence? Reflecting on the death of Salvador Dali, the artist who sought "to systematize confusion and contribute to the total discrediting of the world of reality," Rosenblatt wondered about the "collage of incongruous images" in the news. He compared a "March for Life" by 67,000 anti-abortion protesters to the following day's "march for death" outside the Florida prison where thousands cheered the execution of serial killer Ted

Bundy. "Journalists are born surrealists," says Rosenblatt. "Every form they observe is accompanied by a distortion of that form."[42]

Reporters everywhere face confusion and challenge. Small-town America, itself an endangered species, now mirrors big-city problems. As one reporter explores drug abuse in Detroit, another is pursuing the same subject in Waynesville, Mo. We must hope that both of them succeed.

EXERCISES

1. Ask someone whose knowledge and judgment you respect to recommend a book that influenced her or him greatly. Read the book and then discuss it together. Make the same request of other persons you respect; set a goal of reading one important book each month.

2. Volunteer for work that will heighten your multicultural perspective, such as work at a nursing home or inner-city preschool. Keep a diary of what you observed and learned.

3. Test your listening and observational skills. As you talk with a friend or colleague, watch and listen for their unspoken language—gestures, facial expression, posture. Then discuss your interpretations to determine your ability to accurately assess another person's nonverbal communication.

NOTES

[1] H.L. Mencken, *Newspaper Days* (New York: Knopf, 1941), p. 7.
[2] James W. Carey, "The Press and the Public Discourse," *Center Magazine*, March–April 1987, p. 17.
[3] Walter Lippmann, *Public Opinion* (New York: Macmillan, 1922), p. 81.
[4] Quoted in Jeannette Batz, "Who Needs to Know?," *Universitas*, Winter 1989, p. 6.
[5] Jack Newfield, *The Education of Jack Newfield* (New York: St. Martin's Press, 1984), p. 1.
[6] "We're Interested in What You Think: A Sampling of a Year's Letters to the Chairman of Times Mirror" (Los Angeles: Times Mirror Corp., 1987), p. 9.
[7] Gaye Tuchman, *Making News* (New York: Free Press, 1978).
[8] See Leon V. Sigal, "WHO: Sources Make the News," in Robert Karl Manoff and Michael Schudson, eds., *Reading the News* (New York: Pantheon Books, 1987), pp. 9–37.
[9] Mark Fishman, *Manufacturing the News* (Austin: University of Texas Press, 1980), pp. 3–13.

[10] *Absence of Malice* (Burbank, Calif.: Columbia Pictures, 1981).

[11] Quoted in Shirley Biagi, *NewsTalk I* (Belmont, Calif.: Wadsworth, 1987), p. 149.

[12] Wesley G. Pippert, *An Ethics of News: A Reporter's Search for Truth* (Washington, D.C.: Georgetown University Press, 1989), p. 5.

[13] Gerald Priestland, *The Dilemmas of Journalism* (London: Lutterworth, 1979), p. 113.

[14] Quoted in Michael Schudson, *Discovering the News* (New York: Basic Books, 1978), p. 68.

[15] Melvin Mencher, *News Reporting and Writing*, 4th ed. (Dubuque, Iowa: Wm. C. Brown, 1987), p. 262.

[16] John Calhoun Merrill, *Existential Journalism* (New York: Hastings House, 1977), p. 124.

[17] Deborah Tannen, *That's Not What I Meant!* (New York: Ballantine Books, 1986), p. ii.

[18] See Edward T. Hall, *The Silent Language* (Garden City, N.Y.: Anchor/Doubleday, 1981).

[19] Mary Jo Melone, "Who's the Real Bad Guy Here?," *St. Petersburg Times*, Oct. 5, 1988, p. 6B.

[20] E.D. Hirsch Jr., *Cultural Literacy* (New York: Vintage Books, 1988), p. 7.

[21] Rick Simonson and Scott Walker, eds., *Multicultural Literacy* (Saint Paul, Minn.: Graywolf Press, 1988), p. xii.

[22] Molly Sinclair, "A Feminist Confronts Aging," *St. Petersburg Times*, March 5, 1989, p. 8F.

[23] Carole Rich, "Don't Call Them 'Spry'," *The Quill*, Feb. 1989, p. 12.

[24] Frances FitzGerald, *Cities on a Hill* (New York: Simon & Schuster, 1986), p. 15.

[25] Joan Didion, *Miami* (New York: Simon & Schuster, 1987), p. 77.

[26] Felicity Barringer, "U.S. Racial Composition Has Changed Dramatically," *St. Petersburg Times*, March 12, 1991, p. 10A.

[27] Tim Miller, "The Data-base Revolution," *Columbia Journalism Review*, Sept.–Oct. 1988, p. 35.

[28] Joseph C. Goulden, *Fit to Print: A.M. Rosenthal and His Times* (Secaucus, N.J.: Lyle Stuart, 1988), p. 75.

[29] Melvin Mencher, paper presented at the Poynter Ethics Conference, Poynter Institute for Media Studies, Nov. 1990.

[30] Ron Dorfman and Harry Fuller Jr., eds. *Reporting/Writing/Editing* (Dubuque, Ia.: Kendall/Hunt, 1982), p. 79.

[31] Christopher Scanlan, *How I Wrote the Story*, 2nd ed. (Providence, R.I.: Providence Journal Co., 1986), p. 68.

[32] Nat Hentoff, "Brave Reporters—and the Other Kind," *Village Voice*, March 14, 1989, p. 18.

[33] Louis M. Lyons, *Reporting the News* (Cambridge, Mass.: Belknap Press, 1965), pp. 236–241.

[34] Randy Shilts, *And the Band Played On* (New York: St. Martin's Press, 1987).

[35] Sandy Moore, "Expand Your Horizons," *The Quill*, Sept. 1989, pp. 21, 22.

[36] Ellen Hume, "Why the Press Blew the S&L Scandal," *New York Times*, May 24, 1990, p. A25.

37 David S. Broder, *Behind the Front Page* (New York: Simon & Schuster, 1987), p. 128.

38 *Making Sense of the News* (St. Petersburg, Fla.: Modern Media Institute, 1983), p. 5.

39 Norman Shaw, "Dioxin Contamination in Missouri: The Evolution of an Environmental Issue as Covered by Two St. Louis Daily Newspapers," thesis, Southern Illinois University at Edwardsville, Nov. 1988, p. 14.

40 James Reston, *The Artillery of the Press* (New York: Harper & Row, 1966), p. 83.

41 Bob Greene, *American Beat* (New York: Penguin Books, 1984), pp. 15, 16.

42 Roger Rosenblatt, "The Journalist as Surrealist," *U.S. News & World Report*, Feb. 6, 1989, p. 10.

Chapter Two

Reporters make use of computer technology to help cover the 1984 Olympic Games in Los Angeles. (J.P. Laffont/Sygma)

The Ways
and Means
of Reporting

Charlie Bosworth stood quietly to one side of a conference room at an Illinois State Police complex just outside of St. Louis. As Bosworth watched and took notes, a dozen television and print reporters questioned police officials about a massive drug bust that had taken place a few hours earlier. In another room, the state troopers displayed the spoils of the raid: sawed-off shotguns, cash and drugs.

When the briefing ended, Bosworth went to work. Talking easily to state police officers he addressed by first name, Bosworth sought information that went beyond the press release and news conference. Other reporters received polite, standard, no-frills responses, but he obtained details—names, addresses, anecdotes, background.

Bosworth, a tall, trim man in his late 30s, covers public affairs news in Madison County, Ill., part of the St. Louis metroplex. Cops trust him. "He's one of the best in the business," says a state police sergeant. Judges know he understands the law. Politicians appreciate his integrity and fairness. When you ask Madison County public officials to name a reporter they respect, invariably the response is "Charlie Bosworth."

Bosworth likes to joke about being kept on an electronic leash—his beeper. Actually, his editors at the *St. Louis Post-Dispatch* trust Bosworth to work independently, juggle multiple assignments, meet deadlines, and, most of all, produce accurate, complete stories.

He is not a flashy superstar of journalism, but he is solid and dependable. His byline appears regularly on the front page. Bosworth is a public affairs reporter—a good one—with the attributes needed to succeed in a tough job.

Covering public affairs calls for resourcefulness, knowledge, curiosity, street *and* people smarts and, when warranted, aggressiveness. Public affairs reporters are expected to know what is going on, night or day. Editors count on them to generate significant stories, in depth, but only after they first cover the routine news—from sewer backups to fender benders—quickly and accurately.

It is not a job for the meek, naive or lazy. Beat reporters must face tears and curses, recognize snow jobs and scoop the competition. In the course of a career—perhaps in the course of a day—a public affairs reporter will be set up, put down and chewed out. Why, then, do it? Writer Martin Mayer puts it simply: "The reporter wants to know what is happening—I mean, really happening."[1] Mark Twain once explained the lure of the job:

> No other occupation brings a man into such familiar sociable relations with all grades and classes of people. The last thing at night—midnight—he goes browsing around after items among police and jail-birds, in the lock-up, questioning the prisoners and making pleasant and lasting friendships with some of the worst people in the world. And the very next evening he gets himself up regardless of expense, puts on all the good clothes his friends have got—goes and takes dinner with the Governor, or the Commander-in-Chief of the District, the United States Senator, and some more of the upper crust of society. He is on good terms with all of them, and is present at every public gathering, and has easy access to every variety of people.[2]

Twain's feelings still apply, as Charlie Bosworth would agree. Reporting is an invitation to ask questions, an entree to people and places and a front-row seat to the day's big stories. That is why Bosworth and thousands of other journalists across the country find their work exciting and satisfying.

REPORTING AS AN ATTITUDE

One of journalism's recent catchwords describes an interpersonal technique successful reporters have long practiced without necessarily giving it a name. The technique is *empathy.* Empathy involves a sincere attempt to identify with the experiences and emotions of others. Practicing empathy does not mean reporters must abandon skepticism or deny their own feelings. But empathy does require reporters to listen and evaluate with a open mind, which is not always easy. Consider this situation: Based on hearsay the newly assigned courthouse reporter concludes that the county treasurer is a bumpkin incapable of balancing his own checkbook, much less managing a $15 million budget. Now the reporter must interview the treasurer to explore charges by political opponents that his office is mismanaged. Without a commitment to empathy, will the reporter be able to give the man a fair hearing? Empathy cannot be feigned or misused as a manipulative interviewing tool, however; it must be genuine and honest.

In the journalist's world, empathy can coexist with skepticism and assertiveness. It is often a question of balance and moderation. Communication professor Michael Schudson offers this advice: "Journalists, like other seekers, must learn to trust themselves and their fellows and the world enough to take everything in, while distrusting themselves and others and the appearances of the world enough not to be taken in by everything."[3] The words of philosopher Max Ehrmann also serve as a guide for journalists: "Speak your truth quietly and clearly; and listen to others, even to the dull and the ignorant; they too have their story. . . . Exercise caution in your business affairs, for the world is full of trickery. But let this not blind you to what virtue there is; many persons strive for high ideals, and everywhere life is full of heroism."[4]

Unfortunately, surveys indicate the public generally considers journalists as anything but empathic. They are seen as an arrogant, rude and insensitive lot, inflicting pain wherever they go. Movies and prime-time television programs contribute to the image by depicting reporters as little better than ruthless news vultures. In 1989, writer Janet Malcolm began an article in the *New Yorker* magazine with this blanket indictment of the press: "Every journalist who is not too stupid or too full of himself to notice what is going on knows that what he does is morally indefensible. He is a kind of confidence man, preying on people's vanity, ignorance, or loneliness, gaining their trust and betraying them without remorse."[5]

Malcolm's description of journalists unfairly and inaccurately generalizes, but her words deserve to be heard and considered, particularly when she talks about reporter-source relationships: "The catastrophe suffered by the subject is no simple matter of an unflattering likeness or a misrepresentation of his views; what pains him, what rankles and sometimes drives him to extremes of vengefulness, is the deception that has been practiced on him. On reading the article . . . in question, he has to face the fact that the journalist—who seemed so friendly and sympathetic, so keen to understand him fully, so remarkably attuned to his vision of things—never had the slightest intention of collaborating with him on his story but always intended to write a story of his own."[6]

Stripping away Malcolm's hyperbole, you will find the root of many reporter-source problems. Those problems frequently begin with the tendency in reporting to dehumanize "news subjects." Reporters should never treat or view people as objects to be used and discarded. It might help to remember that a story is not the reporter's alone; it belongs, as well, to the people quoted, described and represented in the story. Reporters must also remember that above all, people—presidents and postmasters alike—want to be treated with decency.

A few journalists, as *Washington Post* reporter Lou Cannon says, exhibit an "annoying self-righteousness" that they are "performing a sacred calling."[7] Some adopt a scorched-earth approach to gathering the news, burning bridges and destroying resources they might need later on. Some become unnecessarily aggressive, kicking down doors without first gently knocking. And some confuse skepticism and cynicism, forgetting that one is helpful and the other destructive.

Despite the public's poor image of reporters, journalists seldom deceive, betray or exploit deliberately. Nonetheless, even well-intentioned journalists hurt people at times. Trained, conditioned and rewarded to nail down stories and make deadlines, they sometimes overlook the feelings and needs of others. Part of that conditioning includes devotion to a seductive principle: the public's right to know. It is an ambiguous and, at times, self-serving term. Other than journalists themselves, few people argue fiercely that the public has a *right* to know. Besides, which "public" does the press serve? And if a public's right to know does exist, who says the public always *wants* to know? "The press justifies itself in the name of the public," says professor James Carey. "The canons of journalism originate in and flow from the relationship of the press to the public. The public is totem and talisman, and an object of ritual homage."[8] Even "objects of ritual homage" do not entitle reporters to ask anyone anything at any time and at any cost.

Lofty principles of journalism are invoked most passionately on public affairs beats. Waving the right-to-know banner on high, certain reporters demand answers and accountability. Indeed, the mythology of journalism casts the press and public officals in adversarial roles. Should reporters and officials constantly butt heads? *Washington Post* ombudsman Richard Harwood questions the value of an adversarial orientation. "[I]t does not contribute to intimate or confessional relationships in which 'truthtelling' . . . is a common transaction," he says. Journalists should worry less about becoming too cozy with public officials, he says, and worry more about becoming too removed. "It is rather the problem of being too distant from those whose personalities, beliefs, knowledge, hopes and fears are essential to the understanding we would communicate to our countrymen."[9] Although Harwood's thoughts apply most directly to reporters covering the centers of political power, they are relevant, as well, for reporters covering school boards or zoning commissions.

Harwood's approach does not mean reporters should stop asking hard questions and pressing for answers. But public officials are not always obligated to talk to reporters or provide information. Certainly they are not inclined to cooperate with demanding, combative reporters. In the mid-1960s, journalist James Reston used the metaphor "artillery of the press" to urge reporters to unleash "a relentless barrage of facts and criticism, as noisy but also as accurate as artillery fire."[10] Reston's concept tends to reduce public affairs reporting to a form of warfare. War is dirty business; artillery shells do indiscriminate damage and sometimes hurt non-combatants. Before firing the heavy artillery, first determine whether a barrage will elicit answers and responses that are complete and forthright. After the dust clears, what will be the condition of the reporter-source relationship? Always consider whether a non-confrontational, empathic approach will work as effectively—and cause less damage. Although all journalists should be concerned about a healthy, fruitful reporting environment, those on the front lines of journalism—the public affairs beats—have the most to gain; they also have the most to lose.

THE BEAT SYSTEM

The beat system became a standard method of gathering news in the 1830s. Beginning with Benjamin Day's *New York Sun*, newspapers for the average citizen appeared and prospered in cities like Boston,

Philadelphia and Baltimore. Stressing news rather than political commentary, the *Sun* and its imitators sold for a penny a copy, replacing the six-penny journals that fit neither the interests nor the budgets of most people. The Penny Press era marked the advent of news in its modern sense. Salaried reporters were posted at the city hall, courthouse, police station and capitol to search out and report the news.

Beat coverage remains a relatively efficient, effective method of surveillance. Working a beat allows reporters to develop expertise, contacts and continuity in news coverage. But the system has its weaknesses.

Reporters in general tend to overemphasize official viewpoints, a tendency that is greatest on beats. According to a series of studies, reporters rely heavily on a small circle of news contacts and experts, many of them white, male, government executives.[11] Stationed as they are at police headquarters or the courthouse, reporters naturally develop cooperative, regular relationships with certain "reliable" sources.

If an empathic approach is more productive than an adversarial one, then professional "relationships" between reporters and news sources are desirable. But beat reporters who limit their relationships to a handful of official contacts risk becoming unwitting practitioners of "establishment" journalism. In extreme cases, reporters become trapped in arrangements that regress from cooperation to dependency, especially if public officials release or withhold information as a form of reward and punishment. News, then, becomes a hostage, and reporters become vulnerable to pressures they could normally resist. To avoid becoming either a pipeline or pawn of official, elite points of view, the reporter needs to draw constantly on a diversity of news sources.

Although over time it is natural that reporters and the people they cover develop associations that extend outside the beat, complications can arise. A reporter accepts the city attorney's invitation to play on a local softball team; later, both of them find it hard to separate their social and professional roles. The city attorney cannot understand why his buddy, the reporter, refuses to keep a lid on an internal investigation of the police department; the reporter cannot understand why his buddy, the city attorney, would try to stop him from telling an important story.

Some complications are hard to avoid. Reporter Kurt Rogahn of the *Cedar Rapids* (Iowa) *Gazette* encountered awkward situations on the education beat because his wife is a teacher. He explains: "One morning I got a call from her new principal. He wanted me to come over and talk about an early childhood education institute he had just attended in Washington, It sort of put me on the spot. We don't usually do much with institutes, but I agreed to talk to him. Maybe with somebody else, I would have turned him down on the phone. I think it's a good illustration of what can happen when you know sources."[12] On the other hand, knowing sources well and personally can be beneficial, as Rogahn points out: "The familiarity works the other way, too. People know me. They trust me. They tell me stories they wouldn't have told me on my first year on the beat. Some have even become whistle-blowers."[13] Reporters walk a tightwire in trying to maintain good relationships on their beats. Ideally, good reporters avoid the extremes—of the adversary or the ally.

Peer pressure also poses problems, particularly on highly competitive beats. Some reporters covering the statehouse, for example, may be reluctant to stray from what other members of the press corps consider the "news" in the governor's budget message. They might confer among themselves about what to emphasize or might fall back on a safe approach—going with a variation of a wire-service summary lead. This follow-the-crowd approach to reporting is called "pack journalism." Timothy Crouse describes a variation of the "pack journalism" phenomenon in his book about coverage of the 1972 presidential campaign, *The Boys on the Bus*. Reporters covering a debate during the campaign literally peered over the shoulder of Walter Mears, ace of the Associated Press staff, to see how he would begin his story. As Crouse explains: "They wanted to avoid 'call-backs'—phone calls from their editors asking them why they had deviated from the AP or UPI. If the editors were going to run a story that differed from the story in the nation's 1,700 other newspapers, they wanted a good reason for it. Most reporters dreaded callbacks. Thus the pack followed the wire service whenever possible. Nobody made a secret of running with the wires; it was an accepted practice."[14]

Pack journalism is a danger whenever reporters on beats compare stories or react to each other's signals. For example, a reporter new to the city hall beat discreetly watches veterans take notes during an aldermanic meeting. When they scribble furiously, the rookie figures the ordinance being discussed is significant. But when the old hands slouch listlessly in their seats as the treasurer's report is read, the rookie concludes—perhaps wrongly—that the report is of little news value. Even among the veterans, there is a reluctance to break away from the pack. As a result, news coverage on beats becomes standardized and reporters eventually lose confidence in their ability to judge news independently.

Computer technology puts another form of pressure on journalists. Years ago, beat reporters rarely wrote stories; they relayed information downtown where the rewrite desk adroitly and speedily converted facts into stories. Once modems and portable terminals allowed beat reporters to file stories direct to the newsroom, the days of "rewrite" were numbered. Today, rewrite persons are about as rare as pastepots and manual typewriters, a development that veteran journalists lament and not merely on sentimental grounds. News executive Michael Gartner remembers his initiation to journalism: "In those days . . . the rewriteman would pepper the reporter with questions. In effect, the rewriteman was the reporter, and the reporter was the source. I knew that I couldn't turn in any story with holes because (they) would always spot them. So I decided stories I wrote had to be complete and fair and thorough and accurate—in those days, I was thinking more of saving my job than of helping the reader—and that's how I learned to report."[15] Now beat reporters largely learn those lessons on their own, through trial and error, not under the tutelage of a skilled rewriteman.

Advice for Working Beats

Orientation for new beat reporters usually involves tagging along for a day—a week at most—with an old hand. It is not a very systematic or effective way to learn a beat. In some cases, the new reporter simply acquires the same routines and sources the old hand relied on. Learning a beat cannot be reduced to a list of tips, but as a starting point, here is some advice:

Introduce yourself. Start with the top person on your beat. It might be the police chief or the chief circuit judge. Meet to explain your goals and perhaps go over some ideas for coverage of the beat. Ask for a tour, if that is appropriate. Some stories may come immediately to mind as you are shown around. Ask to be introduced to employees you encounter and remember their names—including custodians, clerks and secretaries. Introductions by the boss will open doors and loosen tongues. Ask the boss for access to people and records.

Then you can say to a reluctant police department clerk, "Chief Jones said it was okay for me to check the incident log personally."

Make a good first impression. A simple way to quickly gain a positive reception on your beat is to do a "good news" story. Focus on awards, achievements and accomplishments. As long as the story is of legitimate news value, you will not blemish your journalistic integrity.

First impressions also influence editors. To start off positively and productively, send your editor a list describing stories you intend to pursue. A good source of ideas is the clip file of previously published stories; propose follow-ups for continuing issues and problems on your beat.

Reconnoiter and make acquaintances. Wander your beat; become familiar with the territory. If people seem willing to talk, "waste" some time in aimless conversation about the weather, ball games and today's teenagers. Remember birthdays; invest in a card. By doing so, you become a part of the place, not an intruder. Drop in on offices and collect directories, annual reports, budgets, in-house publications, organizational charts—anything that will help you get to know the beat. Find out where records are kept. Look about; a memo tacked to a bulletin board may yield a good story.

Educate yourself. Determine the key periodicals and publications on your beat. In colleges and universities, for example, many administrators and professors read or hear about articles in the *Chronicle of Higher Education*. Urge people on the beat to send you copies of important, interesting articles from their professional reading. Ask people what they do with old copies of publications; maybe they will give them to you. And encourage them to recommend books of relevance to your beat coverage. Then read the books and discuss them together.

Be available. Encourage people on your beat to call you. Give them a card with your home and business phone numbers. Investing in an answering machine pays off quickly. Try, as well, to maintain a schedule of when you will be on the premises of your beat. Some reporters establish a routine: coffee at the city manager's office at 9 a.m. on Mondays; a chat with the mayor at 3 on Wednesday afternoons. When people know your schedule, you make it easier and more likely for them to contact you.

Get organized. If you can, arrange a place to use as a home base, especially one with a telephone and a drop-off point for mail and messages. On a big-city beat, there might be a press room.

Keep track of the whereabouts and agendas of key people on your beat. If you check the mayor's appointment book with a secretary, you may discover the mayor is lunching the next day with Mr. Yamashita and Ms. Osaki. Later the mayor confides, "They're from the Honda company. We're just starting to explore the possibility of Honda opening a plant here. We were hoping to hold off a story until next week, but since you've found out . . . "

Another organizational tool is a personal file of experts or authorities. Whenever you seek information from someone, add his or her name, phone number, title and speciality to your file ("Jane Murray, grant coordinator, St. Clair County, 555-2323—authority on urban redevelopment"). Include several notations of the person's preferences and interests ("Doesn't like phone interviews, big contributor to the Notre Dame alumni fund"). In fact, some reporters are as valued for their extensive "Rolodex" contacts as for their writing or reporting talents.

Start other files as well—a "futures" file to help you remember upcoming events and follow-up assignments, a clip file of published articles so you will not have to depend on the main office for background information, an anecdotal file of material from people on your beat that might be used later for a profile or an obituary, an idea file of material for features or depth stories.

Get out of the office. A beat is more than a building. Reporters who hang out at city hall or do their legwork by telephone get stuck in ruts and miss important stories. Robert Jackson of the *Los Angeles Times* used the term *goyakod* to describe what beat reporters need to do more often: "The word is an acronym around our bureau for 'Go out, you all, and knock on doors.' The more you do that, the more you think you ought to throw away your telephone. . . . You get more out of somebody by seeing them in person. I kick myself every time I've given in out of weakness and simply called somebody on the phone."[16] Reporters who get out and about develop a broader spectrum of sources and different slants on news. Who knows more about traffic jams, dangerous intersections and poorly marked exit signs—a cab driver or a highway engineer? Reporters tethered to their beat are not likely to find out.

METHODS OF REPORTING

Reporters learn about people and issues through *observation, interviews, data-document searches* and *social-science research.* Increasingly, they draw on all four methods. Interviewing, while still the mainstay of reporting methods, often yields what scientists call "impressionistic, anecdotal" evidence, and journalists who draw conclusions based solely on impressions and anecdotes flirt with error and distortion. Interviews remain important, especially for revealing personalities and reliving events, but human sources are fallible. Ideally, stories should be buttressed with multiple evidence—what researchers call *convergent validation.* One-dimensional, pencil-and-pad reporters may find some stories beyond their reach, particularly those requiring research and quantification.

Observation

Social science provides journalists with models for observation. Urban expert Jane Jacobs demonstrated how to observe city life in her book *The Death and Life of Great American Cities,* and sociologist Ulf Hannerz lived in a black neighborhood to produce his study *Soulside.*

Journalists continue to borrow social-science techniques and apply them to a variety of stories. Gloria Steinem established herself in journalism by landing a job as a Playboy bunny and writing about her experiences; Gay Talese regularly relies on observational reporting, but never so intimately as in *Thy Neighbor's Wife,* his excursion into the sexual revolution of the 1970s; reporter Ben Bagdikian posed as a convicted murderer to write about Cell Block A, his identity unknown to anyone at a Pennsylvania state prison; and Hunter Thompson risked life and limb to ride and party with the Hell's Angels.

What does observational reporting yield? Sights-and-sounds reporting or what Gene Roberts, former editor of the *Philadelphia Inquirer,* calls *visual journalism.* Roberts' first boss, editor Henry Belk, was blind. When Roberts' stories lacked vividness and detail, Belk would admonish him, "You aren't making me see; make me see."[17] The idea is to put the reader at the scene, creating a you-are-there feeling. Drawing on an array of physical and emotional senses, observational reporters try to capture mood, symbolism, action, dialogue and characterization. The results can be powerful, as Hunter Thompson shows in the opening scene of his Hell's Angels story:

> California, Labor Day weekend . . . early, with ocean fog still in the streets, outlaw motorcyclists wearing chains, shades and greasy Levis roll out from damp garages, all-night diners and cast-off one-night pads in Frisco, Hollywood, Berdoo and East Oakland, heading for the Monterey peninsula, north of Big Sur. . . . The Menace is loose again, the Hell's Angels, the hundred-caret headline, running fast and loud on the early morning freeway, low in the saddle, nobody smiles, jamming crazy through traffic and ninety miles an hour down the center stripe, missing by inches, like Genghis Khan on an iron horse. . . .
>
> Little Jesus, the Gimp, Chocolate George, Buzzard, Zorro, Hambone, Clean Cut, Tiny, Terry the Tramp, Frenchy, Mouldy Marvin, Mother Miles, Dirty Ed, Chuck the Duck, Fat Freddy, Filthy Phil, Charger Charley the Child Molester, Crazy Cross, Puff, Magoo, Animal and at least a hundred more . . . tense for the action, long hair in the wind, beards and bandanas flapping, earrings, armpits, chain whips, swastikas and stripped-down Harleys flashing chrome as traffic on 101 moves over, nervous, to let the formation pass like a burst of dirty thunder.[18]

Beat reporters rarely enjoy Thompson's degree of literary freedom, but readers appreciate descriptive journalism, even in city council stories. Listen to the engaging narrative style in *St. Petersburg Times* reporter Alicia Caldwell's opening for a short, simple story about a public forum on the city's proposed budget:

> Willard 'Tiny' Weins had worked up a healthy sense of outrage by the time he took the microphone at the first public forum on the city's budget Monday night.
>
> He ranted at City Council members, calling them the "masters" and the residents "slaves." He denounced the city's downtown redevelopment projects. He said he is leaving the city as quickly as he can.
>
> "All the big projects we're building downtown, I know I won't live long enough and you won't live long enough to see them make a profit," said Weins. "This is really, truthfully disgusting. I can't get out of St. Petersburg fast enough."

Observational reporting also provides firsthand insight and experiential knowledge. As Ben Bagdikian explains, "Prison experts agreed that perception of what it means to be imprisoned in America remains dim unless you are on the other side of the bars. They were right. Months of interviewing prisoners, former prisoners, corrections administrators and research scientists, as well as reading dozens of books and reports, had not prepared me for the emotional and intellectual impact of maximum-security incarceration."[19] Can you write powerfully and perceptively about the dangers faced by coal miners without going deep into a coal mine? Can you write effectively about the homeless without at least sharing a meal and a park bench with a street person?

Observation allows you to describe places, study people, watch from multiple vantage points and, perhaps most important of all, formulate questions. When *Miami Herald* police reporter Edna Buchanan goes to crime scenes, she is looking for details to add not only color but accuracy to her stories. The police report may say two bodies were found in a first-floor bedroom, but by visiting the scene, you observe that all the bedrooms are on the second floor. "What gives?" you ask. Some questions occur to you only by being there and seeing for yourself.

Does observation ensure truth and accuracy? Not always. There may be truthful *versions* of the truth. Reporters must always observe carefully, aware of the potential for distortion, and they must approach the observations of others with similar care and skepticism.

Interviewing

Interviewing is as much an *attitude* as it is a *process*. As the word *inter*-view implies, it is not something one person *does* to another but rather something that is done *together*.[20] Reporters who adopt such an outlook naturally engage in empathic communication. They attempt to see the world of the other person, even if the person across from them is a convicted child molester.

Donald Murray, a journalist, educator and writing coach, encourages this style of reporting. He offers a list of questions reporters should ask themselves before, sometimes during and even after an interview:

- How does the news source see the world? (Take a moment and view the world as the person you are interviewing sees it.)

- What does that person value?

- What does he or she fear?

- Why should the news source give you information? (And why is that person giving you information?)

- What are the news source's beliefs?[21]

Explaining why such questions are important, Murray says: "It is one of the great failures of our profession that we assume that everyone inhabits our world. . . . We need to step behind our sources for a moment and imagine what we would see from behind the mayor's desk, from a bed in the charity ward, from a conference table in the corporate lawyer's suite, from a seatless hopper in the prisoner's cell. If we can get out of ourselves and enter into the lives of those we interview then we may ask perceptive questions and may receive perceptive answers."[22]

Reporters who practice empathy usually operate from a position of strength, not weakness. Rarely do you have to "come on strong" to get answers. A key to empathic reporting is understanding why people are reluctant to talk. Rather than write off an apparently recalcitrant police chief as "a jerk," an empathic reporter tries to determine why the chief frequently says "No comment" or offers monosyllabic answers to questions. Among the internal questions the reporter might ask are these: "Is my method of questioning a turn-off?" "Is it the subject?" "Is the chief fearful of being burned by the press?" "Has he been burnt before?" "Is he under pressure from the mayor or city manager to keep quiet?" "Is he, indeed, a jerk with something to hide?" Putting yourself in another person's skin also tends to hold biases in check: As a result you will listen more non-judgmentally and assess more objectively.

Interviewing need not be a selfish act of reporter *taking* and the news source *giving*. Nor should it be seen as a contest, a test of wills or an interrogation. When reporters and news sources clash or play games with one another, can we expect a story that is fair, meaningful or complete? In many instances, the *amount* and *quality* of the "news" that emerges in an interview depend on how successful the reporter and interviewee are in a *mutual* quest to understand and be understood. Remember, however, that this approach assumes that the interviewee is not withholding information or lying. Occasionally, interviewees do not wish or intend to cooperate.

As a reporting method, interviewing allows journalists to probe for details, collect anecdotal material, verify conflicting information and capture the unique expressions of news sources. In combination with observational reporting, interviewing produces vivid, potent portraits of events and people. It is wrong, however, to assume that interviewing is simply a natural extension of talking—something that is intuitive for most of us. It is far more complex than that. Conversational ability certainly helps, but glibness is no guarantee for success. Successful interviewing depends on a reporter's attitude and communication literacy. Glibness cannot overcome self-centered attitudes or communication incompetence.

With time and experience, reporters learn lessons and mature as interviewers. But what happens while they are learning by experience? And what happens if they learn all the wrong lessons? Largely because interviewing is a personal process, advice is difficult to summarize. There is no one universal model for reporters to follow. An interview set in a professor's den may produce dynamics far different from one conducted in an inmate's cell. A style of questioning that works with a police officer may not work with a priest. Because a multitude of variables—personalities, time of day and type of story, to name a few—influence how an interview is conducted, any advice on interviewing must be qualified and generalized.

Like other reporting methods, interviewing is an imperfect process. When people communicate, no matter what their attitudes or how hard they try to mutually cooperate, messages go astray. (Chapter 3 offers guidance on how to best minimize the errors and distortions that occur during interviews.)

Obtaining interviews. For routine interviews, such as collecting eyewitness accounts of an accident, reporters usually identify themselves and start asking questions. Interviews demanding more time and involvement from the news source often warrant a formal request. Veteran reporters advise against seeking an "interview," a word that sounds imposing and intimidating to some people. It is often more useful to seek someone's "thoughts," "ideas" or "background."

Public affairs reporters on beats generally know sources well enough to dispense with the formalities and immediately get down to business. With strangers or "difficult" sources, though, patience and sensitivity may be needed. If someone is "too busy" to see you, be persistent and accommodating ("I really need to compare your perspective with Rep. Smith's, senator; maybe I can drive you to the airport for your flight back to Sacramento"). Remember that a "diffi-cult" source might merely be anxious, insecure or inhibited. Practice empathy to gain a stranger's confidence and cooperation.

When arranging most interviews, state your purpose, review key questions you plan to ask and set a realistic time limit. Keeping an interviewee in the dark usually is counterproductive; being up front encourages openness and enables the interviewee to prepare. If you are calling the city attorney for reaction to a Supreme Court ruling, let her know what you intend to discuss; then she'll be able to do her homework and answer more authoritatively. There is a flip side to forewarning your news sources, however: Notice also gives them a chance to manufacture an artificial answer or concoct an alibi.

Preparation. Preparation enables reporters to ask perceptive, original questions; it also demonstrates to news sources that you are thorough and professional. People tend to trust a prepared reporter. With background information on nearly any subject available at a keystroke through data-base services, there is seldom an excuse for not being prepared.

Greetings and rapport. When meeting news sources for the first time, consider first impressions—yours and theirs. Reporters can-not go wrong using a business-like greeting. Guard against letting first impressions affect your ability to assess and listen fairly. If a politician greets you with, "Well, well. A *lady* of the press," do not devalue what he later says because his seemingly condescending manner offends you. Remember, too, that some people are reluctant to talk to reporters. It may take time to build rapport. If you sense uneasiness, try some ice-breaking small talk to help others relax and feel comfortable talking with you.

Questions and probes. As the interview unfolds, additional questions naturally will surface. Be prepared to alter or abandon your original story focus along the way, if necessary. Guiding you should be this thought: Why is this story worth telling to others? Try to determine what questions readers would ask if they had the chance. If the assignment is to investigate the murky brown water coming out of faucets on the city's southeast side, the first question on the minds of readers will be, "Is it okay to drink?" A simple, "Yes, it's perfectly safe" from city officials will not suffice. Readers will want a fuller explanation and detailed reassurances.

Asking a question is not necessarily going to elicit a good answer—at least immediately. A variety of follow-up questions usually are needed. Some of these secondary questions are called *probes,* which serve to encourage fuller responses. Some probes are nonverbal, like the nod of the head or a smile, suggesting, "Go on; I'm with you." Others are more specific, seeking clarification or amplification: "Could you give me an example?" Above all, never be afraid to say, "I don't understand."

Questions are potent tools of communication whose effect on interview subjects need to be considered. Some questions hurt, some soothe; some inspire, some bore. Rather than a volley of question-asking and question-answering, try to elevate interviews to the level of dialogue. Studs Terkel, noted for his penetrating interviews with "non-celebrated" persons, tells how he gets others to speak so openly: "I think people . . . want to talk about their lives, if they feel you're interested and if they feel it isn't sleazy, cheap, gossipy stuff. The people want to talk about their feelings about work or their memories of the Depression and how it affected them. So people open up. It's conversation, more or less, not really an interview."[23] Instead of following a strict question-answer format, Terkel talks and listens.

Listening. Hearing and listening are different. You can have perfect hearing and be a terrible listener. Listening, like interviewing, depends on cultivating an appropriate attitude. Good listeners concentrate, blocking out internal and external distractions. Empathy enhances your ability to listen; empathic reporters are receptive listeners.

Reporters ought to listen, too, with their eyes. Steady eye contact signals your involvement. Your eyes also help you "listen" for nonverbal communication. If the interviewee wrings his hands, what is the message? Anxiety? You may need to inquire or regulate your interviewing approach if you are making the person uncomfortable.

Indications that you are listening will be reassuring to the interviewee and rewarding for you. Simply leaning toward the speaker and nodding your head—not in agreement but to send the message "I'm with you"—reinforce your involvement. Knowing you are listening, the speaker is likely to reciprocate with greater energy and involvement.

Validation. Interviewing, even face to face, poses possibilities for garbled messages, misunderstandings and errors. Immediate feedback helps clear the air. A simple step to prevent mistakes is the *perception check*. It amounts to a restatement or paraphrase of previous communication. "Judge Owens, let me make sure I understand this *nolo contendere* plea. Correct me if I'm wrong, but it works this way. . . . " The perception check often reveals subtle yet significant shades of difference between what you understand and what the interviewee means.

There will be times when news sources lie, deceive or evade. Detecting lies is not easy, but doing your homework helps. A well-prepared, well-informed reporter can often expose lies and evasion by pressing the speaker for details and particulars. Later, if necessary, you can seek corroboration through other sources or reinterview the original source to discuss contradictions and discrepancies. Try, though, to resist the urge to automatically question the motives of others. It is right to be alert for hidden agendas, but reporters who are on constant guard for lies or other forms of manipulation might not be able to judge messages objectively.

Tight spots. From the reporter's perspective, the toughest interviews are those related to a tragedy. No advice will remove the discomfort of having to question the mother whose 6-year-old died in a hit-and-run accident. When those occasions arise, try to be composed, professional and sensitive. Do not be alarmed by tears; they are to be expected. For people in grief, talk about a loved one is a step toward healing the hurt. By asking questions about the tragedy, you may be helping the survivors learn *what* happened and *why* it happened, providing details and answers they have not received from the authorities. Nonetheless, reporters who cover stories of death and suffering must proceed cautiously and caringly. Resist probing grieving people too deeply about hurtful details of a tragedy; these are usually available from others less directly affected. When people do not want to talk, respect their wishes.

People in grief are not the only interviewees who are vulnerable. Skilled reporters can reach deep within people, especially those unaccustomed to talking to the press. Journalist Elisa Bildner feels a responsibility when people confide in her. "They'll be holding my hands, pouring out their stories. As you spend hours and hours talking to someone they still know you're a reporter but they think of you as a friend."[24] At times, reporters are obligated to remind people that they are not simply talking to another person; they ultimately are talking to an audience of 100,000 or more.

Working the phones

The telephone is an indispensable reporting tool that saves time, beats deadlines and opens clogged avenues of communication.

Paul McLaughlin, author of *Asking Questions*, offers several good reasons for using the telephone to interview and gather information. Among them:

- The phone can neutralize power games. If a reporter faces an interviewer noted for intimidation or angry outbursts, the phone serves as a buffer zone. In some cases, it might save a reporter from a physical confrontation.

- The phone can cover an interviewer's insecurities; some reporters are less inhibited when communication isn't face to face. Conversely, some interviewees are more comfortable being interviewed by phone.

- The phone is familiar; North Americans are used to talking by phone and divulging information.[25]

The telephone, however, can be a crutch if reporters use it as an excuse to remain deskbound. Telephone interviews do not allow for observational reporting; they do not allow you to listen with your eyes; they are not conducive to establishing rapport.

On sensitive stories, especially ones containing damaging allegations, never let the telephone lead to irresponsible reporting, such as, "Mayor Murray could not be reached for comment" or "Mayor Murray failed to return numerous phone messages left by a *Tribune* reporter." Even if readers do not question such behavior, libel lawyers will: "How many times did the reporter call?" "At what time of day?" "How many messages were left?" "Did the reporter explain the importance of the call?"

With certain stories, fairness demands an exhaustive effort, which includes going to the news source's home and office when phone calls are not successful or sending a certified letter or telegraph to request an interview. Then if litigation results, the reporter at least can show he tried. No jury is going to be impressed by a reporter who says, "I called several times to get a comment, but I kept getting a busy signal."

Documents and Data

The explosive growth of information, together with advances in computer storage and retrieval, is both blessing and bane for journalists. Reporting in the Information Age can be overwhelming: Which materials should I use? How do I get at them? How much information is enough? Rather than cope, some reporters retreat to the methods of yesterday. As Lauren Kessler and Duncan McDonald note, "Lack of information about the electronic world coupled with an unhealthy awe of the technology keeps many reporters from moving into the future."[26] Investigative reporting expert John Ullmann reinforces the point: "The technology is readily available and relatively inexpensive, especially when compared to any alternative—hours in the library or on the phone, or a story that lacks crucial information."[27]

Not all stories, of course, warrant extensive data-document searches. The importance and complexity of a story determine the extent of a reporter's search. But let computers do much of the legwork. Increasingly, newspapers are going to on-line data-base services that provide access to printouts of articles from hundreds of news organizations.

Reporters enjoy speed and access to information on a scale unthinkable a few decades ago when there were fewer options. Reporters visited public libraries, if proximity and time permitted, or gathered bits of information in standard reference books or encyclopedias. Usually, though, they simply relied on the newspaper's own story clippings. The "clips" ended up being kept in tattered, soiled envelopes, filed in rows of olive-drab cabinets and organized under an idiosyncratic subject system only the newspaper's librarian could decipher. Clip envelopes—invariably the ones you desperately needed—often got buried under a stack of trash on a reporter's desk. No wonder journalists called the resting place for old stories "the morgue."

Today the enhanced ability of journalists to conduct data-document searches complements other methods of reporting. If the assignment is to produce an in-depth story on dangerous chemicals in drinking water, a thorough reporter might draw on background information from the published record of a congressional hearing, a cover story in *Newsweek*, a report by the state health department and a four-part series from the *Los Angeles Times*. This material is bricks and mortar for a story—dates, statistics, history and names of expert sources. Using data-base services, for example, reporters for the *Louisville Courier-Journal* developed a 1,600-item bibliography, the foundation of a 30-part series on toxic-waste dumps.[28]

By conducting an extensive background search reporters also acquire expertise and insight. If you learn, for example, that not all cities put fluoride in drinking water, then you will know to ask whether your city's water is fluoridated. From your search, you become well informed about the various ways municipalities chemically treat water. Your new knowledge makes you a better observer, questioner and evaluator when inspecting the water plant with the public works director and at other points in your pursuit of the story.

Information is everywhere, but first journalists must be aware of what exists and where to find it. Here in a nutshell are the main sources:

Libraries. "Libraries must always be lumberyards to use, houses of building supplies," says journalist James J. Kilpatrick. "There we go for the facts, dates, documentation that are the cinderblocks and cellar beams of our work. But we also go there for the columns and pediments and finials that add grace and adornment."[29] Libraries contain thousands of books, periodicals, government reports and reference works. Some material can be taken directly from the shelves; other documents may be on microfiche cards, which hold hundreds of miniaturized reproductions of printed material for viewing on a projector. Many libraries now use electronic card files for their book holdings. Some, through telephone modems, allow computer access from a user's home or office.

The basic reference source for background information, especially for those who do not have access to electronic data bases, remains old reliable—the *Readers' Guide to Periodical Literature*. It provides indexing for approximately 200 magazines. A newer reference source, *Magazine Index*, indexes articles from more than 400 publications by author and subject, and is updated monthly. It is more extensive than *Readers' Guide* but not as widely available. Other fields, such as law, have indexes to periodicals comparable to *Readers' Guide*; these specialized indexes can be found in large libraries. One of them, for example, is the *Education Index*, which contains entries from periodicals such as the *American Music Teacher* and *Young Children*, published by the National Association for the Education of Young Children.

Of the guides to newspaper articles, the oldest and most complete is the *New York Times Index,* which indexes every article from the *Times'* late city edition by subject, geographic region, organization name and personal name, with ample cross-references. Under the heading "accidents and safety," for instance, are hundreds of "see also" entries, such as "baby carriages" and "skateboards." Abstracts of articles are included and often are detailed enough to save the user from having to examine the full story from the library's microfilmed back issues of the *Times.*

Most newspaper reference rooms possess basic works, such as *Statistical Abstract of the United States.* (It is a cornucopia of facts about American life. Among the tidbits of information found in the 1989 edition were these: 841.4 million credit cards were in use in 1987, more than three cards for every man, woman and child in the United States; there were 1,441 heart transplants in 1987, up from 62 in 1981.) But many newspaper libraries do not possess lesser known, valuable works like the *Encyclopedia of Southern Culture,* with entries ranging from Henry Aaron (major league home run king) to zydeco (Cajun music played with an accordion); *What's What: A Visual Glossary of the Physical World,* a collection of illustrated definitions of thousands of items, such as the nomenclature of a revolver; or *Maps on File,* which contains a vast assortment of maps, including, for example, one of the United States that highlights the states that suffered the greatest crop losses of the 1988 drought. A well-stocked library has an extensive reference section that detail-hungry reporters turn to regularly.

Other important, frequently used library sources include:

Blue books: Blue books are directories of the executive, legislative and judicial branches of state government, although not all blue books are blue. For years, Missouri's blue book carried a green cover because the secretary of state was an Irishman. Most blue books contain profiles of state officials and information on agencies, departments and commissions. At times they yield newsworthy nuggets of information. A recent Illinois blue book, for example, describes the functions of the Illinois Department of Nuclear Safety, noting that nearly half of the state's 5,000 X-ray machines checked the previous year failed to comply with safety standards after two inspections. The federal government's equivalent of the blue book is the *United States Government Manual.*

Statutes: Public affairs reporters often turn to bound collections of state or federal statutory law. The statutes cover a broad, detailed range of laws passed by lawmakers. A dozen pages might be devoted to meat-packing regulations; another section might deal with procedures for drunk-driving arrests. Knowing the statutory law is essential in a society so entangled with legal issues. When the district attorney cracks down on adult book stores, an alert court reporter will study all applicable anti-obscenity laws. Annotated versions of statutes contain the legislative histories and legal interpretations of laws.

City and telephone directories: R.L. Polk Co. of Detroit publishes directories for more than 1,400 U.S. cities. Each directory contains the name, address, telephone number, occupation and place of employment for adult residents of the city. Information is cross-listed by address. Polk directories also provide historical and statistical information about the city. Phone books and city directories are basic tools with which reporters check names and addresses. If you must track down out-of-town names and addresses, many libraries subscribe to *Phonefiche,* a microfiche collection of about 3,000 telephone books, including white and yellow pages, from around the country. Keep in mind, though, that any directory may contain dated, incomplete or erroneous information that should be double-checked.

Biographical references: Who's Who in America provides sketches of more than 75,000 noteworthy living people. *Webster's Biographical Dictionary* briefly profiles 40,000 historically significant figures. Lengthier biographical profiles of famous living persons are found in *Current Biography.* A recent four-page entry in *Current Biography* profiles Charles Fuller, a writer noted for his 1982 Pulitzer Prize—winning play that later inspired the movie *A Soldier's Story.* There also are specialized biographical references for notable figures in art, journalism, medicine and science, for example.

Business references: Moody's Manual of Investments, American and Foreign is a five-volume reference source covering transportation, public utilities, municipal government, banks and financial institutions and industrial firms. *Moody's,* for example, provides background information on major corporations, including history, personnel and structure and current developments. You may know Anheuser-Busch produces beer, but Moody's contains details about the brewery's diversified holdings. Complementing *Moody's* is *Poor's Register of Corporations, Directors and Executives.* It contains biographical information on 70,000 executives and lists industrial products and the companies manufacturing or selling them.

Directories: The directory is a key to warehouses of background material. Directories connect reporters with organizations and associations that function, in part, to provide services and information to the public. Five important sources are *The Foundation Directory, Consumer Sourcebook, Directory of Newsletters, Encyclopedia of Associations* and *Directory of Directories*. Using a directory as a guide, a reporter looking into U.S. Department of Transportation rules on wheelchair access to airlines might end up talking to a helpful spokesperson for the Paralyzed Veterans of America. Prior to referring to the directory, the reporter probably had no idea an organization of paralyzed veterans existed. *The Washington Journalism Review* annually publishes its "Directory of Selected News Sources," which contains listings of associations, unions and agencies under more than 40 headings as diverse as "beverages," under which you will find the Beer Institute and the International Bottled Water Association, and "metals," where you will find the Aluminum Association and the Institute of Scrap Recycling Industries.

Dictionaries: In newsrooms, the preferred source is *Webster's New World Dictionary* (third college edition), largely because it supports the Associated Press stylebook on questions of spelling and usage. For precision in the use of words, writers refer to sources such as the *Harper Dictionary of Contemporary Usage*, which will, for example, explain the difference between *continual* and *continuous* or provide the etymology of terms like *mickey finn*.

Investigative sources: A comprehensive guide called *The Reporter's Handbook*, produced by Investigative Reporters and Editors Inc., covers documents and techniques, such as detailed strategy for investigating nursing homes. Other helpful books include *Knowing Where to Look*, by Lois Horowitz; *How to Locate Anyone Anywhere*, by Ted L. Gunderson with Roger McGovern; and *The Guide to Background Investigations*, published by the National Employment Screening Services, which includes, for example, information on how to read social security numbers, the "universal identifier."

Government. A river of information, fed by dozens of tributaries, flows from government on the federal, state and local levels. Although government information is sometimes as murky and polluted as some river water, journalists cannot ignore or underestimate the studies, surveys and reports churned out daily by government offices. Reporters use government documents to produce important stories—on dangerous chemicals in fruits and vegetables, safety lapses at nuclear power plants, violent assaults on school teachers, near collisions of passenger aircraft.

The single best guide to federal documents is the *Monthly Catalog of United States Government Publications*. Published by the U.S. Government Printing Office, the *Monthly Catalog* indexes material in seven ways. Most often journalists use the subject index, which identifies material by number, such as "89-9565." For example, a reporter scanning the index for information about drug smuggling finds a hearings report by a Senate subcommittee investigating terrorism, narcotics and foreign policy. The hearings report is likely to be listed under several subject headings, such as "narcotics" or "foreign policy." The index number is used to find a descriptive entry on the report in the main body of the catalog. If the report seems promising, the reporter can obtain a copy from either a library designated as a depository for government publications or directly from the agency or government branch that issued the report.

Two other GPO publications are the *Congressional Record*, a daily, edited account of House and Senate proceedings, and the *Federal Register*, a daily compilation of rules and information issued by federal regulatory agencies. Not everything in the *Congressional Record* comes directly and verbatim from debate or discussion on the floors of the House or Senate. Members of Congress may edit remarks and insert assorted trivia and extraneous material, such as newspaper editorials, into the *Congressional Record*.

Commercial publishers provide help in tracking down government documents with guides that augment the *Monthly Catalog*. The best of these guides is *Congressional Information Service Index*.

Remember that information produced by federal agencies and offices holds promise for local reporters as well as those assigned to Washington, D.C., bureaus. *Congressional hearings*, in particular, are valuable for background. Not only do they contain testimony by expert witnesses and their exchanges with congressional members and staff, they also frequently include appendices of published material relevant to the subject of the hearings. Comparable indexes and government publications are also available on the state level.

Private sector. The pursuit of information may lead to dealings with lobby groups, special-interest organizations, business and trade associations, non-profit institutions and universities. Reporters are right to question information, especially from those trying to enhance images, sell products, shape public opinion or influence legislation. But do not automatically dismiss information from the private sector on grounds that it may be slanted. Be receptive but discriminating.

Companies and organizations often have free 800 telephone numbers, which help reporters obtain background information. During the brouhaha over the gambling troubles of Cincinnati Reds' manager Pete Rose, two *Chicago Tribune* reporters called 1-800-GAMBLING, the phone number of the Illinois Council on Compulsive Gambling. Answering the phone was the organization's executive director, who provided quotable responses about compulsive gamblers. AT&T publishes an 800 directory, or call 1-800-555-1212 to obtain a number.

Often reporters must work through public relations representatives to obtain access to news sources or information in the private sector. To some reporters, public relations is practiced by unprincipled hacks; they are "hired guns." Actually, many people in public relations come from respectable careers in journalism. Normally public relations people are as accommodating as their roles permit, provided the reporter is fair and decent in return.

Data bases. With more and more information being stored and retrieved electronically, thousands of sources of information—court decisions, magazine articles and government reports—are available to anyone with a computer, a telephone modem and a checkbook. Electronic collections of information are commonly called *data bases.* For reporters, the most useful data-base services provide full-text printouts of material. Data bases are being used for many common reporting tasks, such as developing story ideas, checking facts, preparing for interviews, collecting background information, surveying national trends, locating experts and comparing local against national conditions.[30]

"It's amazing how much information reporters now can find through computers, without having to talk to anyone," says Nora Paul, the *Miami Herald*'s library director. When a reporter asked for background information on Eric Dubins, who wounded his girlfriend, killed her sister and then shot himself, Paul's data-base search, which took less than an hour and cost about $100, yielded valuable leads and sources. Dubins' paper trail included a physical description from state license records available through Compu-

Serve; information from Lexis on a lawsuit filed by Dubins, which provided his lawyer's name; and Dubins' employment history and previous residences from the National Address Identifier data base.[31]

Despite how easy Paul makes it seem, computer searching requires skill and strategy. "It's not a matter of pressing a few keys and—*voilà*—there is the information you seek on a silver monitor," say data-base experts Ken Kister, an authority on reference sources, and Jo Cates, formerly chief librarian at the Poynter Institute for Media Studies.[32] There are too many data-base services and too many variables in search techniques for electronic-information retrieval to be a snap. Even computer-savvy reporters might, at first, ask an experienced librarian or information specialist for instruction and assistance. On the horizon, however, are interactive, voice-generated systems that are expected to allow information searchers to telephone a data-base service, ask simple questions ("Are the Japanese buying New York real estate?") and receive, in return, detailed answers and lists of reference material.[33]

The data-base service most familiar to journalists is Nexis, which offers full-text access to the electronic clippings of more than 160 newspapers, magazines and newsletters, including the *New York Times.* Another popular service is DataTimes. It focuses on indexed, electronic clippings from regional newspapers, such as the *Dallas Morning News* and the *Chicago Sun-Times.* One of the largest services is Dialog, but it is complicated to use. Dialog encompasses dozens of specialized data-base services, including Medline and Aidsline, but these services often provide only a citation to a magazine or newspaper and not the full text. To obtain a copy of an article may mean a trip to a public library.

Data-base information from government and legal sources is available through commercial services like Federal Register Abstracts, Legi-Slate or Lexis. The GPO Monthly Catalog is the electronic version of the *Monthly Catalog of Government Publications.* Eventually, reporters will gain greater access to public information directly from government-run data bases, saving trips to the courthouse or federal building. Reporters already are telephoning federal departments to tap into electronic bulletin boards and other data-base services. Michael Meyers, a reporter for the *Minneapolis Star Tribune,* uses the U.S. Commerce Department's bulletin board to obtain figures and data about economic conditions and trends. Meyers, of course, is limited to information the Commerce Department elects to make available. Even then, some information is not easy to extract. "[A bulletin board] makes a very cooperative source," he says, "if you know how to ask the right questions."[34] A reference work called the *Federal Database Finder* lists more than 300 data bases available from the government, but not all are available through an on-line dialing service; some are on computer tapes.[35]

Seeking information from a 6-foot, 200-pound clerk of the court is one thing; getting it from a computer is another. The clerk can delay or bargain, deceive or disclose, intimidate or cajole. The answer might be, "I'd like to help out, but those records are not public." Thwarted or rebuffed by human sources, computer-age reporters will be tempted to do some electronic snooping. If a 12-year-old hacker can penetrate sophisticated corporate computers, then a 32-year-old reporter ought to be able to get into a county clerk's IBM PC system. Obviously, electronic reporting presents a bubbling cauldron of ethical and legal problems. (Chapters 4 and 10 explore some of those problems.)

The computer is a powerful ally for people engaged in gathering news, but, like the telephone, it can further tie reporters to the office when they should be out interviewing and observing. Reporters are advised not to use data-base services as a shortcut or excuse to bypass other methods of reporting. Nor should journalists accept everything from computers as gospel; all material from data bases should be checked for accuracy.

Professional reading. Prepared, informed and enterprising reporters are eclectic readers. They do not subsist on a diet of big-city newspapers or *Time* and *Newsweek*. Instead, they seek insight and ideas from a diversity of sources, such as *Rolling Stone*, the *National Review*, *Mother Jones*, *Fortune*, *Money*, the *Village Voice*, *Cosmopolitan*, *Washington Monthly*, *Columbia Journalism Review*, the *New Yorker*, *Esquire* and *Compute*, to name but a few. They not only read; they clip and file articles for future use.

Alert reporters also monitor the trade press, which often provides tips and background of their own reporting. The *National Mortgage News* (formerly *National Thrift News*) broke the story of the Keating Five—the U.S. senators linked to a key figure in the savings and loan scandal, Charles H. Keating Jr. Another trade publication, the *Chronicle of Philanthropy*, scooped the mainstream press in 1988 with its investigation of a direct-mail charity scam.[36]

Social-Science Research

Communication theorist Alexis Tan describes the casual, non-scientific methods many people, including journalists, use to explain why things happen or conditions exist.[37] The methods are fraught with potential for error. One is the *method of tenacity.* Many beliefs are held simply because people always considered them to be true. How many children, for example, heard their mothers say, "If you play with frogs, you'll get warts"? Who has not used the expression, "Lightning never strikes the same spot twice"? By repetition, certain knowledge becomes engrained and feels unassailable. Tenacity, however, does not equal proof.

When evidence is conflicting or unclear, people turn to experts for proof—the *method of authority.* Seeking out experts is not inherently bad. Too many experts, though, are media ordained. In journalism circles, the method of authority involves "rounding up the usual suspects." The suspects are what *Newsweek* writer Jonathan Alter calls "quote-meisters" who "traffic in opinion."[38] They often become experts because of a job title they hold (or held) or a hot-selling book they have written. After being interviewed repeatedly by reporters and television hosts, they meet the basic criteria for authority status: availability and quotability. Whether they are indeed knowledgable and authoritative is another matter.

Sometimes people let their gut feelings or common sense suffice as proof. Tan calls this the *method of intuition.* Intuition may be on target, but guard against being led astray by "gut feelings." A reporter whose intuition tells him "the mayor is a crook" may look for "evidence" that supports his intuitive sense and dismiss "evidence" that weakens his case.

Reporters who care about accuracy and fairness know the value of the *scientific method.* The scientific method takes various forms, but basically it involves a systematic, objective, vigorous search for answers. Scientific inquiry usually begins with a problem or question: "Why can't Johnny's father read?" Preliminary explanations are explored, and eventually an hypothesis is developed: "Johnny's father can't read because the educational system failed him and thousands like him." Next comes careful study, observation and verification to confirm or refute the hypothesis. Finally, the findings and conclusions are presented in a report, which itself is subject to further scrutiny.

Although reporters may not follow the scientific method step by step, they should be guided by the spirit of scientific inquiry, particularly its emphasis on *doubt*. The scientific method demands that facts, theories, causes and effects be challenged and, if found suspect or wanting, rejected. Fallacies of reasoning and observation are considered; the potential for error is weighed; variables are explored; criteria are established and defined. A scientific-method reporter who wants to identify America's most dangerous city does not simply telephone a handful of quotable experts, plug in FBI crime statistics, relate some juicy anecdotes and call it a day. She questions the statistics, looking for variables; she pins down criteria to avoid loosely using the term *most dangerous;* and she asks a qualified social scientist to review her methods and conclusions. In journalism, the scientific method is most evident in political polls, opinion surveys, statistical interpretation and field experiments.

Surveys and polls. Opinion research is tricky business, but if done well, it reveals important and sometimes surprising findings. Opinion surveys challenge the conventional wisdom of experts and politicians who claim to know what the public thinks. According to conventional wisdom, let's say, Americans want to see drug-using pregnant women criminally punished for putting their unborn children at risk; an opinion poll reveals that 75 percent of the people polled believe society's proper response is counseling and medical assistance, not jail terms.

Care is needed in measuring opinions. Reporters, used to doing person-on-the-street polls, may assume that a random sample involves questioning people leaving a shopping center. There is randomness to such a method, but to be considered "random" in scientific terms, the sampling must be representative of the population defined in the study. Measuring opinion requires planning, pretesting and precision. Objectives are set; sample sizes determined; questionnaires constructed and reviewed; sample errors estimated; data collected, processed and interpreted. It is not a task for the uninitiated. Do not, though, let the methodology of polling discourage you from doing opinion measurement. Some newspapers employ researchers to help conduct polls; a reporter with little experience in opinion polls can seek assistance from a social scientist, who probably is as nearby as the local university. Experiment in scientific polling on a small scale, asking a professional to critique your work. Remember, too, that shoe leather and door knocking remain valuable as informal, non-scientific ways of sampling how people feel about issues and events.

Even a well-constructed survey cannot be counted on to provide a perfect representation of the population studied. All sound surveys build in a *margin of sampling error.* The margin of error is based on several factors, among them the size of the sample population. Normally, the larger the sample, the smaller the margin of error. Let's say the margin of error is a plus or minus 5 percent. If a poll shows that 52 percent of the voters favor the incumbent, Sen. Thomas, that means Thomas' support could range from 57 to 47 percent. With such a wide margin of error, the reliability of polls to predict outcomes clearly is limited.[39]

Whether reporters conduct opinion surveys themselves or report the results of surveys conducted by others, they must be wary of the power of polls, particularly voter surveys, to influence people and events. A common problem with campaign polls arises when they are used, like a scorecard, to keep tabs on who is leading and who is trailing or to predict, even before voting places close, winners and losers. A better use for campaign studies is to explain the bases and implications of voter behavior.

When relying on surveys conducted by outsiders, reporters are responsible for ensuring that polls do not manipulate or deceive. One safeguard is to include a "truth-in-polling" disclosure in all stories or broadcasts reporting the results of opinion surveys. The statement should disclose who sponsored the poll, how many people were sampled, what questions (with exact wording) were asked, who did the interviewing, how accurate the results are (the margin of error) and how the results were tabulated and analyzed. The *New York Times*/CBS News Poll includes a comparable disclosure statement.

Recently, political analysts renewed fears that voters sometimes lie to pollsters, particularly over questions they are not willing to answer honestly, such as feelings about black candidates. In all instances, polls must account for the reliability of respondents. Surveys still involve a degree of guesswork, which is why political scientist Larry Sabato advises, "Let's pay a great deal less attention to polling. . . . You cannot precisely predict what human beings are going to do."[40]

Statistical analyses. Frequently, the grist for statistical analyses comes from readily available sources, like census data or court records. The term *statistics* refers both to a science and to the process of assembling, classifying and tabulating numerical data. Journalists long have used quantitative data in stories, shifting through piles of records and collecting numbers by hand.

Use of statistics is more common and meaningful now that "number crunching" by computer allows reporters to quickly test hypotheses and seek correlations. Suppose a court reporter decides to determine whether the state's new drunk-driving law is resulting in increased arrests and stiffer sentences, as its proponents claim. If driving-while-intoxicated cases are computerized, those claims can be put to a test quickly. *USA Today* uses computers to conduct nationwide statistical studies. A few years ago, the newspaper examined crime on college campuses, using a team of reporters to collect numerical data and conduct thousands of interviews. In one aspect of its computer analysis, *USA Today* identified and charted a campus "fear index" by region.[41]

When public records, such as crime statistics, are available on computer, a printout or tapes of raw data ought to be easy to obtain. New software packages enable news organizations to take government records stored on tape drives and transfer them to personal computers for easier use and analysis. But raw data alone is not enough. A saying describes the problem of feeding questionable statistics into a computer: "Garbage in, garbage out." Reporters using statistical material must be sure data are sound and accurate.

Those preparing for careers in journalism ought to consider studying computer science, information systems and statistics. Some social-science methodology involves sophisticated computer-generated tabulation and manipulation of data that can only be conducted by highly trained researcher-reporters. Help is also available from several news organizations, among them the Missouri Institute for Computer-Assisted Reporting at the University of Missouri–Columbia and the Gannett Center for Media Studies at Columbia University in New York, which conduct seminars and workshops on data-base journalism projects.

Field experiments. Reporters should feel at home with field research that employs *controlled experiments*. Reporters have used field-experiment methods to determine whether ZIP codes get mail to destinations faster or whether small-town residents are more likely than urban residents to help a lost child. In controlled experiments, the researcher manipulates conditions or situations—the *independent variables*—to observe and measure effects. Independent variables are factors believed to cause or influence certain conditions. Suppose that real estate agents in the town of Pine River are rumored to discriminate against blacks. Since people are unlikely to admit they are breaking fair-housing laws, a field experiment might be the best way—perhaps the only way—to determine whether discrimination exists. So a black reporter and a white reporter separately visit all the town's real estate offices, posing as prospective home buyers. All field experiments, however, must be carefully designed, structured and controlled to ensure validity. Otherwise, there is a high probability that evidence will be flawed. For example, something other than race, such as differences in age, dress or manner, could influence how real estate agents treat the reporters.

As with other types of social-science research, problems arise in drawing conclusions based on field findings. In checking the honesty and competence of auto-repair shops, a reporter takes a car in perfect condition to several shops. Later, another car, with spark-plug wires intentionally crossed, is taken to a half dozen other garages. When a shop charges $100 for an unnecessary tune-up, does that mean the owner cheats—or merely employs inept mechanics? Reporters have to be prepared to accept that the results of some field experiments may be inconclusive.

Field experiments can also be harmful, illegal or unethical. In 1989, two French journalists were caught trying to test security at New York's John F. Kennedy airport by sneaking fake bombs into baggage compartments of several airlines.[42] When field experiments involve breaking the law or endangering people, they are difficult to justify.

The information this chapter provides on methods of reporting is not definitive. It is intended to point you in the right direction and to alert you to the reporting *problems* and *possibilities* ahead. Build on the fundamentals. Continue to learn and develop. Ask for help when unsure of what to do. Never forget that the ultimate objective of all reporting methods is accuracy and *the best obtainable version of the truth.* All reporters stumble and err. Chapter 3 is intended to help you recognize and avoid the errors most common to reporting.

EXERCISES

1. Test the accuracy of your note taking by tape recording your next interview and then comparing your handwritten notes to a tran-

script of the tape recording. Identify your mistakes and try to determine how or why they occurred.

2. Enlist the help of a documents librarian to track down congressional hearings or government reports on a subject of current interest, such as Medicare.

3. Attempt a field experiment to test a theory of your choice. You and other students might, for example, travel by various taxi companies to investigate suspicions that fares between downtown and the airport differ because some cab drivers charge higher fees for luggage or take roundabout routes.

NOTES

[1] Martin Mayer, *Making News* (Garden City, N.Y.: Doubleday, 1987), p. 9.
[2] Quoted in Mayer, *Making News*, p. 2.
[3] Michael Schudson, *Discovering the News* (New York: Basic Books, 1978), p. 194.
[4] Max Ehrmann, *Desiderata* (Los Angeles: Brooke House, 1972).
[5] Janet Malcolm, "The Journalist and the Murderer," *New Yorker*, March 13, 1989, p. 38.
[6] Malcolm, "The Journalist and the Murderer," p. 38.
[7] Lou Cannon, *Reporting: An Inside View* (Sacramento, Calif.: California Journal Press, 1977), p. 31.
[8] James Carey, "The Press and the Public Discourse," *Center Magazine*, March–April 1987, p. 5.
[9] Quoted in *Making Sense of the News* (St. Petersburg, Fla.: Modern Media Institute, 1983), p. 9.
[10] James Reston, *The Artillery of the Press* (New York: Harper & Row, 1967), p. vii.
[11] Jane Delano Brown, Carl R. Bybee, Stanley T. Wearden and Dulcie Murdock Straughan, "Invisible Power: Newspaper News Sources and the Limits of Diversity," *Journalism Quarterly*, Spring 1987, pp. 45–54. See, as well, Leon V. Sigal, *Reporters and Officials* (Lexington, Mass.: D.C. Heath, 1973).
[12] Barbara Hipsman and Carl Schierhorn, "Sharpening the Eyes and Ears of Your Newspapers," *ASNE Bulletin*, Jan. 1989, p. 14.
[13] Hipsman and Schierhorn, "Sharpening the Eyes and Ears of Your Newspapers," p. 15.
[14] Timothy Crouse, *The Boys on the Bus* (New York: Random House, 1973), pp. 21, 22.
[15] Quoted in "The Making of Journalists," *Gannet Center Journal*, Spring 1988, p. 38.
[16] Quoted in Gary Atkins and William Rivers, *Reporting with Understanding* (Ames, Iowa: Iowa State University Press, 1987), p. 6.
[17] Gene Roberts, address before the American Society of Newspaper Editors, 1984.

18 Hunter S. Thompson, *Hell's Angels* (New York: Ballantine Books, 1967), p. 11.

19 Ben H. Bagdikian, *The Shame of the Prisons* (New York: Pocket Books, 1972), pp. 35, 36.

20 See George M. Killenberg and Rob Anderson, *Before the Story: Interviewing and Communication Skills for Journalists* (New York: St. Martin's Press, 1989).

21 Donald M. Murray, "Writing on Writing," No. 3, *Boston Globe*, Jan. 1988, p. 1.

22 Murray, "Writing on Writing," p. 2.

23 Michael Hart, "An Interview with Studs Terkel," *Washington Journalism Review*, Oct. 1989, p. 56.

24 Elisa Bildner, remarks at a seminar of the Poynter Institute for Media Studies, St. Petersburg, Fla., June 5, 1989.

25 Paul McLaughlin, *Asking Questions* (Vancouver: International Self-Counsel Press, 1986), pp. 37–42.

26 Lauren Kessler and Duncan McDonald, *Uncovering the News* (Belmont, Calif.: Wadsworth, 1987), p. 112.

27 John Ullmann, "Tapping the Electronic Library," *IRE Journal*, Summer 1983, p. 9.

28 Ullmann, "Tapping the Electronic Library," p. 10.

29 James J. Kilpatrick, *The Writer's Art* (New York: Andrews, McMeel & Parker, 1984), p. 51.

30 Thomas L. Jacobson and John Ullmann, "Commercial Databases and Reporting: Opinions of Newspaper Journalists and Librarians," *Newspaper Research Journal*, Winter 1989, pp. 22, 23.

31 Nora Paul, "The Killer Left a Paper Trail," *IRE Journal*, Winter 1990, p. 11.

32 Jo Cates and Ken Kister, "Researching Your Feature Story," unpublished manuscript, Poynter Institute for Media Studies, St. Petersburg, Fla., July 1989.

33 Jerome Aumente, "The New Wave of Computer Information Services," *Washington Journalism Review*, Nov. 1988, p. 43.

34 Quoted in Craig Webb, "Government Databases," *presstime*, April 1989, pp. 18, 19.

35 See Michael Hartman, "A Few Databases to Get You Going," *The Quill*, Nov.–Dec. 1990, p. 26.

36 See James R. Ross, "When Trades Lead the Pack," *Columbia Journalism Review*, Nov.–Dec. 1990, p. 18.

37 Alexis S. Tan, *Mass Communication Theories and Research*, 2nd ed. (New York: Wiley, 1985), pp. 10, 11.

38 Jonathan Alter, "Round Up the Usual Suspects," *Newsweek*, March 25, 1985, p. 69.

39 See Jean Ward and Kathleen A. Hansen, *Search Strategies in Mass Communications* (New York: Longman, 1987), pp. 195–218.

40 John Diamond, "Unexpected Outcomes Mean Voters May Be Lying to Pollsters," *St. Petersburg Times*, Sept. 24, 1990, p. 5a.

41 Jerome Aumente, "New PCs Revolutionize the Newsroom," *Washington Journalism Review*, April 1989, p. 42.

42 "Reporters as Stunt Men," *Newsweek*, Jan. 16, 1989, pp. 47, 50.

Chapter Three

Some newspapers were so sure that New York Governor Thomas E. Dewey would defeat Harry S Truman in the 1948 presidential election that they published news of the victory before all the votes were counted. In this photo, the newly elected Truman holds aloft a newspaper erroneously proclaiming his defeat. (UPI/Bettmann)

To Err Is Human—
but
Often Avoidable

Expecting a reporter to produce perfectly accurate stories day in and day out is like counting on a shortstop to cleanly field hundreds of sizzling grounders and twisting line drives in a season without making an error. No baseball aficionado boos the shortstop for missing a few tough-to-handle balls. Yet when a reporter is caught in an error, criticism follows—often in waves. Reporters who commit too many errors end up looking for another line of work.

No one is perfect. At some point, all reporters err in print or on the air. Consider how confusing, complex and ambiguous stories can be. Consider, too, the fallibility of human communication, and then add deadline pressure. Columnist-commentator Andy Rooney, remembering his reporting days, understands how mistakes are made. "I am constantly amazed at how difficult it is to get accurate information about anything," he says. "No reporter sets out to print an inaccurate story but the truth is hard to come by."[1]

Despite the inevitability of errors, journalists must begin every assignment with Joseph Pulitzer's legendary refrain ringing in their ears—"Accuracy, accuracy, accuracy." More is at stake than professional pride or press credibility. When reporters err, lives can be affected. Although there is much talk about the power of the press to influence public policy and issues, that sort of power is abstract and difficult to measure. More concrete and measurable in human terms is the power of the press to confuse, inconvenience, embarrass, damage and harm through erroneous reporting.

Look at what happens, for example, when a reporter fails to double-check information about a public hearing on plans to reroute a state highway. Instead of confirming the time, date and place of the hearing, the reporter assumes the press release is current and correct. It is not. The hearing is important to Tom and Ethel Gordon, whose home is in the path of the highway department's plans. So the Gordons and a dozen other homeowners, relying on information in the hometown newspaper, turn up on Thursday night at city hall. They find the building dark and empty; a handwritten notice tacked to the door says, "Meeting postponed." Inconvenienced and angry, the Gordons are reminded of other mistakes in the newspaper, like the time a family member's name was misspelled in an obituary. "You can't depend on them to get anything right," Ethel Gordon says. The next day, they call to cancel their subscription.

Another reporter, rushing through a stack of incident reports at the police station, takes sloppy notes, later misidentifying a woman in an auto accident as a shoplifting suspect. The woman, a respected, popular first-grade teacher, must face the embarrassment of repeatedly explaining the newspaper's error to friends and colleagues who inquire. A brief retraction, carried on page 12A, does little to ease the hurt or quiet wagging tongues.

Unfortunately, unless the error is serious and blatant, it probably will go undetected by editors or unreported by news subjects, who usually are not provoked enough to complain by letter or phone call. In far too many instances, the offender moves on to other errors, unaware and unaffected by the mess left behind. If lessons are learned, they are apt to be learned the hard way—and at the expense of others. After the damage is done, says one observer, reporters react like people in shooting accidents who say, "I didn't know the gun was loaded."[2]

WARNING: POTENTIAL ERRORS AHEAD

Errors come in many forms and sizes. Some are products of haste, carelessness or inattention. A distracted reporter might scan his notebook and transpose the name "Davis Raymond" as "Raymond Davis." Other errors are barely detectable, rooted in the subconscious. A reporter's biases toward homosexuals, for example, may distort her ability to cover a gay rights march. Occasionally, a gullible reporter falls for a hoax story. Most mistakes, however, are as avoidable as they are intolerable, provided reporters know how to read warning signs and follow precautionary steps.

Recognizing Interviewing Errors

At the heart of many interviewing errors is the reporter's failure to make an accurate, thorough record. No reporter enjoys perfect recall; most take notes, but with varying degrees of precision. Reporters who are careless or casual about note taking are bound to err. When they find that their disorganized, sloppy scribblings are difficult to translate later on, they may begin to assume—a dangerous, unacceptable practice.

Journalists who take a disciplined approach to note taking neatly record interviews, usually in a reporter's spiral notebook that fits in a purse or coat jacket. At the outset, they record the date, time, place of the interview and the name, including middle initial, and the precise title of the interviewee. They take pains to produce legible, functional notes, which they save long after the story is published. Careful reporters often use a tape recorder to back up their notes. Transcribing takes time, but a tape recording is the reporter's best insurance policy against inaccuracy. A tape recording silences critics, reassures editors, guarantees accurate, precise quotes and forgives reporters for moments of distraction or lapses in concentration in an interview.

When reporters do misquote or err, the usual excuse begins, "I assumed" or "I guessed." *Reporters should never assume or guess; they should know.* They cannot engage in assumptions to fill in the gaps after an interview. "I am very concerned at how inaccurate reporting is," says editor Wendell Rawls Jr. "[Reporters] don't take good notes. They are listening to only half the quote, then get back to the office and can't remember what the other half was and are embarrassed to call the person back to ask for a clarification."[3] As soon as possible after an interview, review your notes to determine whether they are clear and complete. If questions surface, contact the interviewee, saying, "I just wanted to make sure that I have this right." Do not be embarrassed. After all, what is more embarrassing: making a polite call to prevent an error or receiving an angry one after the error is published or broadcast?

Veteran investigative reporter Steve Weinberg said that for the first 15 years of his journalism career he adhered to the profession's conventional wisdom: *Never show a story to a news source before publication.* Now he practices prepublication review—for purposes of accuracy only—and is convinced it results in more accurate, fair and thorough news reports.[4] Another veteran reporter, Richard M. Clurman, endorses a "checkback" on important stories for a related benefit—clarity. "Rather than being a violation of journalists' rights or a threat to their independence, it can result in many appropriate instances . . . in new illuminations and nuances that otherwise would have escaped even careful reporting and checking."[5] Not every story requires review; some may simply need a recheck on the accuracy of a particular quotation or passage. But a checkback or prepublication review is often a step worth taking.

Even with the precautions of checkbacks, careful note taking and tape-recorded interviews, errors can tiptoe past reporters, especially when they are lulled into a false sense of security by authoritative news sources. Reporters naturally gravitate to people they have come to expect to be accurate and articulate. But once reporters begin to anticipate the reliability of certain sources, they tend to become less demanding, less questioning and more receptive. If the superintendent of schools tells you, her voice brimming with certainty, "This is the first time we've ever had to close one of our schools," do not assume she is right. To be safe—and correct—check it out.

The weight of authority works in other seductive ways. In the presence of a prominent, powerful figure, reporters may find the interview a heady, disorienting experience. If the governor grants you an exclusive interview, treats you like an honored guest, strokes your ego and whispers confidences in your ear, will your determination to ask hard questions melt away? Quite possibly. Try to maintain your resolve.

In another form of seduction, reporters sometimes uncritically lap up the words and opinions of notable, informative, quote-producing news sources. Consumer activist Ralph Nader, for example, enjoys special influence with reporters. As his biographer notes, "Nader [is] a reporter's dream because he not only had accurate, and sometimes sensational, information, but he knew how to present it to a newsman in a way that often saved the reporter from having to do much work."[6] No matter how reliable and quotable a news source has been in the past, reporters should never accept the latest information as gospel.

Potential interviewing errors also lurk in the wording of questions. Guard, in particular, against ambiguity or murkiness in your questions. Interviewing expert Stanley L. Payne finds that even common words can be misinterpreted. Several repairmen, for example, were separately asked, "How many radio sets did you repair last month?" Payne says the wording of the question seemed perfectly fine until one repairman said, "Who do you mean, me or the whole shop?" To the repairman, *you* had a collective meaning.[7]

In most cases, use simple, understandable, jargon-free language that is familiar to the average person. Avoid leading questions that suggest answers, such as: "Would you say the city was negligent in failing to put warning lights at the intersection?" Some news subjects may respond testily, "Don't put words in my mouth." Often, though, people try hard to please and will eagerly follow the reporter's lead: "Yeah. Somebody ought to be locked up. Any fool could see that an accident was bound to happen there." Reporters who use loaded, suggestive words may elicit juicy quotes, but do the "coached" quotes represent true feelings and opinions? Perhaps not.

With long, complicated questions, a simple, common-sense proposition applies: The longer the question, the longer the response.[8] Thus, convoluted complex questions tend to produce convoluted, complex answers, compounding the chances of misunderstanding, misinterpretation and misquotation.

As an interview progresses, inwardly ask yourself, "Am I being clear; am I being understood?" Then, aloud, ask the interviewee, "Am I being clear? Am I understanding you clearly and correctly?" Far from alienating interviewees, your concern over the clarity of communication will be reassuring.

Less easy to recognize are errors resulting from the interviewer-interviewee relationship. A reporter who sends negative messages—indifference, boredom or hostility—can expect a less expansive, less cooperative interview partner than the reporter who sends positive messages. Biases, in particular, can poison interviews. A reporter assigned to interview a convicted rapist may lose emotional control and allow his feelings of contempt to show in his demeanor and questions. Those feelings also subvert his ability to listen and evaluate.

Besides keeping emotions in check, reporters must remain alert during an interview, assessing both speech and body language for meaning. Does sweat on an interviewee's forehead suggest she's lying? Does an obviously inappropriate response to your question indicate that the interviewee misunderstood you? If an answer is vague, is the interviewee being evasive? Do not jump to conclusions; consider and explore a full range of other possibilities. Perspiration may be a sign of nervousness, not lying. A disjointed answer might indicate lack of knowledge or a poorly phrased question on your part, not misunderstanding. Instead of being evasive, an interviewee may simply be at a loss for a concrete example. Being sensitive and open-minded helps you anticipate communication problems and avert mistaken impressions that can lead to errors.

Above all, recognize the limitations of interviews. Have realistic expectations: How well can you get to know a person in a 45-minute interview? Remember, too, that the odds of interviewing error decrease as the scope of your pursuit of truth and accuracy expands. Question and confirm; do not expect accuracy if you rely on one or two sources.

Seeing and Believing

No one's observational acuity is 20/20. One source of distortion involves a principle of physics known as Heisenberg's Rule of Indeterminacy: Some particles cannot be accurately studied because the light needed for examination alters the particles.[9] The rule applies to behavioral science as well. Reporters need to remember that their presence as observers can influence the behavior of others. Reporter Mary Lou Janson spent 80 days in a first-grade classroom, observing how children learn. At first she watched quietly from a first-grader-sized chair in the back of the room. She related her experience: "The first few weeks they would occasionally stare at me. But by mid-year they ignored me. Late in the school year, they would ask me how to spell words, or show me pictures they had drawn."[10] Janson's approach gave her—and her readers—an unusual exposure to education. But was it a *true* view? How did the students and teacher react to being watched? Did they really ignore her presence? Did they change as a result of Janson's presence?

Secretive observation and masquerades allow reporters to watch more discreetly, but such methods do not eliminate the possibility of distortion. In fact, a reporter posing as an abused wife risks affecting the dynamics of a therapy group at a women's shelter. Over time, the reporter might lose her objectivity as she begins to see the subjects as friends. She may become a leader in the group. Moreover, the reporter's perceptions change as she becomes immersed in the experience. Initially she felt a detached sympathy for battered women; now she fights to suppress feelings of outrage. Changes cut both ways: The reporter changes others as *she* herself is changed.

Observation is affected by another form of distortion known as "the *Rashomon* effect." The term comes from a classic Japanese film that explores four accounts of the rape of a woman and the murder of her husband. In turn, each character in the film tells a markedly different story; ego and ulterior motives shape their versions. By the film's end, viewers find it impossible to know what really happened. Witnesses to news events react similarly. A bank guard describes how he kept his cool during an armed robbery; a teller, however, recalls seeing the guard cowering behind a post. Both versions are likely to be subjective. Although the *Rashomon* effect cannot be neutralized, obtaining and comparing as many accounts as possible helps minimize its role. A thorough investigation can lead to dramatic results. In 1989, an acclaimed documentary, *The Thin Blue Line*, helped free a man wrongly convicted of murder by re-enacting and, in several instances, discrediting the conflicting stories of witnesses to the crime.

As *Rashomon* and *The Thin Blue Line* demonstrate, vantage points and emotional states contribute to observational distortions. Watching an anti-abortion rally from the speaker's platform yields one slice of reality; observing from the middle of the crowd offers another; standing with a contingent of police produces a third view. That is why reporters are encouraged to move about at news scenes, gathering and assessing various pieces of the picture, and to try to keep their own emotions in check.

The likelihood of observational distortion is high when a news event is chaotic or traumatizing. Witnesses, for example, to China's bloody removal of student protestors from Tiananmen Square in the summer of 1989 described horrors previously unknown to them. "We expected tear gas and rubber bullets," said Huang Jing, a graduate student at Harvard. "But they used machine guns and drove over people with tanks. One line of students would stand up and then get shot down and then another line of students would stand and the same thing would happen. The soldiers were shooting everyone."[11] The account is powerful and emotional. Under trying, emotional conditions—through tears, outrage and pain—the vision of witnesses and journalists alike can become blurred.[12]

Reporters generally are sound observers, but they, too, are prone to perceptual errors. What you see is not necessarily what others see. Cultural differences, for instance, affect observation. To an Anglo observer, two older Hispanics haggling over the price of tomatoes appear to be so angry they may come to blows. In reality, the men are friends who re-enact the scene endlessly; it is part of a give-and-take heritage of bargaining.

A cognitive process called *selective perception* also influences the ability to observe. Selective perception affects reporters and news sources alike. People tend to see events and people through filters. Sometimes the process involves seeing what we *expect* to see, not actually what happened or what exists. A reporter who strongly believes career soldiers are hardened warriors may fail to see a general's peaceful, gentle side. Being aware of the power of selective perception can help reporters observe with greater care, and remind them to seek out people and details to check the validity of their observations.

As with interviewing, reporters should have realistic expectations about the ability to observe. At best, observation yields an *approximation* of human experiences.

Counting on Numbers

To some people, there are lies, damned lies and statistics. Much public mistrust of statistics dates to Darrell Huff's 1954 widely read monograph, *How to Lie with Statistics*. Actually, numbers do not lie until someone twists them or misreads them. A couple of relatively uncomplicated uses of statistics by reporters illustrate the potential for error.

Several years ago, the *St. Louis Globe-Democrat* published a story with the headline, "Suicides Highest Among the Elderly." Based on information from the reporter, a chart of suicides by age groups accompanied the story. The chart put the suicide rate for people age 65 and over at 21 percent per 100,000 people. The next day, with considerable embarrassment, the newspaper reported what should have been obvious to the reporter and editors handling the story: The suicide statistics were based on the *number* of persons per 100,000 people, not on a *percentage*. For every 100,000 people in the state over the age of 65, 21 committed suicide, not 21 percent.

The second example is a classic case of statistical overstatement based on too small of a sampling. It dates to the New York City power failure of 1965, when about 30 million people went without electricity for up to 12 hours. Exactly nine months after the blackout, the *New York Times* tested a theory: With no television to watch, movies to attend or lights to read by, couples turned to each other for diversion.

Surveying eight New York hospitals, the *Times* reported a dramatic increase in the birth rate. Later, though, an inclusive report from 100 local hospitals revealed that the numbers of births nine months from the blackout date was actually slightly lower than normal.[13]

Drawing conclusions from statistics is especially risky. Care must be taken to see that all variables—conditions that might affect conclusions—are considered. If the police department hires 50 additional officers and the number of home burglaries drops significantly the next month from the burglary rate of a year before, the statistics suggest a correlation: More police equals less crime. When the variables are considered, however—perhaps the new officers were sweating through training and not deterring burglars that month, perhaps changes in the weather, the economy or the unemployment rate were factors—it may not be possible to draw the obvious correlation.

Errors also occur when reporters confuse *percentages* with *percentage points.* In an election poll, for example, if 60 percent of the voters favor Candidate X in August, and her support wanes to 45 percent in October, she has not experienced a 15 percent drop in support. Her support dropped 15 percentage points; translated to percentages, she experienced a 25 percent loss of support.

Numbers impress people. They carry the weight of authority. But whose authority? Question numbers; apply common sense when looking for errors; seek substantiation. (Chapter 9 addresses the problems of political polls.) A wire-service story says a faucet leaking one drop a second wastes 2,300 gallons a year. Using a cookbook table that cited 60 drops in a teaspoon, a skeptical reader figured the water loss at 684 gallons.

Out of Context

The story is familiar: Two politicians of the old school are commiserating about the press. Sen. Blowhard, shaking a copy of the *Daily Bugle,* snorts, "There they go again, quoting me out of context verbatim." Reporters enjoy the story because, from their perspective, it rings true. In many instances, a newsmaker's complaint that "I've been quoted out of context" actually means, "I've been quoted correctly, but *now* I don't like the way my words read in print or sound on the air." But do not dismiss Sen. Blowhard's charges; people, indeed, are embarrassed and wronged by reporters who have quoted or paraphrased them accurately—but out of context.

An example from the *Alton* (Ill.) *Telegraph* illustrates what happens when context is overlooked or ignored. Assigned to cover a panel discussion on "What It Means to Be a Christian in Today's Society," a reporter, paraphrasing one of the participants, wrote: "Professor Huntley believes that in order to be a Christian you must be against equal rights, Dungeons and Dragons (because that is the occult), abortion, humanism (whatever that is) and evolution." In a strict sense, the paraphrased passage is correct. Huntley used those very words. Missing, however, is the context—the crucial qualifiers that prefaced and amplified his remarks. Embarrassed by coverage of his presentation, Professor Huntley sent the newspaper a copy of his opening remarks. Examined in their entirety, Huntley's words revealed the clearly satirical nature of his presentation. He began by saying,

> Unfortunately, in this day and age too many people believe that in order to be a Christian one must be for: prayer in the public schools; a strong defense policy, which means you have to be for killing, as long as you do it in great numbers and to the sound of fife and drum or other appropriate flag-raising music; capital punishment, which means you can also be for killing in small numbers as long as it is done by firing squad, hanging, gas, electrocution or lethal injection, or any other humane means; creationism, which means you cannot take such ungodly and sinful courses as biology, paleontology, geology, natural history.

He continued in a similar vein and concluded with the passage that drew the reporter's attention:

> Christians must be against: Sin, which probably includes sex, alcohol, pot, rock and roll and anything else that is done after dark and might be fun; Communism; the Equal Rights Amendment; Dungeons and Dragons, as being occult; humanism, whatever that is; evolution; abortion, which is killing; and the Supreme Court.

Reporters frequently find themselves forced to condense and paraphrase, which sets the stage for another form of contextual error. Leo Della, ombudsman for the *Arizona Daily Star,* explains the problem. "There are times . . . when the editing philosophy of trim, trim, trim should be junked. Important details, supporting arguments and vital nuances can't always be subjected to telegraphic treatment."[14] That is particularly true of stories based on the ideas of expert news sources who need time and space to explain their views. Expert sources who find their words distorted by abridged treatment will be reluctant to share information the next time a reporter asks for an interview.

Quoting or paraphrasing people out of context is a serious problem for reporters. Rene J. Cappon, author of *The Word,* a book that focuses on news writing problems, cautions about errors of context. "Next to getting the actual words right, the most important thing is to keep quotes in context. Failure usually arises from careless compression that makes a statement appear more emphatic than it is. A qualification may be dropped or buried, a speaker's elaboration of a point overlooked, or a remark intended as jocular reported deadpan."[15]

Be careful if a catchy quotation or an isolated remark becomes the central focus of your story or lead. As a safeguard, ask this important question: Do the words—without their context—fairly and accurately represent the speaker's *overall* views? If, for example, an interviewee spends 45 minutes saying positive things about the city's mayor, is it fair for a reporter to write a lead that highlights the one critical remark made during the interview?

Care also is needed with regard to two other contextual problems. One is juxtaposing remarks. When words spoken early in an interview or speech are placed next to words that came much later, reporters flirt with contextual problems. Let's say state Sen. Mary Bartlett comments to a reporter, "This is a rotten piece of legislation, and Sen. Davis knows it." She then spends 10 minutes explaining her point of view. Bartlett ends by saying, "He really sold out on this one." The reporter splices the two quotations, leaving the impression that Sen. Davis acted improperly or illegally. But the full context of the interview clearly indicates that Bartlett believes Davis "sold out" in the sense that he reneged on an earlier pledge to Bartlett to vote against the legislation. Is this sloppy reporting? Is it unethical? By juxtaposing the comments the reporter, at the very least, distorted Sen. Bartlett's position.

Cappon underscores the other contextual problem: "You can . . . skewer a quote by converting a long, involved question into the subject's answer." He offers this example:

Reporter: "Do you feel the verdict was wrong, that it was a gross miscarriage of justice?"

News subject: "Well, yes."
Copy: He said "he felt that the verdict was wrong and a gross
    miscarriage of justice."[16]

Unfairly and inaccurately, a brief, qualified response, "Well, yes" is
converted into a full-blown, unequivocal statement.

Whenever there is doubt about misrepresenting someone's comments or views, consider consulting with news subjects and allowing them to hear what you have written. Remember, you are not
asking them to edit or censor your story; you are merely trying to
ensure that justice is done for everyone concerned—you, the news
subject and the audience.

Not Getting Fooled

Be prepared. People will to try to fool you. Gullible, careless,
naive, arrogant or mean-spirited reporters are especially tempting
targets for someone's hoax, setup or revenge.

In particular, watch out for pranks. Some are intended to embarrass an unpopular reporter; others amount to an initiation for a
newcomer to a beat. A detective, for example, baits a hook, not really
expecting the cub reporter to bite. "Hey, Joe, we've got a lead on a guy
who steals steaks, chops and ribs right off people's grills. We call him
the 'barbecue bandit.' " The reporter, pleased the detective is helping
him on a story, dutifully asks questions and takes notes. The detective, grinning throughout, says to himself, "Who'd swallow such a
story?" He is shocked when a brief story about the "investigation"
appears in the newspaper. When practical jokes go this far, everyone
gets in trouble. Admittedly, even a veteran journalist initially might
believe the detective's story; it promises to be a decent "brite" on an
otherwise dull news day. But few reporters would publish without
asking for details and talking to victims, steps that would expose
most pranks.

Occasionally, people orchestrate elaborate hoaxes, holding media events, issuing press releases, publishing studies and construct-
ing identities to entrap the press. A few years ago, Joseph Skaggs, a
New York journalism teacher, staged an event to prove his conten-
tion that the press is easy to dupe. Posing as Dr. Josef Gregor, a
fictitious scientist from South America, Skaggs held a news conference to discuss Gregor's group, Metamorphosis, and his experiences
with the curative powers of cockroach pills. The hoax was inspired

by Franz Kafka's story in which Gregor Samsa awakens to discover he has changed into a cockroach-like creature. United Press International covered the news conference, and dozens of newspapers carried the story of Gregor and his cockroach pills. Skaggs believes it is easy to fool the media, especially with sensational, sexy or funny stories, because reporters fail to check the facts.[17]

How do you expose the Dr. Gregors of the world? Skepticism and digging remain the best weapons against a hoax. Verify credentials and claims. Ask for documentation. Unless there is no doubt about the newsmaker's authenticity, routinely check the background of everyone you cover. Certain stories are, indeed, too good—or too bizarre—to be true; some, however, despite straining credulity, are true. It is up to you to uncover the bogus stories without blithely dismissing legitimate ones. Reporters who seek multiple confirmation rarely fall victim to pranks.

A close relative of the hoax is the media event, staged to attract press coverage. Media events may generate bonafide news, such as a politician's tour of a flooded town or an NAACP march in front of the mayor's house. In fact, groups and individuals outside normal news channels resort to media events simply to gain a hearing. Although their methods may be contrived, remember that their message might have merit.

Most efforts to fool or manipulate reporters are not malicious. There are exceptions, however, like this one:

> A man posing as a well-known assistant district attorney calls the newspaper's courthouse bureau 20 minutes before deadline to report the out-of-town arrest of a local business executive. The news is not unexpected; the executive has been in legal trouble previously. Moreover, the assistant DA is quite convincing; although the reporter has not met him, she recognizes the name and knows the assistant DA's reputation for being a straightshooter. The attorney even leaves an off-duty number. "You can reach me there in an hour or so, in case you have other questions," he says.

The trap snaps shut, and a fake story is published. Later, the business executive threatens to sue for libel. Was the newspaper set up so the executive could have grounds for a libel suit? Did an enemy of the executive use the newspaper to get even? Did someone in the district attorney's office play an irresponsible joke on the reporter?

In any case, the antidote is the same: Planted stories quickly unravel when reporters take a few minutes to verify the identity of news subjects and the authenticity of information.

Finally, there are stories so captivating or plausible they gain news legitimacy by being retold and embellished repeatedly. Jan Harold Brunvand calls these accounts "urban legends." They usually begin as orally transmitted folklore. In his books *The Vanishing Hitchhiker* and *The Choking Doberman*, Brunvand relates the history and meaning of such stories, which include, he says, pets accidentally cooked in microwave ovens, alligators lurking in New York City sewers and convertibles filled with cement by jealous husbands. Most often, reporters recognize the stories as rumors and try to dispel them. Now and then, though, overeager, imprudent journalists fall prey.

One seemingly irresistible urban legend centers on drug dealers who try to entice children by lacing Mickey Mouse lick-and-stick tattoo transfers with LSD. The story achieved credibility because of a 1980 bulletin issued by the narcotics bureau of the New Jersey state police, warning that some drug-laced "blotter sheets" were imprinted with cartoon-like figures that children might find attractive. The bulletin carried an illustration of a "sorcerer's apprentice" that vaguely resembled Mickey Mouse. A year later, the superintendent of the Ohio Bureau of Criminal Investigation inadvertently lent further credibility to the legend by being identified as the source in several stories recounting the arrest of a drug dealer caught with 5,000 tabs of blotter acid in his car. Reporters covering the case asked about the rumored Mickey Mouse connection. Patiently and repeatedly, says Brunvand, the superintendent denied the existence of Mickey Mouse–inspired acid stickers, but the rumor persisted, thanks, in part, to irresponsible press hype.[18]

Exaggeration

Be wary of overstating the importance of events, such as court rulings, election outcomes or scientific discoveries. Certain words— *landmark, unprecedented* and *breakthrough*—should sound an alarm. Ask yourself whether you are inflating or overestimating the story. Ask, too, if the source of the news is exaggerating the importance. To avoid errors of exaggeration, check with other knowledgable news sources to see whether they see the event or development similarly.

Contributing to errors of exaggeration is the pressure to produce stories that prompt editors to tell the reporter, "Good stuff." Historian David Hackett Fischer used the term *prodigious fallacy* to describe accounts that attempt to equate sensation with significance. Prodigious fallacies, he says, are widely disseminated by journalists, who freely use terms like *historic* for anything from state funerals to transatlantic canoe trips.[19]

People depend on journalists to help them measure the importance of events. Cancer patients, for example, eagerly read stories about new drugs or treatments. Reporters should not raise false hopes by producing overblown accounts, nor should they unduly cause alarm. Is scientist Richard Lipsey correct when he says sensationalized press coverage has created a generation of "chemophobics"?[20] Criticism like Lipsey's cannot be brushed off as self-serving. Sensationalism remains a problem of journalism, which is why in some newsrooms, reporters are told to be mindful of a simple rule: If you err, err on the side of restraint. There is always tomorrow's—or next week's—newscast or newspaper.

Shaping the News?

Few stories are outright fabrications, premeditated and calculated. More often, reporters produce pseudo-stories, creations inspired by a personal agenda or moral indignation. Media observer Bob Garfield cites *USA Today* for manufacturing a brouhaha over an advertisement for a sunscreen product. The advertisement shows a bikini-clad little girl reclining on a chaise with her mother, identically attired. A headline in *USA Today* said, "Bain du Soleil ad has critics burning." According to the story, feminists and media critics were outraged by the provocative nature of the advertising. The story indicated that there had been a spontaneous uprising. Not so, says Garfield. "None of the quoted critics had been moved to say a thing about the ad *until solicited for comment,* whereupon they suddenly became aggrieved on demand." Garfield, his own outrage showing, noted: "Waving a controversial ad before the National Organization of Women and Media Watch is like gluing antlers to a cow on the first day of hunting season; old Elsie's gonna get blasted, even if it isn't a legitimate beef."[21]

Countless news stories follow a similar pattern. A congressman, for example, is arrested for soliciting a prostitute; reporters rush to seek reaction from his friends and foes. The reporters probe in leading ways: "Shouldn't the congressman resign?" "Isn't his credibility so seriously damaged that he can no longer be effective in the House?" "Isn't this going to kill his chances for re-election?" The answers generate a story that says: "Friends and foes of Congressman X, saying he has lost his credibility to be effective in the House, believe he ought to either resign or not seek re-election." In another instance, a judge, prodded by a reporter's line of questioning, criticizes police for sloppy arrest procedures in a rape case; the reporter conveys the judge's remarks to police officers, who respond in kind. The story that emerges begins: "Judge X and police officers are feuding over the handling of a rape arrest earlier this month." Can you say such stories "existed" before reporters entered the picture? To be sure, the press plays an important catalytic role in bringing society's issues and problems to public attention. And reporters are right to ask tough questions and, at times, even leading questions. But whenever journalists cross the line from reporter to *agent provocateur,* they tamper with reality.

Haste and Waste

News consumers expect news quickly, but they dislike reports containing contradictory information. Reporters are caught in the middle: If they move too quickly, they risk error; if they move too slowly, they risk being scooped.

Television reporters are particularly vulnerable to haste-induced errors. Working from mobile units equipped for live, on-the-scene broadcasts, they compete to see which station airs the news first. Channel 5's reporter rushes to a reported kidnapping of a 16-year-old girl by two black men. In a live broadcast, the girl's sister describes how the teenager was grabbed off the street. The teenager's tearful father holds a picture of his daughter, pleading with the abductors to release her unharmed. It is a powerful, potentially inflammatory story. The police, however, are non-committal, with reason. The following morning, the sisters admit to concocting the story so the teenager could spend the night with her boyfriend.

Official sources, confused by events and pressured to deliver facts to reporters, err, too. A dramatic example of hasty, faulty reportage occurred in 1971 when inmates at New York's notorious Attica prison revolted and seized guards as hostages. In a bloody counterattack, police and state troopers reclaimed the prison. With tear gas and gunsmoke still in the air, shaken law enforcement officials met the press, describing how inmates slashed the throats of the hostages. One hostage was castrated, the *Washington Post* reported. The next day, however, autopsy reports revealed that all hostages died of gunshot wounds and none was castrated. Furthermore, prison officials acknowledged that no guns were found among the inmates' collection of hand-made weapons. Apparently, the hostages were killed by police bullets.

What happened? One reporter on the scene believes journalists were mentally conditioned to believe the official account even prior to the attack. "Before they went in," he said, "everybody was telling us about knives pointed at throats, that these guys weren't joking, and so on. Your mind was prepared for the idea that the prisoners were going to be violent. Then when the troopers and prison people came out with stories of throats cut, everything seemed to dovetail."[22] No reporters actually saw any of the Attica killings. They were kept outside the prison, piecing together stories from an assortment of available witnesses and participants. Had reporters and officials questioned accounts more carefully or waited for autopsy results, serious mistakes could have been avoided. Of course, with breaking stories of such magnitude, reporters sometimes have little choice but to rely on information provided by officials. But always question official accounts, insisting on as many details and particulars as possible.

With certain stories it is difficult to know just when to go public. Rumors and innuendo fall into this category. In 1989, premature media reports, fed by unnamed Navy sources, implicated a young gunner's mate, Kendall Truitt, in an explosion on the battleship *Iowa* that killed 47 sailors. According to published rumors, Truitt and a shipmate who died in the blast were in a homosexual relationship that soured. Adding fuel to the rumors was a single fact: Truitt was the beneficiary of the dead shipmate's life insurance. For weeks, Truitt denied the rumors and proclaimed his innocence. Finally the Navy officially cleared Truitt of any involvement in the explosion. By then, though, Truitt said, the Navy and news media had ruined his life. Were reporters too hasty in covering the Truitt story? Once the Truitt story surfaced in one newspaper, did other reporters rush like lemmings after a titillating rumor? Is it too much to ask the news media to wait for concrete, on-the-record evidence of Truitt's guilt or innocence? Jean Otto, associate editor of the *Rocky Mountain News*, urges reporters to be particularly skeptical about the motives of government sources. In her view, the press often reacts too quickly—and without regard for errors of haste. "Why do we grab it and go with it? It's partly competition. 'Get it first and correct it later' is still an operating principle, if not a motto. Having to correct it later can be devastating to some individuals' lives. And we frequently, in pursuit of a story, don't think about the target of that story. . . . After the fact is terrific, but after the fact doesn't save the destruction of somebody's reputation."[23]

Reports from the police beat also force reporters to make tough decisions. Because allegations by victims may turn out to be concoctions, police carefully challenge all serious accusations. How long do you wait, for example, before identifying a minister accused of indecent exposure? And what about possible false alarms? If a teenager is reported missing by her parents, do you wait to see whether she is an overnight runaway and not a victim of foul play? With other stories, procedures are clear. For example, you do not report the names of accident victims prematurely; reporters wait until identities are confirmed and relatives are notified and cared for by family or friends.

Although we live in a fast-paced, media-intensive world, certain stories and situations call for deliberation and restraint. Reporters should not let deadlines, peer pressure or competition for a scoop force them into filing a hasty, ill-advised story.

A Question of Taste

A story can be factually correct and still wrong in the sense of inappropriate language or bad taste. Although reporters strive for vivid writing, some details are too gruesome for the sensibilities of most readers and viewers. Accounts of sex crimes and traffic accidents often are sanitized.

But deciding where to draw the line can be difficult. A reporter obtains a dramatic, wrenching transcript of a 911 call. It contains the sobbing pleas of a 10-year-old who accidentally shot and killed his little sister: "I shot her. I didn't mean to. Please don't die. Please, God, please, don't be dead. Oh, please help me." In print the words are disturbing; an audio replay might be extremely distressing for audiences. Yet put in the context of a significant increase in accidental shootings, perhaps people need to feel the full impact of a tragedy to prevent further tragedies.

Around newsrooms people talk about the breakfast test: Could you read or view the story over a bowl of cereal without your stomach turning? This subjective test would kill some stories that should be told regardless of how they affect someone's appetite, but as a general rule, if details or words would disturb a sensitive person you know, soften or withhold them.

Letting Ignorance Show

Nearly all errors by journalists are embarrassing in one way or another. But errors of ignorance are among the most embarrassing of all.

Surprisingly, some reporters stumble over language usage. They mix metaphors, such as "He's been keeping his ear to the grindstone" or "It's time the project be sent back to the cutting board." They translate unfamiliar words to familiar ones, spelling "microfiche" as "microfish" or "taut" as "taught." Writer Bob Swift collects hybrid abominations, calling them "malaphors"—the fusion of mixed metaphors and malapropisms. "They almost make sense, then you do a double take," he says. A friend of Swift's puts malaphors in the realm of "fruitworthy English," named for Chicago Mayor Jane Byrne, who once said she hoped an investigation would "prove fruitworthy." Among Swift's favorite malaphors are "He's a ragged individualist;" "I was up at the crank of dawn;" and "He's a fly in the oatmeal."[24]

Journalists with deficiencies in basic knowledge also make mortifying mistakes. What constitutes basic knowledge? Conversational familiarity with a variety of subjects is one measurement. A knowledge of history and culture is another. In Chapter 2, reporters were encouraged to read extensively. Reading the *New York Times* or *Newsweek* regularly is a step in the right direction, but it is not enough. Well-read journalists accumulate story ideas, expand their vocabulary and stay abreast of current affairs.

Familiarity with important moments in history is particularly important. What do you know about Franklin Delano Roosevelt's court-packing scheme? What's the historical significance of *Lebensraum*? History provides perspective and context for today's news. Unschooled reporters, for example, might assume that Ronald Reagan was the first American president to send Marines to Lebanon, not knowing that Dwight Eisenhower dispatched troops there in 1958. Knowledge of local history is just as important.

Columnist Meg Greenfield, however, warns us not to mistake a mountain of information for actual understanding. As she explains: "It is one of the ironies of the current well-documented information explosion with all its instantaneous transmission of news and data around the globe and right into your car radio that we get the impression that we know more than we do. . . . Our heads are stuffed full of snippets of lore that give us the false impression that we know something when we don't or when what we do know is only the most superficial skimming of the pond."[25] Her warning is particularly applicable as reporters attempt to understand people and events foreign to them. Instead of accounting for cultural and political differences, underinformed journalists tend to superimpose an American template on developments elsewhere. One way to avoid errors of ignorance is to be smart enough to ask questions whenever you do not *know* or are not *sure.*

Evaluating and Selecting Information

It is time to write. Before you are notes, observations, documents, figures—the raw material for your story. Reporters should evaluate material throughout the reporting process to determine whether it is logical, accurate, valid and fair. Now, though, you must evaluate yourself—your decision making—as you put together the story.

Do not expect to be absolutely sure of doing the right thing. In fact, uncertainty will keep you vigilant. Each story poses its own set of problems, questions and uncertainties. But evaluative errors frequently creep into journalistic writing, and reporters should be especially alert for them.

One involves what David Hackett Fischer calls the *lonely fact.*[26] The lonely fact follows a sweeping generalization. Often the lonely fact is prefaced by the telltale phrase "for example" or "for instance." Generalizations in news stories follow a familiar form:

> Feminists are up in arms over the president's failure to appoint a woman to the cabinet.

On the heels of the generalization is an authoritative quote or two:

> "It's a slap in the face to all women," says Sally Porter, spokesperson for Women for Women.

There is nothing wrong about using a single supporting example, as long as it is representative of a convincing stack of uncited evidence. Are "all" or even most feminists *really* "up in arms," or is it just a few? Never use a single fact to prop up a fallacious generalization.

Journalists readily reach for words that appear to convey authority and significance, such as *many, most* and *widespread*. These, too, are generalizations, and without the support of numbers and evidence, they are weak, meaningless words. Reporters who casually use such words without being sure they rest on a solid foundation of facts are imprecise at best and misleading at worst.

Other words carry a connotative power that should never be underestimated. In evaluating the tone or emphasis of your story, ask whether you are using what semanticist S.I. Hayakawa calls "snarl words" or "purr words."[27] These words suggest approval or disapproval or promote negative or positive images. In describing a civil rights activist a reporter could call her "committed," "intense" or "obsessed." A story about a first-year legislator might describe him as "timid" instead of "cautious." When a police chief will not answer questions about a murder, does he "decline" or "refuse" to comment? Reporters must recognize whether they are using words that snarl or purr, check their biases and, at times, substitute less judgmental language.

Fischer's observations also apply to another journalistic tendency—the *fallacy of responsibility*. The fallacy, he says, is most likely to arise when people try to explain bad news.[28] A bridge collapses, a space shuttle explodes, a riot erupts. At first, reporters ask, "What happened?" and "What caused it?" Soon, though, the question becomes, "Who is to blame?" and the focus, he says, usually turns to finding a human agent. Reporters are supposed to ask questions to determine cause and to fix accountability, but they cannot assume that a culprit exists. In fact, they must consider the possibility that no one is to blame.

What's in a name?

What is signaled by a mistake in a name?

Name errors quickly and decisively reduce the credibility of journalism and journalists. Can you expect people to have much confidence in other details of a story if they know a name is not reported accurately?

Reporters should unfailingly check every name and title in a story—double-check, in fact. Always ask people to spell their names—first, middle initial and last. Ask how they prefer to be named and identified. Never assume you know how a name is spelled. Years ago, you could expect common spellings and common names—*Tom, Mary,*

Robert. Now you can count on fanciful, unusual names and spellings. You cannot even assume that family members spell their last names the same. In an Associated Press story, an alert reporter learned that one news subject spelled his name Marasciullo, but a sister, also quoted, had dropped an *l* from her name years before.

Foreign names present special problems. Is Libya's leader *Muammar Khadafi* or *Moammar Qaddafi* or *Muammer al-Gadafy?* News organizations spell his name different ways because there is no correct English spelling. Each version is an attempt to capture the correct phonetic transliteration of his Arabic name. Korean names generally consist of a family name followed by a two-element personal name, but not always. While Park Chung Hee is referred to as *Park* on second reference, Syngman Rhee is *Rhee* on second reference.

Do not count on directories, nameplates or business cards to be correct or up-to-date; whenever possible, ask the person directly.

Continue to check and be exact in using the names of organizations and businesses. Is it *K-mart, Kmart, K-Mart* or *K mart?* Does *Corp., Inc.,* or *Ltd.* follow a company name? Is it the *Sunshine Foundation*—or the *Sonshine Foundation?* Be sure.

Roy Peter Clark, dean of faculty at the Poynter Institute for Media Studies, relates an experience with incorrect names. It involved a story about a young man who drove a truck through the window of a donut shop. The young man was identified as a student from Sunnybrook College in New York. "Since I spent four years there, I know that's not the name of the school," Clark said. The next day the paper corrected the error; the school was the State University of New York at Stonybrook, Long Island. "That's closer," Clark said, "but the correct spelling is Stony Brook."

Clark suggests this antidote for errors: "The best lesson on the need for accuracy is to have a story written about you."[29]

TELLING THE WHOLE STORY

"Woman jumps from bridge," a headline says. At first glance, the story that follows is a precise account—accurate and complete. It includes details about the search for the woman's body, a description of how she was dressed, comments from a state trooper who saw the woman jump. Still, there is an error. It could be called an error of omission. An important detail is missing: How high is the bridge? The answer to that question raises another: Could someone survive a jump from that height?

Another story tells how a 24-year-old mentally impaired woman killed a motorist in a traffic accident. The woman, police say, has never had a driver's license and cannot read or write. Details about the accident are included, but unanswered is a series of questions that seem so apparent: How did she get a car? Who owns the car? How did she learn to drive?

Police officers interrupt an attack on two women in the parking lot of a fast-food restaurant. They heard the women scream, the newspaper reports, and they chased the man, arresting him after he circled back to the parking lot. No other details were provided. But questions remain: Where were the officers when they heard the screams? In a patrol car? On foot? Coming out of the restaurant? How did they chase the suspect? On foot? By car? Both? How long did the chase go on? How did they capture the man? At gunpoint? Did he resist? Did he say anything? Space is not an excuse; the story is 14 paragraphs long.

A high school student dies early in the morning after his sports car hits a horse wandering on a lonely stretch of road. The story is a sparse, mechanical account, like too many traffic-accident stories. There are no details about the boy or explanations about what he was doing out at that hour. Was he an honor student? Was he working as a bus boy to earn money for college? How did he die—thrown from the car? Who found him? Where did the horse come from? And what happened to the animal?[30]

Police arrest three people suspected of wounding a guard, shooting open display cases and fleeing with $250,000 in jewelry in a daring mid-day holdup of Tiffany & Co., a jewelry store. The story simply says the three were arrested at 11th and Market streets. Could it be so simple? How did police find the suspects? Were they armed? Did they resist? What's at the intersection of 11th and Market? A church? Tavern? Were the suspects standing on the corner, sitting in a car or sleeping inside an apartment building? Given the nature of the crime, the arrest seems anticlimactic. Was it? Readers never find out.

Some might quarrel that these missing details are not errors. But if you define error as "something incorrectly done through ignorance or carelessness," then their carelessness makes them errors. They certainly are every bit as damaging to press credibility as misspelled names or incorrect facts. Broadcast journalist Paul Davis, speaking for many viewers and readers, expresses the feelings of frustration caused by errors of omission. His remarks, aimed at radio news, apply to all fields of reporting. "At times," he says, "so much basic information is missing that I yell at the radio. Having a cellular phone in my car has become a burden because I want to immediately call the staion and register my objections to the short-sheeted story I have just heard. Missing locators, missing names, missing details. Aaargh!"[31]

When readers and viewers get a steady diet of underdeveloped stories and unanswered questions, they rarely write letters to the editor or call the station. They do not even let out an "Aaargh!" Passively, many readers and viewers expect to be left guessing. Those who are especially frustrated and dissatisfied finally turn away from the newscast or newspaper to watch a game-show rerun or read a book.

Davis offers advice to curb errors of omission. "Writers who can distance themselves enough to check their copy as if they were a casual reader will probably spot the copy's weaknesses, the contextual assumption or missing detail."[32] His point is vividly evident in the following story taken from a metropolitan newspaper. It reports the apparent suicide of a doctor. As you read it, look for questions the average person might ask.

MIDDLETOWN—The body of a 27-year-old woman physician, missing since Oct. 30, was found near some railroad tracks in Middletown Sunday, police reported.

The woman was identified as Dr. Linda Kline, of 1952 Greenpoint Drive, in Greenbriar Apartments, at Central Avenue and Interstate 120.

Lt. James Gregory of Middletown Police said he was told Saturday that the woman had been depressed and had told her husband that she had taken an overdose of an antidepressant drug.

Her fully clothed body was found about 3:30 p.m. Sunday about 300 yards northeast of the Reading Railroad tracks at Baylor Road just north of Pinewood Avenue by a helicopter hired by her father, police said.

Police said there was no reason to suspect foul play. Gregory said he was told that the woman telephoned her husband, Dr. Larry Kline, about 11:45 a.m. Oct. 30 and told him she had taken an overdose.

Gregory said Dr. Larry Kline told his wife to induce vomiting and rushed home. When he arrived, his wife was missing, Dr. Larry Kline told police.

Police said the woman's purse was still at her home and nothing was missing from the house.

The story is sterile and cold. It sounds as though a computer wrote it. Moreover, the reporting is lazy and insensitive. Lack of effort, lack of empathy and lack of imagination combine to result in a story riddled with holes. Among them:

- Who are the Klines? Where are they from? If they both held jobs, where did they work? What branch of medicine? What kind of people are they? Friendly? Reclusive? Driven?

- What made Linda Kline depressed? Was she having problems at work or at home? Was she ill?

- Was an empty bottle of an antidepressant drug found at the apartment? Was she taking drugs? If so, what kind and who prescribed them?

- Who is the father? Would men of normal means hire a helicopter to search for a missing daughter? He sounds extraordinary. But his story is untold.

- What about where her body was found? What's there? An empty lot? Brush? Where is the site in relation to the Klines' apartment? Could she have walked there? If it is miles away, how did she get there?

- Why didn't the husband first call the police or an ambulance when his wife said she had taken an overdose? How far is the apartment from his work? How long did it take him to get home? What did he do once he got there? His is another untold story.

At the core of the story's many problems is poor journalism. It appears the reporter relied on police records and one live source, Lt. Gregory. And Lt. Gregory, it seems, is either a secondhand or third-hand source. There's no indication that Gregory talked to Larry Kline or went to the scene. The reporting—or what passes for reporting—probably was conducted via telephone, perhaps by a single call to Gregory.

Most stories are not this glaringly devoid of detail and life, but nearly every day nearly every newspaper or newscast contains nagging errors of omission. Some errors of omission are attributable to sloppy reporting, but many more are the result of unimaginative, one-dimensional reporting. Unimaginative journalists are not very curious. They fail to ask enough "How?" "Why?" and "Why not?" questions. Certain questions never occur to them. Of course, no two reporters handling the same assignment are going to ask identical questions. But some questions are so compelling they beg to be asked no matter who is covering the story. And these are the questions that will occur to discerning news consumers.

Consider another example. A man, 77, and his wife, 74, set out in their pickup truck to visit a daughter 40 miles away. When they fail to show up, the family calls the police. After a nine-day search that includes use of a divining rod and a psychic, police find the two at a motel 150 miles from their home. Motel receipts, canceled checks and witness accounts indicate they crisscrossed several states in their unexplained odyssey. But only one news account of their travels answered what should have been an obvious question: "How far did they travel?" The sharp reporter who asked the question got an answer from the couple's nephew—"4,000 miles." How did the nephew know? It turns out that shortly before the couple disappeared, he changed the oil on the truck, noting the mileage on the odometer. When he later retrieved the truck, he checked the odometer again.

How do you know what to ask? It helps to try to put yourself into the story. Close your eyes and visualize what happened and why. Speculate if necessary. Your picture of what unfolded may conflict with official accounts. Witnesses, for example, describe how a hand-cuffed burglary suspect manages to escape in a police car and later, after a standoff, kills himself with an officer's gun. Puzzled, you might ask, "Why did the officer leave his gun in his car? Doesn't he carry it in a holster strapped to his waist?" By asking those questions you learn the gun used in the shooting was a spare the officer kept under the seat of his patrol car. That twist in the story sets off another round of questions: "Do officers generally keep a spare gun in a patrol car?" "What's department policy on spare firearms?"

Sometimes reporters avoid errors by simply applying common sense. If the coroner says a duck hunter drowned when his john boat went through the lock, common sense tells you that the mechanics of going through a lock are not going to cause a fatal accident. A lock is an enclosed section of waterway, equipped with gates, to raise or lower boats from one level to another. The process of going through a lock is slow and usually routine. "Hmmm," you say to yourself. "This doesn't sound right. Something's missing." Checking, you discover the boat went *over the dam,* not *through the lock.*

One of the benefits of the computer revolution in journalism is the increased use of diagrams and illustrations. In turn, the emphasis on graphics is sharpening the reporting and observational skills of reporters. They are now expected to help artists recreate scenes and events by providing a detailed, step-by-step chronology. The illustration on page 86 shows how reporter-generated information from police and witnesses was used by a *St. Petersburg Times* artist to produce a five-point graphic depicting what happened when a feud between two men erupted into gunfire.

Reconstructing an event can begin with a simple question: "Show me what happened." For particularly complicated happenings, offer witnesses and officials pencil and paper and encourage them to tell the story through drawings and diagrams. Ask questions that help elicit details. "What's the approximate size of the room?" "What happened next?" "Where was the suspect when he opened fire?" Reporters who attempt to graphically recreate news events will be less likely to leave key questions unanswered. They will be more likely to catch the mistakes of others and less likely to introduce mistakes of their own.

Reporters do not ask questions merely to satisfy the curiosity of readers, listeners or viewers. Much more is at stake. As the public's surrogates, reporters are obligated to tell the whole story so officials and newsmakers can be held accountable for their actions and decisions. When the prosecuting attorney drops a case, reporters are obligated to ask *why.* When the highway commission votes to relocate a neighborhood so a road leading to a shopping center can be widened, reporters are obligated to name the commissioners and ask them to explain their vote. If a court of appeals votes to overturn a murder conviction, reporters are obligated to name the judges and how they stood on the issue.

Occasionally journalists can be excused for not telling the whole story. One of those times is when a story is too difficult, hidden or complicated to be told in a single account. Watergate is the classic example. *Washington Post* reporters Carl Bernstein and Bob Wood-

The day began with gunfire

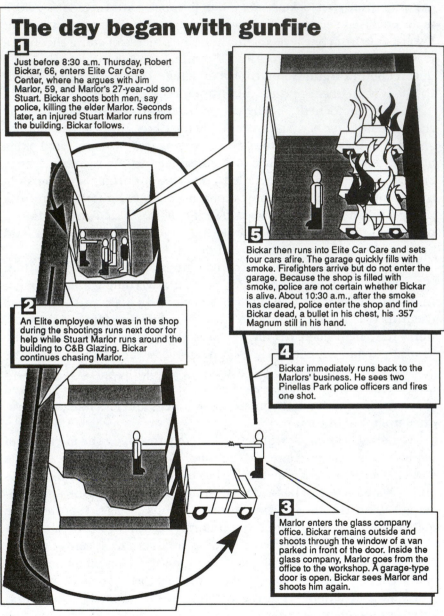

1 Just before 8:30 a.m. Thursday, Robert Bickar, 66, enters Elite Car Care Center, where he argues with Jim Marlor, 59, and Marlor's 27-year-old son Stuart. Bickar shoots both men, say police, killing the elder Marlor. Seconds later, an injured Stuart Marlor runs from the building. Bickar follows.

5 Bickar then runs into Elite Car Care and sets four cars afire. The garage quickly fills with smoke. Firefighters arrive but do not enter the garage. Because the shop is filled with smoke, police are not certain whether Bickar is alive. About 10:30 a.m., after the smoke has cleared, police enter the shop and find Bickar dead, a bullet in his chest, his .357 Magnum still in his hand.

2 An Elite employee who was in the shop during the shootings runs next door for help while Stuart Marlor runs around the building to C&B Glazing. Bickar continues chasing Marlor.

4 Bickar immediately runs back to the Marlors' business. He sees two Pinellas Park police officers and fires one shot.

3 Marlor enters the glass company office. Bickar remains outside and shoots through the window of a van parked in front of the door. Inside the glass company, Marlor goes from the office to the workshop. A garage-type door is open. Bickar sees Marlor and shoots him again.

Source: St. Petersburg Times art

ward never dreamed that what began as coverage of a burglary report would put them on a tortuous trail that ultimately led to the Oval Office. By necessity, the Watergate saga emerged story by story. Publishing pieces of an incomplete puzzle, Bernstein and Woodward kept the Watergate investigation alive so that additional facts could be discovered.

After a long-running story is told in bits and pieces, some journalists need to climb to a high vantage point for a panoramic, retrospective view. The result may be a comprehensive piece that weaves the threads from dozens of stories into a tapestry. Readers who have followed the piecemeal coverage appreciate the big picture.

Reporters can expect frustrations as they attempt to tell stories fully and accurately. Some find the task too frustrating. That is why Russell Baker of the *New York Times* turned to column writing. Reflecting on his reporting days, Baker said: "It's almost impossible to get it right. The deadlines are too quick, and you don't have time to go into the background. It's *Rashomon;* you interview four different people, you get four different answers."[33] Conscientious reporters share Baker's feelings. But rather than surrender to the uncertainty and frustration of reporting, they persevere. Let the uncertainty and frustration motivate and energize you to do your very best to get it right.

Chapter 4 examines what happens—and what can be done—when people, rules and laws make it difficult for reporters to tell the whole story.

EXERCISES

1. Interview a classmate and ask the classmate to interview you. Then each of you write a miniprofile of the other. Together, go over the stories to check for accuracy. If you find mistakes, try to determine how they occurred.

2. Test the reliability of witness accounts. With your teacher's permission and assistance, stage a fast-moving, unexpected happening in your classroom. You might ask two theater students to pose as an odd-looking couple who disrupts class, going from student to student asking for a handout. (A more effective test might be one that is shocking, such as a staged holdup. But give the class warning before any enactment that could be frightening.) Afterward, interview students separately, asking them to recount what happened and describe the participants. Later, as a class, discuss the differences in accounts.

3. Look for a news story that catches your attention but fails to deliver with enough detail or explanation. Study the story carefully, and then develop a list of questions you believe *should* have been asked and answered.

NOTES

[1] Andy Rooney, "Thinking It Over," undated column.

[2] Herbert Strentz, *News Reporters and News Sources* (Ames, Ia.: Iowa State University Press, 1978), p. 3.

[3] Quoted in Martin Gottlieb, "Dangerous Liaisons," *Columbia Journalism Review*, July–Aug. 1989, p. 26.

[4] Steve Weinberg, "So What's Wrong with Pre-publication Review?," *The Quill*, May 1990, p. 26.

[5] Richard M. Clurman, *Beyond Malice* (New York: New American Library, 1990), p. 11.

[6] Quoted in David Bollier, "Ralph Nader: News Creator," *Columbia Journalism Review*, May–June 1990, p. 52.

[7] Stanley L. Payne, *The Art of Asking Questions* (Princeton: Princeton University Press, 1951), pp. 158–176.

[8] Andreas H. Jucker, *News Interviews* (Philadelphia: John Benjamin, 1986), p. 32.

[9] Maxwell McCombs, Donald Lewis Shaw and David Grey, *Handbook of Reporting Methods* (Boston: Houghton Mifflin, 1976), p. 216.

[10] Mary Lou Janson, "Mrs. DeBoe's First Grade," reprint, *Tampa Tribune*, 1983.

[11] "What I Saw Is Bodies, Bodies, Bodies," *Newsweek*, June 19, 1989, p. 22.

[12] See S. Holly Stocking and Paget H. Gross, "Understanding Errors, Biases That Can Affect Journalists," *Journalism Educator*, Spring 1989, pp. 4–11.

[13] George S. Hage, Everette E. Dennis, Arnold H. Ismach and Stephen Hartgen, *New Strategies for Public Affairs Reporting* (Englewood Cliffs, N.J.: Prentice-Hall, 1976), p. 115.

[14] Quoted in Richard P. Cunningham, "Distortion Through Brevity," *The Quill*, July–Aug. 1986, p. 9.

[15] Rene J. Cappon, *The Word* (New York: Associated Press, 1982), p. 82.

[16] Cappon, *The Word*, p. 83.

[17] See Fred Fedler, *Media Hoaxes* (Ames, Ia.: Iowa State University Press, 1989), p. 219; John Consoli, "AP and UPI Hoodwinked by Reporter and J-Prof," *Editor & Publisher*, Oct. 3, 1981, p. 44.

[18] Jan Harold Brunvand, *The Choking Doberman* (New York: Norton, 1984), pp. 162–169.

[19] David Hackett Fischer, *Historians' Fallacies* (New York: Harper Torchbooks, 1970), p. 71.

[20] Alan Caruba, "Has Everything Become Toxic Today?," *Editor & Publisher*, Sept. 21, 1985, p. 52.

[21] Quoted in "Sunscreen Snobbery," *Chicago Tribune*, July 14, 1989, sec. 2, p. 2.

[22] Brian Donovan, "The Attica Errors," *The Quill*, Oct. 1971, p. 38.

23 "Get It First, Correct It Later," *The Quill*, Dec.–Jan. 1990, p. 16.

24 Bob Swift, "You'll Need an Eagle Eye to Spot Best 'Malaphors,' " *Miami Herald*, May 2, 1989, p. 2C.

25 Meg Greenfield, "Misled by the 'Facts,' " *Newsweek*, June 26, 1989, p. 76.

26 Fischer, *Historians' Fallacies*, p. 109.

27 S.I. Hayakawa, *Language in Thought and Action* (New York: Harcourt Brace Jovanovich, 1978), pp. 38–40.

28 Fischer, *Historians' Fallacies*, pp. 182, 183.

29 Roy Peter Clark, "Diary of a Newswriting Guru," *ASNE Bulletin*, April 1981, p. 15.

30 This example comes from Carl Riblet Jr., *The Solid Gold Copy Editor* (Washington, D.C.: Falcon Press, 1972), p. 374; other examples come from published stories.

31 Paul M. Davis, "Simplicity Not Always the Answer; Add a Graph," *The Quill*, Feb. 1989, p. 40.

32 Davis, "Simplicity," p. 39.

33 Quoted in "It's Almost Impossible to Get It Right," *Newsweek*, June 12, 1989, p. 65.

Chapter Four

Signs (and a police officer's glove) warn away non-official visitors from the U.S. Capitol building in Washington, D.C. (Art Stein/Photo Researchers)

Closed Meetings, Sealed Records and "Off Limits" Signs

Muzzled, leashed watchdogs cannot bark or prowl. If the press is, indeed, society's watchdog, what happens when meetings are closed, records sealed, mouths gagged and news scenes put off limits?

- Reporters are denied records of an FBI investigation into the mysteriouis death of a worker who uncovered safety violations at a nuclear plant.

- With incident reports screened and police officers under orders not to talk to the press, a half dozen brutal home invasions are hidden from public attention.

- Just 25 minutes into its meeting on teachers' contract demands, the school board goes into a closed-door session to weigh strategy in the event of a strike.

- A judge closes a potentially explosive rape trial involving four youths while the victim, a minor, testifies.

The watchdog analogy works best when the press is sniffing out wrongdoing. The sun offers an alternate analogy. Applied to government as freedom of information, sunshine illuminates what is dark and hidden from view. In fact, many open meetings and open records statutes are known popularly as "sunshine laws."

Increasingly, however, shadows are falling on areas once exposed to sunshine. Important stories are becoming difficult to tell because public officials are denying reporters access to information and imposing restrictions on newsgathering. In late 1988, the Society of Professional Journalists released results of a survey showing that the news media's principal legal battlefield had shifted from libel defense to pursuit of access. Despite the profession's emphasis on freedom of information, journalists continue to lose crucial contests. In March of 1989, for example, the U.S. Supreme Court ruled that the public has no right to see "rap sheets"—criminal records—compiled by the FBI on private individuals. "What does the decision mean in real terms?" asked an editorial in the *News Media & the Law* magazine. "If a school bus driver is arrested for drunken driving 18 times in 15 jurisdictions, that is no longer the public's business. If a high school coach has been convicted of child molestation somewhere in the United States, the public cannot learn about it."[1]

Even when a request for information is not denied outright, instances of foot-dragging by government agencies are common. Eric Nalder, a *Seattle Times* reporter who made 20 freedom-of-information requests from federal agencies in 1986, described his experiences: "If you make your request too broad, the agency will reply that what you have asked for is too general and that it would take 250 years to fill your request. I had an answer like that from the U.S. Department of Energy. If you are too specific, the agency will often say it doesn't have the document you've asked for—and you find out later that you left out one word of the title."[2]

If news organizations are forced to sue for access, the cost in time and money mounts. Waging a court battle may take years and thousands of dollars in legal fees, as the *Appleton* (Wis.) *Post-Crescent* found out when it asked a judge to release sealed police records of the stabbing death of a young woman. "We started in February of 1987 with a simple letter to a judge I knew, a good-old-boy letter, asking for help," said the paper's managing editor. "The next thing I knew, we were in court. It snowballed and at times it seems there's no end in sight." In the fall of 1988, he estimated the paper's legal bill already had reached $25,000.[3] While the *New York Times* could absorb such a cost, a $25,000 bill in Appleton is serious business.

Determination goes far to unlock records and open doors, but when the only option remaining is legal action, journalists must be prepared to pay the price. As Clarence Pennington, editor of the *Review Times*, a 7,500-circulation newspaper in Fostoria, Ohio, sees it, "It's part of the cost of doing business, and if we don't do it, we ought to just quit the [journalism] business and run pickle factories or something."[4]

Access to information is at the heart of the news enterprise. If journalists cannot get to the people, places and information that make up the news, other legal questions become moot. Access is treated separately in this chapter rather than in Chapter 10, which explores libel, privacy and journalists' privilege.

ACCESS AND THE RIGHT TO GATHER NEWS

Freedom of information is a democratic principle rooted deeply in the American experience. "We the people" begins the preamble to the Constitution. In our self-governing society we delegate authority to legislators, judges and political leaders, and we depend on a free flow of information to help us understand, debate and decide public issues, including who will be our governors. As James Madison said 200 years ago, "A popular government without popular information or the means of acquiring it is but a prologue to a farce or a tragedy; or, perhaps both. Knowledge will forever govern ignorance: and a people who mean to be their own governors must arm themselves with the power which knowledge gives."[5]

To develop and sustain this self-governing, informed citizenry a controversial principle—the "public's right to know"—has evolved. Most Americans lack the means and time to stay fully informed, so the press has assumed the role of surrogate, exercising and defending the public's right to know.

The right to know, however, is not guaranteed under the Constitution. Members of the Constitutional Convention met in secrecy, and they produced a document that says little about openness and access to information. Nowhere does the Constitution mention the public's right to know or the press's right to gather information on the public's behalf. Moreover, the United States Supreme Court, although repeatedly acknowledging the importance of a well-informed citizenry, has never expressly recognized a constitutional right to know.

On the other hand, newsgathering enjoys a degree of constitutional legitimacy as a result of Supreme Court rulings. But any right to gather news apparently excludes a broad *right to access* to government and its information sought by the press. In a 1977 case involving press access to a jail, Chief Justice Warren Burger said this about freedom of information: "This Court has never intimated a First Amendment guarantee of right of access to all sources of information within government control."[6] In more forceful words, William Rehnquist, now chief justice, concluded in another decision: "This Court emphatically has rejected the proposition . . . that the First Amendment is some sort of constitutional 'sunshine law.' "[7]

The First Amendment may not be a sunshine law, but it does give reporters considerable latitude to pursue the news, provided they are ready to expend the effort. In 1974, Supreme Court Justice Potter Stewart aptly described the issue of press and access in these words: "The press is free to do battle against secrecy and deception in government. But the press cannot expect from the Constitution any guarantee that it will succeed. There is no constitutional right to have access to particular government information, or to require openness from the bureaucracy. The public's interest in knowing about its government is protected by the guarantee of a free press, but the protection is indirect. The Constitution itself is neither a Freedom of Information Act nor an Official Secrets Act. The Constitution, in other words, establishes the contest, not its resolution."[8] Indeed, some reporters welcome the challenges of a contest. Reporter Steve McGonigle, recipient of the Breacher Award for Freedom of Information Reporting, lightheartedly says, "I love secrecy. It enables me to write stories nobody can get. I don't know what I'd do without it."[9]

ACCESS TO GOVERNMENTAL MEETINGS

In the 1950s and 1960s, before sunshine laws became commonplace, public bodies occasionally made a mockery of the democratic process of government by meeting at odd hours, without notice and in out-of-the-way places, such as gathering on Christmas Eve in the back room of the Kozy Korner cafe. Today, with statutes in force, officials sometimes resort to novel tactics to stay technically within the law. In Walla Walla, Wash., for example, the county commission adopted an annual schedule, as law required, setting regular meetings on "each workday of every week of the year." Rick Doyle, managing editor of the *Walla Walla Union-Bulletin*, saw the schedule as a ploy to discourage the press and public from attending meetings. "This means they can meet at any time any day of the week," he said. The newspaper countered by suing the commission and stationing a reporter in the council chambers eight hours a day throughout the week.[10]

On occasion, secret meetings cover misdeeds and corruption. Most often, though, public officials sincerely believe they can work more effectively if the process of government is not complicated by the presence of nosy reporters and meddlesome citizens. Officials still meet in private to debate and discuss sensitive matters and arrive at conclusions—no fish bowl for them. Later, when these same officials go through the motions of a public meeting, they vote in apparent harmony, without debate or discussion. Reporters ought to look suspiciously on a pattern of no debate and unanimous votes by a public body.

William Small, author of *Political Power and the Press*, explains the mentality that leads to closed meetings and closed records: "If there is a law in press-government relations it is that information is provided in reverse proportion to the amount of controversy involved. Cooperation decreases in direct relationship to the sensitiveness of the subject matter. What the politician does not share willingly is that material which either reflects unfavorably on his administration or that which he judges must be kept from the public for its own good. It is the arrogance of political power that those who have it always know best when the public should know least."[11]

Not all public officials are infected by the arrogance of power Small describes. Nevertheless, the tendency in government circles is to interpret sunshine laws narrowly and negatively, not affirmatively, as the term *open meetings* implies. From that perspective, the statutory *exceptions to openness* are twisted to become *imperatives for closure*. No law gives the press and public absolute, unconditional rights of access. But with all open meetings laws, there is an underlying *presumption* of openness, and that presumption gives the press leverage to pry open shut doors.

Although every state has an open-meetings law, they vary dramatically in scope, strength and specificity. An intimate knowledge of what the law permits and prohibits is essential if reporters hope to gain access. That knowledge includes how the law has been interpreted in court decisions and in legal opinions by the state attorney general's office. Such information is available from several sources.

In some states, the attorney general's office publishes an annotated version of the law, including legal interpretations. As a public service, various state bar associations provide detailed handbooks for reporters. To date, the best comprehensive reference work is *Tapping Officials' Secrets*, a state-by-state guide to open-meetings and open-records statutes. It is published by a Washington, D.C.–based organization, the Reporters Committee for Freedom of the Press.

Your knowledge of the open-meetings laws should include these points:

What public bodies are covered? Usually the law applies to any agency or body that receives or expends public money. Still, there are many gray areas. Is the faculty senate at the state university covered? What about the board of directors of a non-profit organization contracted to run a city-owned hospital? It may take a time-consuming, costly court fight to find out.

Some bodies are specifically excluded—and with good reason. An example is a state investment board; premature disclosure of its deliberations could lead to improper speculation in securities. But other bodies, like parole boards, may be excluded for no better reason than tradition or political expediency. Parole boards, entrusted to decide when convicted criminals can safely re-enter society, ought to be subjected to scrutiny; too often they operate in secret, fueling suspicions of payoffs and favoritism.

What constitutes a meeting? Florida is noted for a strong record on access, but its open-meetings statute is brief and general; it does not precisely define *meeting*. When Florida officials discuss public business at a cocktail party or golf club, is that a "meeting"? Fortunately, court rulings in Florida have established that a meeting occurs whenever two or more members of the public body meet to discuss official business. In Illinois, by contrast, the law is more definite but not necessarily stronger. A "meeting," the law states, "means any gathering of a majority of quorum of a public body held for the purpose of discussing public business."

When laws are vague in defining a meeting, reporters can expect public officials to wiggle through the loopholes. In Minnesota, for example, three members of a seven-member school board met at the home of one of the board members to discuss the superintendent's performance. Meanwhile, three other members of the board met at a bank for the same purpose. Later, notes were compared in a telephone conference between an attendee of each meeting. A court, asked to determine whether a meeting occurred, decided that the law did not apply to groups too small to officially make a decision.[12] The school board followed the letter of the law but violated its spirit.

What does it take to close a meeting? Must a motion be made? Is a vote taken? Is a majority needed? Two-thirds? Must officials cite a statutory exemption to the open-meetings law? *A strong law puts officials on record, requiring a voice vote and a specific, declared, legal reason for meeting in secret.*

What subjects or topics are exempt under the law? Not all exemptions are found within the text of the open-meetings law. Some are provided for in separate statutes. Often, open-meetings laws include a catchall disclaimer: "All meetings are open except those involving matters specifically exempted from disclosure by federal or state law." The disclaimer might cover hundreds of subjects.

You will find that the language of sunshine laws can be misleading. The law might sound sweeping and unconditional—"All meetings of public bodies shall be open"—but several paragraphs later may list a half-dozen exceptions. These exceptions allow customarily open public bodies, like school boards and city councils, to go into "executive session," a euphemism for a secret meeting.

"Personnel matters" and "litigation" are the two most frequently cited reasons for holding an executive session. Other areas often exempted are discussions of disciplinary cases, collective-bargaining negotiations, real estate transactions, employment and dismissal of public employees and litigation involving the public body. In almost all instances, votes on matters discussed in closed session must be conducted in an open session.

Be sure to know the parameters of general categories such as "personnel" or "litigation." Usually, laws that exclude discussion of personnel matters apply to individual cases, most commonly the hiring and firing of a particular employee. But some public officials will stretch the meaning of *personnel* to cover nearly every subject dealing with employees. Comparable problems apply to use of the term *litigation*. Does the open-meetings law distinguish between imminent litigation or cases presently being adjudicated? Discussion of an *existing* lawsuit against the city might be exempt; discussion of a *threatened* lawsuit might not, a distinction city officials could try to blur.

What notice is required to postpone, reschedule or move meetings? Notice provisions were enacted because unscrupulous public officials in many states manipulated the law by changing meeting sites and dates without informing the press or public. Nearly all state laws require public bodies to post an annual schedule of meeting dates, times and places. Of course, emergencies may force officials to make changes, but a strong law requires at least 48-hour notice of changes to the regular, posted schedule. In some cases, though, reporters must annually request in writing that the agency notify them of changes.

When a meeting is closed, what record is required? Most states require a record of meetings, although it may amount only to a "general description" of the matters discussed, not a verbatim audio or video recording. The record also may be hard to obtain. Although many laws set a time limit for release of minutes, there sometimes is a *caveat*: Minutes are to be made available only after the public body determines that it is no longer necessary to protect a public interest or the privacy of individuals. Such a caveat puts reporters at the mercy of officials who can, by inaction or refusal, set an indefinite time limit on release of minutes. Legal action may be the only way to wrest the minutes away from them.

What legal relief is available to contest closure or non-compliance? Legal action often is not practical when reporters are locked out of a meeting. By the time a complaint can be heard in court, the news may be stale. If, for example, the city council is considering disciplinary action against the police chief, the news value is in being there to report what was said and done.

Still, when a legal challenge is needed to prevent future abuses of the law or to send a message to public officials, the press will not get far without the cooperation of law enforcement officials. Often, a key figure is the local state's attorney, who may be empowered to bring civil action for non-compliance. Among the legal tools available are the *injunction*, a court order that prohibits officials from further violations, or a *writ of mandamus*, another form of court order that requires officials to fulfill their duties under the law.

Proving non-compliance is not easy if public officials, in a united front, proclaim they acted properly and leave no evidence that they acted improperly. Who is to know? The law may require a judge to examine the minutes of a closed meeting privately, but nothing keeps dishonest public officials from editing or falsifying that record. If there is a will to deceive, usually there is a way.

What are the penalties for violating an open-meetings law? Do not expect violations of sunshine laws to be accompanied by thunder and lightning. Although some open-meetings statutes include criminal penalties, they are misdemeanor offenses that seldom include jail time. Fines are more common, usually ranging from $100 to $1,000. The penalties, civil or criminal, may not be enough to deter lawbreakers; some penalties are so slight that officials feel free to flout the law.

What do you do when a meeting is closed?

You are covering a meeting of the Pottsville City Council. After about a half hour of routine business, a council member says, "Mayor Davis, I move that we go into executive session to discuss this next matter." The motion is seconded, a quick vote taken and the council members rise and move to the mayor's private meeting room. What should you do? Here are some suggestions:

Know the law. Remember, your best defense against evasive tactics is to be an authority on your state's open-meetings statute. Make sure officials know the law, too. Usually an attorney retained by the public body attends meetings and offers guidance when officials propose to go into executive session. But the attorney, despite an air of assuredness, may have only a casual knowledge of the law. By establishing that you know the law and are determined to see it properly applied, you might convince officials to yield to its authority. Or you might raise enough doubt in the attorney's mind that he or she will recommend against closure.

Speak up. Do not be timid about your rights. The First Amendment Foundation suggests that when public officials try to close a meeting, reporters read a statement modeled after this one:

> Florida Statute 286.011, the government-in-sunshine law, requires that all meetings of state or local governmental boards or commissions be open to the public unless there is a specific statutory exemption. If I am ordered to leave (or forbidden to enter) this meeting, I ask that you advise me of the statutory authority for your action. Otherwise, my editors have instructed me to insist on my right to attend this meeting.[13]

Get it on record. Insist that public officials specifically identify the exemption being cited to close a meeting. A reference to "personnel matters" is inadequate. Ask the presiding officer to identify exactly what personnel matters are involved—the hiring of a new city manager, disciplinary action against a housing inspector, labor negotiations? Be persistent, although you still may not get a satisfactory answer.

Stay under control. To physically resist expulsion from a closed meeting is counterproductive and may lead to your arrest. Instead, state your objections, then retire to fight again with the help of your editor and attorney.

Publicize closed meetings. Let people know whenever a public body meets in private. Negative publicity has a way of making officials reconsider past ways.

What do you do when officials invite you into a closed meeting— but with strings attached? You may be told you can stay if you agree not to publish what transpires. Do you accede to conditions that gag you? Taking a vow of silence might be preferable to being left in the dark. Then again, it may be best to fight for openness or seek information by other means. Before accepting any conditions, consult with your editor.

ACCESS TO GOVERNMENT RECORDS

John Walsh fumed. As executive director of St. Louis' Visitors Bureau, he had been ordered by the chairperson of the board—his boss—to surrender records to a *St. Louis Globe-Democrat* reporter investigating use of public money to host the Miss Universe Pageant. Since hotel and restaurant taxes heavily financed the Visitors Bureau, the *Globe-Democrat* argued that expense figures should be open for public inspection. The newspaper won its point.

The records revealed that the pageant, which cost $1,479,000 to put on, earned $694,000, leaving $784,000 to be paid by tax money. Among the expenses were $300,000 for scenery, $30,000 for local transportation and $122,000 in local hotel bills. Walsh's comment: "You [reporters] have this fascination with nit-picking details like why we spent $143 on a luncheon somewhere." His parting shot: "If I had my way, I wouldn't talk to you at all."[14]

A sure way for public officials to stir journalists is to say, "You can't have it." As one observer put it, "In some ways, journalists are like children. The more they're told to stay away from something, the more interested in it they become. Their motive is more than childish curiosity. They know that the person or group warning the media away must consider the information important, and if it's important, it's probably something the public should know."[15] Here is what to expect when you seek government records:

Loopholes and Exemptions

Like miners panning for gold, reporters routinely inspect records to see what is happening on their beat. They review travel vouchers, purchase requisitions and real estate assessments, for example, as part of their watchdog role. Perhaps the odds are against it, but one day their panning could turn up irregularities that warrant coverage. It took a freedom-of-information request, but *Detroit News* reporter Angie Cannon gained access to the city's employee overtime records. She discovered that annual overtime amounted to $40 million, half of Detroit's deficit.[16]

By custom and practice, access to certain records, such as land deeds and tax rolls, is almost taken for granted. But statutory law now encompasses and codifies much of what was covered by common law. Ironically, in some instances, the passage of state sunshine laws gave legislators the opportunity to enumerate a long list of records and materials *exempt* from public disclosure.

Illinois provides an example of how exemptions weaken open-records laws. For years, Illinois operated under a narrow law that vaguely covered fiscal records of "obligation, receipt or use of public funds." No one was quite sure what the law covered. Were invoices and payrolls, for example, subject to the law? A haze hung over other records of government, such as police reports.

Beyond the law's lack of specificity and scope, it contained three conditions that encouraged public officials to deny requests: At their discretion, officials could require 24-hour written notice before allowing inspection of records, insist that those seeking information precisely specify the records they intended to examine and refuse to release the material requested if it was "in use" by "authorized" personnel.

In 1984, however, Illinois enacted its first comprehensive open-records statute—the Freedom of Information Act. It lists 14 types of information that fall under the statute's definition of "public record." Yet more than one-half of the text of the law is devoted to describing the types of records *exempt* from disclosure requirements—26 exemptions in all.

One group of exceptions relates to invasion of privacy, such as a ban on release of the names of individuals receiving public aid. Another set pertains to law enforcement records. Nearly all investigative records are closed; arrest logs are open but only to the extent that the information they contain does not constitute an "unwarranted" invasion of an individual's privacy. The names of persons filing criminal complaints are not public. A third category covers documents related to internal operations of public bodies, such as "preliminary drafts of memoranda in which opinions or policies are formulated." The fourth category of exemptions is designed to protect business or financial interests of both private persons and public bodies. Among the exemptions in this category are bids for contracts, which, if disclosed, would frustrate procurement or give an advantage to anyone proposing to enter into a contract with a public body.

Important public interests are evident in several of Illinois' exemptions—for example, non-disclosure of engineering and architectural plans for public buildings, which would jeopardize security if they fell into the hands of terrorists or criminals. There is usually, though, a reverse side to this type of non-disclosure. If a walkway in a public building collapses, killing dozens of people, the engineering plans might reveal a structural defect attributable to negligence on the part of public officials responsible for overseeing construction. When a statute like Illinois' is riddled with escape clauses, those wishing to withhold information can readily find an exemption to apply.

With customarily open records, such as court documents, access rarely is a problem. It is the nebulous, fringe areas of the law that most often are troublesome. One recent legal debate centers on private developers who receive low-interest, tax-free *industrial-revenue bonds* to finance construction of hotels, factories and shopping malls. Are those developers agents of the municipalities that arranged for the industrial-revenue bonds and therefore subject to provisions of the state open-records law? This type of access debate usually requires a court challenge to settle.

Inconsistent application is another problem. The police chief in Jonesboro gives reporters unlimited access to arrest reports; 15 miles away in Smithville, the chief, fearful of invasion-of-privacy lawsuits, filters all arrest reports through shift commanders, who are instructed to remove any information that might embarrass victims or witnesses. The police chief of Smithville cautiously puts privacy interests ahead of the press's interest in informing the public. Perhaps he is overly sensitive, but you cannot say he is corrupt or, for that matter, wrong. He has his perspective; the reporter has another.

Tips for Obtaining Information

Before going to the trouble of filing a written request for information, try an informal approach. A polite, persuasive request made in person is likely to raise fewer objections than a stiff, formal statement received in the mail. In person, you can state your reasons for requesting the information, counter reservations officials might have about releasing records and negotiate conditions for inspecting and copying the records. Investigative reporter Jim Steele of the *Philadelphia Inquirer* offers additional advice: Do not be stymied by clerks. He suggests carrying copies of the open-records law and politely reading them aloud. If that fails, speak with a supervisor or stand around until the clerks relent.[17]

When informal methods prove to be futile, consult statutes on access to government information. They contain procedures detailing how written requests are to be handled. Usually officials must act on requests for records within seven to 10 working days, but time limits tend to expand, especially if the request involves large amounts of information scattered among several offices. The law generally permits public bodies to charge a fee for copying records, but a number of states allow fees to be waived if it is established that release of the information benefits the public.

Some laws explain how to make a request for government documents. Several news organizations also provide sample letters of request.[18] An example is provided on page 104.

If a request is denied, the laws also contain appeal procedures. Typically, an open-records statute gives state courts jurisdiction to conduct *in camera* (private) examination of the documents in question. The burden of proof usually is with the public body, which must establish that its actions comply with the law. If the appeal

SAMPLE LETTER OF REQUEST

Agency head [*or Freedom of Information officer*]
Name of agency
City, state, zip code

Re: Freedom of Information Act request

Dear [*FOI officer*]:

I request that a copy of the following documents [*or documents containing the following information*] be provided
to me: [*identify as specifically as possible*].

In order to help to determine my status to assess fees, you
should know that I am [*insert description of requester and
purposes of request such as "a representative of the
(name of newspaper, broadcast station, etc.)"*], and this
request is made as part of newsgathering and not for commercial use.

[*You may also offer to pay fees up to a certain amount or
request a fee waiver.*]

Thank you for your consideration of this request.

Sincerely,

determines that public officials withheld the information without a
basis in law, then some states allow courts to order the public body
to pay attorney fees connected with the appeal.

In truth, though, open-records laws are only as good as the willingness of public officials to honor them. Even when records are
clearly public under the law, it still may take repeated requests followed by lengthy litigation before files are made available for inspection and copying. Key passages may be blackened out, leading to
another legal tug of war. Before long, the story is likely to be old
news, and the reporter who made the request may be at a new job,

thousands of miles away and hundreds of assignments beyond the original assignment. If records are the path to an investigative story, reporters are likely to find tracks covered and the trail cold by the time the information is handed over.

Access to records is difficult. Do not, however, let discouraging complaints from reporters deter you from seeking records; do not assume the answer will be no. Many public employees are committed to the principle of open government. They help and cooperate with information seekers. Remember, too, the importance of good relations with news sources. The front door to records may be barred, but files may be slipped out the back door to a conscientious, trustworthy reporter. Lauren Cowen of the *Oregonian* reinforces the importance of good sources: "Even if the FOIA were perfect and acted the way it was supposed to, and we got all of the information we were asking for within 10 days, I would never substitute the use of personal contacts within the agency and strictly use the act. You still need those officials within the agency to explain the documents. I would do both."[19]

Access to federal records and meetings

Since July 4, 1966, records of the federal government have been open under the Freedom of Information Act. The father of the law, Rep. John E. Moss of California, began his quest for open records in 1953. Moss, then a freshman in Congress, found he could not obtain information about Sen. Joseph McCarthy's allegations of disloyalty among federal employees even though Moss was a member of the Post Office and Civil Service Committee. Recalling those days, Moss said, "I thought if the committee couldn't get any information who the hell can."[20] It took 13 years, but Moss eventually helped open the records of government to the public and press. Today, Moss says, the FOI Act has met his "minimal expectations, but not my highest hopes," adding that the law has suffered "widespread abuse."[21]

In 1977, the Government in Sunshine Act, which requires open meetings by a range of federal agencies and departments, became law.

Together the two acts constitute a commitment to openness in government, but, by no means, are the laws perfect. Reporters find themselves fettered and frustrated by a spate of exemptions, uncooperative officials, restrictive amendments and narrow interpretations by the courts.

Many exemptions under the FOI Act parallel those found in state open-records laws. That's not surprising; the federal FOI Act served as a model for laws in a number of states. In brief, the act's nine exemptions cover documents relating to

- national security
- internal agency personnel rules
- information specifically exempted by other federal statutes
- trade secrets
- internal agency memoranda and policy discussions
- personal privacy
- law enforcement investigations
- federally regulated banks
- oil and gas wells

Note that government officials are permitted, but not required, to suppress information under the FOI Act exemptions.

Exemptions to the federal open-meetings law cover many of the sensitive areas exempted under the FOI Act. They include matters of national security, law enforcement investigations and trade secrets.

Like state open-meetings laws, the exemptions offer numerous excuses for closing doors. Moreover, the federal law does not apply to cabinet-level departments or advisory bodies closest to the president, such as the National Security Council.

In short, the law leaves much to be desired. Bodies that make some of the most important decisions affecting the public are not covered. But the Government in Sunshine Act is a first step toward making the sprawling federal bureaucracy open and more accountable to the public.

ACCESS TO THE JUDICIAL SYSTEM

At the heart of many access disputes involving the courts and the press are the sometimes competing interests of the First and Sixth

Amendments. Reckless news coverage can threaten a defendant's Sixth Amendment rights to a fair trial by an impartial jury. On the other hand, aggressive yet responsible reporting can help ensure that justice is done. Today's reporters generally are sensitive to the issues of *free press versus fair trial.* Where to draw the line, though, poses problems. Reporters must ask themselves which interests are paramount—those of society or of the accused?

Much of today's friction between the press and courts dates to a series of developments that occurred in the 1960s. In 1964, the Warren Commission, formed to investigate the assassination of President John F. Kennedy, criticized the police and press for releasing incriminating information and statements about Lee Harvey Oswald, the accused assassin. Two years later, in the case of *Sheppard v. Maxwell,* the U.S. Supreme Court overturned a murder conviction of a prominent doctor on the grounds of prejudicial pretrial publicity. In doing so, the Court chastised the judge for failing to maintain order in the courtroom and control over the release of non-admissible *extrajudicial* information.

Finally, in 1968, the American Bar Association released the report of its Advisory Committee on Fair Trial and Free Press, better known as the Reardon Report. Inspired, in part, by the Warren Commission's findings and influenced by the *Sheppard* case, the Reardon Report urged judges to use their powers to guard against prejudicial publicity. The committee's recommendations to judges included closing pretrial hearings if a fair trial appeared to be in jeopardy, ordering participants in the case and reporters covering it to adhere to gag orders governing release of information and punishing violators of court orders by issuing contempt citations.

In the wake of these developments, some judges overreacted to the possibilities of "trial by mass media." Rather than risk the embarrassment of having a ruling overturned or a case retried because they failed to maintain control, judges began to get tough—issuing gag orders, closing pretrial hearings, sealing records and even closing trials. Clashes between the courts and the press increased, forcing the Supreme Court to intervene. In a string of cases, the Court reminded lower courts to impose restrictions on press coverage only under serious circumstances.

Helping ease tension between the press and courts are voluntary press-bench-bar guidelines that protect the rights of individuals while also recognizing the important watchdog role of the press. Not all journalists think such guidelines are a good idea because they tend to curtail aggressive, independent news coverage of the courts. Understandably, skirmishes continue to occur. The following overview outlines what reporters can expect regarding access to the courts:

Grand Juries

The principal role of the grand jury is to determine whether evidence against an individual accused of a crime is strong enough to send the case to trial. Grand jury proceedings are one-sided presentations by the prosecution; normally, the accused cannot contest the evidence presented or mount a defense. In addition, the rules of evidence are not as strict as those governing trials. Grand jurors themselves occasionally are free to question witnesses. Secrecy is needed, court authorities contend, to safeguard the Sixth Amendment rights of accused persons, to encourage witnesses to come forward and give frank testimony without fear of retaliation and to protect the good reputations of those who are investigated and cleared.

As a result, grand jury proceedings are closed to the public and press, and grand jurors and court officials who work with the grand jury are bound by an oath of secrecy, at least as long as the grand jury is in session. Reporters can cover grand jury proceedings indirectly by questioning people before and after they testify, provided the court system's rules of procedure allow witnesses to discuss what they said or heard inside the grand jury room. Not all do. In some jurisdictions, secrecy obligations continue even after a grand jury investigation has concluded. Reporters who aid or abet grand jurors or court officials in breaking their oaths venture into a legal and ethical morass. Fortunately, in 1990 the U.S. Supreme Court ruled that once a grand jury is discharged, a state's interest in preserving secrecy is not sufficient to warrant a ban on speech by witnesses.[22]

Reporters are entitled to reports and documents coming from the grand jury at the conclusion of its deliberations. One exception is a sealed indictment. When a grand jury decides that evidence warrants a trial, it issues an *indictment,* which becomes the basis for an *arrest warrant* to apprehend an accused person who is not already in police custody. If the press reports the indictment before police can serve a warrant, the suspect named in the indictment might flee. When an indictment is sealed, its contents are kept from the press until an accused individual is confronted in open court with the allegations in the warrant's charges.

Juvenile Cases

Juveniles receive special treatment from the courts. Hearings and records often are kept confidential to shield minors from potentially injurious publicity. There is a tendency to think of juvenile court as a place for trying young offenders, but other legal issues, such as child abuse, adoptions and parental rights and duties, also are heard in juvenile court. The juvenile court system generally is committed to aiding, educating and protecting young people.

Access to proceedings and records involving juveniles is not impossible, however. A number of states give judges discretion over access, although as a condition for access, reporters might be asked to keep the identity of juveniles confidential. There are signs that the press's rights to cover juvenile courts are increasing. Recently, several state supreme courts, for example, affirmed the right of reporters to attend proceedings held to determine whether juvenile murder suspects should be tried as adults.[23] Regardless of improved access, the tendency by officials to protect juveniles from press scrutiny remains strong and widespread, which means reporters must be prepared to be persistent.

In many states, statutes prohibit public officials from releasing the names of juvenile offenders. Despite such prohibitions, it is not unusual for reporters to learn identities by standard newsgathering means, such as tips from sources or interviews with witnesses. Law enforcement agencies typically withhold—or at least expect reporters to withhold—the names of juveniles identified in police reports. Although reporters often comply voluntarily, they cannot be prohibited by statute from publishing names. In 1979, the U.S. Supreme Court struck down a West Virginia law that made it a crime to identify juvenile offenders without a written order of the court.[24] A related problem is less clear: What if a *judge* orders a reporter not to publish the name of a juvenile? Violating a judge's direct order could lead to punishment by a contempt-of-court citation. If faced with a judicial order, seek legal advice.

Pretrial Proceedings

Reporters are most likely to confront closed doors at pretrial hearings or proceedings, which are conducted under a less formal set of judicial rules than trials. An example is the *preliminary hearing*, also known as a *probable cause hearing*. It is used to determine whether sufficient evidence exists to prosecute an individual. Secondhand information called *hearsay evidence* is usually permitted. For instance, when an arresting officer cannot be present for the hearing, his account may be read by a detective handling the investigation. Some incriminating evidence presented at a preliminary hearing may not be admissible at the trial.

Another pretrial proceeding is called a *suppression hearing,* which is held in advance of the trial to determine whether evidence or statements should be withheld from the jury. If a judge, for example, accepts a murder suspect's argument that the police forced him to confess, the confession will be suppressed and cannot be used in the trial. Problems arise, though, when evidence the court decides to suppress is nevertheless revealed to prospective jurors through news reports of the hearing.

To guard against a mistrial or an overturned conviction due to prejudicial pretrial publicity, some judges take the safest course and close a hearing at the defendant's request. In the 1979 case of *Gannett v. DePasquale,* the U.S. Supreme Court gave judges even greater latitude to decide whether closure serves the rights of the accused. In an opinion that evoked severe criticism, the Court said the Sixth Amendment guarantee of a public trial pertains directly to defendants and did not entitle the press and public access to courtrooms. Since several judges referred interchangeably to pretrial hearings *and* trials, the *Gannett* case left the impression there were no First Amendment rights of access to any criminal proceedings, including trials.[25]

Certainly, there is much more at stake than defendants' rights if trials can be conducted in secrecy. But even closure of hearings is a serious matter largely because so many criminal cases—up to 90 percent in some jurisdictions—never go to trial. For example, in New York's Seneca County, origin of *Gannett v. DePasquale,* not one felony case went to trial in 1976, the year the *Gannett* case arose. In those cases, the hearing is the trial. Because many criminal cases end in *plea bargains,* or what court officials prefer to call *negotiated settlements,* it is important for the press to monitor hearings. An open system allows the public and press to evaluate the performance of police, prosecutors and judges. If reporters are present, judges are not likely to reduce a DWI charge against a political bigwig to reckless driving; prosecutors are not likely to pad their conviction ratio by allowing an accused rapist to bargain for a reduced charge of assault; and police are not likely to go to court with a weak case built on a questionable confession.

Trials

Access to trials is less of a problem for reporters since the Supreme Court's 1980 decision in *Richmond Newspapers v. Virginia,* which came in the wake of the *Gannett v. DePasquale* storm. Despite its confusing position on access to courtrooms a year before, in the *Richmond* case the Court recognized a First Amendment right for the public and press to attend trials. Chief Justice Warren Burger, writing for the majority, did not, however, rule out closure of trials, but he did make it clear that only under extreme circumstances could a judge justify such action. Still unclear, though, is whether Burger's opinion about the First Amendment applies to pretrial hearings. Nonetheless, lower courts are bound to be influenced by the strong endorsement of open trials contained in *Richmond Newspapers v. Virginia.*[26]

What to do when a courtroom is closed

Reporters, unaccustomed to speaking out in a courtroom, might be reluctant to protest a closure motion. But if they hear no objections, judges may conclude that closing the courtroom is the path of least resistance. Reporters must be prepared to object. Some news organizations provide a sample statement to be read in court, such as this one:

> Your honor, I am _____, a reporter for _____, and I would like to object on behalf of my employer and the public to this proposed closing. Our attorney is prepared to make a number of arguments against closings such as this one, and I respectfully ask the court for a hearing on those issues. I believe our attorney can be here relatively quickly for the court's convenience, and he will be able to demonstrate that closure in this case will violate the First Amendment, and possibly state statutory and constitutional provisions as well. I cannot make the arguments myself, but our attorney can point out several issues for your consideration. If it pleases the court, we request this opportunity to be heard through counsel.[27]

If the judge refuses to grant a hearing, legal experts advise reporters to then ask the judge to *stay,* or postpone, the proceeding that is about to be closed. You still may fail and be ordered to leave. Resisting ejection is asking for trouble; it is better to retreat and seek legal counsel. In emergencies, the Reporters Committee for Freedom of the Press offers free legal advice at a toll-free number: 800-F-FOI-AID.

Restrictive Orders

Judges use *restrictive orders* to keep a lid on potentially prejudicial information. *Gag orders,* as the press prefers to call them, come in a variety of forms: some cover testimony, others apply to records and evidence. A judge in Baton Rouge, La., for example, conducting a preliminary hearing for a civil rights activist accused of conspiring to kill the city's mayor, announced from the bench: "It is ordered that no report of the testimony taken in this case today shall be made in any newspaper or by radio or television, or by any other news media."[28] Judges can gag both reporters and trial participants. But gagging the press puts judges squarely on a collision path with the First Amendment. The U.S. Supreme Court, addressing the problem in a 1976 decision, said gag orders are prior restraints on the press and therefore presumptively unconstitutional. Gag orders against the press are justifiable, the Court said, only when there is no other way to ensure a fair trial.[29]

A gag order against trial participants is another matter; their free speech rights are less clear. Reporters who elicit information from people who have been placed under a gag order are likely to cause them trouble. The reporters involved might even be viewed by the court as accomplices to an illegal act. Reporters who plan to circumvent a gag order on participants ought first to ask an editor for advice and legal counsel.

The Supreme Court helped curb but not eliminate the use of gag orders against the press. Under normal conditions, reporters are free to report anything they see or hear in an open courtroom. A gag order changes the rules. The reporters may rightly conclude that the judge acted without legal justification, but anyone who ignores a gag order, even one that appears to be patently unconstitutional, risks being cited for contempt and jailed. In the Baton Rouge case, reporters ignored the judge's order, and although an appellate court eventually ruled the gag order invalid, the court *also* upheld the contempt-of-court citation against the reporters, saying, "[Journalists] may not now escape the inescapable legal consequence for their flagrant intentional disregard of the mandate of a court."[30]

Court Records and Documents

More courts are sealing records, some permanently, to protect a variety of public interests, usually those centering on the privacy rights of individuals. A judge, for instance, handling the case of a big-league pitcher decides to seal all records of the ballplayer's arrest for scuffling with police officers at a bar. The judge says he was influenced by the exemplary way in which the ballplayer carried out the terms of his three-year probation. Another judge decides to seal videotapes of police sting operations that show a prominent lawmaker accepting a bribe. The judge fears broadcast of the tapes might make it difficult to find an impartial jury if the lawmaker, on appeal, is retried. Judges sometimes seal the names and addresses of jurors to protect them from outside pressure, including, at times, inquiries from reporters. Details of divorce actions, such as testimony about peculiar sexual behavior, may be put off limits to prevent damage to reputations and to shield the parties' children from embarrassment. Frequently, courts recognize a need to protect the identity of informants or undercover police officers whose names appear in court records.

Gaining access to sealed records may prove to be difficult without a court challenge. As with other questions of access, consult your editor and media attorney. A written request to the judge who sealed the records is a first step and should include a diplomatic reminder about the presumption of open records. If the judge denies the request, ask for the denial in writing. Even going to court to challenge the sealing of records may not help. The law is much clearer and stronger on reporters' rights to attend court proceedings and listen to testimony than it is on access to records.

Actually, many so-called sealed records are not physically sealed or locked away. Sometimes they are kept with other open records of the case. Veteran reporters with ready access to offices and records in the courthouse may be able to inspect sealed materials. The important point to remember is that publication or broadcast of sealed records might hurt innocent people or jeopardize someone's rights. There are often good reasons why the press and public are denied access. Nevertheless, if it can be shown that a judge has sealed records for improper motives, reporters are right to publish what they are able to obtain.

Civil Law and Access

Reporters and courts clash most often over access to criminal records and proceedings. But problems arise, as well, in civil law. Of concern lately is the increasing number of secret out-of-court *settlements* in civil lawsuits, especially in product-liability actions, such as a string of cases against General Motors Corp. by crash victims who accused GM of negligence in the design of its gas tanks. GM, the *Washington Post* reported, paid millions of dollars to settle cases before trial. The settlements typically included agreements barring the parties and lawyers in the case from revealing records in the case or talking about the design of GM fuel tanks. The reporters said they learned from documents that GM officials were told in 1970 that the gas tanks were vulnerable to punctures in high-speed crashes.[31] Companies usually argue for secrecy to prevent disclosure of the size of the monetary settlement or to protect trade information from competitors. But reporters covering sealed cases around the country, some of which are identified in court files only as *Sealed vs. Sealed*, contend secrecy keeps important information about dangerous products and practices hidden from the public.[32]

Unfortunately for reporters, access rights in civil courts are not as well defined as those in criminal courts. The Supreme Court, for example, has yet to clarify whether the public and the press have a First Amendment right to attend civil proceedings. Additionally, arguments for access are less convincing in civil litigation because many cases involve primarily private matters. Nonetheless, reporters ought to challenge closed civil courtrooms and records, particularly in matters that extend beyond merely private litigation to encompass important societal questions. Recent examples include disputes over the right to die and surrogate motherhood. In both instances, litigation focused intense media attention on private individuals in painful situations. But the cases could not be ignored because they involved moral and legal questions of great magnitude.

Contempt Power

Complicating access to the courts is the contempt power. Judges can back up their orders and actions by subjecting violators to swift and serious consequences. Melody Perkins, a reporter for the *Great Falls* (Mont.) *Tribune*, found out how thin-skinned some judges can be if they perceive that their authority is being challenged. When Perkins, following instructions from her editor, asked the judge to delay his decision to close a hearing until the newspaper's attorney could be consulted, the judge called her "insolent," cited her for contempt and fined her $300.[33]

Judges are most likely to react when reporters directly violate judicial orders or encourage others to break the rules. Bob Woodward and Carl Bernstein were scolded for tampering with justice during the Watergate investigation of the Nixon administration. Woodward and Bernstein contacted several grand jurors, hoping some of them would talk about their Watergate deliberations. When John Sirica, the judge overseeing the grand jury, learned about the reporters' inquiries, he sent a message to Woodward and Bernstein through *Washington Post* lawyer Edward Bennett Williams. Woodward and Bernstein described the scene in their book, *All the President's Men.* Williams sternly told them Sirica, known as "Maximum John" for his tough sentences, meant business. "Judge Sirica is some kind of pissed at you fellas," Williams said. "We had to do a lot of convincing to keep your asses out of jail." Williams offered some parting advice: "Keep your noses clean."[34]

DEALING WITH "OFF LIMITS" SIGNS

What began as a protest against construction of a nuclear power plant near Tulsa, Okla., ended in a setback for journalists' rights to report breaking news events on private property. Reporters covering the 1979 demonstration followed several hundred protestors onto the power company's property. Not only were the protestors arrested and charged with trespassing, but so were six journalists.[35]

In appealing their convictions, the reporters raised a number of important arguments in support of access. To begin with, the reporters accused the power company and county authorities of conspiring to minimize publicity about the protest. The power company tried to restrict the reporters to a viewing area a mile away from where the protestors planned to enter the property. The sheriff stationed officers on the site to begin making arrests as soon as the demonstration began.

The public, the reporters argued, needs to be informed about developments in the national debate over nuclear power, even when the debate spills onto private land. They asked for the right of reasonable, unimpeded access to private property to observe peacefully and report on a newsworthy event in progress. Their arguments applied to any number of "hot news" situations, such as an explosion at an oil refinery or a fire at a condominium complex.

The reporters argued to no avail. The U.S. Supreme Court declined to hear the case and let stand the criminal trespass convictions against them. Their experiences reflect the difficulties journalists face in gaining access to newsworthy events and places. Not surprisingly, few judges would interpret the First Amendment as a license to trespass or break the law in pursuit of news. There is little help from the Supreme Court; on several occasions the justices have said the Constitution does not entitle the press to special rights of access to information or places beyond those afforded to the general public.[36] Many journalists feel that the Court could be more sensitive to the press's role as a watchdog and guardian of the public's right to know.

The power plant protest also illustrates the problems of access to private places when reporters are unwelcome or uninvited. By customary practice, reporters enter private property to cover accidents or disasters. But police and other public authorities are not necessarily empowered, for example, to invite reporters to accompany them on a drug raid of a private home. At the very least, reporters who enter private property without permission risk an invasion-of-privacy suit.

Covering news occurring on public land or government-owned property usually presents fewer problems, but there are always exceptions. Police officials, in particular, may bar reporters from crime scenes or accidents in the name of maintaining order and protecting lives and property. Although police officers usually are cooperative when dealing with reporters they know and respect, their behavior may alter under pressure or trying conditions. They might, for example, banish reporters from otherwise public places, like sidewalks, parks or government buildings. Reporters who resist flirt with arrest for criminal trespass, disorderly conduct or interference with a police officer.

Although police can be obstinate about press access, sometimes their demands are reasonable. At crime scenes, police and firefighters must be sure that evidence is preserved and untouched by outsiders. During an emergency, reporters cannot expect to peer over the shoulders of police as a negotiator tries to talk a gunman into releasing hostages. In many circumstances, a solid professional relationship with police and emergency crews will be a surer means of access than a First Amendment demand.

Reporters can also expect to encounter restricted access to penal institutions, partly because of several U.S. Supreme Court opinions on the subject, including one in 1978. The case involved a California sheriff who limited press access to the county jail to once-a-month guided group tours for the public. A San Francisco television station sought permission to inspect and videotape the jail after an inmate committed suicide. The tours did not permit use of cameras or tape recorders and did not include disciplinary cells or the section of the jail where the suicide occurred.

Chief Justice Warren Burger, delivering the majority opinion, rejected the role of the press in serving the public's right to know. As he put it: "Unarticulated but implicit in the assertion that media access to the jail is essential for informed public debate on jail conditions is the assumption that media personnel are the best qualified persons for the task of discovering malfeasance in public institutions. But that assumption finds no support in the decisions of this Court or the First Amendment."[37] Burger said the sheriff's rules did not prevent the press from learning about jail conditions, albeit "not as conveniently as they might prefer." Reporters could receive letters from inmates that criticize and report conditions, interview their lawyers, talk to prison employees and public officials and seek out former inmates and jail visitors, Burger advised. Success at following his advice, of course, depends on whether inmates and people connected with the jail speak freely without fear of retaliation. Despite the Supreme Court's stance on prison access, not all prison or jail officials turn away reporters. In fact, some jail superintendents welcome the press and proudly show off their facilities.

Access to voting places presents another problem for reporters. A number of states attempted to limit reporters from conducting *exit polls*, which involve interviewing voters immediately after they cast their ballots. Washington, for example, banned exit polling within 300 feet of voting places. The limits came partly as a result of intense criticism over the networks' use of exit polls to predict election results while people were still voting. Exit polls, however, also yield important information that is used to interpret voter patterns and behavior. Several court challenges suggest that limits on exit polling are unconstitutional, but reporters can anticipate continued resistance from public officials who say the privacy rights of voters take precedence over the newsgathering rights of reporters.

Legislative chambers, municipal buildings and courthouses are among the most public of buildings; still, unlimited access to any government facility is rare. Reporters, for example, may be restricted to a press gallery when the legislature is conducting business. Occasionally, a mayor will ban "unfriendly" reporters from her office or press conferences. Obviously, during emergencies, any public building might be put off limits to the press.

NEW BATTLEGROUNDS OVER ACCESS

New access battles continue to erupt. Among the latest issues pitting journalists against public officials are access to military operations, electronic records and videotapes.

The Grenada invasion of 1983 broke with a tradition of reporters following American troops into action. The military has long engaged in various forms of news management—VIP treatment, denial of travel to "restricted" areas, staged news events and separation of reporters from fighting troops. But Grenada set a new standard for government control and manipulation of the news media.

In mid-October of 1983, reports circulated about U.S. plans to invade the Caribbean island of Grenada after a violent coup by a Marxist military leader who imposed a 24-hour-a-day, shoot-on-sight curfew. On October 24, White House press spokesperson Larry Speakes told reporters that the invasion rumors were "preposterous." The next day, American troops landed on the island. Later, officials said they invaded Grenada to protect and evacuate about 1,000 Americans on the island, most of them students at a medical school. Secretary of State Caspar Weinberger said secrecy was necessary to ensure the mission's success.

A few journalists tried to slip onto the island by boat or plane, but the military turned them back, in several cases at gunpoint. When enterprising reporters used ham radio operators to seek information from islanders, the Federal Communications Commission issued a warning, saying regulations prohibited use of amateur radio for newsgathering. Two days after the invasion, a 15-reporter pool, escorted by military personnel, arrived on Grenada. Finally, on October 30, the military gave reporters unlimited access. But the initial reports, photographs and videotape Americans received came from the Pentagon, not the press.[38] Left behind, reporters could not judge for themselves the dangers posed to American citizens, the strength of Cuban troops on the island or the conduct of American forces.

Complaints by the press led to formation of a commission that recommended a rotating pool of reporters to cover future military operations. Under the rules, reporters would accompany troops, but not necessarily the first wave; moreover, they would be sworn to secrecy until the military lifted any news embargo. Early non-combat tests of the pool concept went smoothly, but under battle conditions or during secret missions, the press may still be left behind the lines or kept at bay by tight restrictions on travel and access to troops. That has been the pattern for the post-Grenada military operations in Panama and Saudi Arabia. In 1990, the first press pool was not taken to Saudi Arabia until five days after the U.S. deployment began. *Time* reported that American journalists suspect the unstated purpose of the press pool is to prevent serious coverage during the early stages of military actions.[39] With operations in isolated areas under strict military control, there may be little choice but to follow rules, as journalists covering the Persian Gulf war discovered.

Access to electronic records poses an array of legal, logistical and policy problems unanticipated when most open-records laws originally were enacted. Public records stored in computer data bases present a tempting opportunity for officials to keep electronic records away from public scrutiny. With government agencies at all levels moving toward "paperless," electronic storage of vast amounts of information, the press has good reason to fear more access difficulties.

The battle lines are being drawn. Some public officials, for example, believe that an electronic search for data an agency does not ordinarily compile creates a *new* document; public-records laws, they say, cover only *existing* documents.[40] Of course, with computer security an understandable consideration, it is not likely that reporters will be given passwords and clearance to search randomly for information in government data bases. One government source said the only solution may be a new generation of "Electronic Freedom of Information" statutes.[41] On the federal level, the Justice Department in 1990 was working on rules for obtaining computerized government information under the Freedom of Information Act. But implementation and interpretation of any rules covering access will take time and undoubtedly lead to legal challenges.

Another development in government record keeping promises to further complicate access. To reduce costs and waste in government, some agencies transfer data collection and storage to private, profit-making companies, which, in turn, sell the data to their subscribers. Communications lawyer Donna Demac is alarmed by this trend, which has been referred to as *privatization* of government information. "Since these private entities are not subject to federal rules regarding public access and are able to charge whatever the market will bear, privatization has the effect of further promoting government secrecy."[42] Other critics of privatization fear that the high fees private companies are expected to impose for retrieval of electronically stored information will prohibit reporters, especially those with limited budgets, from investigative journalism.[43]

Videotape is fast becoming a contested "visual record." Police are making wider use of videotapes for statements and evidence, such as filming drivers suspected of being intoxicated. In some crime-infested cities, citizens are using camcorders to discourage criminals and collect evidence of drug deals, theft and prostitution. With video equipment inexpensive, compact and ubiquitous, nearly every news event is apt to include someone's videotaped record. In Los Angeles, for example, an amateur videographer captured police repeatedly beating a helpless suspect. The standard arguments for withholding print records—privacy, security and fair trial rights—will be applied to videotape records.

Because this is an emerging area, legal precedent is limited. A California appellate court ruling, however, suggests what journalists might anticipate when requesting videotape from public officials. The case involved a police videotape of the execution of a search warrant at the home of a psychotherapist who allegedly possessed evidence needed in a murder investigation. The videotape covered several sections of the home, including bedrooms, and showed the therapist's wife dressed in a robe. In arguing for release of the videotape, CBS and ABC cited the watchdog role of the press to monitor how police and court officials carry out their duties. The appellate court decided the videotapes were not subject to the state's public records law unless the tapes were admitted into evidence. Historically, the court said, the public has not had pretrial access to items seized under a search warrant. The court also raised the issue of privacy, concluding that examination of the videotape constituted an invasive search of the therapist's home by the media.[44]

FEAR OF TALKING

Overshadowing all access problems is the real or implied threat of retaliation against public employees who, without authorization, provide information to reporters. Increasingly, rules and penalties governing release of government information are making it difficult and dangerous for employees at all levels of public service to talk to the press. Police departments, for example, often invoke a "spokesperson only" policy to centralize and control release of news. The policies usually forbid officers on beats or at crime scenes from answering reporters' questions.

Some institutions and government agencies take an indirect approach to control communication, but the message usually is clear. A state university in the Midwest, for example, operates under a five-page set of procedures for "media relations and information dissemination." Employees are "urged" to go through the university's director of news services whenever a reporter calls for an interview or information. Throughout the document are strong hints that employees are duty bound to avoid answering inquiries that might "embarrass" or "hurt" the university. And there are the direct approaches. In 1989, U.S. Attorney General Richard Thornburgh announced that the Justice Department would criminally prosecute federal employees who leaked information about government investigations to the press.[45]

In response to the Justice Department's policy, media attorney Bruce Sanford remarked, "The good ship of government is probably the only ship that operates best with leaks."[46] Sanford alluded, in part, to leaks by "whistleblowers"—people who follow their conscience to expose wrongdoing in government or the private sector. From aerospace companies to the State Department there are examples of recriminations, dismissal or prosecution against whistleblowers. Employees who violate policies or go against the wishes of their superiors also face hidden acts of punishment, such as being passed over for promotion or denied a merit raise. In some government offices, workers are so concerned they fear even being seen with a reporter.

A few safeguards for whistleblowers exist. Federal and state laws protect some private-sector employees, such as miners or workers at nuclear plants, who disclose safety hazards at work. Whistleblower laws generally protect workers from being fired, threatened or discriminated against. But protection is not universal, and where laws exist, whistleblowers still face forms of retaliation and censure for speaking out.

Newsgathering in the Information Age is increasingly difficult and complicated. Gaining access to people, places and records involves more than knowing what information is available, where it can be found and who holds the keys to its release. Effort and persistence are required. Journalists must aggressively seek information and access. Those who resignedly settle for news releases and tamely submit to agency rules on access to records and meetings only encourage public officials to keep the people's business private.

Computers and information-retrieval systems are opening vast, unexplored territories of news and analysis to reporters. But conversely, as more information is converted to electronic form, technology poses serious threats to freedom of information if reporters fail to lay claim to those new territories. The sheer volume of information and the speed with which it is generated and disseminated calls for journalists with the ability and determination to keep a self-governing people informed and its leaders accountable.

EXERCISES

1. Carefully read your state's open-records law. Then make a freedom-of-information request for public records at your school. Do not pursue records that are clearly unobtainable under the law. Seek those on which you can build a story. For example, you could ask for parking-ticket receipts to see how much money the school collects each semester. Is your school about to hire a new dean or administrator? As part of your coverage, ask to examine the applications. If you attend a private school, you cannot count on support from the state's open-records law; it applies only to public institutions. But you still might consider making a request for similar information and writing about the experience— as long as it does not get you into trouble with school officials.

2. Interview several local journalists who cover public boards or agencies. Ask them to assess how true public officials are to the spirit and the letter of the state's open-meetings law. Next, obtain the perspective of the public officials involved. In a story, compare and contrast the different positions.

3. Talk to the manager (or public relations spokesperson) of a nearby factory, power plant or refinery about policies on press

access to their facilities in the event of an emergency. Some companies have detailed procedures for handling journalists, but officials may not want to reveal those procedures or speak openly about press relations. Try your best to find out why companies often see a need to manage news coverage in an emergency.

NOTES

[1] "Editorial," *News Media & the Law,* Spring 1989, p. i.

[2] Jack Briggs, "Federal Agencies Under Reagan Slow to Respond to FOI Requests," report of the Freedom of Information Committee, Associated Press Managing Editors, Sept. 1987, p. 6.

[3] Guy Munger, "FOI Court Battles Can Be Expensive," report of the Freedom of Information Committee, Associated Press Managing Editors, Oct. 1988, p. 25.

[4] Munger, "FOI Court Battles Can Be Expensive," p. 25.

[5] Gaillard Hunt, ed., *Writings of James Madison* (New York: Putnams, 1900–1910), 9:103, letter to W.T. Barry, Aug. 4, 1822.

[6] *Houchins v. KQED,* 438 U.S. 1(1978).

[7] *Gannett v. DePasquale,* 443 U.S. 368 (1979).

[8] *New York Times,* Nov. 3, 1974, p. 37A.

[9] Steve McGonigle, "Media Access to Government: An Open or Shut Case?," Fifteenth Annual Media Law Conference, Florida Bar, Orlando, Fla., Feb. 25, 1989.

[10] Quoted in M.L. Stein, "Reporter Stationed in Council Chambers Eight Hours a Day," *Editor & Publisher,* Jan. 21, 1989, p. 18.

[11] William J. Small, *Political Power and the Press* (New York: W.W. Norton, 1972), p. 382.

[12] "The Open Door to Government in Minnesota" in *Tapping Officials' Secrets* (Washington, D.C.: Reporters Committee for Freedom of the Press, 1989), p. 9.

[13] First Amendment Foundation, Tallahassee, Fla.

[14] Les Pearson and Bill Smith, " 'Nit-Picking Details' of Pageant Add Up," *St. Louis Globe-Democrat,* Oct. 25, 1985, p. 1.

[15] Jane T. Harrigan, *Read All About It!* (Chester, Conn.: Globe Pequot Press, 1987), pp. 14, 15.

[16] Angie Cannon, "How Much Overtime Does Your City Pay," *Editors' Exchange,* July 1990, p. 2.

[17] Jim Steele, "Tips on Investigative Reporting," *Editors' Exchange,* Sept. 1990, p. 4.

[18] "How to File an FOIA Request," *The Quill,* Nov.–Dec. 1990, p. 51.

[19] Quoted in Richard P. Kleeman, "Life on the FOIA Front," *The Quill,* Dec.–Jan. 1990, p. 19.

[20] Laird B. Anderson, "FOIA Founder Looks at Law Today," *1988–1989 FOI Report,* Society of Professional Journalists, p. 13.

[21] Anderson, "FOIA Founder Looks at Law Today," *FOI Report,* p. 13.

[22] *Butterworth v. Smith,* 17 Med. L. Rptr. 1569 (1990).

[23] "Media Gain Juvenile Court Access," *News Media & the Law,* Spring 1989, p. 21.

24 *Smith v. Daily Mail Publishing Co.,* 443 U.S. 97 (1979).

25 *Gannett v. DePasquale,* 443 U.S. 368 (1979).

26 *Richmond Newspapers v. Virginia,* 448 U.S. 555 (1980).

27 *Legal Handbook* (Syracuse, N.Y.: New York State Newspapers Foundation, 1980).

28 *United States v. Dickinson,* 465 F.2d (5th Cir. 1972).

29 *Nebraska Press Association v. Stuart,* 427 U.S. 539 (1976).

30 *United States v. Dickinson,* 465 F.2d 496 (5th Cir. 1972).

31 Elsa Walsh and Benjamin Weiser, "Public Court, Private Justice," *Washington Post National Weekly Edition,* Nov. 28–Dec. 4, 1988, p. 6.

32 Anne Lucey, "Secrecy in the Courts Rises, Leaving Public in the Dark," *The Quill,* Nov.–Dec. 1990, p. 13.

33 "Judge Fines Reporter $300 for 'Insolence,' " *Editor & Publisher,* May 20, 1989, p. 24.

34 Carl Bernstein and Bob Woodward, *All the President's Men* (New York: Warner, 1975), pp. 236, 237.

35 "Justices Allow Reporters' Convictions for Trespass," *News Media & the Law,* Jan.–Feb. 1984, p. 7.

36 *Branzburg v. Hayes,* 409 U.S. 665 (1972).

37 *Houchins v. KQED,* 438 U.S. 1 (1978).

38 "Coverage Efforts Thwarted," *News Media & the Law,* Jan.–Feb. 1984, p. 6.

39 Stanley W. Cloud, "The First Casualty," *Time,* Sept. 10, 1990, p. 69.

40 "When Does Electronic Data Turn into a Public Record?," *ASNE Bulletin,* Nov. 1988, p. 9.

41 "OIP Takes 'Electronic Records' Survey," *FOIA Update,* U.S. Department of Justice, Spring 1989, pp. 1, 2.

42 Donna A. Demac, *Liberty Denied* (New Brunswick, N.J.: Rutgers University Press, 1990), p. 119.

43 See Mitchell Hartman, "Investigative Reporters Use Databases to Break Stories," *The Quill,* Nov.–Dec. 1990, p. 21.

44 *Oziel v. Los Angeles,* 18 Med. L. Rptr. 1113 (1990).

45 George Garneau, "Clampdown on Sources," *Editor & Publisher,* Aug. 12, 1989, p. 11.

46 Garneau, "Clampdown on Sources," p. 11.

Chapter Five

The Wenham Town Hall in Wenham, Mass. (Fredrik D. Bodin/Stock, Boston)

Government News
for the People

The business of government is conducted at polished walnut desks beneath the fresco-adorned ceilings of massive statehouses. It also is conducted at folding tables set up on the patched linoleum floors of cinder-block community halls. No matter what the setting, and no matter who governs, the average citizen wants to know an essential point about the business of government: "How am I going to be affected?" That question should guide all government reporters, whether they cover sessions of Congress or meetings of the village board. Here is how Mark Davis of the *Tampa Tribune* keeps his perspective on government reporting: "You sit in some old county commission meeting, and they're talking about developmental impact or some old crummy ordinance, and you forget that basically they're dealing with people. Somebody's going to be affected, and you have to keep your eye on those details: who the people are, how it's going to affect them for better or worse, and how they view it."[1] As Davis knows, the key to effective, appealing government reporting is the people factor. First, tell the news of government *through people.* Second, relate news of government *to people.* Writing coach Don Murray adds this advice: "Invite the reader in—it's the reader's government."[2]

Government reporters who care about "inviting the people in" avoid becoming pipelines for "officialdom." Officialdom is not so much a place as a state of mind. It is a stultified realm populated by politicians and bureaucrats who speak *governmentese,* a hybrid of jargon and gobbledygook. Reporters have to function in officialdom, but they must not succumb to its numbing influence. Otherwise they are apt to end up writing by formula, concentrating chiefly on meetings and events, relying on a handful of favored official sources and dealing in the inanimate objects of government—bills, reports, studies and pronouncements. The dull stuff.

Too many news accounts of government are poorly written and poorly read. Readers often skim government stories, assuming they offer little of interest or value. But government is not a vast, barren wasteland. For resourceful and enthusiastic reporters, there is action, intrigue, drama and significance on government beats, as Mark Davis demonstrated in his five-part series "Anatomy of a Road." By turning what could have been a tedious subject into a lively journey through a tangle of heavy machinery and traffic jams, Davis won the American Society of Newspaper Editors award in 1989 for government reporting.

Mark Davis and other reporters who have shared his experiences know the task is not easy. Government at all levels is becoming increasingly complex, specialized and far-flung. To find important stories, reporters must sift through layers of bureaucracy—agencies, commissions, boards and departments. Moreover, much of the debate, bargaining, compromise and decision making of government occurs away from public view. Simply covering meetings and events is not enough. To do the job adequately, much less well, means understanding the intricacies of policy making, legislation, public finance, law and politics. The most successful government reporters learn to attend to both the important actions of government and the significant issues and problems affecting—or soon to affect—citizens.

City hall coverage is at the core of government reporting and prepares journalists for other beats. Chapter 5 begins with and focuses heavily on city hall, where many reporters, some while still in school, start their careers.

COVERING THE CITY AND THE HALL

A city hall reporter ought to be a walking encyclopedia of community life. Intelligent, accurate, thorough coverage begins with a foundation of knowledge. Do not assume you know the city until you can answer the following questions—and many others:

- What is the city's history? Who founded it and when? How did it get its name? Who were the leading settlers? What were crucial events in the city's history? What does the city's history say about its *present* and suggest about its *future*?

- Who are its people? What are their ethnic roots? What is the city's demographic profile? Where do people live? Is there segregation by race, ethnicity or age? Discrimination? Are segments of the population frustrated? Involved? Angry?

- What about development? Is the city growing? Stagnant? Withering? Is there a sufficient tax base to maintain city services? Which businesses and institutions are the largest employers? What's the jobless rate? Are people taking out building permits? Business licenses? Does the city have a master plan for development? If so, what does the plan propose?

- What's the condition of the city's infrastructure? Are water and sewer lines adequate and in good repair? How about housing? Roads? Bridges? Public buildings? Who does the inspecting and how diligently?

- What about amenities and services? Is it a good place to live in terms of health facilities, police protection, arts and culture, transportation, recreation and education?

- Who are the political, social and economic power brokers? Who are the opinion leaders? The religious leaders? Who are the experts and authorities?

Although you cannot learn about a city overnight, there are shortcuts. Often the city government or Chamber of Commerce prepares a community profile for use in planning and economic development. Get a copy and read it. Then go exploring. Ask to accompany a social worker as she visits clients. Ride around town with a supervisor in the streets department. Drop by the municipal recreation center and explore the city parks. Invite a housing-rights activist to give an assessment on the city. Chat with the city's unofficial historian. Share a cup of coffee and a view of the city's future with the executive director of the Chamber of Commerce. Discuss the city's progress with a labor union official.

If you make an effort to know the city, you will better understand personalities, events and activities; ask more penetrating questions; acquire the background to issues and problems; build a file of valuable news sources; and discover untold stories. For example, you might find out that dozens of older residences still lack indoor plumbing—or that no new homes have been built in the city in the past six months, all of which could surprise even the most well-informed citizens.

Functions and Role of City Government

Reporters who carefully monitor a city's functions understand the greatest concerns of citizens. In an ideal sense, cities function to ensure order, provide essential services, nurture civic life and protect public health, welfare and safety—with varying degrees of success and efficiency. When a city fails to perform its basic functions, that is usually news.

An urban scholar studying government-citizen contacts in Kansas City found that people were most often concerned about service problems, such as uncollected trash or barking dogs. Next in degree of concern were safety problems, like fear of walking city streets at night. Least frequently mentioned were social problems—for instance, unsupervised teenagers.[3] Should reporters, then, devote more attention to junked cars than aimless youths? Rather than prioritize news coverage based on Kansas City's experiences, remember that each city has its peculiar problems. To understand citizens and their concerns, leave city hall and visit neighborhoods, talk to people and listen to what is on their minds.

Knowing a city also involves understanding its relationship to the state. Cities are not autonomous entities that can do as they please. In fact, political scientists sometimes describe cities as "creatures of the state" because, in many cases, charters granted by state legislators define a particular city's powers, functions and structure of government. For example, most states, by statute, determine how cities set tax rates, annex land and borrow money. Certain cities, though, operate under a principle known as *home rule.* States with home-rule charters allow cities a greater degree of self-determination, particularly in selecting a form of government and method of elections. Home-rule communities still must abide by the state's constitution and statutes. If nothing else, home-rule cities enjoy a psychological sense of freedom. If your city has a charter, be sure to study it.

The Structure of City Government

In part, journalists are responsible for the structural characteristics now widely found in city governments. Lincoln Steffens and other muckrakers helped expose the shame of the cities—the boodle and bossism of the late 19th and early 20th centuries. They wrote about election fraud, bribes, influence peddling, patronage, nepotism and other sins of the boss-led political machines that controlled many big cities. Their stories helped fuel a reform movement that tried to rid cities of corruption and chaos and restore honesty and efficiency in government. The reform package often included non-partisan, at-large elections, city manager–council structure and civil service merit employment, all intended to make city government more democratic, professional and honest.

Actually, reform presented its own problems, some of them unanticipated. For example, with management of government in the hands of unelected professionals, city officials began to be less directly accountable to the people; you cannot vote a city manager out of office. By ousting boss-controlled political cronies from their patronage jobs in city hall and replacing them with bureaucrats, government tended to become less responsive to complaints. In the old days, people knew whom to call to get a pothole repaired or a stop sign installed. And when at-large elections replaced election by wards or precincts, some neighborhoods and classes of citizens lost their direct representation on the city council.

Most cities now operate under one of three common forms: *mayor-council, city manager–council* and *commission.* City hall reporters need to know the characteristics, strengths and weaknesses of each form of government, since the structure of government tends to create different sets of tensions over who wields power, sets policy and makes decisions.

The *mayor-council* form includes two main variations—weak mayor and strong mayor. The distinction pertains to the powers held by a city's chief executive. As a rule, strong mayors are authorized to hire and fire administrators, initiate policy, prepare and administer the budget and veto legislation. Weak mayors frequently are ceremonial figures with little administrative power. An administratively strong mayor, however, could be ineffectual; on the other hand, a weak mayor may possess great influence and power. Personality, ability and political connections help determine whether, in practice, a mayor is strong or weak. Henry Maier, mayor of Milwaukee for 28 years, observed: "The mayor of New York has considerable strength by statute. And Mayor (Richard) Daley of Chicago had the weakest power by statute in the U.S. So which is the strong mayor?"[4] Mayor Daley dominated Chicago politics. As Maier suggests, do not put too much stock in "statutory power."

The *city manager–council* form is common in midsized cities of 25,000 to 250,000 population. It began as a product of reform, but today it makes sense for cities that are governed by part-time mayors and legislators who often lack the expertise or time to oversee day-to-day operations. A competent, professionally trained city manager can bring cost-effective, expert administration to a city.

City managers often run the show, particularly if the mayor and council members are busy at their full-time jobs. Reporters, naturally, will turn to city managers for opinions, reactions and information related to city government. But keep in mind that a powerful, policy-making city manager may be knowledgable, witty, urbane *and* politically savvy, at least in dealing with the mayor and council. But is he or she as attuned to citizen concerns or knowledgable about the community? Keep in mind as well that many city managers lead a nomadic life, relocating frequently because of career ambitions, a tiff with the city council or election of a new administration. This is the price of being a hired hand. City managers often will admit that it is a precarious, stressful position. "People expect you to do miracles," says Robert Obering, city manager of St. Petersburg, Fla. "Then if you have a city council that doesn't like you very much, that's much more stress. If you have a split council, they will put the city manager in between."[5] City managers walk a tightrope and are cautious about what they say and do. Reporters should not overly rely on the city manager as a source for news or insight. As always, seek a diversity of viewpoints.

The *commission* form is an awkward breed of government. By most accounts, the commission form developed in 1900 after Galveston, Tex., struggled to recover from a hurricane that killed 6,000 of the city's 37,000 residents and destroyed half of the city's property. The state legislature appointed a five-person commission of business leaders to run the city. Each commissioner directed a municipal department. But as the commission form evolved and spread to other cities, its disadvantages became apparent. Not all commissioners, even those who are successful in the business world, prove to be adept at managing municipal departments. In addition, the commission form fails to provide for a separation of powers between executive and legislative functions of the commissioners and leads commissioners to frequent turf battles. The mayor, often holding no more power than the other commissioners, may lack authority to intercede when commissioners fail to act in the best overall interests of the community. Today, fewer than 200 cities, mostly small communities, operate under the commission form.

The structure and size of city government also influence how much day-to-day contact reporters can expect with officials. In big cities, the mayor's office may be structured like the White House, which means a reporter must deal with a chief of staff, an appointments secretary, a press secretary and assorted aides before—or instead of—seeing the mayor. As a result, some big-city reporters must either be satisfied to ask questions at the mayor's occasional press conferences or wait for a personal interview, which might have to be scheduled well in advance. Big-city mayors are busy, but they are also in a good position to dictate and manage media coverage, particularly by staging events and "happenings" for television coverage. At the other extreme, small-town mayors answer their own phones and share coffee and chitchat with reporters. And if you miss the mayor at city hall, she can be reached at her full-time job as a State Farm insurance agent.

Council members, sometimes called aldermen, usually are available and eager to talk to the press. Even in the largest of cities, few are full-time lawmakers. But they are politicians, and, if they wish to remain in office, they need to be visible to their constituents.

Who's Who in City Hall

Regardless of the size of the city, certain officials—both elected and appointed—play key roles as newsmakers and information providers. In midsized or small municipalities and villages, the office of the *city clerk*, often adjacent to the front lobby of city hall, is the hub of activity. (In the case of a village, substitute "village" for "city" in the titles.) Here is where you will find the bulk of the city's records, such as minutes of council meetings, applications for building permits, lists of property-tax assessments and sets of ordinances. In smaller communities, the city clerk may be the only full-time elected official. In almost all cases, the clerk knows who's who and what's what in city hall. The clerk is one of the first people you should get to know on the city hall beat, especially when you need background information, access to city documents, schedules of meetings and copies of agendas.

The *city attorney*—sometimes called the corporation counsel— is a source of information on nearly every facet of city government, including ordinances, municipal bonds, contracts and labor negotiations. You can anticipate that other city officials, including the mayor and city manager, will seek the city attorney's advice on a wide range of issues and problems. Usually, the city attorney is an appointed official on a retainer who serves at the pleasure of the administration. In large cities, it is a full-time position. City attorneys tend to be politically astute and well connected, but most prefer to remain in the background, staying clear, if possible, of tugs of war over city policy. When there is a division among city council members and the mayor, you might be able to tap the city attorney for a moderate, less partial viewpoint—although it may be given off the record.

Municipal money flows to and from the *city treasurer.* That does not necessarily mean the city treasurer is a fiscal expert. In fact, many city treasurers are elected officials who know only the rudiments of accountancy and budget management. In large cities, the city treasurer frequently oversees a professional staff and a multimillion-dollar budget. Even when there is no reason to suspect problems, the city treasurer's office requires constant vigilance. Many conscientious city hall reporters routinely inspect invoices, purchase requisitions, bills and monthly budget updates.

Municipalities that seek orderly, sound development often hire a professional *city planner.* Part of the city planner's job is to design and implement a blueprint for land use and growth called a *master plan.* City planners frequently find themselves in controversies over rezoning, annexation, condemnation of property and other touchy aspects of city growth.

Operation of city services is delegated to department heads who are likely to be well-trained professionals. Nearly all cities have a *public works director* or city engineer responsible for, among other things, water and sewage-treatment facilities, which are subject to increasingly strict, complicated and expensive requirements set by federal and state agencies. Other common municipal departments include housing, recreation, streets, and public safety.

HOW TO COVER COUNCIL MEETINGS

Covering city government means going to meeting after meeting. Too often, the meetings are overly long, slowly paced and sparsely attended, unless a controversial issue is on the agenda. Dreary as this may sound, dedicated reporters approach government meetings with a serious sense of purpose. They know that reporting the activities of government is a responsibility they owe to the public, and they also know that what happens at a city council meeting may reveal the tip of a larger story. What if an engineering report, given scant attention by the council members, reveals a serious, impending shortage in the city water supply? Unless reporters are present—and alert—the story may go undetected, which could be exactly what city officials hope will happen.

Experienced city hall reporters also know that much of the work, discussion and resolution of differences over ordinances and other municipal business occurs at meetings of the *standing committees* of the city council. These, too, must be covered.

Preparation

Preparation is a key to competent coverage of city government meetings. A starting point is careful review of the agenda and the packets of materials the council members receive in advance of meetings. The packets contain, among other things, copies of reports, correspondence and proposed ordinances. Most often, the city clerk's office prepares and distributes the packets.

Preparation includes, at times, *advance stories* to alert citizens about what is going to happen at the city council meeting. Advance stories also help reporters stay on top of their beats. By talking to council members and city officials prior to a meeting, you can begin to anticipate, plan and organize meeting coverage.

What to Expect

Government meetings are not reported in chronological order, otherwise most leads would begin: "The City Council opened its meeting Tuesday night with a solemn pledge of allegiance, followed by a snappy roll call and unanimous approval of the minutes."

The order of business will vary, but generally meetings include these categories: petitions and communications, reports of city officers, council committee reports, new business and old business. Time may be reserved at the beginning or end of meetings for citizens to speak from the floor.

In small and midsized communities, the mayor presides over meetings of the city council. In larger cities, an alderman, elected by his or her colleagues or by citywide vote, may preside as president of the board of aldermen or council. Whoever presides often controls the pace, tone and flow of meetings.

City council meetings often are informal and disorganized. People, including council members and reporters, move around the council chambers, shuffle papers, clear throats and carry on conversations when others are trying to speak and conduct business. For the uninitiated, the apparent lack of decorum may be disconcerting, but it usually is not worth reporting—unless, of course, a meeting turns into a three-ring circus of fisticuffs or epithets.

Legislative Process

The meat of most city council sessions is passage of *ordinances*—the laws of municipalities. Ordinances originate in several ways. A citizen, for example, may approach a city council member, asking for a parking ban on the north side of a dangerously narrow stretch of Elm Street. Or a problem may arise, such as keg parties at city parks, requiring specific rules governing consumption of alcohol on municipal property. Regulations coming from a federal or state office, like the Environmental Protection Agency, might require passage of a new ordinance detailing how sewer lines are installed. In some cases, ordinances satisfy a public official's whim or address a pet peeve. In suburban Chicago, the mayor of Evergreen Park spent more than an hour stuck at a railroad crossing by a stopped freight train. Soon afterward the village board passed an ordinance calling for a $100,000 fine against trains that unnecessarily blocked crossings.[6]

In its earliest stage, an ordinance may be scribbled in pencil on the back of an envelope. Eventually, it is refined and put into legal form and language by the city attorney or the city manager. Once introduced before the city council, the proposed ordinance receives what is called the *first reading,* and normally it is perfunctorily passed on first reading so that it may move to the next stage, which usually is review by a standing committee of the city council. If, for example, the ordinance involves parking, it is sent to the committee responsible for streets. In special cases, the standing committee holds one or more public hearings to allow citizens an opportunity to respond to the proposed legislation, particularly if a tax levy or expenditure of public money is involved.

As a proposed ordinance undergoes review, it can be modified or refined before returning to the full city council for the *second reading.* At this point the proposed ordinance normally is subject to discussion and debate by members of the entire city council, who may seek additional amendments or alterations from the floor or return it to committee. Some cities require a *third reading,* followed by a majority vote of the council, to pass an ordinance. The process is deliberately slow so that citizens and lawmakers alike can read, consider, amend or reject legislation. In an emergency, an ordinance can be passed on first reading, but usually a two-thirds vote is required to prevent laws from being "railroaded," or rushed, through the city council. The final steps of the process include approval by the mayor, who may have the power to veto the legislation, and publication of a legal notice of the ordinance in a local general-circulation newspaper.

Understanding the process is important, but, above all, reporters must know the origins and motives behind any important piece of legislation. Who, for example, are the opponents and sponsors, including those in the forefront and those behind the scenes? David Broder, a political correspondent for the *Washington Post*, once described coverage of Congress in terms that apply, as well, to coverage of city government: "When I started working on Capitol Hill, the wire service did a lot more of what I would characterize as railroad timetable reporting of Congress, which tells you what train (or bill) has just left what station and what its next stop will be. It tells you a little bit about what's on the train, but almost nothing about how the train was put together and why it is carrying that particular cargo."[7] Reporters who provide consistently accurate explanations attend committee meetings where they can better observe how the train is put together, learn what it is carrying and find out where it is headed and why it is headed there.

Do not confuse ordinances with two other official actions subject to a vote of the council—*resolutions* and *motions*. Resolutions are used to set city policy (telling the street department to cut high weeds on vacant lots and bill the owners) or express community sentiment (declaring the council's moral support for the United Way campaign). Motions made and approved by the council usually direct city administrators to take action on a variety of routine matters, such as instructing the city clerk to rehire two part-time employees or authorizing the treasurer to pay the city's monthly bills.

Writing Meeting Stories

For inexperienced reporters, the greatest challenge of meeting coverage is determining what to emphasize among a number of actions of apparently comparable importance—or unimportance. As the meeting progresses, dozens of agenda items may be swiftly dispatched to committees or disposed of with little comment and no vote. Do not assume such matters are inconsequential. Conversely, do not assume a lengthy, heated debate over a request by the fire chief to attend a convention in Las Vegas is important. Stay alert and ask questions if you are unsure of what is significant and what is not. Let the people factor guide you. As a rule, the news value of city business increases proportionately with the number of people affected.

It is much easier to determine significance when you are familiar with the background of major business before the city council. That is especially true regarding matters the council has discussed repeatedly over the course of months or even years. Because there is no need for council members to review the history of a long-running agenda item, they compress details, speak obliquely and still understand each other—losing reporters who fail to do their homework.

Government officials also speak in bureaucratic shorthand. In the course of a few rapidly delivered sentences, a city official might refer to "IEPA," "C-3 zoning," "special-use permit" and "non-performance bonds." To survive, you must be conversant in the language of government. If necessary, ask public officials to help you define specialized terms in lay language.

Another challenge of writing meeting stories is to translate the legalese of ordinances into plain English. Ordinances normally are collections of "whereas" paragraphs that explain the background and rationale of the legislation. They lead to the "therefore" clause: "Therefore, be it ordained by the City Council of Pottsville. . . ." After that, the details of the ordinance are enumerated by series of sections. When ordinances are especially long and technical, do not be too proud to seek the city attorney's help.

With any major legislation, you will want to explain the background, anticipate the impact, gather reactions and provide the analysis, none of which is to be found in the text of the ordinance. One reason that accomplished city hall reporters do their homework is to prepare themselves to flesh out the story. By itself, an ordinance provides little more than the story's skeleton. In fact, with a controversial ordinance, reaction-background coverage begins with its first reading. If, for example, the city council proposes to ban overnight parking of all trucks, including pickups, on residential streets, there will be no shortage of reaction. Just be sure to seek reaction both inside *and* outside of city hall.

To some extent, what you write—and how you write it—depends on a number of external factors. Among them are the amount of news space in that day's paper, your editor's desires and needs and news developments elsewhere that are competing for space. It is vital for beat reporters to consult with editors frequently, especially to plan and coordinate meeting coverage. Consultations between reporters and editors should be a mutual enterprise, with ideas flowing in both directions.

Most city hall reporters prefer to present council news in several small doses rather than cram everything they know into a comprehensive piece. When coverage is limited to a single, long story, readers may overlook other important city business reported deep in the story. If forced to go with a single piece, be sure to insert a paragraph near the lead of the story to summarize major developments. Here is an example:

> Despite objections from local merchants, the city council voted unanimously to increase parking meter rates downtown from 10 cents to 25 cents an hour.
>
> In a meeting marked by angry debate, the council also approved a zoning variance that will allow Pizza Palace, Inc., to build a restaurant adjacent to Washington grade school and granted a liquor license to Mayor John Williams' son-in-law.
>
> The strongest protests, however, came when the city council prepared to act on parking rates. . . .

Sometimes, particularly in small communities, there is not much on which to pin a lead. One possible solution is to find a connection among otherwise unrelated, minor actions, as the opening of the following story does:

> In a brief but busy session last night, the city council took several steps to replace wornout equipment.
>
> Among other things, the council:
>
> - appropriated $1,000 to buy tires for a city fire truck
>
> - authorized the city clerk to call for bids on a police car
>
> - asked the city engineer to estimate the cost to replace a faulty sewer pump at the Beacon Hills lift station
>
> - approved a low bid of $10,500 for a new tractor for the streets department

News emerging from city council meetings seldom is momentous. Even when more pressing issues beg for attention, much time and effort may be given by the council to seemingly mundane matters, such as sewer backups, junked cars and potholes. But life's mundane side occasionally produces everyday irritations that should not go unaddressed or unreported.

Coverage Tips

Arrive at least 30 minutes early for a city council meeting. If nothing else, you may need the extra time to battle traffic or find a parking space. More productively, you can use the time to gather background information, conduct interviews or engage in useful small talk.

Position yourself close to the action. A table for the press may be provided, but is it the best vantage point? Try to get an unobstructed view of the council so you can better see and hear what is being discussed. If you have never met the council members, do not assume that the person sitting at a desk marked "Alderman Mary Davis" is Mary Davis. Learn the identity of all the city officials prior to the start of the meeting.

After the meeting, line up people you need to interview. You might say, "Councilman Perkins, I have to ask the mayor a few questions, but if you could wait, I'd like to talk to you, too." If people are in a hurry to leave, find out where they will be later and how you can reach them by phone.

Talk to citizens who attend. Find out who they are and why they are present, even if they were silent during the meeting. They still may have a story to tell. "Few people come to a meeting for entertainment," says Fred Palmer, managing editor of the *Johnson City* (Tenn.) *Press-Chronicle*.[8]

Identify in your meeting story any city council members who were absent, and find out why they were absent. Do not be satisfied with a vague explanation, such as, "She's away on city business" or "He's attending to a personal matter." The council member away on "city business" might be meeting with representatives of a corporation who are scouting the city for a factory site. The council member attending to a "personal matter" could be at a college graduation or in the hospital for cardiac tests.

FINANCING CITY GOVERNMENT

Running a city is big business. In the 1980s, the budget for the City of Chicago passed the $2 billion mark. Three hundred miles downstate, the 1989 budget of Breese, Ill., population 3,500, topped $5 million. Municipal finances actually are not complicated, however, once you become familiar with their four basic components—*revenues* and *expenditures* and *budgeting* and *borrowing*.

Revenues and Expenditures

For most communities, property taxes constitute the main source of revenue, although increasingly, especially in suburban cities with profitable shopping malls, the sales tax is overtaking the property tax. The property tax remains a crucial and controversial source of revenue, partly because it is a tax that city officials can manipulate to help balance the municipal budget. Indeed, understanding the budget-making process begins with an understanding of property taxes.

The property tax is based on a unit called a *mill*, which is 1/10 of a cent, but most commonly, the tax rate is expressed in cents or dollars per $100 of assessed valuation of the property being taxed. The *assessed value* generally is based on a percentage of the fair market value of the property. County or municipal assessors inspect and photograph real estate property, noting, among other things, lot size, square footage of living space, type of construction and condition of nearby property as factors in determining the market value. When a home is sold, the purchase price normally is used to set a new assessed value. Otherwise, property is supposed to be reassessed every few years to account for appreciation and improvements that might affect the market value. Assessments of commercial, industrial and farm land are more complicated, based on various formulas to determine income-earning use or potential.

The tax rate is set by a city or county official, such as the county clerk, based on information provided by the taxing body. The mayor, budget director and other municipal officials figure the city's revenues and expenditures and then calculate how much in locally generated property tax revenue is needed to balance the budget. Once collected, tax revenue often goes into a general fund, although sometimes a city's tax rate is subdivided, and revenues are diverted to several separate funds dedicated for special use, such as employee pensions or library expenses.

Most city residents live within the boundaries of several taxing authorities, so a typical homeowner may pay taxes to the city, county, township, airport authority, sewer district, community college district and the local school district, which usually requires the largest share of the tax dollars. A sample tax bill, based on a $60,000 home assessed at one-third its market value ($20,000), breaks down this way:

County	.56 per $100 assessed valuation
Township	.09
City	1.18
School	3.34
Community college	.27
Airport district	.18
Sewer district	.23

The total comes to a tax rate of $5.85 per $100 of assessed valuation. Multiplied by 200 (20,000 divided by 100), the taxpayer's bill comes to $1,170.

Long before the taxpayer revolts of the late 1970s, property owners protested the inequities, financial burdens and corruption associated with the tax-assessment process. Among a litany of complaints are these:

- Property is not always assessed uniformly or accurately.

- There is little incentive for owners to improve property if it means an increase in taxes.

- The poor and people on fixed incomes are hit hardest by the property tax.

- Dishonest public officials continue to assess private, commercial and industrial property for political favor or personal gain.

For homeowners, however, one of the most controversial aspects of the property tax is *equalization.* When assessments in a county or city fail to correspond with selling prices of property, state or county officials are empowered to raise or lower taxes automatically and uniformly by a legal means sometimes known as a *multiplier.* In theory, multipliers and other instruments of equalization are supposed to maintain equity in assessments from county to county or city to city, but in practice, multipliers penalize property owners whose assessments already are in line with prevailing market values.

Other major revenue sources are the city's share of various state-collected taxes on incomes, motor fuel (gasoline), tobacco and alcohol. A few large cities, such as St. Louis, impose an earnings tax on all people who work in the city, regardless of where they reside.

Grants and aid from state or federal agencies, user charges, impact fees, licenses and franchise fees also constitute income for cities, but as revenue sources, they generally are not as dependable or substantial as taxes. City officials try to avoid funding programs with grant money: They usually come with strings attached, and they can be cut off at any time by Congress or the state legislature. In 1986, Congress eliminated the federal revenue-sharing program that many cities depended on as a major source of outside funding. Most user fees are generated by city-owned utilities, which frequently augment income by selling water or electricity to homes and businesses in unincorporated areas. In some areas, developers and builders must pay impact fees to help finance public roads and utilities needed to service new developments. Licenses range from auto stickers to liquor-sale permits. And franchise fees often are collected from cable operators, ambulance services and other companies that seek special or exclusive arrangements to do business in the city.

Reporters need to monitor all aspects of city finance. But tax levies and assessments deserve extra attention, largely because they nearly always generate debate and disputes. Do not underestimate the emotional and economic impact of taxes. When city officials propose a half-cent increase in the city's share of the state sales tax, it is of less consequence for a merchant selling greeting cards—or for customers buying the greeting cards. But applied to someone who sells $15,000 automobiles, increasing the sales tax from 6 to 6.5 percent adds $75 to a customer's bill, which is enough to drive some customers to a car dealer outside the city limits. Whenever taxes go up or down, do your best to determine what the change means in dollars to the average citizen.

Of course, nearly all of a city's income is quickly converted to expenditures. For most cities, the largest outlay—often one-third or more of the budget—goes to fire and police protection. In addition, cities that borrow money through the sale of municipal bonds may earmark 5 percent or more of the budget to retirement of debt, which could be substantial if the city decides to finance a major project, such as a sports complex or convention center. Other big-ticket items are employee pensions and insurance policies.

As cities age, more money has to be spent on replacing, repairing or upgrading the *infrastructure*—expensive physical facilities, such as water lines, sewers, streets and bridges. New needs also arise and call for new services, such as care for the homeless in big cities. And some variables are beyond the control of city officials.

One of them is the weather, which affects spending on road repairs and snow removal.

City hall reporters cannot be expected to examine and assess every expenditure, but they can and should be experts on municipal fiscal policies, procedures and records. The late Clark Mollenhoff, a prize-winning investigative reporter before he turned to teaching, encouraged reporters to concentrate on how equipment is purchased, contracts are awarded and bills are paid.[9]

Knowing bidding procedures is particularly important. Most cities are required by law to seek competitive bids for all purchases over a set amount, such as $1,000. The bidding process is designed to ensure that both the city and its vendors operate fairly and honestly— something that does not always happen. At times bid specifications are written in a way to favor a particular vendor; occasionally someone in city hall conspires with a vendor to fix a contract by improperly disclosing the amount of the competitors' sealed bids.

Always be alert for conflicts of interest or questionable spending. Is the city, for example, buying insurance from an agency co-owned by the mayor's son-in-law? Is it paying $15 for brooms that should cost $5? Are officials spending lavish amounts on travel expenses? Often a city council will pay hundreds of accounts by voice vote. Reporters, however, should spot-check payments. Moreover, they should check the monthly budget for spending patterns. (Is the city headed toward red ink on telecommunications?) And they should examine any audits closely. If an outside, independent audit has not been conducted in years, they should find out why.

Corruption is not the only reason for your vigilance. By incompetence or neglect, city officials may not be handling public money wisely or economically. Are the city's surplus funds, for example, sitting idle in a non-interest-bearing account? Could the police department save money by hiring its own mechanics rather than sending patrol cars to an auto dealer for repairs?

Borrowing

A city borrows money for many of the same reasons its citizens borrow—to make improvements, build facilities, pay off an unexpected expense, buy a needed piece of equipment or weather a temporary financial shortage. When cities or other governmental bodies, such as school districts, encounter a cash-flow problem, they generally borrow money from a local bank and repay it as soon as tax revenues come due. Most short-term borrowing is by way of *tax-* or *revenue-anticipation warrants.* It is not uncommon for a government body occasionally to need to borrow money while awaiting tax receipts, but frequent short-term borrowing suggests deeper fiscal problems that should be examined.

For large, long-term projects or problems, cities usually issue *municipal bonds* to raise needed money. There are two principal types of bonds—*general obligation* and *revenue.* General-obligation bonds are guaranteed by the municipality and backed by its taxing powers. A general-obligation bond might be used to build a new city hall. Revenue bonds, however, are not guaranteed and are repaid by revenues the project generates. Revenue bonds might be used, for example, to finance building a municipal skating rink or expanding the airport, with user fees and other income brought in by the project, such as food-concession contracts, used to help retire the debt.

Municipal bonds are usually sold in denominations of $5,000 or higher, and they may be repaid or retired over a period of 20 years or more. They offer a lower pretax return than some other types of investments, but the interest they pay is not taxable. Because investors today are able to choose from among a number of tax-deferred or tax-exempt options, municipal bonds are less attractive than they once were.

Two other methods of borrowing are *special-assessment bonds* and *industrial-development bonds.* When a project, such as installing a sewer line to a newly annexed neighborhood, primarily benefits one segment of the population, the property owners may be asked to bear the cost of the project through a special assessment. By sponsoring tax-exempt industrial-development bonds, cities encouraged the construction of numerous private projects, ranging from luxury hotels to furniture factories. Businesses and developers once flocked to these bonds because they could build projects with money borrowed at below-market interest rates. Federal laws, however, now limit the amount of tax-exempt funds that may be used for private development.

Some communities believe in a pay-as-you-go policy. But when cities do borrow, they encounter factors that affect all borrowers: interest rates, borrowing power and credit ratings. High interest rates may force a city to postpone projects, and state laws set ceilings on the amount of money a city is allowed to borrow. Moreover, the city's financial condition affects the bond rating it receives from investment services, among them Moody's or Standard & Poor's. An

"Aaa" rating from Moody's, for example, reflects a solid fiscal base and record and helps sell a city's bonds. A "Caa" reflects a weak fiscal base and record, thus making it harder to attract investors. Watch the city's borrowing practices. Like its citizens, a city might indulge in impulse spending on unwise or unneeded projects that threaten to put the community too far in debt.

The Budget-Making Process

Reporters who fail to follow the budget-making process from start to finish will not be able to adequately interpret the final product when it is presented to the people and the city council for reaction and adoption. The annual budget represents a city's estimate of expenditures and revenues for operation of the municipal government and its services. The budget covers either a calendar year or a fiscal year, which is usually July 1 to June 30 of the following year. The budget-making process begins in the executive branch and is overseen by the mayor and the mayor's staff. (The budget process of municipal government resembles the process for state, county and federal units of government as well.) In general, the municipal budgets evolve in these stages:

- submission of proposed spending plans for the year by department heads to the mayor, city manager or budget officials
- assessment of anticipated revenues for the year
- meetings and conferences between department heads and budget-making officials
- drafting of the budget
- submission of the budget and budget message by the mayor (or designee) to the city council
- study, debate and adjustments by the city council
- public hearings
- adoption of the final budget

Reporters ought to be stationed at every stop along the route.

Each city goes about preparing and adopting a budget in its own way, but one study of government problem solving found that nearly all city officials *strive* for a balanced budget that maintains existing services and provides for wage increases for municipal employees— without raising taxes.[10] They do not always succeed.

If revenues cannot keep pace with the costs of government, which is often the case, city officials have little choice but to raise taxes, find new revenues or make cuts. Often equipment and supplies are the first to be trimmed. Plans to hire new employees or launch costly programs are likely to be postponed. Who wins or loses the budget-cutting game may indicate who wields the greatest or least power in city hall.

Here's how *St. Petersburg Times* reporter Thomas C. Tobin reported the city's continuing struggle with its budget:

> City Council members tentatively agreed Tuesday to raise property and business taxes but still fell almost $3 million shy of balancing the 1990 budget. That shortfall, they said, will mean reduced services for thousands of residents.
>
> The council decided to complete its work at an afternoon session on Thursday. "That's when it's really going to get tight," City Manager Robert Obering said. "I think Thursday's going to be a rather critical time."
>
> Obering has suggested a variety of cuts that would leave some city departments with up to 15 percent less operating money than they have this year.

Tobin's story goes on to detail areas that might be hit hardest, among them the city libraries and recreational facilities. It also explained the impact of the proposed tax increases. The story was one of dozens already published about the budget, and dozens of other stories followed before the city's financial condition was settled for the next fiscal year.

As the proposed budget is developed and debated, it helps for reporters to retain a degree of healthy skepticism. Are fiscal conditions as dire as city officials proclaim? Guard against either understating or overplaying budget-making rhetoric.

It is also important to see the budget as more than a spending blueprint. According to political scientist David L. Martin, "The city budget can be viewed as public policy spelled out in dollars and cents, and expenditures decisions represent the allocation of certain kinds of values (priorities) as well as resources."[11] Reporters, therefore, should examine and assess those values and priorities to determine whether they correspond with needs and demands of the community. Are the city's priorities misplaced if $25,000 is allocated annually to manicure the city's golf greens while nothing is spent for child-care programs?

Once completed, a big-city budget can fill several dictionary-sized volumes. A village budget may be held together with a paper clip. Regardless of the budget's size and bulk, citizens—as always—will be concerned about how they are going to be affected. Reporters who regularly attend budget meetings and hearings will not be in a last-minute rush to decipher the pages and columns of figures and percentages. In addition, the budget message by the mayor or chief financial officer will help highlight major points. Nonetheless, a careful review of the final budget is essential.

All budgets include two parts—revenues and expenditures—but the organization, format and detail of budgets vary considerably. Usually revenues and expenditures are listed for a number of funds or accounts. The largest of these is the *general fund,* which includes most of a city's operational costs, such as administration, public works and public safety. Some cities have dozens of lesser funds, covering everything from retirement and pension programs for public employees to support of the municipal band.

The budget submitted to the city council for consideration might be divided into several columns for ease of comparison and study. Here is a sample section for the municipal swimming pool of a small city:

Budget categories	Current budget FY 1990	Department request FY 1991	Mayor's recommendation FY 1991
Payroll	$30,000	$35,000	$30,000
Repairs	10,000	15,000	5,000
Utilities	3,500	4,000	4,000
Advertising	500	1,000	750
Supplies	7,000	7,000	7,000
	$51,000	$62,000	$46,750

Notice the column marked "mayor's recommendation." Under a weak-mayor system, budget preparation and recommendations might come from a special committee of the city council instead of the executive branch. But many municipalities operate under the *executive-budget plan,* which means the budget is prepared by the mayor or a budget officer, who is an employee of the executive branch.

Notice, as well, that the proposed expenditures for the swimming pool are individually specified. This is an example of a *line-item budget*. Line-item budgets emphasize costs and purchases, as opposed to services, and tend to lock cities into spending patterns. A more flexible alternative is the *performance budget,* under which a department receives a lump sum for the operation of its various activities. Suppose usage of the swimming pool is down from last year's attendance figures. Under a line-item budget, the pool supervisor might be limited to spending $500 on advertising. But under a performance budget, he would be able to make adjustments, such as ordering fewer supplies and increasing advertising.

The chief executive's control over the final budget varies.

A reporter's analysis of the budget begins with several central questions:

- How does the budget compare to the budget from last year or the year before?

- What, if any, services and programs are being cut or added?

- What taxes and fees are being added, changed or increased?

Of course, answering these questions thoroughly and clearly may require dozens of hard-earned stories spread over a period of weeks. Using the swimming pool example, if the mayor's recommendation holds, the recreation department will have to live with a smaller budget than the previous year, and some planned repairs will have to be put off.

Helpful, informative budget coverage humanizes, explains and anticipates the city's fiscal condition, which, in turn, takes time, effort and enterprise. Focus on the implications for those in the community who can least afford higher fees or reduced services— the aged, the poor, the young.

Budget coverage may culminate with the adoption of the city's *budget ordinance,* but it should not end there. Citizens certainly want to know how public money is supposed to be spent, but they also want to be assured that budgeted money actually is being spent properly and wisely. As the fiscal year unfolds, be alert for rates of spending and whether they are under or over budgeted amounts of the previous year.

CITIES AND LAND USE

Cities address planning and zoning in different ways. Some rely on a professional administrator to plot the city's course of development. Other communities prefer to place planning in the hands of a commission, usually comprised of citizens appointed by the mayor or council. Still other cities have both a professional planner and lay commission.

Occasionally a single body oversees a city's planning and zoning, but most often there is a separation of responsibility. The separation is logical: Planning establishes priorities and policies for a city's land use and development; zoning, by means of various ordinances and codes, enforces city planning.

The practice of giving citizens key roles in planning and zoning began as an attempt to minimize the influence of politics and private interests. But no matter where a city places responsibility for planning and zoning, politics are involved and battles ensue. In fact, the composition of many planning commissions—realtors, bankers, engineers and land developers—ensures conflicts of interest and potential corruption.

Planning and zoning disputes often involve big stakes—property values, jobs, housing—and little consensus. One segment of a city may value rapid growth and industrial development; another may cherish a tranquil status quo. A condominium builder could profit from a rezoning decision that allows him to build beside a subdivision of expensive single-family residences; the homeowners' property could decrease in value if the rezoning is approved. Residents may ban together to oppose plans to build low-income housing in their neighborhood; civil rights activists may ban together to promote housing rights.

Disputes often end up before the *zoning board*, sometimes called a *zoning board of appeals*, which must decide how—or whether—to enforce land-use laws. Most commonly, the board is asked to consider a rezoning petition or a request for a *variance*, an exception to a zoning ordinance or building code. A typical rezoning petition might be brought by a homeowner seeking to change a single-family designation to a multiple-family, which might result in an influx of rooming houses into a single-family neighborhood. An applicant for a variance or a *special-use permit*, another type of exception to land-use laws, might seek permission to convert a garage of a single-family home into a beauty shop. Sometimes the rezoning process requires on-site public hearings, which can yield lively human-interest stories.

Many zoning and planning issues ultimately end up before the city council, which acts on recommendations from planning and zoning bodies. The city council usually is authorized to overrule the zoning and planning bodies, but a vote of two-thirds of the council might be required. If the stakes are high enough, a land-usage issue can be counted on to attract a crowd of vocal proponents and opponents. Even when a land-use decision attracts little attention, reporters should be vigilant. If big money is involved, there is always the possibility of graft and illicit dealing.[12]

City hall reporters deal with two other land-related issues— annexation and eminent domain. *Annexation* is the process by which cities acquire additional territory. Most often, people residing in an enclave adjacent to the city will either court annexation or agree to overtures from the city. At times, land-hungry cities on either side of a piece of property will compete for annexation, particularly if the land has great tax-generating potential. Rarely, though, can a city absorb another area against its will; normally a referendum by both sides is required. Although annexation may look good in theory, officials sometimes discover too late that there is a high price for bringing city services to fringe areas.

Eminent domain gives municipalities and other government bodies the legal right to take private property for public use, such as widening a road or building a stadium. Because it does little to enhance a city's image with residents, city officials are reluctant to employ eminent domain. Displaced property owners are supposed to receive just compensation for their property, but when people are forced to give up a beloved home or a business, they tend to fight back—and citizens tend to side with them.

COVERING LOCAL GOVERNMENT

Local government comes in a variety of sizes and forms. There is county government, township government, regional government and the largest category of all—special-district government. In a metropolitan area there may be dozens—perhaps hundreds—of governmental bodies supported in whole or in part by tax revenue. Some small, obscure units of local government operate in near seclusion;

only rarely do outsiders attend meetings, even when important issues are on the agenda. It is important for journalists to give attention to *all* government bodies entrusted to serve the public.

County Government

The role and power of county government vary from urban to rural areas. County government may be important or powerful in a sparsely populated region and, in fact, may be central to the lives of people living there. In metropolitan areas, county government not only provides essential services, such as police protection and road maintenance, to unincorporated areas, but it also typically assumes responsibility for areawide problems or operations, such as jails, airports, parks and flood control.

County governments differ in organization, but most share these features: a chief executive; a legislative body, named variously the county board, county commission or board of supervisors; a half dozen or more elected officials, such as sheriff, coroner and recorder of deeds; and a number of appointed officials, who oversee departments and services, among them libraries and roads.

In rural areas, the offices and departments of county government are likely to be housed in the courthouse, which may be an old, ornate edifice of doric columns and limestone that occupies the center square of town. In fast-growing metropolitan counties, government business is more likely to be conducted in modern, corporate-style buildings that may be attractive and efficient but lack the lore and appeal of the old courthouse.

Regardless of where government business is conducted, you can expect the atmosphere in a county building or courthouse to be politically charged. Unlike the non-partisanship of many city governments, most elected county officials proudly campaign and vote along party lines. Workers in the offices of elected officials often earn and keep their jobs through political loyalty, which may include a monthly contribution to the boss's re-election fund.

Reporters covering the county beat frequently are responsible not only for government news but court news as well. (The judicial system is covered in Chapters 7 and 8.) Part of the job naturally entails meeting coverage. Although frequently larger in size, the county legislative branch operates like a city council, with much of its work being done by standing committees. In organization and the conduct of business, meetings of a typical county commission and a typical city council display few differences.

The county's chief executive may be elected at large or selected by the membership of the county board. Chief executives often lack direct power or control over the county's elected officials. But if a chief executive controls the legislative branch, which controls the budget, then the power of the purse strings applies. The political clout of many county executives goes far to compensate for any built-in administrative weaknesses.

County beat reporters should monitor all county offices and services, but several merit special mention. One is the office of *county clerk,* where most of the county's records are stored. Besides maintaining minutes and records of the county legislative body, the clerk's office usually holds license records, birth, death and marriage certificates, voter registrations and campaign-disclosure reports. When reporters are unsure where to find a piece of information or the answer to a question, they usually start with the county clerk's office.

Another key office is the *recorder* (register) *of deeds.* It may not be a daily stop on a county reporter's rounds, but the recorder's office can help you find out who owns and who is buying and selling property in the county. Deed records, for example, will reveal whether foreign investors are buying thousands of acres of local farmland. *Revenue stamps,* a fee paid to the county by sellers of property, indicate the sale price, which often is not listed in public records. A common charge for a revenue stamp is $1, with each stamp representing $1,000 of purchase price. A deed transfer that requires 100 revenue stamps means the property sold for $100,000. Buyers have been known to buy extra stamps on their property to make it appear more valuable than its actual price.

The *county treasurer's* office is also an important stop on a reporter's beat. The treasurer, of course, generally handles the county's fiscal transactions through payments by checks called *warrants* and keeps track of the budget funds. But the office also is valuable for its tax-related records. They usually include assessment books for all property in the county, filings of people protesting taxes and records on property owners who are delinquent in paying taxes. Records on unpaid taxes might, for example, indicate that a prominent business in town is failing.

Counties, like many other large units of government, often have a department, independent of the executive branch, to monitor the fiscal activities of other departments and public offices under its jurisdiction. Heading the department is an official usually called an *auditor* or *comptroller.* Financial records, including copies of vouchers (receipts or statements certifying an expenditure or receipt of money) and purchase orders, are kept by the auditor, who also periodically checks the efficiency of services and the need for purchasing supplies and equipment. The auditor's office is a principal source when reporters are investigating the management and use of the public's money.

Some counties have a *supervisor of assessments,* whose office oversees property assessment throughout the county. The supervisor of assessments' office often includes a board to review complaints from citizens who believe their property assessment is too high. Because of the potential for corruption and controversy in tax assessments, the office bears watching.

Several other offices that typically fall under the county beat, including the sheriff's department, coroner's office, prosecuting attorney and clerk of the court, are discussed in detail in other chapters.

Township Government

Township government is largely an old-time form of government that manages to stay alive in several states. (It is also a six-mile-square unit of measurement in U.S. land surveys.) Years ago, when people were scattered across the countryside, hours by horse or wagon from the county seat or nearest city, township government served them best. With urbanization, the role of township government has diminished, but in some unincorporated areas outside the boundaries or attention of other governmental bodies, the township remains an effective provider of services, particularly road maintenance, public aid and support for such improvements as sewer systems.

Township government often gives citizens a direct say in decision making through a vote at annual or semiannual town meetings. The township hall may be one of the few places where reporters can still see grassroots democracy in action.

Regional Government

Regional government units, normally comprised of elected officials from local governments in a region, serve to address areawide problems and issues. Some are merely quasi-governmental bodies that undertake studies, issue reports, suggest cooperative ventures. Others go beyond those roles and administer programs and disperse grant money.

Regional bodies came into existence beginning in the 1950s, partly as a means of unifying and coordinating the fragmented web of local government.[13] The concept spread as federal officials tied more aid and grant programs to areawide cooperation among local government officials. If local officials wanted federal money for rapid-transit systems or air-pollution control, they were told they had to work together. In some instances, though, regional agencies only intensified infighting and conflict over who gets what. Reporters rarely find coverage of regional bodies glamorous, rewarding or exciting, but when large-scale projects or problems are involved, regional government generates news.

Special Districts

Special districts are units of government that possess taxing authority. Many exist to provide services to a large region. There may be hundreds of special-district bodies of varying size and authority within a metropolitan region, serving such purposes as mosquito abatement, sewage disposal and public housing. In some areas, special districts enable residents outside of the reach of municipal services to organize and raise tax money to provide, for example, fire protection. (The most common form of special unit—the school district—is discussed in Chapter 9.)

By sheer numbers alone, special districts pose challenges for news coverage. On a given Tuesday, a popular night for meetings, several dozen special districts might be in session. But special districts cannot be ignored or given cursory attention; to do so would invite expansion of a hidden layer of government with great power but little accountability to taxpayers.

COVERING STATE AND FEDERAL GOVERNMENT

For most reporters, experience in public affairs reporting begins with city hall or the courthouse, and only after years of proven service is a reporter assigned full time to the statehouse. Few reporters have the opportunity to cover the federal government from Washington, D.C. A beginning reporter's coverage of state and federal government typically is done locally or as part of a temporary assignment.

State Government

A state capitol is an imposing sight of marble floors, mosaic walls and dark-stained woodwork. It is a dignified setting for a process that is not always pretty to behold. As an old statehouse saying colorfully puts it, "If you love sausage and law, don't watch either being made."

If laws are like sausages, then each is made from many ingredients. Lawmakers, the governor and the governor's staff are involved in lawmaking, as are the staffs of state agencies. Behind the scenes, but not too far behind, are the lobbyists. In fact, in some state capitals there are three or more registered lobbyists for every lawmaker. In general, lobbyists possess a tarnished reputation, but reporters quickly learn that some lobbyists are gold mines of information.

Much of state government coverage naturally focuses on the legislative process. The flow chart on pages 158–159 shows how laws progress through the Illinois General Assembly, which is a bicameral (two-house) legislature, comprised of a 59-member Senate and a 118-member House of Representatives. The process is complicated. At any point along the path to passage, a proposed piece of legislation, called a *bill*, can be killed or left for dead. Bills that run the entire legislative gauntlet are often the products of compromise and bargaining by many players. The legislative process is similar to what happens when a city council passes an ordinance; bills receive readings and go through committees where they may be reshaped by amendments. But there are differences. Chief among these is the requirement that *both* houses of a bicameral legislature must approve the bill. If there are disagreements, the bill may be sent to a joint *conference committee* that attempts to work out a version acceptable to both houses.

Legislators' positions on a particular bill usually are based on political considerations. For one thing, legislators weigh how a bill is going to be received by constituents in the home district. Sometimes legislators support a colleague's bill with the understanding that the favor will be returned at a later date. Throughout the process, lobbyists are at work to either kill or advance legislation. A legislator is most vulnerable to pressure by lobbyists who represent a contributor to the legislator's election or re-election. When the trucking industry, for example, backs Sen. Thompson, the senator's support on industry-related matters is expected in return. Lawmakers who accept campaign contributions from organizations seeking influence over legislation often find themselves in compromising positions. Sen. Thompson personally may believe the large cross-country trucks operating on state highways endanger motorists, but his campaign "debt" forces him to vote against a bill that would restrict the weight and length of tractor-trailer rigs. Reporters covering the legislature should know which senators and representatives are beholden to special interests.

A key player, of course, is the governor, who influences legislation by many means, among them arm-twisting of legislators to support or defeat a bill. The governor's ultimate power is the veto, which the legislature can override with usually a two-thirds or three-fifths vote of its members. Competent statehouse reporters thoroughly understand the legislative process and know all the players.

States enact thousands of new laws each year. Not all can be reported, but the news media provide a service by informing the public about the major laws, especially as they are about to take effect. On New Year's Day, when many California laws become effective, the *Los Angeles Times* provides a capsule description of important pieces of legislation. In 1987, for example, one of California's 1,504 new laws, a response to a spree of freeway shootings around Los Angeles, made it a felony for anyone to threaten an automobile driver or passenger with a firearm on a public road. Another law required health-care plans to pay for mammograms used to detect breast cancer in women.

Statehouse reporters get a good deal of newsgathering assistance, which they need to keep track of the steady stream of legislation. State-run information services help journalists and lawmakers alike by publishing daily schedules of meetings and providing updates and chronologies of bills. At a glance, reporters can tell where a subcommittee on agriculture, for example, is holding a hearing on inspection guidelines for imported fruits and vegetables. Less valuable but useful are the press releases and reports pouring daily out of state agencies, departments and the governor's office. In some states, reporters operate out of offices, provided at taxpayer expense, in the capitol building that are wired with closed-circuit audio or television systems to allow reporters to work in their offices while still monitoring sessions of the House and Senate.

Although it may take years to understand the intricacies of state

HOW A BILL BECOMES A LAW

FIRST HOUSE

Bill drafted by Legislative Reference Bureau

Introduced

Read 1st time (perfunctory), referred to Committee on Assignment

Assigned to substantive committee

Hearing. Amendment(s) may be added.

Recommended "do pass" or "do pass as amended"

Recommended "do not pass" or not recommended

Full house votes to discharge

Full house doesn't discharge

Bill dead.

Read 2nd time. Committee amendment(s) may be accepted; floor amendment(s) may be added.

Read 3rd time. Voted on.

Fails

Passes

Bill dead.

Sent to second house

SECOND HOUSE

Sponsor found by sponsor in first house

Introduced

Read 1st time (perfunctory), referred to Committee on Assignment

Assigned to substantive committee

Hearing. Amendment(s) may be added.

Recommended "do pass" or "do pass as amended"

Recommended "do not pass" or not recommended

Full house doesn't discharge

Bill dead.

Full house votes to discharge

Read 2nd time.

Committee amendment(s) adopted or floor amendment(s) added

Sent to 3rd reading without amendments

Read 3rd time. Voted on.

Read 3rd time. Voted on.

Fails

Passes

Bill dead.

Sent to Governor

Fails

Passes

Bill dead.

Sent to first house for concurrence with second house amendment(s)

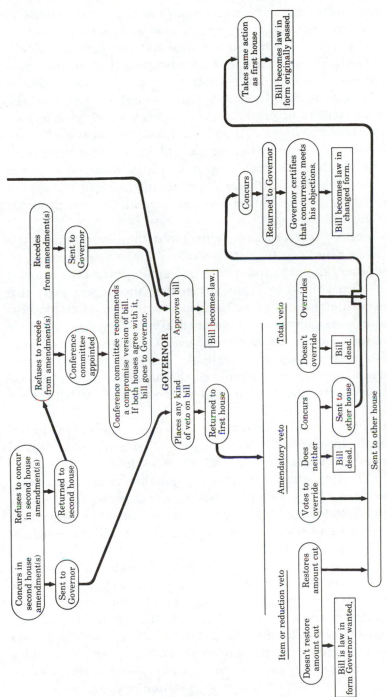

Source: Illinois Legislative Council, Springfield, Illinois.

government and develop the sources and background needed to cover the statehouse properly, reporters who become entrenched in the job tend to acquire habits of coverage and lose a fresh perspective. That is why reporters are now spending less time on the statehouse beat before moving on to other assignments, a cycle that is largely by design. Younger, mobile reporters sacrifice the close relationships journalists of previous generations shared with legislators. As one observer notes, "The distance between press and politicians has widened in the past generation, pushed by evolving ethical standards on both sides, [resulting in] a mutual wariness that has mounted over the years with each new scandal."[14] But the loss of "coziness" in statehouse journalism has advantages that probably outweigh the disadvantages.

Reporters are correct to concentrate on the governor and the legislature for news, but important work of government goes on in dozens of other buildings and offices in a state capital city. In most states, the Department of Transportation is the largest executive branch department in terms of budget and number of employees. Other major, newsmaking departments deal with corrections, public welfare and child abuse and family services. The state organizational directory, often known as the "blue book," describes the full range of governmental operations, including administrative agencies and commissions. Even obscure units of state government hold news potential.

The executive branch includes the governor's cabinet of elected or appointed officials, such as the lieutenant governor, secretary of state, treasurer and attorney general. Because the office focuses on substantial legal matters, the *attorney general* tends to generate more news than other cabinet officials. In several states, an increasingly active role for the attorney general is consumer protection through high-profile prosecution, for example, of insurance frauds and nursing-home violations.

Because coverage of many administrative agencies and executive departments, even the larger ones, is infrequent or sporadic, stories abound outside the legislative chambers for reporters who make the effort to collect them. Remember that when the legislature passes a law, responsibility for its implementation most often falls to a state department or office. After the fanfare of the bill's passage subsides and the law takes effect, government reporters should continue coverage to determine how well the new legislation or program is working. Too frequently, such follow-up reporting is absent.

Administrative agencies and departments also offer bountiful opportunities for feature stories, especially ones that tell readers or viewers how various components of state government work. What, for
example, does the public health department do? In many states, the
department provides prenatal care for mothers with high-risk pregnancies. What does that responsibility entail? Another common function of the public health department is milk and food inspections.
How is milk tested—and for what? A reporter's role includes educating citizens about the processes and functions of government.

Some government stories are so close at hand they tend to be
overlooked. As metropolitan editor of the *Des Moines Register*, Richard Paxson regularly tapped a simple source of good stories:

> Almost every weekday in our newsroom, a big envelope
> arrives from the state unemployment agency, containing doz-
> ens of written decisions from hearing officers on whether
> out-of-work Iowans should get jobless benefits. Most of the
> cases are appeals from unemployed workers who originally
> were turned down. Others are from businesses protesting
> the awarding of benefits because it raises their taxes.
>
> These decisions provide terrific keyhole peeks into the
> workplace. . . . Some of the stories make you angry—like the
> nursing home worker who got unemployment benefits even
> though she was fired for hanging paper cups from the ears of
> a victim of Alzheimer's disease.
>
> Many make you laugh—like the baker who was fired be-
> cause he bared his behind to co-workers so often that they
> adopted "Blue Moon" as their theme song. . . .
>
> Almost every reader can relate to such stories because
> almost everyone has a job and a boss.[15]

As Paxson points out, it pays to check out what at first glance might
appear to be "junk mail" from state offices.

Coverage of state government goes on well beyond the city limits
of the state capitol. Scattered throughout the state are branch offices of departments and agencies. Legislators, too, operate offices in
their home districts. Not all actions or policies of state government
originate in the statehouse and flow downward to regions and communities. The conduit linking government and the people is two-
way, and news can be covered from either end. An agriculture agent,
whose office may be a few blocks from your newspaper or broadcast
station, might be working with local apple growers to control the

spread of a plant blight that threatens to damage next season's crop. Local reporters who build and nurture contacts within branch and regional offices of state departments will be rewarded with good stories and news tips.

Federal Government

Experienced Washington correspondents acknowledge that federal government is too big and complex to ever understand fully. Besides the 14 departments of the executive branch, more than 60 independent or quasi-independent agencies fuel the federal government. They range from the Central Intelligence Agency to the Tennessee Valley Authority.

The White House is the glamour beat of federal coverage, although coverage of the president and his staff is so tightly managed that enterprise reporting is difficult. What amounts to "news" quite often is generated by staged events, like a presidential appearance to welcome a visiting dignitary or news briefings conducted by White House staffers. According to political scientist Timothy Cook, White House reporters have more contact with *their own colleagues* than with other news sources. "They are quickly aware of the stories and angles pursued by their colleagues and cannot help following each other's leads. . . . Because of the beat, then, the White House press corps is a textbook example of pack journalism, more corporate than permeable."[16] In many respects, the White House is less complicated to cover than other federal government assignments but, in the long run, is probably less satisfying as a beat.

Congress, on the other hand, offers almost too many sources and too many possibilities for news. So much is happening on Capitol Hill, primarily the "nuts and bolts" variety of government business, that reporters find it easier and more appealing to focus on "sexy" issues, according to Tom Freedman, a former legislative aide for a New York congressman. As he recalls: "While Washington's establishment—its politicians, reporters and administrators—is whipped into motion by the mere whiff of an emotional issue or scandal, there is no reward in today's Capitol for fixing the broken mechanics of government or solving the huge problems that haunt us. . . . There was always extensive press coverage at [congressional] hearings if a star from the entertainment world, or better yet, a dramatic hooded witness was testifying. . . . In Washington, there is widespread acceptance of the idea that the public doesn't want complicated news."[17]

Do people prefer simpler news—sexy news? Reporters have been known to underestimate the public's interest in hard news. Solid government reporting, told in a style and language people can understand, will find an audience. Based on information from the National Highway Traffic Safety Administration, the *Miami Herald* highlighted the high fatality rate in minivan accidents. Christopher Scanlan humanized the story with this opening:

> To Alan Janofsky, his new Chevrolet Astro minivan was a dream vehicle—with enough interior space to use in his cosmetics business and ample room for his two daughters to spread out on trips.
>
> But the van frightened his wife, Barbara. "I have a feeling if we ever get hit broadside, it's going to flip over," she recalled warning as they drove it home from the dealership in November 1985. "It's your imagination," he said.
>
> Eight months later, Barbara Janofsky's fears came true.

The story went on to dramatize the growing number of accidents, pointing out that minivans, despite their popularity with families, continue to be exempt from safety standards required for automobiles.[18]

Despite the wealth of stories elsewhere in Washington, the White House and Congress attract the greatest attention, partly because they are convenient to cover. According to veteran White House reporter Lou Cannon, "Off Capitol Hill, with the exceptions of the White House, the State Department and the Defense Department, coverage of the vast, overlapping federal bureaucracy is sporadic at best and non-existent at worst."[19] As a result, important news or actions of the federal bureaucracy may go unreported until a scandal or disaster surfaces. An example is the history of fraud and mismanagement at the Department of Housing and Urban Development that came to light in 1989, but only after Congress finally investigated HUD. *Newsweek* accurately reported that the press "failed miserably" in its watchdog role over HUD.[20]

The tentacles of federal government crisscross the nation; offices are not relegated to metropolitan areas. A quick check of the local telephone directory will tell you which agencies and departments are in your area. Sometimes reporters overlook local federal operations, such as the U.S. Postal Service, the Veterans Administration hospital or Civil Aeronautics Board office at the airport. There are also the district offices of members of Congress, which are usually staffed year-round. Congressional aides in district offices can reach Washington quickly by telephone, computer or facsimile machine. Sometimes the district aides are former journalists who are sensitive to newsgathering needs and deadlines.

All reporters ought to be alert for ways to localize developments in Washington. If Congress is considering an important piece of legislation, the political editor should tell the public where their legislators stand. When the Department of Interior promulgates a new regulation on camping in federal forests and parks, the outdoors writer can explain its impact on the region.

Several sources of information can help local reporters stay abreast of developments in Washington. Among the more important are the *Congressional Record* and the *Federal Register.* Regular reading of the *New York Times*, the *Washington Post*, news magazines and specialized publications, such as the *National Journal* and *Congressional Quarterly Weekly Report*, also yields ideas for local reports on the activities of the federal government. A recent issue of *Congressional Quarterly*, for example, devoted 32 pages to 1990's sweeping amendments to the federal Clean Air Act, which include new standards on auto-exhaust emissions. Information Age reporters do not have to be ensconced in a Washington, D.C., bureau to reach newsmakers, collect data or write stories about Congress, the executive branch or the federal bureaucracy.

Government reporting does have its dull side at times. Sitting through a public meeting might require several cups of strong coffee and a firm resolve to find a way to enliven a story of what transpired. But by casting themselves as guardians of the public's right to know, journalists assume an obligation to spend hours, if necessary, listening to windy lawmakers or poring over tax rolls. When dull meetings or dusty records yield nothing more than a news-digest item, reporters can at least say they did their duty as society's watchdogs and surrogates for the people.

No matter where you are stationed and no matter what you cover as a beat, keep this thought in mind: If government is *of* the people, *by* the people, and *for* the people, reporters should bring government at all levels *to* the people through appealing, useful and informed coverage.

EXERCISES

1. Develop a state-of-the-community feature based on an interview with the mayor, city manager or another key municipal official. Concentrate on major conditions, such as city services, crime, economic conditions, city finances, public housing, homelessness and social services. Examine both positive and negative sides of the city's condition.

2. Profile a state agency or office in your area. Explain its functions. Introduce key personnel and show them at work. Perhaps the state Department of Agriculture has a livestock and poultry inspector stationed nearby. Besides describing the inspector's work, accompany her on rounds, such as a check of an egg-producing complex where you will see the process that leads to tomorrow's omelets.

3. Localize a story out of Washington, D.C. You will probably want to focus on a federal law or regulation that will affect your community. For example, when the Interstate Commerce Commission in 1990 banned smoking on all regularly scheduled interstate buses, there were opportunities around the country for reporters to learn how the news was being taken at the city bus terminal.

NOTES

[1] Don Fry, ed., *Best Newspaper Writing 1989* (St. Petersburg, Fla.: Poynter Institute, 1989), p. 297.

[2] Donald M. Murray, "Making Politics Dull," *Writing on Writing*, Sept. 1988, pp. 1, 5.

[3] Elaine P. Sharp, "Citizen Demand-Making in the Urban Context," *American Journal of Political Science*, Nov. 1984, pp. 654–670.

[4] Jane Mobley, "Politician or Professional? The Debate over Who Should Run Our Cities Continues," *Governing*, Feb. 1988, p. 48.

[5] Amelia Davis, "City Managers Learn to Live with the Job," *St. Petersburg Times*, May 22, 1989, p. 3.

[6] David Elsner, "Suburban Mayors Hold On—and On," *Chicago Tribune*, March 5, 1989, pp. 1, 24.

[7] David S. Broder, *Behind the Front Page* (New York: Simon & Schuster, 1987), p. 224.

[8] Fred Palmer, "Editorially Speaking: The Meeting Story," *Gannetteer*, Jan.–Feb. 1985, p. 4.

[9] Clark R. Mollenhoff, *Investigative Reporting: From Courthouse to White House* (New York: Macmillan, 1982), pp. 361–368.

[10] John P. Crecine, *Governmental Problem Solving* (Chicago: Rand McNally, 1969), p. 74.

[11] David L. Martin, *Running City Hall* (University, Ala.: University of Alabama Press, 1982), p. 100.

[12] See David Anderson and Peter Benjaminson, *Investigative Reporting* (Bloomington, Ind.: Indiana University Press, 1976), pp. 68–81.

[13] Mitchell Gordon, "Councils of Government: A Better Approach to Metropolitan Complexities," in Robert L. Morlan, *Capitol, Courthouse and City Hall*, 5th ed. (Boston: Houghton Mifflin, 1977), pp. 254–258.

[14] Rob Gurwitt, "In the Capitol Pressroom, the Old Boys Call It a Day," *Governing*, July 1990, p. 27.

[15] Richard Paxson, "The Best Local News Idea I've Had in Five Years," *ASNE Bulletin*, April 1986, p. 5.

[16] Timothy E. Cook, *Making Laws and Making News* (Washington, D.C.: Brookings Institution, 1989), p. 34.

[17] Tom Freedman, "While Journalists Chase 'Sexy' Issues," *New York Times*, Sept. 16, 1990, p. A14.

[18] Christopher Scanlan, "Critics Question Safety of Popular Minivans," *Miami Herald*, Aug. 14, 1989, p. 1A.

[19] Lou Cannon, *Reporting: An Inside View* (Sacramento, Calif.: California Journal Press, 1977), p. 196.

[20] "The HUD Ripoff," *Newsweek*, Aug. 7, 1989, p. 22.

Chapter Six

A police officer detains and searches a suspect. (N.R. Rowan/Stock, Boston)

Public Safety: Crimes to Corrections

Edna Buchanan knows the police beat, having spent more than 20 years covering murders, muggings and mobsters in a city made infamous by the television program *Miami Vice*. Here is how she once described the job:

> Nobody loves a police reporter.
>
> You are often an unwelcome intruder. People blame you for the bad news. It is human nature. Somebody gets in trouble, you report it and he turns on you as though it were your fault, not his, that he is into this mess.
>
> The job can be lonesome and arduous. I have been threatened with arrest, threatened physically, had rocks thrown at me. I've gotten threatening letters, subpoenas and obscene phone calls, some of them from my editors.
>
> It is tiring, haunting and truly wonderful.[1]

Buchanan elevated the stature and visibility of the police beat by winning a Pulitzer Prize in 1986 for her crime coverage in the *Miami Herald* and by writing a lively book about her work, *The Corpse Had a Familiar Face*. As the magazine *presstime* noted: "For a while it was a stepchild beat. Then Edna Buchanan won a Pulitzer. Now covering the police beat is glamorous."[2]

For Buchanan and a handful of other reporters, the police beat is the ultimate assignment. Yet many of journalism's finest, who started out on the police beat, saw it mainly as a prerequisite to more respectable, substantial assignments. Russell Baker, later to achieve fame as a *New York Times* writer and columnist, went to work on the police beat at the *Baltimore Sun,* not knowing that "a police reporter was the lowest form of life in the *Sun*'s universe."[3] In those days, as Baker quickly learned, police-beat reporters rarely wrote their own stories or worked out of the main office of the newspaper. Baker wanted to be a newspaper *writer.* Phoning in details about a holdup or murder to the city desk, where a re-writeman would rapidly mold them into a story, was not his idea of a career in journalism.

The police beat remains a training ground for many young reporters, who now usually do their own writing on portable computers tied to the main office by telephone modems. Still, there is a lingering stigma about police reporting. It is not a beat most reporters volunteer for or fight over. The work is tough and stressful. Much of the job involves writing about life's ugly side. Paradoxically, the job calls for sensitivity and compassion mixed, at times, with toughness and detachment.

Done well and done right, the police beat is more than a rite of passage or a rung on a career ladder. It is a valuable job, full of drama and societal significance. Enterprising police reporters quickly graduate from chasing sirens or listening to police-band scanners. They humanize the beat by including coverage of everyday crime as it touches everyday people. They describe and explain crime and law enforcement in useful, intelligent, responsible ways. They are curious and vigilant, going beyond the surface facts. When a drunken-driving suspect dies after being subdued by police officers, they ask "Why?" and "How?" The questions, in turn, lead to a story about a controversial police policy on use of chokeholds. When three accidents occur at the same intersection in less than a week, they test the casual theories of patrol officers ("There's just too much traffic there") and question engineers and safety experts. When a clerk at a convenience store is robbed at knifepoint, they do not rely on an antiseptic police report. They visit the scene and sensitively ask the attendant to relive the experience.

As with most reporting, there is always a degree of uncertainty. Did I get the story right? Have I been fair to all parties? Should I do more? Edna Buchanan explains why that is particularly true on the police beat:

You never know if you are really finished. There is always something to check, another detail you might glean that could change everything. A newspaper story can ruin a life or come back to haunt it twenty years later. . . .

Police reporters deal with lives, reputations, and careers. So you keep on—ask one more question, knock on one more door, make one last phone call, and then another.

It could be the one that counts.[4]

This is excellent advice for *all* reporters on *all* beats.

CRIME AND THE MASS MEDIA

Is crime in America as bad as it seems? The statistics certainly are alarming, as illustrated by the Crime Clock, a visual device the FBI uses in its annual *Uniform Crime Reports.* The Crime Clock converts crime occurrences to minutes and seconds; for example, a property crime may occur every three seconds or a rape every five minutes. Naturally, people begin to wonder, "Will I be the next statistic?"

Statistics, of course, can be misleading or overstated. Big-city murder rates, for example, leave the impression that the streets of Chicago, Los Angeles or Washington, D.C., are littered with bodies. Actually, Americans are 16 times more likely to die in an auto crash than at the hands of an unknown assailant.[5] Nonetheless, crime is a serious national problem. Scores of stories and volumes of data could be used to highlight the problem, but one example stands out: A 1989 study conducted in Florida's Dade County found that 254 juveniles who used crack had committed more than 86,000 crimes in one year to support their habit—a stunning average of nearly a crime a day for each juvenile.[6]

Despite all the sobering statistics and studies, should people be putting bars on their windows and handguns under their pillows? No, say criminologists like Kevin N. Wright, author of *The Great American Crime Myth,* who tend to blame the mass media for creating excessive, unwarranted fear and anxiety about crime.[7] There is no denying that crime news dominates television newscasts and grabs headlines in newspapers and magazines, especially accounts of violent attacks against people. That is to be expected; these are the crimes the public finds most menacing and disturbing. Several years ago, a pregnant young doctor was raped, strangled and fatally beaten in her office at New York's Bellevue Medical Center. Commenting on the horror of her death, a magazine writer said, "A murder in a hospital? A murder in the cathedral? The mind keeps a list of safe houses in the world, and it is shaken when sanctuaries are violated."[8] As life's sanctuaries are being violated, the press cannot be expected to sanitize or ignore what is happening.

Obviously, the press plays an important role in informing people about the scope and seriousness of crime. It is sometimes hard, though, for reporters to know when they have gone too far—or when they have not gone far enough. A low-key approach to coverage might lull people into a false sense of security. If tourists are being mugged in a popular downtown entertainment district, the story should not be buried in the crime roundup column on page 5A. On the other hand, sensationalized treatment of crime news might unduly frighten people, perpetuate stereotypes or cause societal tensions where none need exist. Moreover, by reporting some criminal acts, do journalists exacerbate conditions or contribute to copycat crime? Did "crack" use, for example, spread partly because of media publicity? When news accounts described how someone slipped cyanide in Tylenol capsules, did the mass media encourage others to poison consumer products? Often, it seems, crime reporting is a case of damned if you do, damned if you don't.

Reporters who cover crime must understand crime—as well as it can be understood. This much is known: Crime is everywhere. It can be found in hamlets and luxury high-rises as well as city streets and housing projects. Criminals and their victims come from every segment of society. Crime is also relative. In a small town, an armed robbery will be given the highest priority by police. In a big city, police must practice a form of medicine's *triage,* deciding which cases are most urgent—and which to deal with as time and resources permit. Press coverage follows a similar pattern. An armed robbery is front-page news in a city of 4,000; in a city of 1 million, a similar armed robbery may go uncovered by the press.

There is much about crime that is unknown or unexplainable. What are the causes of crime? How can crime be curbed? There are no ready answers or quick fixes; if there were, society could begin to control crime as it controls measles or air pollution. Police-beat reporters must continue to seek answers and explanations, even though they can expect to be forever perplexed and troubled by much of what they see and report.

BEHIND THE BADGE

Police officers are nearly always on guard—watchful, suspicious, cynical. It is a survival instinct. Not surprisingly, neither police officers nor reporters demonstrate much trust or understanding in their mutual relationships. Author Joseph Wambaugh, once a Los Angeles police officer, put it this way: "Cops generally trust the press about as much as they trust politicians, judges, lawyers, psychiatrists and the Red Army."[9] Two experienced reporters echo Wambaugh's observations:

> To most police officers a reporter is welcome only as long as he is not only anti-crime, but pro-police. Let that reporter turn a critical eye on the department or any of its knights in blue and immediately the reporter becomes an enemy to be shunned, misled and even arrested, if possible.
>
> No matter how noble a cop might be, he knows that out there among the public are lots of people who fail to appreciate him, who misunderstand him, who instinctively dislike him. At the top of the list of unfriendly people—just below professional criminals—are most journalists.[10]

Considering such bleak assessments, can reporters ever expect to relate to law enforcement officers and vice versa? The answer is yes—at least in terms of a professional relationship. Building the relationship is usually the reporter's responsibility, and a starting point is understanding the fears and pressures facing the police.

Listen, for example, to a patrolman with 18 years on the Detroit police force talk about daily effects of stress: "You run into people that think that you should be invincible, okay? You should be afraid of nothing. You've got a gun on your side. Well, you know, on TV it all looks so good. Pull the gun, the guy runs, shoot him, you know? You see, you have to live with that."[11]

Robert Stewart, selected in 1988 as the St. Petersburg, Fla., officer of the year, lives with the memory of killing a man. "It leaves home with me every day, and it comes back home with me. It's something that I had never wanted to have happen in my career."[12] His chilling story illustrates the reality facing everyone in law enforcement.

> It was about midnight and Stewart, home and off duty, had just paid a pizza delivery man. The delivery man returned to his car, but he didn't leave. He stood in the street, alongside the car, which Stewart thought was strange. Then Stewart heard another voice and sensed something was wrong. As Stewart, armed, approached the car, he saw a figure crouched nearby and realized the delivery man was being robbed. "I grabbed him [the robber] and told him to drop the gun," Stewart recalled. "As I was trying to put him in a neutral position, I saw a gun come up to my face. . . . I never even remember pulling the trigger." For a split second, Stewart was not sure whether he or the robber had been shot.[13]

Many police officers never draw their service revolvers in the line of duty, much less fire them. Indeed, police work can be generally dull and uneventful. But even in the smallest communities, even when answering a call about a family spat, police officers never know whether this will be the day their luck runs out.

The pressures build in other ways. After dealing with fatal accidents, child molestations, rapes, drug dealers and lie after lie, police find it difficult to see the decent side of life and the good in people. "I think you can't help but get a little callous to it after a while," says another Detroit officer. "You just see so much stuff, and I think the hardest thing is trying to remember that you are dealing with people out here all the time."[14] Mark Baker, author of *Cops: Their Lives in Their Own Words,* found that police officers often see the world as nothing but falsehood, evil and death, which helps explain why they sometimes appear hard edged and unfriendly. As Baker got to know police officers, his opinion of them changed: "Having tasted the casual violence and bone-numbing boredom they experience, I am better able to understand their point of view. I don't fear police as a group as much as I used to, because I now know a good number of them as individuals. When I see a police officer today, I look at his face, not at his uniform."[15] Journalists who make a sincere attempt to understand the person behind the badge can anticipate better relationships and ultimately better news coverage. A word of warning: Do not join the police team. Maintain a *professional* relationship and distance. And maintain a critical eye in monitoring the performance of the police.

INSIDE THE POLICE DEPARTMENT

With any beat, you start by learning the lay of the land. For a police department, that includes its organization, facilities, communications system and operating policies.

Organization

The *police chief* is at the top of the organization chart. Often attached to the chief's office is the *internal affairs* unit, which is entrusted to rigorously and independently investigate possible cases of police misconduct. Occasionally a separate civilian board addresses complaints against officers, but all law enforcement agencies should have a formal process for investigating questionable behavior by police.

Many departments are organized along similar lines, with three main bureaus or divisions: patrol, investigations and services.

The *patrol division* handles most day-to-day operations. There are usually three eight-hour periods or shifts of patrols a day, each overseen by a *shift commander*. The patrol bureau might also include a K-9 (police dog) unit, a traffic branch and a unit for reserve officers.

The *investigative division* often includes separate units to deal with juvenile offenders, narcotics cases and crimes against persons or property. Some departments have an undercover intelligence-gathering branch under the investigative division.

Service divisions usually handle administration, records, communications, training and community programs, such as Drug Abuse Resistance Education (DARE), which in several states brings uniformed police officers into grades from kindergarten through high school for a 17-week curriculum designed to prevent use of drugs and alcohol.

Do not be satisfied with simply knowing the organization chart. Learn the duties and responsibilities for all units and offices within the department. If the department, for example, has a research unit, its work could include interesting, important studies into crime trends and psychological profiles of criminals. Ask questions and learn about how the department operates. Study the police budget and how it is subdivided.

Facilities and Equipment

Police department facilities vary, depending on the size of the community and the size of the city budget. Usually, though, a police station has *holdover cells* to confine prisoners temporarily until they can be taken to a county or regional jail. Another common facility is an *evidence room*, where drugs, weapons and property connected with crimes are stored prior to a case going to court. Examine all sections of the police station, if possible, and learn how facilities are used. But the evidence room and holdover cells are particularly important, because these are places where improprieties are likeliest to occur. Suspects are sometimes neglected in holdover cells; firearms and drugs are known to disappear from evidence rooms.

Reporters can also learn about a department—its strengths, weaknesses and approaches to law enforcement—from taking stock of its equipment. Does the department have the latest in radar guns to catch speeders? Does the city provide bullet-resistant vests to all officers? Has the department invested heavily in riot gear and high-powered weapons? Does it have its own criminal laboratory? Is it stockpiling guns and vehicles that it is allowed to seize from drug suspects? What happens to money seized from drug dealers? Can it be used by the department to purchase supplies and equipment? The answers to questions like these may reflect a department's priorities and lead to important stories.

Communications

At the heart of most police operations is the communications center. In smaller departments, one person—usually known by the job title of *dispatcher*—may serve as receptionist, watchman and communications operator. Within the dispatcher's reach are television monitors, radio microphones, computer terminals and telephones. In the period of a few minutes, a dispatcher might greet a visitor, take a call about a stolen bike, run a computer check of a license plate number and dispatch a patrol car to investigate an activated burglary alarm. In large departments, the job is much the same; there are simply more dispatchers. It is important for reporters to know how the communications system works and what type of information it yields.

Federal grant money has enabled nearly all police agencies to tap into computerized crime data from state records centers and the National Crime Information Center in Washington, D.C. The computer is especially important in protecting police on patrol. An officer making a traffic stop, for example, can either use a dash-mounted computer terminal or radio a dispatcher in headquarters to run a computer check of a license plate or a driver's license. Within seconds, the request will be answered by state computers or the NCIC, providing the officer with a variety of information, including whether a license plate is connected with a crime or whether a driver is wanted on criminal warrants. Crime-information computers also hold data about stolen property and missing persons. Reporters, however, cannot expect direct access to information in crime computers. Much of it is considered confidential, especially an individual's criminal history of arrests, charges and convictions, or what officers still refer to as a *rap sheet*. Release of such information to the press might later make it difficult to find jurors who have not been prejudiced by the disclosure. Police chiefs do not want judges or district attorneys accusing them of botching prosecution of a criminal case.

Telephone calls to the police often involve routine, non-emergency matters: "Someone's illegally parked outside my business" or "Those teenagers next door are having another wild party." Because no one knows when the next call will be serious and urgent, many departments tape record *every* call. With increasing use of mobile cellular phones, along with the spread of 911 systems to quickly summon emergency help, drama is being preserved on tape, including, at times, the dying words of murder victims. Although police tapes are not considered public records in all jurisdictions, reporters should always ask to review or transcribe newsworthy calls and persist with higher authorities when the request at first is declined. Besides their potential news drama, the tapes may determine whether the police or other emergency agencies responded quickly and appropriately to an emergency.

Tape recordings are not the only record of calls. Usually a dispatcher, using a time-punch device, records four stages of a call: when it is received, when an officer is dispatched, when the officer arrives at the scene and when the officer is freed from the call. The time card provides a chronology of police response.

In addition, with the widespread use and linkage of computers, police now are more likely to build intelligence files or dossiers on suspicious persons. For example, city police, called to question a shoplifting suspect, complete a field-interrogation report, noting, among other things, a distinguishing physical feature—a tattoo of an eagle on his right wrist. The information goes into a computer file. Months later, a woman in a neighboring suburb may fight off an attempted rape and remember her assailant's eagle tattoo. A computer check quickly pulls up the name of a possible suspect.

In metropolitan areas, police departments are often interconnected by a joint radio frequency to coordinate operations, such as setting up roadblocks or directing a high-speed pursuit. At times, though, a fugitive will escape because police departments are not properly equipped to quickly share information by radio.

Operating Policies

Knowing the department also means knowing its operating policies, particularly ones governing police conduct and procedures. For example, what kind of professional training and psychological screening does the department require of its new officers? What is departmental policy on types of weapons and ammunition officers may carry—and their use of those weapons? Does the department have guidelines on methods to subdue violent suspects? Clear, strict policies covering police behavior indicate whether a department is serious about preventing brutality or unjustified use of force. In the absence of rules and policies, abuses occur. After a suspect in New York died in 1987 while hog-tied—his arms and legs bound together behind his back—the city police commissioner admitted he never realized police routinely but unofficially used such a restraint. New York subsequently banned the practice.[16]

WORKING WITH POLICE

Twenty-five years ago reporters could walk into many police stations and freely inspect copies of incident reports. No more. Scanning television cameras guard exits and entrances to police stations. Visitors, including reporters, are stopped in the front lobby and asked to state their business by clerks or police dispatchers protected behind bulletproof glass. Records often are screened and in some cases withheld from journalists. Many departments filter news through a public-information officer, blocking reporters from talking directly to patrol officers or detectives. At times, the police exhibit a siege mentality.

Once a reporter is a known quantity, however, access to people, places and records is easier and rules are more readily bent. But it takes time before a reporter is trusted. And some reporters, especially those who get facts wrong or violate confidences, never gain police cooperation.

The Blotter

Covering the beat begins with access to police-blotter information. The *blotter* is an old term to describe a book in which police recorded criminal incidents and arrests. Today, blotter information usually is recorded in an *incident log,* which may be computerized. The log generally contains a brief summary of an incident; for fuller details, police and reporters alike must refer to a written incident report completed by the officers handling the case.

You will find that access to records varies from department to department, and even from reporter to reporter. Some differences are a result of statutory provisions—or interpretation of statutes. State open-records laws vary on the types of police information considered public domain. Moreover, some laws are ambiguous in their treatment of police records.

When police-press relations are badly strained, reporters may be permitted access to incident reports only at a designated time and place—say, once or twice a day at the public-information office. Increasingly, nearly all police officials are concerned about protecting the privacy and well being of victims, witnesses and juveniles, so reporters might have to settle for edited versions of incident reports with certain names and addresses deleted.

As a rule, reporters are entitled to details immediately surrounding an arrest, including:

- identification of the suspect by age, address and occupation

- the substance or text of charges against the suspect

- names of arresting officers and law agencies

- time, date and place of the arrest

- descriptions of weapons used or possessed by the suspect

- information regarding how the suspect was taken into custody, such as pursuit or resistance

Additional information will be harder to come by, particularly if it jeopardizes a suspect's rights to a fair trial by an impartial jury. As a result, police often will not disclose the following information:

- the contents of any statement, confession or admission made by a suspect

- opinions about the suspect's character, guilt or innocence

- the results of investigative procedures, such as polygraph examinations, ballistics tests, fingerprints or laboratory evidence

- statements concerning the credibility of prospective witnesses in the case

- the prior criminal charges and convictions of the suspect

In dealing with timid or lackadaisical reporters, police will be inclined to withhold more and more information. Reporters sometimes are obligated to fight for access to police records and information, including the names of victims and witnesses.

To gain the fullest amount of information, especially where open-records laws are vague or weak, reporters must also develop a number of reliable contacts within the department, particularly with detectives who investigate crimes. A good network of sources ensures against being shut out if policies change or unfavorable press coverage chills access to the police chief.

In small departments it is important to build rapport with police dispatchers, who frequently are keepers of the incident log. Because dispatchers are at the center of operations, very little escapes their attention. When police withhold arrest information, sometimes the county jail's daily log of prisoners will be available. But realistically, there will be times when nothing you say or do will yield answers and information, even from your unofficial sources.

Stories from the Police Beat

News organizations have widely divergent approaches to covering the beat. Some papers, for example, report every traffic accident, from fender bender to fatality. Others cover only unusual accidents or ones resulting in injury or death. By policy, a big-city daily may publish the name and address of everyone arrested for driving under the influence; a mid-sized paper may be sporadic in DUI reportage. Television journalists look for crime incidents that lend themselves to visual treatment; therefore, a spectacular pile-up on the interstate may get more attention than a new method to use hair samples to test for the presence of drugs.

Access to incident reports is merely the starting point for a reporter. Police reports provide the skeleton of a story. That is to be expected. Most police officers detest doing paper work, which probably explains why their reports frequently are incomplete and inaccurate, with misspelled names, wrong addresses and skimpy details. The reporter's job is to verify police information, visit the scene, talk to victims, witnesses and officers and then produce a readable, accurate account of what happened and why it happened.

Moreover, police-beat coverage involves far more than daily inspection of police reports and coverage of news items they yield. It includes stories about unpaid traffic tickets, police training, neighborhood crime-watch programs, dangerous intersections, missing children and the recovery of accident victims. The beat extends, as well, beyond the confines of the police station and into the streets, where reporters can hear about crime and law enforcement from the experiences of experts on the subject—people who live in public-housing complexes, work at all-night gas stations or drive cabs.

Too often, police-beat stories are cold and mechanically written. They have a sameness about them, as if composed by a computer; only the names, dates and places change. Police-beat reporters should always humanize coverage, no matter how "routine" a story might first appear. And they should always consider the victim's perspective.

The victim, for example, may be the owner of a ramshackle one-chair barbershop on the edge of town. Three times in the span of a month, neighborhood youths break into his shop, stealing from the petty-cash drawer, breaking into a gum-ball machine and taking bottles of after-shave lotion. Against a backdrop of armed robberies and sexual assaults, his loss, of course, is insignificant. But stories like his should be told periodically to remind us that *all* victims of crime pay a price and have feelings.

Journalists, at times, underplay crime stories, withhold grim details or report with unnatural detachment. In some cases, their behavior is overcompensation for critics' charges that the press and public gorge on crime fare. Then, too, a few reporters become so blasé or callous about crime news they stop being astonished or outraged by it; the burn-out rate on the police beat is high. Still others fear offending sensitive readers, which is a legitimate concern when not taken to an extreme. Whatever the reason, by de-emphasizing crime news, reporters inadvertently insult already injured victims and their families. And by withholding details they deprive the citizens of information they ought to hear or read. Consider this account from a metropolitan newspaper:

> Two North Side women—one of them nine months pregnant—were the victims of sexual attacks Wednesday, police said.
>
> A 19-year-old North Side youth was charged Wednesday afternoon in the sexual assault and vicious beating of a woman, 32, and the beating of her two children—a girl, 10, and a boy, 5—who live in his neighborhood.

Buried eight paragraphs into the story were details of the "assault" and "vicious beatings." At 12:30 a.m., an intruder broke into the 32-year-old woman's home and sexually assaulted her with a board, which he then used to beat her and the two children. All three suffered skull fractures; the mother lost an eye, a lip and part of an ear in the beating. The 12-paragraph story contained not a single direct quote from anyone—police, victims, neighbors or family of the victims.

More commonly, police-beat reporters fail to capitalize on the human-interest value of everyday police stories, such as vehicle accidents. Treated in a routine, unimaginative manner, the report of a tanker-truck accident might go this way:

> A fuel tanker spun out of control and rolled over on Interstate 222 near the 54th Avenue exit Friday, gushing fuel onto the highway.
>
> A passerby helped the driver, Henry Smith, 48, of Middletown, crawl away from the wreckage. He was listed in good condition Saturday at St. Joseph's Hospital, where he was treated for four broken ribs.
>
> No other vehicles were involved in the accident, which tied up traffic for an hour. City firefighters washed the fuel from the highway.

But when a reporter does his or her homework, the human interest surfaces, as in this version of a tanker accident:

> The sound of a tire exploding boomed in Connie Murray's ear as she drove south on Interstate 222 Friday afternoon. Moments later, in her rear-view mirror, she saw a fuel tanker spin out of control and roll over.
>
> "The whole thing looked like a total mess and the cab was on its top," said Mrs. Murray. A private-duty registered nurse, she was on her way from her home in Jonestown to St. Joseph's Hospital.
>
> "All I could think of was, how was I going to get the driver out of the cab?"

The story told *how*.

Now and then, a police story is suitable for light treatment. After taking three police cars on a wild, reckless chase that ended, luckily, without loss of life or limb, a 20-year-old motorcyclist said to one of the police officers, "Man, you aren't going to give me a ticket, are you?" "No," said the officer, "we're giving you 21 tickets." For the most part, your treatment should be serious; crime seldom is a laughing matter.

Press-Police Relationships

It should come as no surprise that police officers have little regard for reporters who make mistakes, ask stupid questions, renege on agreements, get in the way at crime scenes or endanger victims and witnesses. The more you know about police work and criminal procedure, the less likely you will make mistakes and damage your reputation with police officers. Do not, in particular, use legal terminology carelessly. Assault and battery, for example, sound like they go together—as a single charge. But they are distinct criminal offenses that may or may not go together. *Assault* is an attempt or a threat to injure a person; *battery* is actually striking someone. Know the traffic code (what, for example, is the difference between *reckless* driving and *careless* driving?) as well as the criminal code.

At accident or crime scenes, remember that police and emergency personnel are under as much pressure to do their jobs as you are to do yours. They are particularly concerned about maintaining the "integrity" of crime scenes. If you are among the first persons to reach a fire or crime scene, do not tramp about or touch anything. By barging in, at worse, you could damage evidence; at the minimum, you are going to irk police officials.

Do not automatically get testy and demanding when police officers refuse to answer every question you put to them. Generally, police welcome media coverage of unsolved crimes, for it often helps them generate tips and make arrests. Sometimes, though, they must suppress key evidence or information to rule out bogus confessions. If every detail of a crime is broadcast or published, police can anticipate getting calls from people who, for whatever reason, admit to crimes they did not commit. Reporters are trained to seek specific details, but when a suspect is still at large, they might have to be satisfied when police simply say the murder weapon was a "large-caliber revolver" or a "blunt instrument."

For many police officers, the worst offense is for a reporter to prove to be untrustworthy. Journalists who violate a confidence, break an agreement about release of information or act irresponsibly in coverage can expect retaliation from the police. In some cases, police departments blackball untrustworthy journalists; in other instances the retaliation happens, but it is less obvious, such as making the offender wait for hours outside a crime scene and then giving him just scraps of information.

Police officers are known to test newcomers to the beat by passing along a juicy but fabricated piece of information, with the stipulation to the reporter that the information is off the record. "If [the police] see it in print," says Joseph Halliman of the *Indianapolis Star*, "that reporter is burned for the rest of the time he's down here. They'll never talk to him or her again."[17]

It is all part of dealing with police officers. Edna Buchanan's observations are worth sharing:

> Persuade them that you will be fair, absolutely accurate and can be trusted to protect your sources.
> It is inevitable that we clash from time to time. When it happens I do not take complaints to their bosses or mine. . . . It is better, whenever possible, to handle [complaints] yourself, person to person. Police officers perform under pressure. So do we. We should be able to work things out without ratting on each other. Nobody likes a crybaby, especially cops.
> I like to let them know that our jobs are a lot alike. If we wanted to be loved, they would be firemen and I would teach

kindergarten. We both have to do things we don't like. We are both just doing our jobs.[18]

There is a delicate balance to press-police relationships. That balance is severely tested when law enforcement officials ask you to withhold information or help them set a trap for suspects. Are there ever times when reporters should cooperate with police? If so, when does cooperation cross the line to co-option? Two examples, each based on actual incidents, underscore the problems inherent in answering those questions:

> Three times in the space of a week, an abusive-talking man wearing a ski mask has broken into apartments in a six-block area, robbing two elderly women and being scared off in the third incident. Police ask you to hold off on a story about the robberies another day or two so undercover officers, staking out the neighborhood apartments, can catch the man. What do you do?

> A detective asks you and the editor of your newspaper to plant a bogus story that says a local businessman is missing and presumed to be the victim of foul play. The plan is to entrap the businessman's partner, who has offered a hit man, actually an undercover police officer, $5,000 to carry out the killing. What do you do?

If you polled editors and reporters at random, they would struggle over these scenarios, arriving at a variety of decisions based on a variety of reasons. While there is no definitive rule to cover police requests for press cooperation, this perspective, taken from a National News Council report on crime coverage, might help guide journalists: "The primary obligation of the press in reporting about criminal activity is to serve, both in fact and in public perception, as an instrument of public information, not as an arm of law enforcement."[19] Reporters who decline to cooperate with police risk a loss of cooperation in return. But reporters should never abandon principles and credibility to avoid offending the police.

DANGER ZONES

The police beat requires great care in coverage. Here are a few areas where dangers lurk.

Arrests, Warrants and Rights

From the first day on the job until the last, a police reporter must know and remember that there is a big difference between being *arrested* and being *charged* with a crime. When police arrest someone, they detain the person as a suspected lawbreaker. A flexible legal yardstick called *probable cause* is supposed to help police officers determine whether there are sufficient grounds for an arrest. While there is no uniform definition for *probable cause,* it basically amounts to circumstances and facts that would lead a reasonable and prudent individual—in this case, a police officer—to believe someone has committed a crime. If a woman cries out, "Stop, thief!" and officers catch a teenager two blocks away clutching her handbag, the police might decide that possession of the handbag is probable cause to arrest the teenager, particularly if the victim says, "That's the one!" However, a police officer's determination of probable cause may differ from probable cause as seen by a judge, who may conclude the arrest was unwarranted and release the individual. In addition, the facts and circumstances that led to the arrest could quickly change; the victim, for example, might waver on her once-sure identification of the purse snatcher.

To be legally safe and ethically responsible, avoid printing or broadcasting the name and address in an arrest report until formal charges are filed in an official court document, which typically is a *warrant* issued by a judge that names the accused and specifies the charges against him. Once a news report prematurely identifies and links someone with a crime, the damage may be irreversible. The more serious the crime, the greater the damage. Even a report of a shoplifting arrest can cause pain and problems for the individual involved and his or her family. If circumstances dictate that you must report an arrest immediately, try, if possible, to withhold the suspect's identification or blur it by saying, for example, "Police arrested a 35-year-old accountant Monday on suspicion that he is the Oceanview cat burglar, responsible for 20 break-ins locally."

Once charges are filed, reporters should pursue the case aggressively. Nevertheless, there must be limits to coverage, based on a concern for the rights of accused persons. The U.S. system of criminal law rests on the principle that all accused persons are presumed innocent until proven guilty. The principle of a *presumption of innocence* is reinforced by rules and procedures designed to ensure that criminal defendants can exercise their constitutional rights to be tried according to due process of law and before an impartial jury. Journalists should not intentionally jeopardize those rights by publishing inflammatory hearsay or other inadmissible information, even if it comes from the police. What to publish—and what to withhold—may present difficult choices for reporters. Do you, for example, publish the contents of a murder suspect's rambling confession statement, leaked to you by a source in the department? When in doubt, share your indecision with editors and colleagues and allow them to help you weigh options and make a decision.

Crime Statistics

Reporting on crime statistics is tricky. For one thing, crime data are based on *reported* incidents. Since a number of crimes, for various reasons, go unreported, the statistics do not necessarily provide an accurate picture of a city's or region's crime rate. Careless use of percentages adds to the problem of interpreting crime statistics. If a community, for example, experiences nine slayings in a year, up from six the previous year, stories and headlines might emphasize "a 50 percent increase" in the murder rate. With such small numbers, stressing the increase in terms of a percentage tends to be misleading.

Still another problem is lack of adequate analysis of statistics. Raw numbers and percentages alone cannot reveal much about patterns of crime in a city. A more useful account identifies and assesses important factors in determining patterns, such as location, time of day and types of victims. Explanatory stories—accompanied by graphs, maps and other visual devices to explain the crime rate and compare it to previous figures—put the statistics into context.

Reporters are justified in being skeptical about crime figures and police rhetoric. Law enforcement has its political side. Police officials want to look good, so there is a temptation to pad arrest figures or downplay serious crimes.[20] To provide balance, check with insurance companies to see whether they have more reliable data on thefts and burglaries in the city.

Bias and Labels

Stereotypes influence public perceptions of crime. Some people associate crime with skin color and neighborhoods. When a woman is abducted from a suburban shopping mall parking lot and raped, they will assume the victim is white and a black man assaulted her. If a drug dealer is shot to death outside a public-housing building, they will conclude that the killer and the victim are black. In other cases, stereotypes cause us to write off certain crime as insignificant or inevitable; after all, do not some "elements" of society invite or cause trouble? This kind of racist or ethnocentric thinking can be found everywhere, including newsrooms.

Especially troublesome is how stereotypes affect our impressions of black-against-white crime. Columnist Ellen Goodman addressed the problem by describing an encounter on a dark city street:

> One night last winter, a young and white friend left a movie theater and headed down the street to her car. Out of the corner of her eye, she anxiously tracked two black men walking until they were right in front of her.
>
> Finally, eyes cast down, she heard their laughter and when she finally looked up at one of the men, her fear met his smile. He was a colleague from work. In the moment of that exchange, he read her expression. Everything passed between them. Hurt. Anger. Understanding. Sadness.
>
> That's what crime does. That's what racism does. That's how hard it is to tell them apart.[21]

Actually, crime statistics suggest that most crime is *intraracial* (white against white; black against black), not *interracial* (white against black; black against white).[22] Occasionally, though, racism is at the root of criminal violence. Two separate episodes suggest that the press is not always consistent in dealing with racism and crime. When a gang of young whites in the New York City community of Bensonhurst killed a 17-year-old black in August of 1989, race became the focal point of intense media coverage. *Bensonhurst* practically became synonymous with racism. But earlier, in Cleveland, when a black mob killed a young white man, his death, as one critic put it, "occasioned a great silence." Editors of the *Cleveland Plain Dealer* de-emphasized the racial angle, even though the black reporter covering the story said, "There's no question that it was racial. Anybody that can't see that is blind."[23]

A writer who studied the Cleveland killing and compared it to another racial attack of whites against blacks in New York City's Howard Beach area commented:

Twenty-five or 30 years ago, the mainstream American press did a lousy job of being fair to minorities. . . .

News people eventually confessed past sins and repented. And they—the good ones, at least—have tried to make amends. . . . And yet, perhaps news organizations have gone so far in making amends that they now routinely miss certain kinds of stories—stories that revolve around this unpleasant fact: While whites can be racists, so can blacks.[24]

Reporters are wrong to devalue a criminal act—either by underplaying it or not reporting it all—based on where it happened or to whom it happened. Is the mugging of a black grandmother any less disturbing than the mugging of a white grandmother? When a prostitute is murdered, is it any less tragic than the murder of a nun?

Nevertheless, being strictly non-judgmental in crime coverage presents its problems. Did the black mugging victim live in a neighborhood where attacks occur daily? Prostitutes work in areas and engage in activities that put them at risk; they get beaten, robbed and murdered. Nuns usually are not at such risk, and if one is killed, it is unusual and therefore considered bigger news. Crimes against prostitutes—and against street people, the poor, blacks and Hispanics—undoubtedly are underreported by the press because, ironically, crimes against certain categories of people are so commonplace that they *lessen* in news value.

The question of racial identification is even more complicated. In a world still full of hatred and prejudice, how do you determine when—or whether—race is a factor in a criminal act? Moreover, if the press identifies most victims, witnesses and suspects by name, address, age, sex and occupation, should not the public be provided with racial identification as well? Indeed, cannot racial identification *dispel* stereotypes as opposed to perpetuating them?

Clearly, these are difficult questions that defy ready answers. Perhaps they are best addressed through advice from civil rights leader Benjamin Hooks. In the late 1970s Hooks, director of the NAACP, stressed the importance of the media's role in race relations. "The press," he said, "becomes a major link between black and white communities. It can either reinforce prejudices, racial stereotyping and the status quo, or it can take on the role of broadening the horizons of its readers."[25] His words should inspire reporters to seek fairness and balance covering *all* crime news. That includes paying attention to *all* victims of crime.

Handle with Care

Crime news should always be handled with care, but there are times when reporters must be especially sensitive.

To begin with, reporters should recognize that crime victims have certain rights. The principal right is to say no to interviews. Other rights include being able to grieve in private, to refuse to answer certain questions, to know the proposed angle or approach to the story, to select the time and place for an interview and to request a specific reporter as the interviewee.

Try hard to imagine the victim's experiences and feelings; take care in asking questions. When in doubt, ask for the advice and cooperation of a trained counselor who helps victims of crime. Many communities now have victim-assistance units, either independently operated or attached to the local police department. These counselors will tell you that crime victims and their families may be physically and emotionally stunned by what happened; they are vulnerable. Reporters, therefore, must guard against causing additional hurt—a second victimization—by their behavior.

Every victim of a serious crime suffers in some way. Do not assume that an unbloodied victim is unhurt. Psychic and emotional injuries are as painful and real as physical ones. A victim of a holdup, for instance, might be ridden with guilt for not resisting. Reporters should not compound the guilt by insensitive remarks ("At least you weren't hurt") or insensitive questions ("Didn't you fight back when the holdup man hit your son?").

Rape, incest and child molestation are among the most serious and traumatizing of crimes. The victims of sex crimes must be, whenever possible, spared further pain or the possibility of harassment, intimidation or threat of another attack. In most cases, the names of sex-crime victims are voluntarily withheld by the press. There are exceptions, such as a rape-murder or an assault on someone so prominent the identity cannot be protected. Infrequently, a rape victim voluntarily goes public with her ordeal to help other victims, as singer Connie Francis did.

Once again, arriving at ironclad rules is impossible and probably unwise, even when it comes to something so traditionally accepted as protecting the identity of rape victims. Mary Beusoleil, a former editor, believes not naming rape victims "perpetuates the notion that there is some blame or disgrace attached."[26] Other editors say it is sexist and discriminatory to identify rape suspects but not rape victims. Finally there is the question of whether keeping victims anonymous dulls and dehumanizes our views toward rape. Some critics contend that the public needs to know that real people—your child's teacher, a friend's mother, an executive at your bank—are attacked. Despite these different viewpoints on identification of rape victims, most news organizations will not reveal names.

Editors and reporters usually protect the identity of victims and witnesses if there is any possibility that they might be emotionally or physically harmed by the publicity. If a nurse escapes an attack by a rapist, reporters should not give the assailant another chance to attack by publishing her address; if a frail, elderly couple is robbed, do not mark them as a tempting target for other thieves; if a witness can identify gang members who beat a street person, do not help the gang harass or threaten the witness into silence. When police ask you to withhold information, listen to them, but before agreeing or disagreeing, consult with your editors.

It is rare when the identity of a crime suspect is withheld, but it happens, and perhaps it should happen more often than it does. Newspapers, for example, routinely withhold the names of juvenile offenders. At times, the names of parents accused of child abuse are withheld until more evidence is acquired. Or when incest is the charge, usually you cannot identify the assailant without indirectly identifying the victim. These exceptions aside, often the newsroom policy is "show no favorites" and "treat everyone equally." A shoplifter is a shoplifter; a child molester is a child molester.

An equal-treatment policy, however, fails to account for a problem known as *punishment by publicity.* The term is based, in part, on the possibility that mere publication of a suspect's name, address and alleged offense constitutes a harsher penalty than that meted by the sternest jury or judge. In cases of acquittal or dismissal of charges, the "sentence" imposed by the press cannot be easily repealed, even by a follow-up story or a retraction.

A related problem involves the often unclear distinction between what constitutes a criminal condition and what constitutes a medical or psychiatric condition. Is an accused arsonist, sex offender or thief evil—or mentally or physically ill? Police are not trained to determine the difference; neither are reporters. Should people with mental or medical problems—and their families—pay an additional penalty of press publicity? Is there harm in withholding identity until more facts and answers can be obtained? These are questions police-beat reporters should seriously consider before going public with sensitive information.

One of the hardest assignments for any journalist is to interview and collect information from people still reeling after the tragic, sudden death of a child, spouse, parent or friend. Such assignments often go to police-beat reporters. Yet some of the most touching, effective stories about tragedies are based on interviews with survivors. In Oldsmar, Fla., a 5-year-old kindergartner died after she darted into the path of a van. By interviewing her father, reporters learned he was not allowed to accompany his daughter on the medical helicopter. Instead, he and his wife raced by car to the hospital, where they learned she was dead. "It would have been nice to be with her instead of being stuck in traffic," he said. "It's a hollow, sad feeling."[27] Evocative words like his help us feel the loss.

You might wonder, "Why do reporters bother people at such times?" Reporter Charlotte Sutton offers this explanation that reporters should find reassuring: "No reporter wants to be outdone on a story. But competition isn't the only reason for what can look like cold voyeurism. It seems wrong to let pass the violent death of a good person without saying more about the victim than his name and age. To do that would almost be like equating a tragedy with any routine entry in the police blotter."[28]

There is no right way to approach people in grief. Try to be professional, yet compassionate. Briefly offer condolences, then gently and slowly proceed with your questions. A starting point is background information about the deceased. Facts of the accident or tragedy should be elicited carefully, so as not to cause pain. Ask for pertinent details without dwelling on gory particulars. Remember, there are other sources—police, medical examiners, emergency crews, friends and other family members—for many of your questions.

Listen and react non-judgmentally, particularly in regard to suicides. Often, suicide survivors experience fear, guilt, rage and depression. Rather than bluntly ask, "Do you know why your son killed himself?" probe gingerly and indirectly. Henry Seiden, co-author of *Silent Grief: Living in the Wake of Suicides*, offers advice for friends of suicide survivors that applies, as well, to reporters. Say something like, "It's the why of this thing that's really hard to understand, isn't it?" he suggests. "This," says Seiden, "lets the woman know you're there and helps her clarify what she feels."[29]

PUBLIC-SAFETY AGENCIES

While city police may remain the focal point of your coverage, you must develop contacts with other public-safety agencies that deal with crime, accidents and disasters.

State Police

The state police do more than nab speeders and handle traffic accidents. The state police often are among the best trained and most comprehensive of law enforcement agencies. Unfortunately, too many journalists know the state troopers only as "Smokies" who patrol the highways and interstates.

The highway patrol may be one of several diversified divisions under the department of state police. In Illinois, for example, other elements include the Division of Criminal Investigation, an equivalent to the FBI, and the Division of Forensic Services and Identification, which operates crime laboratories around the state.

The work of the state police includes gathering criminal intelligence for dissemination to local police units; investigating auto theft and "chop shop" operations, where stolen cars are cannibalized for parts; regulating gambling and race tracks; inspecting trucks that transport hazardous wastes; reconstructing vehicle accidents; training new troopers and local police officers at the state police academy; and investigating police corruption in cities and counties.

All reporters who cover law enforcement should make it a point to know the people and functions of the state police and visit the regional headquarters regularly, whether or not it is under their beat.

Sheriff's Department

Reporters assigned to cover the county courthouse sometimes get a bonus—coverage of the county sheriff's department. The size and role of the local sheriff's department will vary. In rural areas, it may be the main branch of law enforcement in a sparsely populated but geographically large county. In urban counties, sheriff's deputies may be limited to law enforcement in unincorporated areas that lack a municipal police department. In addition, the sheriff's department normally operates the county jail, since few cities can afford or justify their own facilities to hold suspects awaiting judicial action.

Nearly all police agencies are touched by politics, but that is particularly true of sheriff's departments because most sheriffs are elected, not appointed. Many sheriffs must stand on their record before voters every four years. Political pressure cannot help but influence a sheriff's behavior, decisions and relations with mass media. Raiding the sheriff's own Elks' Club, for example, and seizing its backroom slot machines may be proper law enforcement but dumb politics, so with some so-called victimless crime, the sheriff might adopt a see-no-evil stance. But he may, again for political reasons, arrest clerks at several video shops for renting obscene tapes.

Politics mix with police work in other ways. If the sheriff is Republican and the County Board is predominately Democratic or vice versa, the department's budget may become a political pawn. When an incumbent sheriff is defeated or resigns, you can expect major administrative changes in the department. The new sheriff probably will replace key aides and officers with his or her own politically loyal people, which, among other things, means reporters must rebuild a network of news sources.

Federal Law Agencies

When we think of federal law enforcement, most of us picture the Federal Bureau of Investigation (FBI) and rightly so. It is the largest and most visible federal police force. Its 8,000 special agents, all trained at the FBI Academy in Quantico, Va., operate out of 59 field offices around the United States, including one in Puerto Rico, a U.S. territory.[30] Thousands of other FBI employees support the agents in the field, checking fingerprints, conducting scientific tests of evidence and maintaining computer records of arrest warrants and stolen property through the National Crime Information Center.

The typical FBI agent is well educated, well trained and very disciplined. Agents reputedly are closemouthed, but they can be good news sources under the right conditions. Like all police officers, they will be cautious until they feel a reporter can be trusted. Remember that their work is largely investigative, and therefore they cannot reveal many details without jeopardizing an investigation.

At times, FBI agents will leak—most often under a condition of anonymity—incriminating information about individuals under investigation. Whenever that happens, reporters ought to warily question the FBI's motives. In the past, particularly under the administration of J. Edgar Hoover, the FBI's founder and long-time director, the FBI used reporters to uncover information or put pressure on a public official suspected of being corrupt or tainted. Reporters should not allow themselves to be manipulated by the FBI or *any other law enforcement agency.*

The FBI is part of the U.S. Department of Justice, as are two other agencies with increasingly important roles in law enforcement—the Drug Enforcement Administration (DEA) and the Immigration and Naturalization Service (INS). Under the U.S. Department of the Treasury are the Customs Service, which inspects ports of entry; the Internal Revenue Service, responsible for investigating tax fraud; the Bureau of Alcohol, Tobacco and Firearms, with jurisdiction over alcohol, drug and tobacco sales, gun control and criminal use of weapons, including bombs and explosives; and the Secret Service, which protects the president and, among its other duties, investigates counterfeiting activities.

Many other federal departments have law enforcement components, such as the U.S. Postal Service, which investigates illegal use of the mails. In addition, the president appoints approximately 100 U.S. marshals, backed by deputy marshals, to transport federal prisoners and to enforce federal law. In the past, U.S. marshals have been used to control riots, implement court-ordered integration of schools and protect commercial airliners from skyjackers.

In the 1980s the federal government mobilized to combat violent crime in the United States by establishing the National Center for Analysis of Violent Crime (NCAVC) and the Violent Criminal Apprehension Program (VICAP).[31] Both units collect and assess data and help local police agencies solve, apprehend, prosecute and, ultimately, prevent violent crime.

Crime Laboratories

Today's sophisticated crime-fighting equipment and scientific methods would astound Sherlock Holmes. Computers now analyze and identify drugs; physical anthropologists reconstruct unidentified skeletal remains; scientists link suspects to crimes through use of genetic DNA "fingerprints" taken from blood, semen or saliva samples.

Part of any police reporter's beat is the local crime lab. Only the largest of municipal departments have their own labs; most others rely on state, regional or federal labs.

Laboratory work begins at the crime scene, where evidence is carefully gathered and catalogued. The process can be flawed. In some instances, the police initially may decide a sudden death resulted from an accident or natural causes. Evidence is not immediately collected or secured. By the time police conclude a crime was committed, the evidence may have been mishandled or removed. In other instances, sloppy police work results in mislaid, damaged or incomplete evidence.

Once collected, scientific analysis of evidence is entrusted to crime laboratory technicians, whose effectiveness and thoroughness, obviously, are dependent on how effectively and thoroughly evidence was collected. Well-equipped laboratories can conduct ballistics tests; analyze blood, hair and saliva samples; administer polygraph examinations; classify drugs; examine documents; identify fabrics and other materials; and process, evaluate and compare fingerprints.

Experienced police reporters know how tests are run and what they yield. Fingerprints, for example, can be collected and processed in a half dozen ways, including the use of Super Glue, which helps detect fingerprints on metal and many other surfaces. (The Super Glue is heated on a piece of aluminum foil, and the fumes then adhere to the fingerprint residue, causing the prints to become visible.) In comparing prints taken at a crime scene to those taken from a suspect, police and prosecutors usually want a full enough print to make at least eight distinct points of comparison; the higher the number of comparison points the better. Fingerprints remain an important tool to link a crime with a suspect, but other identification methods, including teeth imprints, lip, palm, heel and toe prints and, most recently, DNA tests of the body's unique genetic code are used as well.

Reporters ought to observe how tests are conducted or, if possible, participate in tests, such as taking a polygraph examination. (How often do journalists refer to polygraph examinations without knowing the procedures, uses and limitations of the examination?)

Medical Examiners

The "death detail" belongs to medical examiners and coroners. Medical examiners are usually appointed, professionally trained public servants; in many states they are required by statute to be a licensed physician, preferably a forensic pathologist, whose medical specialty is to determine causes of death. Coroners, however, are usually elected and often lack formal medical training. Few states require elected coroners to be physicians. Many coroners, in fact, are full-time funeral directors or mortuary employees, which poses a built-in conflict of interest if they solicit business while on official duty.

Both medical examiners and coroners are responsible for issuing death certificates and determining the *cause* and *manner* of deaths that do not appear to have been from natural causes. The cause refers to the medical reason for death, such as a gunshot wound or heart attack. The manner refers to circumstances that led to the death—accident, natural cause, suicide or homicide. Determining cause and manner of death is not always an easy task, and coroners, while they may have considerable practical experience, are limited in their resources. An autopsy, augmented by tests conducted by criminal lab technicians, may be required. Even then, the question of cause and, more often, the manner of death may remain open.

To aid in closing a case, some jurisdictions provide for a coroner's inquest before a jury. Evidence, witnesses and test results are presented to the jury, which tries to decide on the questions of cause and manner of death. Normally such inquests are open to the press and public; moreover, they may yield more details about a case than the police are willing to release. The contents of an autopsy report, for example, might be presented at the inquest. In some states, autopsy reports are not covered by the open-records law.

Coroner and medical examiners work closely with the police and sometimes provide the key to solving a crime. A medical examiner in New York, for example, found a contact lens in one eye of a woman who had been raped and strangled. He told police to search the suspect's car for the other lens. They found it, and the lens helped bring a conviction in the case.[32]

Fire Departments and Emergency Services

Firefighters and ambulance-rescue crews are the stepchildren of public safety. The police usually get most of the attention and the headlines. Now and then, a firefighter will be pictured rescuing a baby from a burning building or snatching a pet kitten from a tree limb. But most of the time, firefighters and emergency-medical technicians (EMT) aid people at great risk—anonymously. Reporters do not get to know them as they do the police. They should.

Actually, firefighters and emergency crews are valuable sources in covering accidents and crime. Frequently they arrive at a crime scene ahead of the police and are the first to assess the situation and talk to victims and witnesses. Cool and well trained, they are highly reliable sources, as well. They also may be freer than the police to talk to reporters.

Reporters need to build contacts and observe the work of emergency personnel. Tour their stations, learn about their equipment, accompany them in training and in action. Well-informed reporters ask better, more focused questions; they know, for example, without asking, why firefighters quickly use axes or power saws to cut a hole in the roof of a blazing building.

At fire scenes and accidents give emergency crews time and room to do their jobs. At first you might concentrate on talking to bystanders, witnesses, survivors—whoever can help you learn who, what, where, why and how. During a lull in the action or once the crisis stage has passed, then talk to fire officials and others involved in handling the fire or emergency. If you have cultivated relationships, the emergency crews will not be strangers.

When a disaster strikes

Earthquakes, plane crashes, chemical-plant explosions, bridge collapses and tornados occur quickly, with little or no warning.

All news organizations should have disaster plans, as far as they can be developed. No amount of preparation can anticipate every development or every problem. But there should be at least a basic plan to provide for the notification, deployment and coordination of the news staff. A list of names, addresses and telephone numbers of key information sources—police, emergency services, hospital officials, state and federal disaster agencies—should be at hand. An emergency power system may be needed to stay on the air or to publish.

Establishing and maintaining effective, reliable communications is a key. In the San Francisco earthquake of 1989, cellular phones continued to provide communication when Pacific Bell's wire lines failed or became overloaded.

When emergency teams rehearse for a disaster, news media people ought to rehearse along with them, not only to assess the strengths and weaknesses of the agencies involved but also to test their own responsiveness.

When the real thing occurs, journalists must engage in calm, accurate reporting; otherwise they risk adding to the initial confusion, misinformation and anxiety. James Holton, an expert on emergency management, urges journalists to verify and reverify information before making it public: " 'Official sources,' " he says, "often disagree with one another. They often lack the overall picture. There may not be an 'overall' picture."[33] Most important, do not rush onto the air or into print with casualty and damage figures; in the confusion, you can expect that they will be inflated.

Joseph Scanlon, another authority on disaster response, further cautions journalists to be patient. "Rather than harass already overburdened officials with demands for precise information—how many injured, how many dead, what's the extent of the damage—the media should understand even the best planned response effort will take time to learn precisely what has happened and what needs to be done."[34]

Be understanding, as well, about the emotional trauma likely to affect victims and rescue workers. When a crippled United Airlines jet crashed in a cornfield at Sioux City, Iowa, in 1989, killing 111, secretaries typing body-identification tags at a makeshift morgue were so overwhelmed by the grim task that psychologists were called in to console them. And survivors who fled the burning wreckage felt ashamed that they left fellow passengers behind.[35]

Journalists covering disasters should focus on five stages of reporting: determining the dimensions of the disaster; providing the public with safety information and advice from officials; alerting the public to present and potential dangers; calming the public by emphasizing positive aspects of the disaster, particularly who and what was spared; and, finally, assessing the situation as to causes or, if complications that contribute negatively to the crisis arise, determining who is responsible for the complications.

Jails and Prisons

While police-beat reporters or court reporters frequently *write* about penal institutions, too often no one regularly and systematically covers the penal system as a *beat.* The result may be missed opportunities for important stories and a serious breakdown in the press's watchdog role.

Steve Green, who covers prisons for the *Sacramento Bee,* explains the lack of thorough coverage this way: "The indifference to prisons in the news media is a reflection of society. People don't give a damn about people in the can. They're out of sight and they are not compelling."[36] But as Green knows, there are compelling stories to be told, one of which is the average annual cost to house, clothe, feed and provide supervision of a single prisoner—reportedly more than $16,000.

Not all jails, prisons, detention facilities and penitentiaries are open to reporters; do not expect to be made welcomed. If reporters are allowed access, it may be limited to portions of the facility. Bans or unacceptable limits on access to facilities or prisoners should always be challenged. While many penal facilities are well run and free of abusive treatment, abuses are more apt to occur when the public and press are not watching.

County jails tend to be more open than state or federal prisons, partly because many of the people detained in county jails are not serving time; they are awaiting trial or judicial action, and, until judged, they are presumed innocent. In most cases, if they had money or property to put up, they would be free on bail. As a result, detainees at a county jail may have comparatively liberal visitor and phone privileges.

Police-beat reporters are wise to make the county jail a part of their rounds. For one thing, crime occurs at jail—stabbings, rapes, murders. Usually the crime is the work of the detainees, but guards commit crimes, too. Unwatched, jail crime may go unreported. In addition, good feature material is to be found in the jail, yielding stories on such subjects as "scared straight" tours for juvenile offenders, the traffic in contraband, prison ministers and their work, educational-vocational programs and letter-writing scams by inmates.

A regular check of the county jail roster to see who has been admitted recently also serves as a back-up system, especially for reporters who suspect the police are withholding records of some arrests.

Do not be timid or reluctant to seek interviews with suspects and inmates. In fact, you might want to encourage particular individuals to call or write you. Communication with an inmate might amount only to jailhouse jive. Then again, a memorable story could emerge.

That is what happened to Peter Franceschina of the *News-Press* in Fort Myers, Fla., when he interviewed, by telephone, Samuel A. Pettit, known as "Wild One," who spoke from the county jail. Pettit, accused of the murder of an assistant state attorney and the attempted murder of a female companion, another assistant state attorney, seemed to gloat over the killing, saying, "I think I should have done better 'cause she [the survivor] lived. . . . I would've killed her, too." In a chilling page 1 account, Pettit described his attack on the pair. Told of the interview, the prosecutor handling the case said, "That's amazing. I still can't believe prisoners in jail have phones. That blows my mind. He has not given us any statement, any statement about the shooting or a confession."[37] Although publication of a "confession" like Pettit's poses questions of free press versus fair trial and could result in the reporter being subpoenaed to testify in court, the episode is a dramatic example of enterprising prison reporting.

In some ways, covering the police beat is like running in a relay race. Police reporters cover crimes and arrests, then the baton is passed on to the courthouse reporters, who run the next leg of the process—coverage of the disposition of criminal cases. Often, however, it is an uncoordinated exercise in news coverage. The next chapter on the courts beat, therefore, begins with criminal law, then moves on to various aspects of civil law.

EXERCISES

1. See whether your city's police or sheriff's department has a "ride-along" program that allows civilians to go on patrol. Although a ride-along tends to be a managed experience, it is still a good way to meet police officers and observe how they go about their work.

2. Crime technicians often labor in relative obscurity. Make arrangements to meet with a crime technician and tour crime-laboratory facilities. Among the interesting work to be observed is ballistics testing and drug analysis. You should find numerous possibilities for a feature story about the technician's role in criminal investigations.

3. Most communities now have counselors or specialists assigned to the police department who assist victims of crime. Interview a

counselor and learn what the job entails. If it can be arranged, also talk to a crime victim who needed counseling.

NOTES

[1] Edna Buchanan, "Advice from One of the Best Police Reporters Around," *ASNE Bulletin*, April 1986, p. 10.

[2] Rolf Rykken, "The Police Beat—Not Exactly a Dead Beat," *presstime*, Sept. 1988, p. 6.

[3] Russell Baker, *The Good Times* (New York: William Morrow, 1989), p. 53.

[4] Edna Buchanan *The Corpse Had a Familiar Face* (New York: Random House, 1987), p. 81.

[5] Alan F. Hoskin et al., *Accident Facts, 1984* (Chicago: National Safety Council, 1983), p. 8.

[6] "Young Crack Users Commit 'Stunning' Number of Crimes," *St. Petersburg Times*, Aug. 4, 1989, p. 1A.

[7] Kevin N. Wright, *The Great American Crime Myth* (New York: Praeger, 1987), p. 29.

[8] Roger Rosenblatt, "Murder in the Safest Places," *U.S. News & World Report*, Jan. 23, 1989, p. 7.

[9] Joseph Wambaugh, *Lines and Shadows* (New York: Morrow, 1984), p. 24.

[10] Harry Jones and Bill Farr, "Law Enforcement," in John Ullmann and Steve Honeyman, eds., *The Reporter's Handbook* (New York: St. Martin's Press, 1983), p. 329.

[11] "Behind the Badge," *48 Hours*, CBS News, Jan. 5, 1989.

[12] Tammerlin Drummond, "Killing Still Haunts Officer of the Year," *St. Petersburg Times*, March 7, 1989, City Times, pp. 1, 3.

[13] Ibid., p. 1.

[14] "Behind the Badge."

[15] Mark Baker, *Cops: Their Lives in Their Own Words* (New York: Pocket Books, 1985), p. 7.

[16] Bob Port, "Merits of Hogtying Suspects Debated by Police Experts," *St. Petersburg Times*, Feb. 16, 1989, p. 8B.

[17] Richard Kobel, "Some Agencies Seek Harmony in Police-Press Ties," *Law Enforcement Newsletter*, Aug. 25, 1988, p. 13.

[18] Buchanan, "Advice from One of the Best Police Reporters Around," p. 12.

[19] *Covering Crime: How Much Press-Police Cooperation? How Little? A Report by the National News Council* (New York: National News Council, 1981), p. 7.

[20] David Johnston, "The Cop Watch," *Columbia Journalism Review*, Sept.–Oct. 1983, pp. 51–54.

[21] Ellen Goodman, "The Confusion of Racism and Crime," *St. Petersburg Times*, May 3, 1989, p. 18A.

[22] See William Wilbanks, "Is Violent Crime Intraracial?," in Delos H. Kelly, ed., *Criminal Behavior*, 2nd ed. (New York: St. Martin's Press, 1990), pp. 94–103.

[23] Ted Joy, "Why Was the Story Kissed Off?," *The Quill*, May 1989, pp. 20–23, 26–27.

[24] Ibid., p. 27.

[25] Quoted in John DeMott, "White Racism in the Newspaper," *The Masthead*, Winter 1981, p. 10.

[26] Deni Elliott, "Anonymity for Rape Victims . . . Should the Rules Change?," *FineLine*, June 1989, p. 2.

[27] Angela Duerson Tuck and Stevan Allen, "Van Strikes, Kills Girl in Oldsmar," *St. Petersburg Times*, Oct. 28, 1988, p. 3B.

[28] Charlotte Sutton, "Trying to Add a Human Touch to News," *St. Petersburg Times*, Nov. 13, 1989, City Times, p. 3.

[29] "How Sharing Grief Can Ease the Pain," *U.S. News & World Report*, Jan. 30, 1989, p. 80.

[30] Sue Titus Reid, *Criminal Justice* (St. Paul: West, 1987), p. 121.

[31] Leonard Territo, James Halsted and Max Bromley, *Crime and Justice in America*, 2nd ed. (St. Paul: West, 1989), p. 246.

[32] Ullmann and Honeyman, *The Reporter's Handbook*, p. 341.

[33] James L. Holton, "Planning for Chaos," *The Quill*, Nov. 1985, p. 20.

[34] Joseph Scanlon, "Media Cover Disasters by Rote," *content*, Nov.–Dec. 1988, p. 37.

[35] Eric N. Berg, "Relief Gives Way to Despair as Horror of Crash Sinks In," *New York Times*, July 21, 1989, p. 1.

[36] Denise Goosby and Kristine A. Kennedy, "Prison Journalism," *ASNE Bulletin*, May–June 1990, pp. 16, 17.

[37] Peter Franceschina, "Pettit Admits to Killing Young Lawyer," *News-Press*, Fort Myers, Fla., Aug. 13, 1989, p. 1.

Chapter Seven

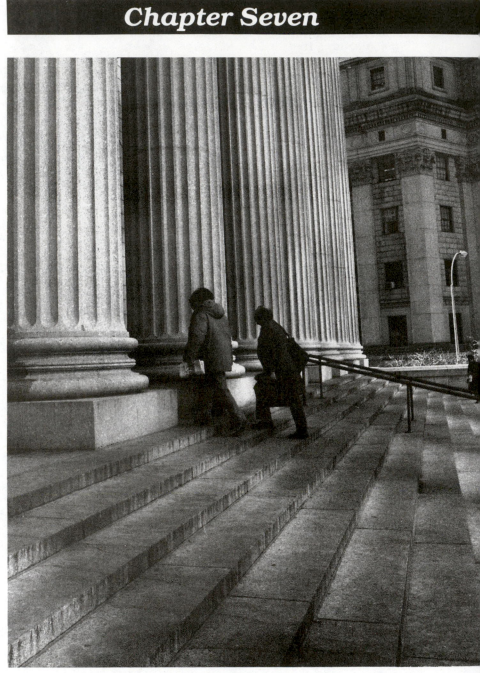

The steps leading into Foley Square Courthouse in New York City.
(Grunzweig/Photo Researchers)

Into the
Legal Maze

Ellen Goodman does not cover the courts, but her columns often involve the law and its sometimes extraordinary implications. In one, she told the story of John Moore, a 43-year-old Seattle sales manager whose treatment for leukemia included removal of his spleen. Moore's doctors, though, did not tell him that tissue from his spleen would be used for important research. The research led to development of a cell-line for treating cancer, which the doctors patented and negotiated into multimillion-dollar contracts with a bioengineering firm and a pharmaceutical company.

Moore eventually filed a lawsuit, arguing that he deserved to share in the profits. A California appeals court agreed, finding that blood and bodily substances are an individual's "tangible personal property." Goodman raises several issues in analyzing Moore's case, including whether it could lead people to "market their tissue as if it were pork bellies or wheat futures. If we discover the cure for AIDS in one person's blood, he or she can offer blood up for auction." To which she added, "None of this paints a very attractive picture."[1]

Ellen Goodman frequently focuses on legal issues because they involve gripping stories of human tragedy—and folly. While trials seem to attract the most attention from the news media, court coverage involves much more than highly publicized spectacles before judges and juries. In fact, few legal matters—civil or criminal— ever go to trial. The vast majority of cases are settled or negotiated, sometimes just minutes before the jury is seated. Yet as scores of reporters record vitriolic testimony in a Hollywood star's palimony suit or report painful details of the beating and gang rape of a jogger in Central Park, portions of the legal beat remain in the shadows.

The preoccupation of press and public with the sensational side of the law sometimes deflects attention from thousands of day-to-day stories, played out not before television cameras and standing-room-only crowds of reporters and spectators, but in near-empty courtrooms, private conference rooms and judges' chambers. Many of these stories are as important and as intriguing as those emerging from more celebrated cases.

Ours is a litigious society, which is not necessarily a problem. As a nation of law, most often we seek justice and resolve disputes through a relatively civilized process of jurisprudence. But unwarranted and insignificant litigation can clog the courts, complicating the work of reporters and judicial officials alike. What happens when enraged Washington Redskins football fans go to court in an effort to overturn a referee's controversial touchdown call or a 24-year-old man sues his parents for $350,000 on grounds of parental malpractice? The courts must deal with an unusual assortment of legal issues, and because some of these issues are outrageously odd, the press reports them. Actually, there is far too much happening in the courts for the news media to cover all that merits coverage. But included among the legal developments that *must* be covered are some of society's most controversial, far-reaching issues, which come before the courts for resolution. The challenges and complexities of our legal system demand that reporters be on duty as explainers, interpreters and watchdogs. In those roles, it is vitally important that reporters know the law in theory, principle and practice.

Lyle Denniston, long-time court reporter and author of *The Reporter and the Law,* reminds journalists to report legal news simply and clearly so lay people will find it understandable and useful. Doing so requires special ability: "To be able to write simply, any journalist—on the court beat or elsewhere—must understand penetratingly. The language of the law and its processes can be excruciatingly precise and arcane. It is an accomplishment of major dimensions to translate it into the popular vernacular, and to lose nothing of consequence in the translation."[2] Denniston values a balanced preparation of legal training and general knowledge so reporters can see the law in terms of its broad social utility. The common denominator for journalists is knowledge and respect for the law. The best court reporters know that hasty, ill-informed and sensationalized treatment does not serve the law or the public.

The law in all of its forms and processes cannot be explained adequately in a few pages of a journalism textbook. This chapter is a departure point for reporters who wish to cover the legal system intelligently and responsibly.

THE JUDICIAL SYSTEM: STRUCTURE AND PROCESS

The United States has 51 court systems—one for each state plus the federal system. Although all share certain characteristics, each system exhibits differences in procedures, rules and terminology. In one state, for example, those who prosecute criminal cases are called *district attorneys;* in a neighboring state prosecutors are called *state attorneys;* in the federal system they are known as *U.S. attorneys.* An *initial appearance* and an *arraignment* usually are two distinct criminal proceedings, but in a few jurisdictions the terms are synonymous. Grand jury witnesses are banned from discussing their testimony outside court chambers in some courts—but not in others. Reporters must know the differences between systems and never assume that what is done in one jurisdiction is surely permissible in another.

The federal system and a number of state systems use a three-tier structure: *trial courts, appellate courts* and a *supreme court.* Not all systems are organized this way; many have additional courts with limited or special duties, such as *family court,* which handles matters like non-payment of child support and adoptions, or *probate court,* which is responsible for supervising the disposition of estates and determining the authenticity of wills.

In both civil and criminal law, nearly all cases—federal and state—begin at the trial level. Verdicts, findings, judgments and rulings made by trial courts may go on to an intermediate level of appellate courts, where they are reviewed for errors or misapplication of the law. Appeals courts, usually comprising three or more judges, do not retry the case, calling witnesses and examining evidence. Instead, sitting either on *panels* of less than full membership of the court or *en banc,* with all members present, they review the facts and the records of a case, deciding whether to uphold or overrule the trial court's action. Although civil and criminal defendants are free to appeal, normally there are no guarantees that a case will receive full review. Appellate and supreme courts exercise broad discretionary power in accepting cases.

The Long and Winding Road

Going to court seldom is a simple matter. Complications, for instance, can arise in determining which court holds *jurisdiction* over a legal matter. Ordinarily, state courts address civil and criminal issues dealing with state law or occurring within the boundaries of the state and involving citizens of that state. Federal courts address violations or questions of federal law or legal issues involving different states or citizens of different states. At times, the distinctions between federal and state jurisdiction become blurred.

In criminal cases particularly, multiple violations of federal and state law are possible, which means multiple prosecutions are possible as well. A husband and wife, for example, are abducted from a shopping center parking lot in New York. The husband is killed while the abductors are still in New York. The wife is taken to a remote area in New Jersey, where she is raped and murdered. State authorities in both New York and New Jersey could pursue charges against the abductors; U.S. authorities could do likewise because federal laws covering interstate crime apply. In criminal cases, jurisdictional problems usually are worked out among the prosecutors involved because of a common goal—the prosecution of criminal acts.

Civil law poses even more problems. When jurisdiction is not clear, lawyers and litigants in civil cases often will seek the court that appears to offer them a strategic advantage. Under the right circumstances, for example, rail or barge workers injured on the job may file suit in a court hundreds of miles from the site of their injuries, provided the railroad or barge company operates within that court's jurisdictional boundaries. As a result, thousands of such lawsuits have ended up in the circuit courts of Illinois' Madison and St. Clair counties, which are known as "plaintiff's counties" for the high monetary damages juries there typically award in personal-injury suits.[3] Struggles over jurisdictional questions might lead to additional legal action, such as a motion for a *change of venue*—a request to have a case heard in another location.

Beyond problems over jurisdiction, the judicial path a case follows can be tortuous and unpredictable. Consider this example: An accountant files a libel suit in the local state court after the hometown newspaper publishes a story in which a half-dozen unidentified clients accuse him of fraud. One of the first steps by the accountant's lawyers is to ask the reporter to identify her unnamed sources.

The reporter refuses, even after the trial judge orders disclosure. The judge finds her in contempt of court and orders the reporter to jail. The newspaper's lawyers then challenge the judge's action through what is called an *interlocutory appeal*, which allows a higher court to settle a disputed point of law that could bear on how the case is tried. As a result, the battle over confidential sources might have to be resolved by an appellate court's ruling before the libel case can progress. Along the way, there may be numerous legal twists and turns before final resolution; it certainly is not a linear process. In fact, the case could meander through the courts for years before running its full course of motions, trial and appeals.

Finally, litigation often is costly, both emotionally and financially. Two dramatic examples in 1989 occupied the news on the same day— October 9. In Atlanta, testimony opened in the first of seven scheduled civil trials in a sex-abuse case involving ex-employees of a treatment center for troubled youths. Lawyers took three years preparing for the trial, which is not surprising for a case with 124 plaintiffs, 31 defendants and 10,000 pages of documents. In Los Angeles, final arguments started in a 30-month-long trial against preschool employees accused of molesting 11 children. According to news reports, it was the nation's longest and costliest ($15 million) criminal case.[4] On appeal, cases like these may drag on for several more years, adding to an already heavy toll.

Roots and Branches of Law

To this point, the word *law* has been used to refer to the U.S. system of courts and judicial processes governing them. *Law*, in another sense of the word, refers to the legally enforceable rules by which society lives.

U.S. law, in its broader meaning, is like a sturdy, pliable tree, with deep roots and a thicket of branches. At the tree's core is the United States Constitution—the law of the land. Forming the branches are state constitutions, federal and state statutes, local ordinances, court opinions, administrative rulings, executive orders and other legal pronouncements, which combine and, at times, interrelate to form our body of law.

Our legal system is rooted in *common law*, which originated in medieval England as a practical means for the king's courts to settle disputes that were not covered by written laws. Today, common law amounts to centuries of accumulated legal precedent, much of it based on sensible resolutions of conflicts. Under common law of many states, for example, unwed couples who cohabit for a period of years are considered legally married. Judges continue to create and interpret common law because it remains a flexible, useful means of addressing life's unanticipated or uncharted legal problems.

Statutory law is legislation passed by elected officials on the local, state or federal level of government. Statutory law is *codified*—that is, it is organized and maintained in books and volumes referred to as *codes;* statutory law includes criminal codes as well. Every year, thousands of new laws are created by local, state and federal legislators. The Pottsville city council, for example, enacts an ordinance requiring a building-safety inspection before any home in the city can be sold and occupied. On the same day, Congress passes a statute amending the federal tax code's provisions on interest deductions. Although both pieces of legislation would be widely reported—one locally, the other nationally—the public may be unaware and uninformed about most areas of statutory law, which on all levels of government is simply too voluminous to report in any comprehensive way.

Administrative law primarily encompasses rules and regulations formulated by state or federal regulatory agencies, such as the Federal Communications Commission or the Internal Revenue Service. These rules and regulations have the same legal effect as a statute. *Executive orders* fall in the same category. These are pronouncements issued by the president or, on the state level, by governors, setting policies and rules for the executive branch of government. The president, for example, might order all federal agencies to establish procedures to punish employees who leak sensitive information to the press.

The U.S. Constitution and the various state constitutions define the powers of government and the rights of citizens. *Constitutional law* generally refers to judicial interpretation of the meaning and scope of these documents. Changing times and newly emerging societal problems pressure the courts to examine and re-examine constitutional law.

The judicial system ultimately touches each element of law— constitutional law, statutory law, common law, administrative law and executive orders—because all law is subject to legal challenge and review by the courts. The city council's ordinance on home inspections, Congress' statute on tax deductions and the president's order to plug leaks are bound to generate controversy and debate, probably leading to legal action of some sort.

All law, however, including law established by state constitutions, is subservient to the United States Constitution. No legislative body or agency can sustain a law that is in conflict with the rights and liberties guaranteed in the federal Constitution. Of course, thousands of legal disputes have focused on what the Constitution's words do or do not protect. The final authority is the nine-member United States Supreme Court, empowered to interpret the Constitution and decide all legal challenges, even if the result finds the actions of Congress or the president unconstitutional, or overrules the decision of a lower court's or even one of its own.

Principles, Characteristics and Qualities

Although not unchangeable, the law is quite stable, based on time-honored principles. One principle in particular distinguishes the judicial system: the *doctrine of judicial review*. Of the three branches of government—judicial, legislative and executive—the judiciary enjoys a special status because it alone can decide the meaning of state and federal constitutions. Therefore a court, exercising its power of judicial review, can nullify the unconstitutional action of any government within its jurisdiction. Of course, a single court's power is not absolute and rarely unchallengeable, which is why the judicial system includes many opportunities to appeal decisions and rulings.

Another fundamental principle is *stare decisis*—the policy of courts to stand by precedent and adhere to points of law settled by previous court decisions. When a legal problem arises, judges and attorneys consider how other courts dealt with similar problems. But even the principle of stare decisis bends. Precedent does not always fit a particular case, requiring courts to seek new solutions. Moreover, courts must depart at times from outdated or faulty precedent to ensure justice or to serve the public interest. If that were not true, America's public schools would still be racially segregated under the "separate but equal" doctrine.

Energizing and fueling the judicial process is the adversarial principle. Our system of justice, in fact, depends on each side in a civil or criminal action to fight with all its legal resources. Ideally, truth and justice emerge from such a spirited contest.

The system, though, is far from perfect. Consider some of its flaws and limitations:

• *The adversarial principle works best when the contest is fought among equals.* The fact is, money often can buy better legal representation. An overworked public defender may see his indigent client for the first time a few minutes before a court appearance. In a nearby courtroom an immaculately groomed criminal suspect huddles with a high-priced, influential attorney in private practice, paid a hefty fee in advance and backed by the research of a team of other lawyers and specialists. Assuming the state's evidence against both is comparable, which defendant stands a better chance of staying out of jail?

• *Truth and justice are abstractions.* Whose truth? Whose justice? Somebody wins, somebody loses, and truth and justice do not always prevail. At times, technicalities and loopholes determine the outcome of cases. A burglary suspect is freed because an inexperienced police officer conducted an improper search of the suspect's apartment; a factory worker who lost an arm in a plant accident loses the opportunity to sue because his attorney waited too long to file the case (although he later might be able to sue his attorney for malpractice). Unfortunately, the judicial system, like other areas of human endeavor, displays ignorance, ineptitude and dishonesty.

• *Ambiguity permeates the law.* Many laws are subject to widely differing interpretations. William P. Statsky, an expert on legal analysis, uses the following statute section as a simple but effective example of this ambiguity:

> Chronic alcoholic means a person who, in consequence of prolonged excessive drinking, has developed a diagnosable bodily disease or mental disorder.

Statsky provides an 18-point list of ambiguities in the statute. For example, what does "prolonged" mean? A period of years? If someone drinks night and day for two weeks, is that "prolonged"? By the time Statsky finishes picking apart the passage, it is easy to see how it could be read in a dozen or more ways.[5]

• *Often the system must make pragmatic compromises simply to keep the wheels of justice from grinding to a halt.* In criminal law, plea bargaining generally results in reduced charges and lighter sentences. In civil law, settlements and deals may or may not serve the best interests of the parties involved. Not every case can—or should—go to trial.

• *Politics and the law are frequently inseparable.* Many judges are either elected or must stand before voters periodically for *retention votes.* Prosecutors, too, are often elected officials; some possess ambitions to hold higher office, including a judge's post. As a result, courthouses can be hotbeds of politics, and court officials may practice the most expedient or personally profitable form of law.

• *The law is dynamic.* The world changes, people change, customs change, technology changes. The law must adapt. Medical advances alone have forced the courts to address extraordinarily difficult questions involving life-support measures, surrogate motherhood, fetal tissue and genetic engineering.

Despite its flaws and limitations, however, the law touches lives, often in deep, lasting ways. From divorce decrees to murder verdicts, people are affected, which is something reporters must never forget. Constantly focus on the law for its human implications. The *Chicago Tribune*'s Linnet Myers, winner of the 1990 ASNE best newswriting award, is a model for producing stories such as this one:

> Murderers walk these halls, and the mothers of murderers, and the mothers of the murdered too.
>
> This is 26th and California.
>
> Step through the metal detectors and enter the multicolored stream of humanity that flows through the Criminal Court building each day. It is the largest felony-trial system under one roof in the United States. In 34 courtrooms, nothing but felonies are heard: murders, manslaughters, sexual assaults, armed robberies, burglaries, drug cases. Last year, 19,632 cases were heard here.
>
> Officially, it is the Cook County Circuit Court, Criminal Division. But those who work here refer to it by its near Southwest Side location, 26th Street and California Boulevard—known simply as "26 & Cal."
>
> Outside, on the building's noble limestone walls, are carved the Latin words *veritas* and *Justitia*—truth and justice.
>
> Inside is a world the average Chicagoan never sees.[6]

As Myers knows by experience, the realities of the law can make covering the courts exasperating and confusing; they also can make coverage challenging and exciting.

CIVIL CASES

Because of extensive press coverage and treatment of criminal cases in movies and television programs, most people have a passing familiarity with the fundamentals of criminal law—from arrest to trial. Civil law not only is less visible; it is also more complex. In civil litigation, one party—whether an individual, corporation, group or government—battles a second party to correct alleged wrongs or seek redress for damages. The variety of proceedings and legal subjects under civil law is practically limitless, with new areas of civil law emerging to meet new problems.

Among the most common civil suits are those arising from traffic accidents. In a typical scenario, a delivery truck and a compact car collide on an icy bridge, leaving the driver of the car paralyzed by a neck injury. The driver sues the delivery person, his employer and the truck's manufacturer, claiming several counts of negligence. If the court finds sufficient evidence of negligence, the jury or judge's award for monetary damages might run into the millions of dollars.

Civil actions involving recovery for damages come under a category of cases known as *at law.* Other actions at law include disputes over breach of contract, invasion of privacy, product liability, professional malpractice or defamation of character.

A second category of civil action is known either as *equity* or *chancery.* Frequently, equity cases involve a request for court-ordered protection against an existing or impending wrong. A historic-preservation group, for example, attempts to stop a shopping mall developer from bulldozing a landmark—a 150-year-old home— to make way for a parking lot. The preservationists ask the court to issue a *temporary restraining order* to gain time to mount a legal argument and develop a plan of action, such as relocation of the building to a nearby park. Later, before both parties, the judge might issue a *permanent injunction,* ordering the developer to leave the home intact. Most often, all factual and legal issues in equity cases are decided solely by a judge and do not go to a jury for determination.

Cases in the category of *extraordinary* (or special) *remedy* usually do not fit the normal conditions of a lawsuit in which damages are sought; often, special-remedy cases involve unusual or urgent issues, such as an alleged deprival of legal rights and liberties. In one widely publicized episode, the American Nazi party, aided by the American Civil Liberties Union, successfully contested the efforts of city officials in Skokie, Ill., to ban Nazis from holding a rally, wearing military uniforms and displaying the Nazi symbol, the swastika. The City of Skokie and the Nazis battled on two main fronts. The first centered on the anti-rally injunction obtained by the city; the second focused on three ordinances the city quickly passed to block the Nazis' plans to gather in uniform. The cases warranted immediate, expedited appellate review because of the serious constitutional questions at stake.

Other special-remedy cases include changing a name, dissolving a corporation and challenging the action of a government official through a *quo warranto* proceeding to determine whether the official has the legal authority to take the action in question.

Combinations and complications are not only possible, they are probable. An entertainer suing to recover money from a business agent accused of misappropriating funds might first seek an injunction to bar the agent from further access to the entertainer's financial and business records. In addition, initial actions sometimes result in a spate of related litigation, as the Skokie-Nazi cases illustrate; in all, a half-dozen courts—state and federal—became involved over a period of 18 months.[7] Because civil actions frequently overlap, a number of court jurisdictions no longer distinguish cases as belonging to "law," "equity" or "special-remedy" categories, which has helped to streamline civil law.

If a civil case goes to trial, it should be decided in favor of the party with the most convincing, credible evidence, or what is known as either *preponderance of evidence* or *greater weight of evidence*. This is known as the "burden of proof" for a civil case decision. The burden of proof for a criminal case is higher—the defendant must be shown to be guilty *beyond a reasonable doubt*.

Commencing a Civil Action

Often the first impulse of an aggrieved person is, "I'm going to sue!" At times, threatening to sue is merely a way to let off steam. Many conflicts are resolved informally, without resorting to litigation. With a few exceptions—mainly petitioning to small-claims court—commencing a civil action requires the aid of an attorney. If the attorney believes there are grounds for a lawsuit, or a *cause for action*, the next step is preparation of a formal, written *complaint* or *petition* that states the facts, arguments and damages or relief sought. The person initiating a civil action is the *plaintiff*, and the action is directed against the *defendant.* The complaint is received, filed, recorded in a *docket book* and given a *case number* by the clerk of the court.

Civil complaints follow a format and procedure prescribed by each court system. Complaints may range in length from several paragraphs to dozens of pages; usually they are written in stilted, formulaic language. The complaint might begin: "Now comes the plaintiff, Jane Doe, by her attorney, John Smith, and for her complaint against defendant Mary Brown, states as follows: . . ." In some complaints, the basis for the suit—the *cause of action*—is detailed in a series of numbered *counts.* The damages or legal actions sought by the suit normally are stated at the conclusion of the complaint: "Wherefore, the plaintiff claims damages in the amount of . . ."

A typical story based on the filing of a complaint would take this readable form:

> BEVERLY, Mass.—Parker Brothers filed suit Tuesday against the manufacturer of a board game that allegedly uses elements of Monopoly.
>
> The lawsuit, filed in federal court in New York, charges the Elusive Dream Marketing Service of El Cajon, Calif., with unfair competition and trademark violations for distributing a game called Cityopoly.
>
> Also named as defendants were the F.A.O. Schwarz and Saks Fifth Avenue retail stores.
>
> Parker Brothers seeks an injunction against the alleged use of Monopoly elements, plus unspecified damages.

If available, the story would include comments by spokespersons for the plaintiff and defendant.

The filing of a suit is followed by service of a *summons*—a legal notice—to the defendant. A summons usually is delivered by an officer of the court or a sheriff's deputy. At times, summons servers must resort to disguises or ploys to reach an evasive defendant. Once properly served, the summons cannot be ignored, no matter how frivolous or unfair the defendant considers the complaint. Failure to respond to the summons could result in the court entering *judgment by default* in favor of the plaintiff.

A defendant is entitled to sufficient time to prepare and file an *answer.* In the answer, the defendant denies the claims in the complaint or enters a defense to the claims. Thereafter follows a period of pretrial motions and a process called *discovery,* during which both sides, under court order, must exchange information and evidence. One method of information exchange is accomplished by *interrogatories,* which are written questions from one party to the other. Interrogatories are supposed to be truthfully and fully answered. Oral interviews under oath are called *depositions,* which allow lawyers to question witnesses and parties in a case to gain information later needed to represent their clients in court.

The steps described amount to the *simplest* of scripts for a civil action. Frequently civil action is complicated by the legal strategies employed. A complaint, for example, might prompt a *motion to dismiss* or a *demurrer,* a request to discontinue a case because the complaint is legally insufficient. Other maneuvers by the defendant might include a legal counterattack in the form of a *cross-complaint.* After the defendant files an answer, more motions, such as one for a *summary judgment,* could follow. A judge's summary judgment decides the case for one party based on the facts presented in the *pleadings*— the complaint and answer. Summary judgments promptly end claims the judge believes to be legally unjustifiable.

Some action in a civil case occurs in private out-of-court meetings and communications between lawyers for the parties, outside the sight and earshot of reporters. During the discovery stage, records may be produced and depositions taken that might not be open to the press. Depositions can be quite newsworthy, but often they are considered the private work product of the lawyer unless officially filed with the court. There also may be several private pretrial conferences by lawyers in the presence of the judge. Pretrial conferences can lead to *stipulations,* which are agreements by both sides pertaining to the proceedings or use of evidence, such as the admissibility of photographs, video tapes or medical records.

Civil cases frequently end in *settlements* to avoid a costly, risky trial; at times, settlements are reached while a trial is in progress. Going to trial is somewhat like throwing dice—for both sides. An automobile manufacturer, sued by a man badly burned when the gas tank of his pickup truck ruptured in a rear-end accident, may emerge from a trial with no damages assessed—or $5 million. The same range of possibilities exists for the plaintiff. So a settlement of $750,000 is reached. Once again, the press may not be privy to the conditions of settlements, which are reached in private sessions. In fact, a firm stipulation in many settlements is that neither party reveal any details, particularly the amount of money paid out.

Covering the Civil Courts

Covering the courts means regular visits to the *clerk of the court*'s office. Reporters on the court beat, in fact, may check with court employees and examine records several times a day, keeping abreast of pending cases and looking for new filings to report. Some reporters check records right before the clerk's office closes to make sure an attorney does not try to slip a filing past the press. For the most part, reporters enjoy ready access to court documents, although they may not be allowed to retrieve records personally.

As civil actions are received by the clerk's office, they are given case numbers and recorded in either handwritten or computerized log books. Without a case number, it is more difficult to track down records. Knowing the names of the parties involved—*Jones v. National Tool & Die Co.*—may not be enough. Workers in the clerk's office are still likely to ask, "Well, what's the case number?" Court employees are busy, too, and do not appreciate being inconvenienced.

Since reporters cannot attend all hearings or keep up with all legal moves and motions, they rely on court personnel and records to stay informed. In most civil actions, documents—such as complaints, pleadings and motions—are kept in a legal-size folder that is accessible to reporters, unless the folder temporarily is in the judge's hands. Customarily attached to the file is the *minute record,* a chronological summary of each stage of the case, citing, for example, when a summons was served or what a judge ruled on a motion to dismiss. As courts install computer systems, records are being stored in data bases, making it more practicable for court officials and journalists to retrieve and analyze cases.

Certain documents are particularly valuable. Access, however, can be a problem. Sensitive records may be sealed by the judge or put off limits by a court ruling. In a 1984 case, the Supreme Court said pretrial depositions and interrogatories "are not public components of a civil trial."[8] Nonetheless, as watchdogs of the judicial system, reporters should continue to argue for access to all court records. Remember that court records that are open one day may be closed the next if the judge decides to seal them. To guard against such a possibility, alert reporters immediately copy every relevant document filed in an important case.

Reporters sometimes spend more time going over court documents than attending hearings or trials. For his book *News Making in the Trial Courts* Robert E. Drechsel observed a full-time court reporter for a metropolitan daily in Minnesota. In the four-day period of observation, the reporter produced eight stories, going briefly into courtrooms on just two occasions. Neither courtroom visit involved trial coverage. One was to cover an arraignment; the other was for a sentencing hearing.[9] Of course, patterns and frequency of courtroom coverage will vary, but reporters normally cannot spend hours listening to testimony that may not yield a story worth publishing. Indeed, they must be extremely selective. Only rarely do court reporters spend extended, uninterrupted periods at a trial or proceeding. Usually they pop in and out of courtrooms, covering important pretrial hearings or a key witness's testimony in a newsworthy trial.

Monitoring all that goes on in the courts is not easy; in some jurisdictions, hundreds of cases may be filed in a single day. With so much going on, reporters need to cultivate people in the courts building who have a good sense of what is newsworthy and are willing to assist with tips and information.

Nearly all courts are inundated by litigation. The challenge for reporters is to decide which cases and legal developments warrant coverage. The news criteria for the courts beat include the old standards: timeliness, prominence, consequence, oddity, conflict, change and proximity. A single story might meet several criteria at once. A 52-year-old woman, for example, sued the heavy-metal band Motley Crue after suffering hearing damage at a concert. Although the suit eventually ended in an out-of-court settlement, the woman's attorney said the case, reportedly the first of its kind, quickly produced results around the country. It led several rock promoters to include noise warnings on the back of concert tickets and issue earplugs on request at theater entrances.[10]

Reading complaints and other court records often presents translation problems for reporters. In "legalese," for example, an auto accident description might read: "On the aforesaid date, the defendant did operate a motor vehicle in a southerly direction along and upon Main Street, in the 3200 block thereof, in a careless, negligent and intoxicated manner, so as to . . ." Reporters must convert the language of lawyers into everyday English, avoiding legal jargon and technical descriptions of injuries or damages.

Writing for and about people helps court reporters cut to the significance of even the most complex of court cases. *New York*

Times writer Andrew H. Malcolm humanized a lawsuit between AT&T and a handful of Ohio farmers in a clear story with an appealing opening:

> ATHENS, Ohio—In an old courtroom with peeling green paint, a college professor and some farmer friends are fighting with a giant telephone company over a hole in the ground.
>
> There is no grand constitutional issue at stake. Both sides fully expect the American Telephone & Telegraph Co.'s new fiber optic cable, 1 inch of rubber wrapped around 42 strands of glass, to go 4 feet under all those farm fields between Washington and St. Louis.
>
> There, beneath Don Flournoy's hay and Scott Ervin's cows, tiny bursts of light will carry 500,000 conversations simultaneously.
>
> What is at stake in this struggle seems more a point of personal pride or principle, with the farmers sending a message to someone, almost anyone, that they feel pushed around by strangers on their own land and they don't like it.

You will not find any *wherefores* or *thereases* in Malcolm's reporting. The issues and history of the lawsuit are explained in lay language, resulting in a relevant story for city and country residents.

There is another aspect of humanizing court coverage: Reporters should never forget that emotions and reputations can be deeply affected by litigation. Care is needed at all times in court coverage but especially at the complaint-filing stage. Nearly anyone can find an attorney willing to file suit, no matter how silly or unfair the charges might be. It is also relatively easy for a reporter to scan a complaint, make a few calls and write a story focusing on the allegations and the damages sought. But a civil complaint merely *begins* the process of determining who is right and wrong or who is at fault and who is not.

Suits asking for multimillion-dollar judgments sound impressive and serious. They may not be. Avoid overreacting to the sheer amount of damages being asked. With the exception of *actual damages,* which are supposed to be based on measurable out-of-pocket costs or losses, the damages cited in a civil complaint may have no relationship to what is reasonable redress—or what the plaintiff ends up being awarded. Remember that by overplaying damages, you might cause readers and viewers—some of them potential jurors—to wrongly assume that a plaintiff's request for massive damages suggests grave wrongdoing on the defendant's part.

Calling the defendant for "reaction" to the complaint may seem to satisfy the reporter's duty to be fair, but often such an obligatory phone call merely is part of a tired formula for lawsuit stories. In fact, the defendant's first knowledge of the complaint may come from a reporter, leaving no opportunity for much more than a brief remark: "I can't comment until I read the complaint." For reporters, the temptation is to publish or broadcast charges in a complaint as soon as it is filed by the plaintiff; to be fair to all parties, a more cautious, restrained approach may be required. Many lawyers and judges would prefer that journalists withhold a lawsuit story until the defendant legally "answers" the charges in the complaint.

When possible, talk to all sides involved in a legal dispute, although you should be prepared for rejection. Lawyers or participants may decline to comment for any number of reasons, among them the fears of being unprofessional, upsetting the judge, violating ethical codes or otherwise hurting their own case. On the other hand, some lawyers and participants will orchestrate press coverage to their advantage. Despite the legal profession's overall objection to "trial by media," some lawyers welcome a hearing in the court of public opinion.

Journalists should attempt to follow up on all lawsuit stories by reporting the final judgment or settlement. A lawyer emphasized that point for *Los Angeles Times* reporter David Shaw: "If a guy sues for $10 million and the court gives $1.98, you ought to print it. Otherwise, the public gets a mistaken, inflated impression of the value of even the most frivolous lawsuits and they file bigger and bigger lawsuits and the spiral of cost goes up and up for everyone."[11] Reporters also should track a reported case to its conclusion, particularly for the sake of the reputations of the litigants. If a lawsuit is worth reporting in the first place, let people know what happened to it.

CRIMINAL CASES

In film and television, from *Perry Mason* and *12 Angry Men* to *L.A. Law* and *The Accused*, criminal law is the star. So it is in real life.

In criminal cases, the government seeks to enforce laws and punish those who violate them. Attorneys employed by local, state or federal governments *prosecute* violators on the behalf of the citizens, which is why criminal cases typically are cited as *"The state* (or the people) *against John Doe, defendant."* A criminal violation is either classified a *felony,* which is a serious offense that can result in imprisonment of a year or longer, or a *misdemeanor,* a "petty" violation for which punishment is a fine or less than a year's imprisonment.

Police sometimes clash with prosecutors and judges over whether a case is strong enough to prosecute. In some jurisdictions, police must present all felony arrests to the prosecutor's gatekeeper, usually an assistant prosecuting attorney, who reviews the facts and preliminary evidence, determining whether the case merits prosecution. If so, the prosecutor's office will have to commit what may be already stretched, limited resources. At times, the decision boils down to the odds of winning or losing the case.

A linchpin of the criminal system is the principle of a *presumption of innocence.* In theory, at least, criminal defendants are not required to prove their innocence. The prosecutor must convince the court and jury that the defendant is guilty *beyond a reasonable doubt.* Jurors who have a reasonable doubt about guilt are instructed—and obligated—to find the defendant not guilty through an *acquittal.*

All criminal defendants possess constitutional rights, particularly those established by the Bill of Rights—the Fourth Amendment (which includes protection against unreasonable searches and seizures); the Fifth (protection against self-incrimation and double jeopardy, among other rights); the Sixth (the right to a fair, speedy trial and associated rights); the Eighth (no excessive bail or cruel and unusual punishments); and the Fourteenth (due process and equal protection of the law). These rights have been expanded by a number of court rulings, such as the U.S. Supreme Court's 1962 *Gideon v. Wainright* decision, which required states to provide legal counsel for indigent felony defendants.

The Genesis of a Criminal Case

A criminal case can begin in a variety of ways. Often, routine police work leads to arrests and charges against individuals caught committing a crime. In other cases, investigative work by the prosecutor's office—such as a "sting" operation to catch a public official taking a bribe—brings about criminal charges.

A key step in the criminal process is the issuance of a warrant of arrest or a warrant to search a person or property for possible evidence. An *arrest warrant* is issued by the appropriate court based on a demonstration of *probable cause* that the person named in the warrant committed a crime or violated conditions of parole or probation. Although its meaning and application vary, probable cause is generally determined by facts and circumstances that would lead a reasonable person to conclude that a crime had been committed.

Under federal and state constitutions, citizens are protected against unreasonable searches and seizures. When law enforcement officials ask a judge to approve a *search warrant,* they must clearly specify the person or property to be searched and identify what is being sought. They also must show probable cause for the search, as well as meet additional conditions set by particular courts or required in various jurisdictions. Comparable conditions, especially probable cause, apply to police requests for telephone taps or electronic surveillance.

Normally, a request for a search warrant is made and reviewed in an informal, confidential *ex parte* hearing, which means a one-sided presentation by the police or prosecutor. The individual named in the warrant is not present nor given the legal opportunity to contest the warrant. Reporters routinely should examine the *affidavits* on which requests for warrants are based. These sworn statements by law enforcement officials may contain important, newsworthy details not included in police reports, such as names and addresses of other persons connected to the suspect and the crime. Unfortunately for reporters, search warrants and the accompanying affidavits fall within a gray area of access, with courts divided on whether the press is entitled to such material.[12]

If an arrest, search or seizure is done in an unconstitutional manner, evidence or statements so obtained may be inadmissible under what is known as the *exclusionary rule.* Defense attorneys frequently attack the legitimacy of searches and seizures, particularly those conducted without a warrant. Warrantless searches and seizures are permitted, but only under special circumstances. If evidence, for example, is found during a routine body frisk for weapons or if it is in plain view at the time of an arrest, it can be legally seized; of course, there is often controversy surrounding how *plain view* is defined.

Some criminal cases fall apart because of improper interrogation methods. For instance, if police question a criminal suspect in custody without a *Miranda warning* to explain the suspect's right to remain silent and right to be represented by a lawyer, any evidence and information collected as a result may be tainted under a legal concept known as *fruit of the poisonous tree.* If the "tree"—the illegally obtained statement—is poisoned, then the fruit it yields in the form of additional evidence is likely to be poisoned, too, and probably cannot be used against the suspect.

Lineup identification is another critical stage. Police cannot coach witnesses or allow them to talk among themselves as they try to pick out a suspect. Nor can they stack a deck so that a witness, who told police a holdup man "looked like a football player," cannot help but focus on a muscular suspect intentionally placed in the middle of a lineup of men with slight builds.

Interesting stories can emerge from clashes between the prosecution and the defense over the propriety of investigative methods and the validity of witness identifications. Competent defense attorneys will attack flawed police procedures or evidence through pretrial motions or, later, through post-trial appeals.

Whether criminal suspects are in custody or still at large, they must be charged formally before the judicial process goes any farther. Two charging procedures are commonly used: *informations* and *indictments.* An information is the prosecutor's means of alleging the commission of a crime and bringing a suspect to trial. Indictments come from a *grand jury,* a panel varying in size from 12 to 23 laypersons and appointed for specific terms of varying duration. The grand jury hears evidence presented by the prosecution and then decides, usually by a majority vote, whether there is sufficient probable cause to recommend that the suspect be charged. Some states require a grand jury hearing for all felony cases; in others, informations are being used more frequently than grand jury indictments to file charges against defendants.

An indictment, also referred to as a *true bill,* is only an official accusation; it is not a finding of guilt. All stories about indictments should stress that point. If necessary, reporters should include a definition of an indictment in grand jury stories. Otherwise, the presumption of innocence is undermined, and the common charge of "trial by media" becomes regrettably more valid.

Grand juries also investigate broader criminal problems, such as organized crime, gambling operations and governmental corruption. Another common function is overseeing public facilities and institutions, including jails and government-operated mental health centers. Thus, a grand jury inquiry might result in dozens of indictments in a drug-ring case or a recommendation for officials to improve medical treatment at the county jail.

The power of a federal or state grand jury goes beyond its ability to issue indictments; it includes the power to force the appearance of witnesses and suspects, even those not yet formally charged in warrants. A *subpoena* is a judge-issued order to appear before a grand jury or other judicial body. A *subpoena duces tecum* is an order to produce documents. Those who refuse to honor a subpoena are subject to a citation for *civil contempt* and jailing until they comply. (*Criminal contempt* applies to direct affronts to the court, such as an outburst during a trial, and is punishable by a set jail term or fine.)

A reporter who covers crime and corruption may someday face a grand jury subpoena. During the late 1960s and early 1970s, in particular, grand juries investigating militant groups, such as the Black Panthers, regularly called journalists to testify. Battles between the press and the judiciary are inevitable whenever reporters are subpoenaed and ordered to reveal names of anonymous sources or turn over confidential information. Most reporters will go to jail rather than break a pledge of confidentiality.

Some reporters who receive subpoenas see them as intrusions on their newsgathering role. And at times, prosecutors or grand juries use subpoenas in an indiscriminate search for evidence, which critics label "fishing expeditions." But no one, including reporters, can ignore a grand jury subpoena. Even a patently frivolous subpoena is serious business that probably will require a lawyer's advice and assistance. (Chapter 10 addresses the legal and ethical issues of confidential sources.)

Because grand jury sessions are closed to the public and the press, coverage can be difficult. In some jurisdictions, everyone connected with the grand jury is sworn to secrecy. In others, reporters may be able to question witnesses after they testify. Often, reporters must wait patiently until the grand jury releases its report. When a grand jury inquiry is especially important, journalists may be tempted to approach grand jurors privately for inside information. But, if they are suspected of being involved in a leak of information from the grand jury, reporters can anticipate being subpoenaed and asked to identify their sources of information. Unless there is evidence of corruption or misconduct in a grand jury's handling of a case, reporters are advised to neither encourage leaks nor publicize them. Being first to break a story of a grand jury's indictment normally is insufficient reason for breaking the law.

In a few cases, the grand jury returns a *suppressed indictment* for criminal suspects still at large. Reporters who prematurely identify people named in suppressed indictments could give them an opportunity to flee.

Regardless of the method used to bring charges, all accused persons are entitled to appear before a judge quickly to ensure that constitutional and due process rights are observed. In many jurisdictions, this proceeding is called an *initial appearance*. As a rule, judges use the initial appearance to determine the identity and age of the accused, read charges, inform the accused of his or her rights, determine whether the accused can afford to retain a lawyer and set bail, if it is permitted.

Most defendants are allowed to be free on bail while the case is pending. *Bail* is a written promise to appear in court as ordered. To ensure compliance, defendants must do one of the following: put up cash in the full amount of the bail; provide a percentage—usually 10 percent—of the cash bail; put up real estate of value equivalent to or greater than the amount of bail; or obtain a surety bond from a bail bondsman, who is responsible if the defendant fails to appear in court. Friends, relatives and neighbors of accused persons sometimes use their own property or cash to meet bond. If the accused flees, all cash and property may be forfeited to the courts. Determine who is liable if a defendant "jumps bail"; you may find a human-interest story.

Many states have made it easier and less costly for defendants to "make bail." Reform in bail rules has minimized the involvement of bail bondsmen, some of whom charge excessive fees for services, knowing that certain suspects have no other options.

In less serious cases involving first-time offenders, a court might accept a *signature* or *recognizance bond* that does not require money or property as a guarantee. Use of recognizance is based on the high probability that the defendant will honor the conditions of bail.

Many people, however, cannot make bail. Studies indicate that jailed defendants are more likely to be convicted and receive longer sentences than those released on bail. Evidently, defendants free on bail can better help in preparing a defense. Even when convicted, bailed defendants often can point to steady employment and good behavior while awaiting trial as reasons for probation or a minimum sentence.[13]

Two other common pretrial proceedings are the *preliminary*

hearing and *arraignment*. "Prelims," as they are called in court-house jargon, serve the same basic purpose as the grand jury session—to determine whether evidence presented by a prosecutor as part of an information is sufficient to warrant a trial. A preliminary hearing differs from a grand jury session in that a judge makes the determination of probable cause. On advice of their lawyers, some defendants waive the right to a preliminary hearing, knowing that the prosecutor's office can easily establish probable cause for prosecution. Rather than go through the formalities of a hearing, the defense attorney and the prosecutor's office simply get down to the business of a negotiated plea and sentence. In other instances, the defense may see the preliminary hearing as an opportunity to assess the strength of the prosecutor's case. If weaknesses are apparent, the defense could use them to its advantage during plea negotiations or, if need be, at the trial.

When the news media's interest in a case is particularly high, the pressure may convince the judge to ban the press and public from preliminary hearings. A judge who closes a preliminary hearing generally does so out of fear that prospective jurors might be prejudiced by the incriminating evidence presented by the prosecutor, including hearsay testimony, which is not admissible in a trial. The preliminary hearing often is a critical stage in the criminal justice process. Important pretrial motions to suppress evidence, for example, might be heard; conditions and agreements might be reached among the judge, defense and prosecution. With so many criminal cases ending in negotiated pleas, the preliminary hearing may be the last opportunity for journalists to hear evidence and rulings in a case.

The *arraignment* usually comes after an indictment is rendered or following a preliminary hearing. At a typical arraignment, the judge formally reads the charges, explains the consequences of a guilty plea or conviction, asks the accused to enter a plea and, if the plea is not guilty, sets a trial date. At this point, discovery generally becomes effective, although rules and procedures vary. *Discovery* in civil law and discovery in criminal law share a common purpose of a two-way exchange of relevant information, evidence and documents.

Several types of plea are possible under criminal law. Some defendants stand silent or *mute* before the judge, who then enters a not guilty plea on the defendant's behalf. A *nolo contendere* plea is permitted in federal courts and certain state courts. Sometimes called a "no contest plea," a nolo contendere technically is not an admission of guilt and therefore cannot be used against a defendant in any civil actions related to the criminal case. Some states permit a plea of *not guilty by reason of insanity*, which often is used in murder cases. The plea has been used successfully by a battered wife accused of killing an abusive husband and by a young mother who twice killed her newborn daughters. It is a controversial plea, largely because the public perceives it as a convenient escape route for someone who has committed a terrible crime.

Although the likelihood of a trial increases for arraigned defendants who plead not guilty, negotiations between the prosecution and defense may continue, leading to a last-minute guilty plea.

Covering the Criminal Courts

Few criminal cases go to trial. In some jurisdictions, up to 90 percent end either in dismissal of charges or a negotiated plea of guilty—a *plea bargain.* To court critics, plea bargaining is an unsavory term; it suggests that criminals are getting off easy, which, indeed, sometimes happens. Without plea bargaining, though, legal experts agree that U.S. courts would be hopelessly snarled by a backlog of cases.

Building additional courtrooms and expanding the judiciary might reduce the number of plea bargains. But if more defendants enter the corrections pipeline as a result, what happens at the destination, where there are too few prison cells? Building more prisons would, in turn, ease pressure on the courts. Nevertheless, increasing the capacity and efficiency of the criminal justice system would not eliminate the need for plea bargaining. At times, there is little choice but to plea bargain. If, for example, the prosecution concludes that jurors will not believe a rape victim's story, a negotiated guilty plea on a reduced charge and sentence might be the only means to impose sanctions on the assailant in some way. Under such circumstances, a plea bargain can appear to be unfair to the victim; that is why reporters should insist that prosecutors explain their reasons for a negotiated plea. Occasionally, prosecutors intentionally overcharge a defendant, citing as many offenses as possible, to encourage a guilty plea on a proper charge. By overcharging, prosecutors will argue they actually are not "bargaining away" anything.

Despite what prosecutors say about plea bargaining, injustices are bound to occur, considering the high number of cases being negotiated within an already pressured, overburdened system. Realistically, too much is going on in most courthouses for any one reporter to monitor. But studying patterns and tapping the court-house grapevine ought to reveal serious improprieties. Reporters, again, should persist in seeking explanations and particulars whenever charges are dropped or reduced, holding judges and attorneys accountable for their actions. Be aware that negotiated pleas are not always a "bargain" for defendants, some of whom receive bad legal advice and are pressured into a guilty plea. Consider, too, what happens when a defendant rejects a negotiated plea. Defense attorneys believe certain judges and prosecutors go harder on defendants who insist on a jury trial.

Obviously, these are potentially volatile subjects to raise with judges or prosecutors; you can anticipate that some of them will express outrage if their motives and integrity are questioned. But to effectively monitor the courts, reporters must be aggressive, as officials of the Virginia State Bar urged at a seminar for news media: "Responsible journalists wouldn't dream of being satisfied with a partial and inadequate knowledge of either the legislature or the executive. Certainly, no seasoned journalist would ever admit to being awed, intimidated or mystified by the legislative or executive branches. The court system should be no different."[14] By asking tough questions, reporters usually serve the best interests of all concerned—the public, victims, defendants and officers of the courts. On the other hand, what interests are served by simply reporting that the "defendant pled guilty to reduced charges"?

A crucial part of a court reporter's job is to maintain close contact with judges, who, of all officers of the court, can appear—and sometimes are—the most intimidating. Although a few judges refuse to talk to reporters under any circumstances, many, if approached properly, will answer questions of clarification or provide off-the-record guidance and background for reporters. It would be appropriate, for example, for a reporter to ask: "Judge Baker, would you explain what an adjournment in contemplation of dismissal entails? Is that like a no contest plea?" Be forewarned, however, that it is ethically improper for a judge to offer comments or opinion that might influence the outcome of *any* pending case; in fact, most judges would find it highly improper for journalists to solicit such comments. However, no amount of indignation on a judge's part should deter reporters from asking questions meant to hold the judge accountable for his or her actions on the bench.

Court reporters must also work closely with attorneys in the criminal courts. In state court systems, persons who hold the title *prosecuting attorney* or *state's attorney* generally are elected to office and, therefore, pay attention to public opinion and press relations. The chief prosecutor can be an important source of information and commentary, but he or she is not likely to be in the thick of courtroom action. On a daily basis, you can expect to turn more often to assistant prosecutors, who do most of the courtroom work. Defense attorneys are either in private practice or serve as *public defenders,* who are employed by the state to represent indigent defendants. In most jurisdictions, the chief public defender is an elected official, accustomed to dealing with reporters.

For the most part, success at communicating with courthouse personnel depends on a reporter's personal reputation for accuracy and fair play. The extent and conditions of your communication with attorneys will vary from individual to individual and case to case. Some attorneys enjoy holding corridor press conferences; others prefer to talk quietly for background only; still others beg off entirely. Often, ethical considerations or office politics limit what attorneys say to the press; less frequently, attorneys are prohibited from talking about a case by a judge's restrictive order to curb potentially prejudicial publicity.

Intelligent questions rarely upset lawyers; dumb ones usually do. Defense attorney M. Hatcher Norris cautions reporters to avoid asking, "Is your client guilty?" "It's the worst question," he says. "What am I going to say? 'He's guilty as hell?' You don't really expect that answer, do you?" Norris further advises: "Don't ask us to characterize the evidence or witnesses. You're not going to get an answer. All you're doing is turning off the lawyer."[15]

A broad network of sources includes those in less lofty positions, such as court clerks, bailiffs and court reporters. Employees in the chief clerk's office not only help court reporters obtain case files. They also compile data and maintain calendars of court dates, usually called *dockets.* In addition, the clerk of the court may issue detailed monthly reports on the disposition of cases. As courts increasingly go to computerized records, it is becoming easier for reporters to keep track of particular cases and to study trends and larger issues based on statistics kept by the clerk's office.

Bailiffs aid judges and supervise courtrooms. When court is in session, the bailiff often seats the jury, announces the judge's entrance, maintains order, guards the courtroom doors, arranges seating for spectators and escorts witnesses to and from the courtroom.

Befriend bailiffs. If so inclined, a bailiff can keep reporters informed, such as explaining why a trial is late in starting, when a particular witness is expected to be called or what issue the judge and attorneys probably are discussing in the judge's chambers. Bailiffs will not be inclined to confide in reporters they barely know or ones they feel are asking them to be disloyal to *their* judge.

Stenographers called *court reporters* are responsible for keeping a verbatim transcript of courtroom proceedings. Journalists who miss a portion of important testimony might convince the court reporter to repeat what was said. Since rules in some jurisdictions prohibit reporters from bringing a tape recorder into the courtroom, the court reporter's record becomes all the more important. If you are a stranger, it is much easier for the court reporter to say, "I'm sorry. I don't have the time." Complete transcripts of proceedings often can be purchased, but generally the cost and time of preparation negate their value as a news tool.

Periodically, visit offices and talk to courthouse personnel informally, not strictly in connection with a particular case or problem. You do not want to acquire a reputation as a reporter who comes around only "to get something."

Be prepared to wait for justice to be served; it is often behind schedule. Reporters find themselves spending precious minutes and hours in frustration, waiting for the judge and attorneys to get on with business. Court watchers attribute some delays to a condition called "courthouse time." If a hearing is scheduled to begin at 9 a.m., it may be 30 to 40 minutes before everyone is prepared to proceed. Delays apply to trials as well, but there is a tendency for judges and attorneys to be less punctual at pretrial hearings.

Pretrial proceedings tend to be relatively informal. The judge may wander in and out of the courtroom, engaging in small talk. The attorneys may kid each other and exchange documents, seemingly oblivious to the defendant, slouching in a nearby chair. At some pretrial or post-trial hearings, defendants may be manacled and dressed in sneakers and jail jumpsuit. You can expect a more serious tone and approach by all participants at a trial.

Although the number of civil and criminal cases going to trial represents a mere fraction of total business before the courts, trials often receive disproportionately high attention from the public and press. The trial—most notably the jury trial—still epitomizes the American system of justice both in terms of public perception and legal principle. Chapter 8, therefore, concentrates on trials.

EXERCISES

1. Try to follow a civil case from its beginnings. It may test your persuasive powers, but see if you can convince a local attorney to let you observe what goes into the filing of a lawsuit. For as long as your schedule permits, follow the case as it moves through the judicial system.

2. Ask the clerk of the court to arrange for you to review the records of a recently completed civil or criminal case that went to trial. Be prepared to wade through hundreds of pages of documents. Remember that the record probably will not include a transcript of the trial proceedings, which generally is prepared only when a case is being forwarded to an appellate court. Even without the trial transcript, the record should be substantial and interesting.

3. Interview a federal or state judge. Some may deny your request, but with persistence, you will obtain an interview. You might ask a local reporter to suggest an approachable judge. Be sure to avoid talking about any pending cases in the judge's jurisdiction. But talking about points of law and the judge's past experiences would be proper. After the interview, observe the judge in court. Drawing on information from the interview and your courtroom observation, produce a profile of the judge.

NOTES

[1] Ellen Goodman, *Making Sense* (New York: Atlantic Monthly Press, 1989), pp. 71, 72.

[2] Lyle W. Denniston, *The Reporter and the Law: Techniques of Covering the Courts* (New York: Hastings House, 1980), p. 52.

[3] See Thomas B. Littlewood, *Coals of Fire: The* Alton Telegraph *Libel Case* (Carbondale, Ill.: Southern Illinois University Press, 1988), pp. 6, 7.

[4] *USA Today,* Oct. 9, 1989, p. 3.

[5] William P. Statsky, *Legal Research, Writing and Analysis* (St. Paul, Minn.: West, 1974), pp. 392–394.

[6] Don Fry and Karen Brown, eds., *Best Newspaper Writing 1990* (St. Petersburg, Fla.: Poynter Institute for Media Studies, 1990), p. 170.

[7] Fred W. Friendly and Martha J.H. Elliott, *The Constitution: That Delicate Balance* (New York: Random House, 1984), p. 85.

[8] *Seattle Times v. Rhinehart,* 467 U.S. 20 (1984).

[9] Robert E. Drechsel, *News Making in the Trial Courts* (New York: Longman, 1983), p. 87.

[10] Paul L. McGorrian, "How Loud? $30,000 Worth," *St. Petersburg Times,* April 25, 1989, sec. B, p. 1.

[11] David Shaw, "Media Coverage of the Courts: Improving But Still Not Adequate," *Judicature*, June—July 1981, p. 19.

[12] See *In re Search Warrant for Secretarial Area*, 855 F.2d 569 (8th Cir. 1988), and *Times Mirror Corp. v. United States*, 873 F.2d 1210 (9th Cir. 1989).

[13] E.W. Single, "The Consequences of Pretrial Detention," a paper presented to the American Sociological Association, New Orleans, 1984, cited in Leonard Territo, James Halsted and Max Bromley, *Crime and Justice in America*, 2nd ed. (St. Paul, Minn.: West, 1989), p. 302.

[14] "Legal Aspects of Reporting and Editing News" Virginia State Bar, 1984, p. 5.

[15] *A Journalist's Guide to Federal Criminal Procedure* (Chicago: American Bar Association, 1988) (videotape).

Chapter Eight

Leona Helmsley's trial for tax evasion was one of a number of "Big Show" trials that dominated the news in 1989. Here she is seen attracting media attention as she leaves the courthouse. (R. Maiman/Sygma)

The Trial
and Thereafter

Every year seems to bring its share of sensational trials. But 1989 set a standard for scandal and melodrama—some of it soap-opera vintage.

Early that year, White House aide Oliver North stood trial for selling arms to Iran, using the profits to aid the Contras in Nicaragua and then lying to Congress. The summer sizzled with television evangelist Jim Bakker answering to charges of defrauding his flock and Leona Helmsley, self-crowned "queen" of luxury hotels, facing a jury of "commoners" who found her guilty of tax evasion. Zsa Zsa Gabor discovered that her histrionics could not convince jurors she had a right to slap a patrolman for giving her a traffic ticket. Miami police wearing anti-riot gear and armed with semi-automatic weapons tensely awaited the verdict on manslaughter charges against a fellow officer, accused of killing two black men during an earlier outbreak of racial violence. The guilty verdict touched off celebrations, not riots, in the black community. As 1989 demonstrated, the criminal trial is the Big Show—the judicial system's scene stealer.

When most people picture a trial, they imagine suspense, tears, angry shouts of "Objection, your honor, objection!" and, perhaps, a surprise, last-minute confession. Real-life trials often fail to resemble the Hollywood versions; they may move slowly and dryly, generating few sparks of excitement or nuggets of news. But since only a select handful of cases go to trial, there is usually legal significance and human interest—or both—in all trials.

Covering a trial is not easy, especially for newcomers to the court beat. While the judicial process itself is relatively uncomplicated, the legal strategy at work and the testimony of witnesses can be difficult to understand and report. Trial coverage also, at times, puts reporters in the position of trying to serve the public's right to know under the First Amendment without doing harm to a defendant's Sixth Amendment rights to a fair trial.

The verdict does not end the reporter's role or responsibility. Although news coverage tends to wane after a trial concludes, in many instances the human drama and legal maneuvers go on for years in a legal purgatory of motions and appeals.

THE BIG SHOW

If the trial resembles theater, then most reporters cover productions of the Community Players rather than Broadway extravaganzas. Although the settings and the characters change, civil and criminal trials follow a similar format. Certain cases, *bench trials,* are tried by a judge alone. Without a jury to impress, attorneys in a bench trial tend to be more restrained and less demonstrative. As a result, bench trials usually lack the tension and clashes of jury trials.

Defendants in criminal trials are constitutionally guaranteed a "speedy" trial, and in applying that guarantee most courts stipulate that cases are supposed to be tried within 60 to 180 days, unless the defendant seeks a *continuance* (delay) or agrees to a delay requested by the prosecution. Civil trials usually are not required to begin within a set number of days.

Once a judge is assigned to a case (which in some jurisdictions means being chosen by lot) and the trial date is set, the next step is jury selection. The trial itself commences with opening statements by the attorneys, followed by presentation of evidence, examination of witnesses, closing arguments, jury deliberation and the verdict or judgment. The sequence of these steps, however, may differ from court to court.

The Jury

In theory, the jury is the cornerstone of the judicial process; in practice, the jury system has weaknesses. One is public apathy; too many people try too hard to stay off juries, citing a litany of excuses when called to serve. Moreover, attorneys may try to remove potential jurors whom they consider too educated, individualistic or assertive for fear they might unduly influence fellow jurors. As one textbook for law students advises, "You want jurors whose minds can be molded."[1]

Concern over pretrial publicity also works against selection of well-informed jurors. Consider the jury selected to hear the Oliver North case in 1989. According to published reports, the 12 jurors and six alternates selected showed little interest in or understanding of national news and knew only the sketchiest details about the highly publicized Iran-Contra scandal of the Reagan administration.[2] In one observer's opinion, a typical jury consists of "twelve prejudiced, gullible dolts incapable of understanding evidence or law involved in a case."[3]

That assessment is too harsh and apparently unfounded. In *The American Jury*, a classic study of more than 3,500 trials, Harry Kalven Jr. and Hans Zeisel found that in about 80 percent of the criminal and civil cases examined, judges agreed with jury verdicts. So despite criticism about who serves on juries and how they are chosen, more often than not, those 12 ordinary citizens listen, weigh evidence, deliberate and reach reasonable, fair decisions.[4]

The normal size for a trial jury, called a *petit jury*, is either six or 12 persons, depending on the type of case and rules governing particular jurisdictions. Several alternates are also selected in case illness or an emergency forces one or more of the original jurors to withdraw from the case. Jurors usually are selected from a pool of residents whose names are drawn from the roll of registered voters. Potential jurors, called *veniremen*, are welcomed by the judge, who may tell them about the case and question them before allowing attorneys to do their own questioning.

The process of selecting a jury is called *voir dire*, a term that means "to speak the truth." Voir dire is an examination by the court to test the competence, ability and impartiality of persons called to serve as jurors. During voir dire, attorneys for either side may exercise a number of *peremptory challenges* to "excuse" (remove) a venireman "without cause." Attorneys can cite an unlimited number of challenges "for cause," provided the judge agrees there is a good reason to doubt a venireman's ability to be fair and impartial. At voir dire, certain types of questions are standard. In criminal cases, for example, defense attorneys are likely to ask questions like these: "Do you know any party involved in this case?" "Have you ever been a crime victim?" "Have you read or heard news media accounts of the case?"

As attorneys question and challenge potential jurors, they may apply a mixture of science and intuition. In major cases, law firms sometimes hire psychologists specializing in jury selection to provide attitude surveys, computerized juror profiles and demographic charts. But hunches and stereotypes still prevail, even among attorneys who use scientific methods. Some prosecutors, for example, prefer black jurors, assuming that as residents of high-crime areas, they are steadfastly in favor of law and order. Conversely, other attorneys assume that blacks mistrust or dislike police officers and therefore will give more credence to the defendant's story. Something as inconclusive and subjective as body language or the tone of a venireman's voice might prompt an attorney to use a peremptory challenge. Several U.S. Supreme Court opinions, however, prohibit attorneys from using peremptory challenges to exclude potential jurors because of their race.

For high-profile trials, reporters cover the jury selection carefully, reporting the occupations and backgrounds of those selected. The composition of the jury may be an important issue as the trial unfolds or later on appeal, particularly if the defense claims the defendant's constitutional right to a trial by an impartial jury was violated.

In a celebrated case, a judge may try to protect jurors from outside pressure by keeping personal details, especially phone numbers and addresses, confidential. In rare instances, jury selection is conducted behind closed doors. Whenever a judge denies access to proceedings or trial-related information, news organizations should protest and seek legal assistance. But it is wrong to automatically condemn the judge's action; extenuating circumstances may put the jurors or the trial itself in jeopardy, possibly outweighing the public's right to know.

A jury selection and other pretrial steps offer reporters an opportunity to introduce the trial's main cast, especially the judge and the attorneys, and set the stage for what is to follow. Just after jury selection in the trial of Wayne Williams, suspected as the killer of 28 children and young adults in Atlanta, the *Chicago Tribune* painted this profile of Williams' chief defense attorney:

> ATLANTA—Alvin Binder is a lawyer who looks as though he stepped from the pages of a novel. He is a big showboat of a man who smokes expensive cigars from Chicago and calls young women "little lady."

There is substance behind all this style, says a private investigator who works with him.

In fact, some say, Alvin Binder is as smart as a professor and can be as tough as a junkyard dog that wags its tail before it attacks.

The story also included observations about the other attorneys in the case, the judge and background details, including reference to the judge's order that reporters not publish the names and addresses of the jurors selected. The *Tribune*'s reporter, Charles Madigan, remained on the scene to cover the trial as it unfolded.

Opening Statements

As law's Big Show, the trial becomes a dramatic production with the participants as actors, whether they care to play the role or not. The outcome of a trial is supposed to be determined by the jury's detached, logical assessment of the facts, evidence and testimony. As humans, though, jurors react to emotional arguments as well as reasoned rhetoric.

A prosecutor's or defense attorney's dramatic performance can be pivotal in an otherwise weak case. Although it may seem unprofessional for attorneys to perform for juries, it happens. The equivalent of acting classes for lawyers offers instruction on the importance of gestures, inflection, timing, props and attire. Occasionally, a "shadow" jury that matches the demographic-psychological profile of the actual jury is hired so the attorneys can rehearse opening statements and examination of witnesses, measure the shadow jurors' reactions and then, if necessary, adjust their strategy or delivery. An attorney's polished, eloquent performance might bomb with some juries; an "Aw-shucks,-I'm-just-a-good-ole-boy-myself" style might work best, unless jurors perceive it as an act.

Regardless of the style and approach used, opening statements must be confined to the facts and evidence that will be presented. In a criminal case, the prosecutor uses the opening statement to tell the jury how he or she intends to prove the defendant guilty "beyond a reasonable doubt." Court rules may permit the defendant's attorney to delay an opening statement until the prosecution presents its witnesses and evidence. Either side may waive the right to an opening statement.

The opening statement gives reporters a clearer idea of how the trial will unfold. In that sense, it is somewhat like a play program, listing the cast and scenes to follow. A word of caution: Guard against inflating the importance of opening statements or any other in-court remarks by the attorneys. Their rhetoric may be spellbinding, but it is not evidence, which is something jurors and reporters alike sometimes forget.

Evidence and Witnesses

The main act of a trial is presentation of evidence and examination of witnesses. In criminal cases, the prosecution begins this stage of the trial; in civil cases, the plaintiff's counsel goes first, calling its witnesses for *direct examination.* In direct examination, each side, in turn, carefully asks questions of its own witnesses and experts to elicit testimony, building a chain of arguments in an attempt to lead jurors to a logical conclusion. The prosecution, for example, typically calls the arresting officer as a witness, asking such questions as, "Please describe what you saw when you arrived at the bank and saw a holdup in progress." There is an unwritten rule for attorneys in direct examination: Never ask a question unless you know what your witness is going to answer. Such answers become known before the trial from the lawyer's interviews with witnesses or depositions taken under oath.

After direct examination, the opposing side is entitled to conduct *cross-examination* of the same witnesses. A goal of cross-examination is to *impeach* (discredit) the credibility of witnesses and devalue the evidence. During cross-examination, questioning can get rough, as it did when a prosecutor cross-examined a 42-year-old woman accused of abandoning her newborn child in a trash dumpster. The prosecutor picked up a photograph of the woman's kitchen and began to question her:

> *Prosecutor:* "This is your kitchen?"
> *Woman:* "Yeah, it looks like it."
> *Prosecutor:* "When those kittens were born in that kitchen, you didn't put them in a box and throw them in a dumpster, did you?"
> *Defense attorney:* "Objection, your honor! He is goading the witness, and it's totally irrelevant."
> *Judge:* "Objection overruled."

> *Prosecutor:* "You didn't get rid of those kittens when they were born, did you?"
>
> *Woman:* "Oh, no, sir."
>
> *Prosecutor:* "That baby wanted you, didn't it? You held it?"
>
> *Woman:* "Only enough to clean it up."
>
> *Prosecutor:* "And then you just got rid of it and threw it like trash by the dumpster, right?"[5]

Exchanges between attorneys and witnesses usually are not so dramatic, but when they do reach this level of intensity, reporters can quote directly and let the participants' words best capture the moment.

Throughout the trial, the judge functions, in part, as a referee; that role is most apparent in witness examination, as the judge is often asked to either *sustain* or *overrule* objections from the attorneys. Many objections center on a witness's *hearsay* testimony or an attorney's *leading* questions.

Cross-examination may be followed by *redirect examination* and *recross examination.* The same process is followed when the defendant's witnesses and evidence are presented. Among those called to testify may be victims, plaintiffs (civil cases), experts and defendants, although in criminal trials, defendants can refuse to testify under the constitutional protection against self-incrimination.

Not all that occurs during presentation of evidence is obvious or spoken; some attorneys try to impress the jury with subtle, nonverbal messages. For example, a factory worker suing over a job-related spinal injury gets these directions from his attorney: "Take your time getting to the witness stand. Let the jurors see how you walk. And bring along that cushion you use at home to sit on." Attorneys sometimes test the limits of propriety in trying to influence the jury. A prosecutor may play to the jury by dramatically handling and snapping shut a sawed-off shotgun used in a murder; another attorney may roll his eyes in mock disbelief as the opposition tries to make a point. Alert judges usually admonish attorneys who distract or disrupt courtrooms through overly dramatic behavior.

Closing Arguments

Closing arguments are characterized by impassioned appeals to the jury, or so people come to expect from fictional trials. In reality, not all closing arguments are moments of high drama, but they do give each side the opportunity to make a final impression before jury deliberations begin.

In their closing arguments, attorneys cannot stray beyond the issues or evidence presented in the trial. Each attorney usually tries to accentuate arguments that best support his or her position. If the judge gives *instructions* to the jury prior to closing arguments, the attorneys might also comment on the instructions and indicate how they apply to the evidence. Defense attorneys in criminal cases normally remind jurors that they must find the accused "guilty beyond a reasonable doubt" otherwise the verdict must be "not guilty." The goal of the defense is to plant the seeds of doubt; the prosecutor tries to remove doubt.

The plaintiff's attorney (or, in criminal cases, the prosecutor) goes first with a closing argument, followed by the defendant's attorney. The plaintiff's attorney or prosecutor may also be entitled to the last word—a *rebuttal argument.*

The Decision

Juries deliberate in secret. On occasion jurors are *sequestered* for the entire trial, which normally means they are confined to hotel rooms while not in court, isolated from family or other outside influence, such as news media coverage. The jurors are under the strict supervision of a bailiff or officer of the court. A jury also may be sequestered when its deliberations go longer than a day. Any attempt by outsiders to communicate with jurors is a serious matter and could lead to a *mistrial.* During the trial of John Poindexter, President Reagan's national security adviser who allegedly lied to Congress in the Iran-Contra affair, a *Washington Post* reporter contacted several jurors to set up post-verdict interviews. The judge reacted angrily: "The reporter, we are told, just came back from Lebanon and didn't know the ground rules. If anyone . . . in government gave such a lame excuse, the press would be justifiably scornful and sarcastic."[6] Reporters, like everyone else connected with a case, must wait until the jury reaches a decision, no matter how long that takes.

The judge usually gives the jury its instructions after closing arguments. Although some jury instructions are "patterned" (standardized) to apply to an entire category of cases, judges usually are free to explain the jury's responsibilities in more detail. For example, the jury hearing the libel trial of Israeli general Ariel Sharon against

Time magazine received a 64-page set of instructions from Abraham Sofaer, the presiding judge. Sofaer's instructions, in fact, helped clarify the question of "fault" in libel law and thereby became an important sidebar story in coverage of the verdict.[7]

Reaching a decision is rarely easy for jurors, and it can be particularly agonizing in criminal cases. In a three- or four-day trial, the evidence and testimony might be sufficiently clear and convincing for a verdict to be reached in a matter of hours. Longer, more involved and less clear cases can take days to decide. After a period of time, the judge might recall the *foreman*, chosen by vote of the jurors at the outset of deliberations, to determine the jury's progress. At this point, the judge might decide to issue "blockbuster" or "dynamite" instructions, which urge the jury to do its duty and reach a verdict. For criminal cases, a verdict must be unanimous in most states. In civil law, a verdict or judgment may require agreement of only two-thirds or three-quarters of the jury. In the event of a *hung jury* that simply cannot reach agreement, a judge could be forced to declare a mistrial, which allows for the case to be retried.

Bench trials conclude with a judge's *finding*, which, at times, can be more suspenseful than a jury verdict because the judge is not compelled to decide immediately. Suspense might build for days or weeks before the finding is announced.

REPORTING TRIALS

A trial unfolds in snatches of testimony and pieces of evidence. Each day brings its own news, but the news may be hard to detect. It is not like covering a baseball game. At a trial, who is scoring or striking out is not always obvious.

With experience—and with insight provided by knowledgeable judicial sources—court reporters learn to recognize key testimony, evidence and strategy. Do not be embarrassed to seek help from court personnel and attorneys before, during and after a trial. Veteran court reporters sometimes get unsolicited tips. At the outset of a criminal trial, for example, the prosecutor approaches a reporter and says, "This is going to be an interesting case. We're bringing in the leading forensics expert on teeth-mark identification. You ought to catch her testimony." A judge presiding in a medical malpractice case volunteers: "The defendant is scheduled to take the stand after our noon recess. That ought to be lively."

Reporters with especially good contacts sometimes are able to discuss strategies or game plans with the attorneys involved. A few attorneys will open the door for fuller discussions of the case by asking reporters for informal opinions: "How am I doing? How do you think the jury reacted to my cross-examination of the victim's wife?" As a trial progresses, there may be many casual, off-the-record conversations between reporters and the judge or attorneys. The off-the-record stipulation may not be stated outright; it is one of those presumably "understood" conditions by which reporters and sources operate. To be safe and fair, reporters ought to know where everyone stands with regard to any conversations related to a trial. Whenever in doubt, always check with sources before quoting them by name in a news report.

A typical trial story opens with the most important development of the day; usually the focus is on testimony. Here is how Linda Deutsch, who covers major trials for the Associated Press, began one day's coverage of the tanker *Exxon Valdez* oil spill case tried in 1990:

> ANCHORAGE, Alaska—The skipper of the *Exxon Valdez* thought the seaman who was at the tanker's helm when it ran aground had problems steering and warned others to watch over him, the ship's second mate testified Wednesday.
>
> Both Capt. Joseph Hazelwood and third mate Gregory Cousins talked about problems with Robert Kagan's steering of the ship, second mate Lloyd LeCain Jr. testified at Hazelwood's trial.
>
> "How would you rate Mr. Kagan's abilities?" the prosecutor asked LeCain.
>
> "I'd say slightly below normal," LeCain said.

Included in nearly all trial stories is a *review of the charges or legal issues involved*, a *summary of past developments* and a *preview of what is expected to occur as the trial continues.*

In another report on the Hazelwood trial, Deutsch helped readers easily see a pattern in past testimony and evidence:

> ANCHORAGE, Alaska—The *Exxon Valdez* could well have been an accident waiting to happen, according to testimony at the ship captain's trial.
>
> When the ship ran aground March 23, 1989, spilling 10.92 million gallons of oil into Prince William Sound, it carried:

- A helmsman, Robert Kagan, who had well-known problems with steering.

- A second mate, Lloyd LeCain, who allegedly had a history of mental problems. Capt. Joseph Hazelwood's defense attorneys have said LeCain boasted of being a submarine commander in the Falklands War, a Green Beret in Vietnam and a figure in the Iran-Contra affair.

- Hazelwood, who has a history of drunken driving convictions and is accused of being intoxicated the night of the spill.

As the prosecution ended its second week of evidence and prepared to wrap up its case, a picture emerged of a cohesive navigational team strengthened by highly educated and experienced officers but weakened by a troubled few.

Readable, informative trial stories also provide context and color. The context is provided through background information and history not found in the day-to-day testimony: Are the litigants in a civil suit former business partners? Is this case likely to set a legal precedent? Is there a connection between the present case and ones of the past? Color coverage focuses on the personalities, setting and mood of the trial—an Ivy League defense attorney versus the homespun prosecutor; the history of the old courtroom; the tension evident as the victim's and defendant's relatives glare at each other from opposite sides of the aisle.

At the conclusion of the trial, coverage continues as reporters attempt to elicit reaction from everyone connected with the case, including the jurors. In celebrated cases, some judges feel obliged to shield dismissed jurors from the press, telling them it would be "best not to answer" reporters' questions about the case. Convincing jurors that they have a *right to speak* to reporters may prove difficult, but always try; the results are often well worth the effort. When the nation's longest criminal trial—a complex child-molestation case involving a Los Angeles preschool—ended early in 1990, seven members of the jury met with reporters. The director of the school and her son had just been acquitted on 52 counts of child molestation, and the jurors attempted to explain why. One juror said, "I believe the children believed what they were saying was true in the courtroom." But she added that she was not sure that "the children were telling what actually happened to them or if they were repeating what they were told by their parents and other people."[8] By talking to jurors, reporters come closer to knowing what unfolded in the jury room. Your questions, for example, might reveal that several jurors felt pressured to go along with the verdict or, as in the preschool trial, that some objected to the way investigators handled the case.

Responsible journalists are keenly aware that what they report and how they conduct themselves in dealing with court officials and participants can affect the outcome of a highly publicized trial. For example, publishing or broadcasting an incriminating story about the defendant's past troubles with the police either before or during the trial might expose jurors to prejudicial information. Do you publish? When? Whose interest is paramount, the defendant's right to a fair trial or the public's right to know? The *Buffalo News* faced a similarly difficult choice in a murder trial, deciding to publish a profile of the defendant despite the judge's request to withhold publication until the trial ended. The judge declared a mistrial and blamed the newspaper.[9]

Did the *Buffalo News* act improperly? There is no "correct" way to handle such a situation. It is highly unlikely that a judge would try to stop publication by legal action; that would be a prior restraint, which is presumed to be unconstitutional. But with the *right* to publish a potentially prejudicial story prior to a trial comes the *responsibility* to seriously consider a story's impact on the case. At the very least, a news organization should have sound, defensible reasons for going with a report that risks a mistrial.

VERDICTS, JUDGMENTS, SENTENCES AND APPEALS

The final scene of the trial is the reading of the verdict. Some verdicts are shocking surprises; some are anticlimactic. Trial's end is not, however, a time for a reporter's coverage to grow lax. Important details are yet to be learned and reported.

Unless deadlocked, juries in criminal trials either find the defendant "guilty" (or guilty of a lesser included charge, such as a manslaughter charge in a murder case) or "not guilty" as charged. In bench trials, the term *finding* commonly is used instead of *verdict.* If the defendant is being tried on multiple charges, the jury might return a guilty verdict on certain counts and a not guilty verdict on others. After returning and reading its verdict, the jury's job usually is over, although certain states ask the jury to recommend punishment or, in a capital murder case, to decide whether the death penalty should be imposed.

For criminal cases, a "not guilty" verdict—an acquittal—ends the case; the prosecutor cannot seek a retrial on the same charges. But if other untried criminal charges are pending against the defendant, the prosecution is permitted to pursue them.

A conviction is likely to prompt one or more post-verdict motions by the defense. Most often, the defense makes a *motion for a new trial,* usually alleging procedural errors committed by the judge, such as allowing the prosecution to make an improper closing argument. Some states require filing of a motion for a new trial to preserve further rights of appeal. Another post-trial motion in both civil and criminal law is an *acquittal* (or judgment) *notwithstanding the verdict.* It asks the judge to disregard the jury's decision and declare a verdict or judgment in the defendant's favor. Since it is a motion judges rarely grant, it is news when accepted by the court.

If the post-trial motion is overruled, sentencing proceeds, with the judge normally asking for a presentencing investigation by state or federal probation officers. Unless the sentence has been negotiated in a plea-bargain agreement, there may be an *aggravation and mitigation hearing* to determine whether circumstances justify stiffer or lesser punishment. Because of mandatory sentencing rules, judges in both federal and state courts increasingly have less discretion in deciding on punishment. In some jurisdictions, being convicted of a serious crime—no matter who committed it and no matter what the circumstances—brings a set mandatory prison sentence with no possible probation, parole or early release. When judges do retain discretion, the presentencing report provides information about such factors as the defendant's criminal history, family situation, employment and prospects for rehabilitation. Sentencing on multiple charges may require the judge to decide whether prison terms should be *consecutive* (served in succession) or *concurrent* (served simultaneously).

Most negotiated pleas cover the charge and the sentence. Ordinarily, judges do not participate in plea discussions between the attorneys until a negotiated agreement is reached. Then, both attorneys usually ask the judge to follow the agreed on charge and sentence. Some judges, however, insist, as they should, on checking the facts of the case and the background of the defendant. When defendants object to the prosecutor's proposed sentence, they sometimes opt for an *open plea,* which leaves sentencing up to the judge. If the judge does not accept the negotiated plea agreement, the defendant has the right to withdraw his or her guilty plea and go to trial.

Sentencing

No matter what form it takes, sentencing is not a simple process of meting out punishment. Sentencing guidelines and options are complicated, and reporters should never take this aspect of the criminal process lightly. Watch, especially, for sentencing disparities. Determine whether offenders who commit similar crimes under comparable circumstances receive similar punishment from court to court or judge to judge. Courthouse reporters quickly learn which judges are reputed to be "soft" or "hard" sentencers. But disparities are not always widely known or easy to detect. Sentencing ideally should be consistent, rational and fair; often it is not, being the result of human judgments. One judge, for example, might consider a car thief's drug addiction a mitigating factor and lessen the punishment. But in a courtroom a few doors down the hall, another judge sees the offender's drug addiction as a reason to impose a tougher sentence. Sentencing by its nature attempts to individualize the punishment. Reporters ought to find out about the person sentenced and the judge's reasons for the sentences selected.

Sentencing stories should routinely explain terms and conditions of punishment. To merely report that "Joe Doe received a 10-year sentence" tends to be misleading. Frequently, well-behaved inmates receive credit for days of "good time," which could, in some states, reduce a sentence by 50 percent or more. If you are unsure how much of a 10-year term a convicted bank robber is likely to serve, ask the judge or corrections officials for assistance.

Finally, sentencing stories should, if at all possible, include the reaction of victims, families and offenders. The superficial emotions shown—or suppressed—at a sentencing hearing do not necessarily fully or accurately reflect feelings. Thorough reporters will ask questions sensitively and explore emotions after a sentence is imposed. For negotiated sentences, one question, in particular, should be asked: Did prosecutors and the judge seek reaction or input from the victim or his or her family in arriving at a plea bargain? The answer will likely be no. As courts rush to dispose of criminal cases, those who suffered because of a criminal act are sometimes overlooked. In their coverage, reporters should strive to avoid similar oversights. Victims seldom have any official role apart from that of a witness, although some jurisdictions now have victim-assistance programs and provisions for the victim to be heard at sentencing. It seems fair that they get a chance to comment, at least in news accounts.

Probation

Probation usually is among a judge's sentencing options. With probation, convicted offenders are placed under the supervision of a probation agency instead of being sent to prison. Probation is used in various ways. A judge, for example, could elect to set a burglar's penalty at five years in prison but suspend execution of the sentence, placing him on probation; if probation is revoked, the five-year sentence usually will be immediately executed. Other judges prefer to reserve the option to impose a sentence if probation fails; that approach affords the flexibility to impose a stiffer sentence than ordinarily given for a burglary conviction. Another variation is called *shock probation*, which involves imprisoning an offender briefly to demonstrate the result if he or she violates the terms of probation. Increasingly, electronic transmitting devices, such as unremovable ankle bands, are being used to monitor the whereabouts of probationers, as well as offenders who are on parole or confined at home on "house arrest." Electronic surveillance is not foolproof, but it offers another alternative to imprisonment.

With most prisons so overcrowded, judges regularly confront sentencing dilemmas: Imprisoning a 19-year-old car thief—a first-time offender—may mean that 35-year-old armed robber with a long record gets an early release. With certain offenders, probation is an appropriate penalty. For example, is justice served by breaking up a single-parent family to jail a working mother convicted of passing bad checks? Not surprisingly, 60 to 80 percent of the sentences imposed by the courts involve probation.[10] But probation often backfires, according to national crime statistics. One study found that 65 percent of convicted felons were rearrested, usually for serious crimes, while on probation.[11] The figures suggest that reporters are quite right to question officials rigorously and dig deeper into a case when previously convicted felons receive probation.

Ironically, despite its widespread use—or perhaps because of it—misconceptions about probation persist. Probation is not, as some people think, a free ride. Typically, probationers must submit to no-notice searches and drug tests, report regularly to a *probation officer*, undergo counseling and follow a strict set of rules governing where they can go and with whom they can associate. Often probation officers play the combined roles of detective, social worker and counselor, watching over and caring for perhaps dozens of probationers at any given time. It is a demanding and frequently dangerous job. Reporters ought to know probation officers and appreciate their work.

Parole and Pardons

Very few laypeople know how inmates become eligible for *parole* or a *pardon*, both extremely sensitive but shadowy areas of the corrections system. News organizations generally do an adequate job of monitoring criminal cases through the sentencing stage. But a gap in coverage often occurs when it comes to parole or other forms of early release based on good behavior and prospects for rehabilitation. Parole is a continuation of the sentence—but outside of prison confinement. A pardon is an absolution of guilt and punishment for a crime and usually entails no conditions.

In a handful of cases, the parole or pardon process receives thorough coverage, such as the case of Sirhan Sirhan, who has sought early release several times since being convicted of the 1968 assassination of Robert Kennedy. But most often, it seems, the press ignores paroles and early releases until something goes wrong. A classic case was the early release of a convicted murderer named Willie Horton, who slashed a Maryland man and raped the man's fiancée after escaping on a furlough (a leave) from a Massachusetts prison. In the 1988 presidential campaign, George Bush repeatedly criticized his rival, Massachusetts governor Michael Dukakis, for that state's system, which allowed Horton out of prison.

Parole and pardon boards operate outside the normal parameters of the court beat, because parole is a function of the executive branch, not the judiciary. Who, then, covers parole boards—a legal reporter or a government reporter? Sometimes no one, which is why reporters covering the court beat ought to check personally—or through a colleague—the activities of parole and pardon boards at least monthly. Parole boards generally include representatives of the state department of corrections and professionals qualified to weigh parole requests. The process of deciding parole requests can be quite subjective and the criteria used vague or non-existent. Given the horror stories about freed convicts who, on release, return to a life of crime, parole and pardon decisions should be watched closely. Reporters, however, can anticipate obstacles. A number of states permit closure of meetings and records of parole and pardon boards in the name of privacy rights.

Civil Verdicts and Judgments

As in criminal law, several motions usually follow the conclusion of a civil trial. These legal requests sometimes are required to reserve the right to appeal at a later date. But unlike criminal law with its outcomes of either guilty or not guilty, civil verdicts tend to be more involved. Reporting a civil verdict might include sorting out several types of damages, which are awarded as monetary compensation for losses or injuries to a plaintiff's person, property or rights through the defendant's unlawful act or negligence.

Three common categories of damages are compensatory, actual and punitive, but those terms differ in meaning from jurisdiction to jurisdiction, sometimes causing definitional confusion. In general, *compensatory damages* are awarded to cover losses or injury, including pain, suffering and disability, that are a direct result of the wrongful act. *Actual damages* cover tangible out-of-pocket losses that followed as a natural consequence of the wrongful act. *Punitive damages* are awarded over and above compensatory or actual damages to punish an offender for aggravated, willful misconduct. Another intent of punitive damages is to make an example of civil offenders to deter others from committing similar wrongs. While damages for tangible loss may amount to thousands of dollars, punitive damages often soar into the millions.

Jury awards that seem unrealistically excessive should not be overplayed by the press. The recipients of a $5 million award in a product-liability suit rejoice and celebrate, and news coverage makes them look like winners of a lottery jackpot. Years later, however, the case may still be on appeal and the plaintiffs have yet to receive a penny. Appellate courts frequently find jury awards excessive and reduce them substantially. A California jury, for example, awarded entertainer Carol Burnett $300,000 in actual damages and $1.3 million in punitive damages in her libel suit against the *National Enquirer*, which published a story describing Burnett as drunk and disorderly in a Washington, D.C., restaurant. An appeals court, though, trimmed the actual damages to $50,000 and the punitive damages to $150,000. Burnett and the *National Enquirer* eventually settled out of court, cutting short the cycle of appeals.[12]

In civil law, certain types of litigation do not involve a jury trial. Included under the non-jury category are equity actions, such as requests for an injunction. Regardless of who decides a case, there is usually a way for most court rulings and judicial decisions to be appealed to a higher authority. Whether an appellate court agrees to hear the case is another matter.

Appeals

After cases leave the lower courts on appeal, it is possible for them to disappear into journalism's twilight zone. Reporters who covered a case through the verdict and post-trial motions usually do not follow the case any further, partly because of geography and partly because of limited resources. The trial court may be hundreds of miles away from the nearest appellate court, and while nearly all news organizations cover the local circuit (or district) trial court, few station reporters permanently at appellate or supreme courts. Consequently only the most publicized of cases are thoroughly monitored as they move through the appeals process. Even then, an appeals case may be passed along from reporter to reporter with little continuity in coverage.

The odds of losing track of a case increase if it happens to move from the state courts into the federal courts. (Appeals from a state court to a federal appellate court are possible when there are grounds to argue that the defendant's rights under the federal Constitution have been violated or denied.) Reporters assigned to cover the courts for a news organization need to meet regularly to share ideas and information and, with the aid of editors, coordinate long-term coverage of important cases.

To appeal a case there must be a will and a way. Not all losers in a court case are eager to expend the time, money and energy on an appeal in the hope that somewhere, somehow and sometime they will be vindicated. Some litigants decide enough is enough. Even those with the will and resources to forge ahead may not succeed in obtaining a review of their case. There are few guarantees of an appeal in federal or state courts, although *one* appeal is a matter of statutory right in many jurisdictions. Most often there must be grounds for an appeal, and then the parties appealing must convince a court to review the case.

The appeals process usually begins with the appealing party— the *appellant*—filing a *notice of appeal,* a brief statement that may or may not specify the issues or points in question. The notice is followed by preparation of the *record* of the case, which usually includes the trial court's transcripts. The record accompanies the appeal. Normally, the next step is submission of the appellant's *brief*, which is a written argument of the issues to be decided on appeal. The other side—the *appellee*—is given time to file a brief to answer the appellant. After submission of the briefs, the appeals court may hold a hearing for *oral arguments,* at which both sides repeat or clarify points made in their briefs. The oral arguments also give the appellate judges an opportunity to question the attorneys.

Access to the records and proceedings of appeals courts is often broader than access to trial courts. A major reason is the absence of jurors, which, in turn, eliminates concern about the impact of prejudicial publicity. In any event, reporters covering the appeal of a major case should, at minimum, examine the briefs and attend the oral arguments. Particularly important cases might include *amici curiae* (friends of the court) briefs, which the appeals court can allow outside, interested parties to submit. The briefs, with their footnotes and numerous citations to other cases, often are as detailed, legalistic and ponderous as law journal articles. The oral arguments, however, can be spirited jousts between and among the judges and the attorneys of record in the case. As veteran court reporter Lyle Denniston notes: "The hearing gives the reporter his first opportunity to gauge the potential reaction of the appeals court to the case." But Denniston quickly cautions that reporters should not assume that how judges react at oral arguments necessarily indicates how they will decide the case.[13] Reporters who study the briefs and attend hearings not only gain newsworthy information; they also prepare themselves for explanatory reporting once the appeals court reaches a decision.

A case, however, may linger in an appeals court for months before the outcome is announced. The outcome seldom is a landmark ruling; in fact, it could amount to an anticlimactic non-ruling, such as a simple confirmation of the lower court's decision without comment. Unless an appellate decision is announced with what amounts to a flourish of trumpets, reporters who are not especially alert and organized in their coverage can easily miss rulings.

The appeals courts—state and federal—deal with newsworthy issues of considerable importance. But some journalists are concerned that appeals courts are not properly covered. John Seigenthaler, editorial director of *USA Today,* commented: "Some news decision-makers have convinced themselves that if the story isn't about fads or fashions or jogging or junk food or polls or personalities, it doesn't touch the lives of readers."[14] Seigenthaler particularly expressed concern about coverage of the federal appellate system—the "anonymous court," as one judge described it. Through interviews with judges and other court officials, Seigenthaler found that most media coverage ranged from "spotty" to "non-existent" to "very superficial" to "shallow at best."[15]

The federal system includes 13 circuits, called U.S. Circuit Courts of Appeal; some of these circuits encompass three or more states. All federal appeals within a circuit go to the circuit court's headquarters, which may be hundreds of miles from the court that originally heard the case and the news organization that originally covered it. In all, the federal appellate courts review approximately 35,000 or more cases a year. News organizations may want to cover the nearest federal appeals court, but the distance separating reporters from the source of the news, together with the size of the task, discourages thorough coverage.

Fortunately, computer technology encourages fuller coverage of all courts. Several courts, for example, are experimenting with electronic bulletin boards that allow reporters to check on rulings and other activities from their offices by use of modems.[16] Computer links with case-reporting data services such as Westlaw or Lexis make it possible for subscribers anywhere to obtain many court opinions soon after they are released.

The final step in the appeals process is the Supreme Court of the United States. Although asked to review as many as 4,000 cases a year by a petition known as a *writ of certiorari*, the Court usually issues full opinions for approximately 150 of these cases. The cases it does decide often are highly significant in both legal and societal terms. The Supreme Court obviously attracts news media attention, and most of its decisions are well publicized. A cadre of a dozen or so experienced reporters covers the U.S. Supreme Court full time. Their stories are widely disseminated through various news services, and, by most accounts, the coverage is quite good. Does that mean, however, that court reporters in Davenport, Iowa, or Bangor, Maine, should leave Supreme Court coverage to others? Reporters who want to keep abreast of legal precedent and measure legal impact will take the time to review the Court's decisions and, if appropriate, relate the Court's decisions to their own readers, listeners or viewers. That job is becoming easier for local reporters. In 1990 the Supreme Court announced a new service to provide near-instantaneous distribution of the entire text of its opinions to news organizations through a non-profit consortium called Supreme Court Opinion Network.[17]

Finding, Reading and Explaining Court Decisions

Many, but not all, decisions of appellate courts are published and collected in volumes called *reporters*. The rulings of trial courts occasionally are "reported"—that is, published—but the vast majority of reported cases come from courts hearing appeals. In some cases, a court's written decisions are first published as *slip opinions*. These are, in a sense, like page proofs. Later the slip opinions are published in final form for inclusion in a bound reporter.

Bound sets of case reporters can be found in courthouses, law offices, universities and libraries. Usually only law school libraries hold a complete collection of federal and state reporters, for there are hundreds of reporters with dozens of volumes. Journalists with access to Lexis or other data-base services can obtain full-text printouts of many federal and state court opinions without a trip to a law library or courthouse. Commercial newsletters, many published by the Bureau of National Affairs, provide weekly digests or full texts of important court decisions in particular branches of law, such as tax law or media law.

Nearly all cases are located and referred to by *citation*, which is a group of names, numbers and abbreviations. An early journalists' privilege case provides a typical citation: *State v. Buchanan*, 250 Ore. 244, 436 P.2d 729 (1968). The citation normally begins by naming the parties involved, with the appellant cited first. The number that follows—250—refers to the volume of *Oregon Reports* (Ore.) that contains the decision. The second number is the page on which the decision begins. For certain cases, there are multiple citations, indicating the case is published in other reporters. *State v. Buchanan*, for example, can be found in one of West Publishing Co.'s regional reports—the *Pacific Reporter*, second series (P.2d). Some reporters and law books are annotated, containing important explanatory notes about a particular case.

Ideally, reporters on the court beat should be well versed in legal research. More practically, what you cannot learn on your own, learn from a legal authority, such as a law school librarian. He or she can introduce you to many methods of examining and assessing the law.

Reading a court decision is not like reading a paperback novel.

Decisions of appellate and supreme courts may be 50 pages or more of legalistic language and complicated arguments. Reporters who skim or flip to the last few pages to find out the outcome invite mistakes of interpretation and meaning. With experience, reading court opinions becomes easier, but it should never be a casual undertaking. A reporter who approaches a court opinion without a clue about its history or significance is asking for trouble.

Most opinions begin with background—the facts, chronology and issues of the case. The background, however, might be sketchy and require augmentation from other sources, such as previously published news stories. The background usually is followed by the court's rationale for its decision. Often, other cases germane to the present case are cited in support of the court's rationale. In stating its rationale, the court typically addresses the various legal arguments raised by the parties in the case, accepting or rejecting those arguments as it deems fit. Opinions generally end with the court's decision, or *holding.* Sometimes the holding is clearly marked in a synopsis of the court's position. In the classic 1964 libel case, *New York Times v. Sullivan,* for example, the Supreme Court said, "We hold today that the Constitution delimits a state's power to award damages for libel in actions brought by public officials against critics of their official conduct."[18] Of course, that summarized statement sheds little light on the importance of the case or the court's rationale. Usually, news stories must go well beyond simply reporting the holding.

The court's decision often includes further action to be taken in regard to the case. The most common actions are to *affirm,* or uphold, the lower court's ruling; to *reverse* the lower court and *remand,* or return, the case for appropriate action, such as a new trial; or reverse the lower court outright, which means there is nothing more to be tried or decided. There are combinations when the court is dealing with cases involving a number of rulings or issues.

The heart of most appeals decisions is the main or *majority opinion.* Appellate court decisions, though, usually involve a panel of three or more judges or justices, so there are bound to be differences of opinion, some of which could be significant and newsworthy. That is especially true of *dissenting opinions,* which reporters should heed and, if appropriate, include in their coverage of a ruling. A full decision might also include one or more *concurring opinions,* which are written by judges who agree with the holding and the action taken by the majority but see the issues or rationale in a different light. In a close vote of an appeals court, a concurring decision could be pivotal and crucial to the outcome of the case.

Poring over the record of a case is important. But useful, explanatory court reporting goes beyond the documents. Robert Coram, formerly a reporter for the *Atlanta Constitution*, reminds us: "Stories that are remembered are not those in which court records are parroted, but rather those in which a knowledgeable reporter went beyond the record and displayed initiative."[19]

SPECIAL COURTS, SPECIAL PROBLEMS

As spectators and reporters flock to a murder trial two floors up, in the basement corner of the courthouse a judge assigned to probate court quietly does her work. Probate is one of several "other" courts that seldom attract much attention. Although often out of the way, special courts deserve coverage. Good stories and features are to be found in special courts, particularly in probate and two other areas—juvenile and bankruptcy courts.

Probate Courts

Each state regulates the disposition of a deceased person's property. The main role of probate court is to judge the validity of wills and supervise the administration of estates. Certainly, reporters will want to check probate court when a renowned citizen dies. News coverage should involve more than merely satisfying the public's curiosity about the lifestyle, money and heirs of the rich and famous. At times, provisions in the will and information about the estate reveal surprising, hidden aspects of the individual's life and relationships. In a sense, the will, if there is one, amounts to a person's last public statement and completes his or her record. Probate court also yields its share of human-interest stories: the apparent pauper who died, it turns out, with a million-dollar stock portfolio or the widow who left her sizable estate to a menagerie of cats, dogs and canaries. There are investigative possibilities, too. Occasionally, *administrators* or *executors*—those entrusted to carry out the will and administer the estate—divert money improperly into their own pockets.

Many people of wealth and power carefully prepare for the passage of property to heirs. When a person's preparation includes a will, it is said that he or she died *testate*; dying without a will is called *intestate.* In the absence of a will, state law provides for how an estate is to be distributed. When a will exists, determining the validity of its content and provisions often presents no problems. But occasionally wills are contested, such as when family members argue that a *codicil*—a modification to an existing will—unfairly changes who gets a share of the estate. Probate judges handle details and disputes over estates without the involvement of a jury.

Another function of probate court is to protect persons who are determined to be incapable of managing their own affairs. Children of elderly parents sometimes face the unhappy but unavoidable step of going to court to establish a mother's or father's incompetence. In such cases, a child, relative or trusted person is appointed *guardian* with the legal power to pay bills, manage property and administer fiscal accounts. It is a position of great trust that most people would never violate, but abuses occur, which is why diligent court reporters should monitor incompetency proceedings.

Juvenile Courts

All states have separate courts for *juveniles,* a designation that typically includes all children under the age of 18. The goal of juvenile courts is to *aid* as opposed to *adjudicate.* People tend to think of juvenile courts as forums for delinquency, and often they are. But juvenile courts deal with other types of cases, such as child abuse, lack of proper medical treatment, truancy and termination of parental rights.

Because juveniles are particularly vulnerable to the negative effects of publicity, the courts traditionally have been quite protective. Some critics will argue that juvenile officials are overly protective. Indeed, with strict confidentiality stressed in most juvenile courts, it is difficult at times for the press to perform its watchdog role.

Some states allow the press access to juvenile proceedings, although prohibitions on disclosure of the juvenile's identity or other confidential information generally apply. Access to records might be limited primarily to law enforcement officials or agencies that deal with juvenile matters. Moreover, paper trails can be wiped clean in jurisdictions that permit *expungement* (removal) of criminal records for juveniles who stay out of further trouble with the law.

Sensitive reporters, of course, consider the welfare of juveniles in their coverage and, most often, honor conditions of confidentiality, even with regard to juveniles accused of committing serious crimes.

Names of juveniles do, though, appear in news accounts. Policies differ among news organizations; moreover circumstances affect decisions to reveal identities. Under the law, however, it appears clear that it is not illegal for reporters to identify juveniles. In two cases in the 1970s, the Supreme Court established that journalists cannot be punished for or prohibited from disclosing lawfully obtained information about juvenile offenders. Civil liability, though, remains a possibility, especially over invasion of a juvenile's privacy.[20]

The toughest disclosure decisions usually involve particularly shocking crimes. The decision-making burden is eased if an accused juvenile is prosecuted as an adult. That happens if the prosecutor, through a motion, can convince a juvenile-court judge that the case warrants special consideration. Factors that determine whether a juvenile is certified as an adult include premeditation, extreme aggressiveness, age, prior criminal record and public safety. More often, though, juveniles are treated differently because they are children, and children make mistakes from which they can be expected to recover. Among the correctional options available to juvenile-court judges are placement in a foster home, assignment of community service or commitment to a detention facility.

Despite the difficulties and sensitive matters associated with covering juvenile law, journalists must observe carefully, if not always report all that they observe. The juvenile justice system is one of society's pressure points. Crime, divorce, sexual abuse, runaways and teenage pregnancies frequently are either the causes or effects of juvenile problems. Important decisions affecting young lives are being made daily, often behind closed doors. The shield of privacy around the juvenile courts obscures as well as protects, increasing the likelihood of hidden problems. The argument that responsible news coverage serves the interests of juveniles therefore appears as strong as the argument for strict confidentiality.

Bankruptcy

Charles Dickens experienced the humiliation of a debtor's prison because of his father's financial problems. In Dickens' day, entire families lived in jails while the debtor was punished. It was a degrading and nonsensical way to deal with debtors, who obviously could not repay creditors from a jail. The specter of debtor's prisons encouraged the framers of the U.S. Constitution to provide for uniform laws governing bankruptcy under section 8 of Article I.

In today's climate of consumer credit, economic downshifts and job layoffs, debt is a problem of major proportions. But U.S. bankruptcy laws now allow individuals, partnerships and corporations relief from all or part of their debt in order to make fresh starts.

Although there are several types of bankruptcy cases under federal law, the two most common are "Chapter 7" or "Chapter 11" bankruptcies. Chapter 7 provides for *liquidation* of a debtor's assets, with the exception of certain exempt property, and distribution of those assets among the creditors. Chapter 11 provides for *reorganization* so that businesses, in particular, can continue to operate under a plan that determines the manner and amount of payments to creditors. A Chapter 11 bankruptcy usually is handled by a court-appointed *trustee* whose duties include administering property, investigating financial conditions and overseeing implementation of the reorganization plan. Trustees in the reorganization of large corporations are often experienced managers or business executives. In Chapter 7 bankruptcies, trustees normally play a lesser role. Both Chapter 7 and Chapter 11 cases can be voluntary, when the debtor files for bankruptcy, or involuntary, when the creditors initiate the bankruptcy petition.

When an unemployed sheet-metal worker with $10,000 in credit-card bills declares bankruptcy, few news organizations could justify telling his story; there are too many more pressing, more significant stories to tell. In fact, the worker probably would not want his story told. But when the man's employer, which employs 800 other workers, files for bankruptcy, that is news—perhaps quite surprising news. Businesses and corporations sometimes quietly, without attracting much attention, fall into debt. A venerable downtown department store, for example, may seem to outsiders financially stable if not solid, until its owner petitions for reorganization.

Once an individual or company takes its financial problems into U.S. Bankruptcy Court, there is no hiding records and debt. The information debtors normally must provide includes the identity of company officials, the names of creditors and the amounts owed. Documents like these often lead to additional, newsworthy details about the company's financial woes and its impact on the community.

Much of the work of bankruptcy courts is done informally and not before a judge. Debtors and creditors, usually aided by the trustee, collaborate on terms. If all goes well, the judge's role is to approve arrangements and discharge the case. Along the way, there may be hearings, but there are no trials or juries in bankruptcy court. Moreover, bankruptcy is the exclusive domain of the federal court system. State courts retain some jurisdiction when creditors seek, for example, to garnish a debtor's wages or foreclose on his or her property. A petition for bankruptcy, however, *stays* (suspends) attempts by creditors to collect on a debt through state courts. In addition, state legislatures can establish statutory exemptions that protect debtors from loss of certain property, such as a home or tools of a trade. Often, debtors can choose between the uniform federal exemptions or the exemptions provided by state law, which can vary greatly.[21]

This chapter and Chapter 7 primarily address the work of reporters assigned to the court beat. But *all* reporters should be able to find, read, interpret, and analyze court decisions. In this society there is not a geographic or subject beat that is litigation-free. The baseball writer or book editor, for example, should be prepared to report on the law as it affects their beats. They cannot say, "Oh, that's something for the courthouse reporter." For one thing, the reporter assigned specifically to the courts might be tied up with several other pressing stories. For another, the court reporter may lack the background and news contacts to deal with, say, an antitrust suit by players against owners or a copyright case involving a biographer's use of a famous person's unpublished correspondence.

As Chapter 9 demonstrates, the challenges of special beats—from religion to business—include issues of social and *legal* significance.

EXERCISES

1. Ask a librarian at the nearest law school to show you reference books, law journals and case reporters available to help journalists cover legal news. Most law schools now have computers to assist law library users as they search for information. Have the librarian help you conduct an uncomplicated search.

2. As an introduction to the criminal courts, spend several hours observing preliminary hearings, which are commonly held at a regularly scheduled time and courtroom. "Prelims" usually offer an intriguing cross-section of offenses, which, on a given day, could range from child abandonment to vehicular homicide. Select a case that particularly interests you and follow its outcome.

3. Scan the news for an important ruling by the U.S. Supreme Court or the state supreme court. (As an option, select a decision

from a nearby state or federal appellate court.) Consider the ruling's local impact. Talk to people who might be affected and to those who have informed opinions about the ruling's meaning. Authorities are probably available on campus. Write a localized story about the case.

NOTES

[1] F. Lee Bailey and Henry B. Rothblatt, *Fundamentals of Criminal Advocacy* (Rochester, N.Y.: Lawyers Co-Operative, 1974), p. 285.

[2] Ruth Marcus, "North Jury: Collection of the Uninformed," *St. Petersburg Times*, Feb. 22, 1989, p. 4A.

[3] Seymour Wishman, *Anatomy of a Jury* (New York: Times Books, 1986), p. vii.

[4] Harry Kalven Jr. and Hans Zeisel, *The American Jury* (New York: Little, Brown, 1966); Lawrence S. Wrightsman, Saul M. Kassin and Cynthia E. Willis, eds., *In the Jury Box* (Newbury Park, Calif.: Sage, 1987).

[5] Sheryl James, "A Gift Abandoned," *St. Petersburg Times*, Feb. 20, 1990, p. 5D.

[6] "Poindexter Judge Scolds Press for Calling Jurors," *St. Petersburg Times*, April 4, 1990, p. 4A.

[7] C. David Rambo, "Judge's Instructions in Sharon Case Weighed by Libel Experts," *presstime*, April 1985, pp. 24, 25.

[8] "Former Preschool Workers Acquitted of Molestation," *St. Petersburg Times*, Jan. 19, 1990, p. 2A.

[9] Mark Fitzgerald, "Judge Declares Mistrial in Murder Case; Cites News Story," *Editor & Publisher*, April 1, 1989, p. 23.

[10] Leonard Territo, James Halsted and Max Bromley, *Crime and Justice in America*, 2nd ed. (St. Paul, Minn.: West, 1989), p. 496.

[11] Joan Petersilia, *Probation and Felony Offenders* (Washington, D.C.: U.S. Department of Justice, National Institute of Justice, 1985), p. 3.

[12] "Burnett Settles Libel Suit," *Editor & Publisher*, Jan. 26, 1985, p. 33.

[13] Lyle W. Denniston, *The Reporter and the Law* (New York: Hastings House, 1980), p. 198.

[14] John Seigenthaler, "News Media Neglect Has Made the Federal Court of Appeals 'the Anonymous Court,' " *ASNE Bulletin*, March 1989, p. 4.

[15] Seigenthaler, "News Media Neglect," p. 6.

[16] David Stolberg, "Pilot Program Aims to Help Newspapers Cover Federal Appeals Courts," *ASNE Bulletin*, July–Aug. 1989, pp. 30–32.

[17] Steve Nevas, "Coming Soon to a Screen Near You," *The Quill*, April 1990, p. 24.

[18] *New York Times v. Sullivan*, 376 U.S. 254 (1964).

[19] Robert Coram, "Assume That Assumptions Are Wrong," *The Quill*, Feb. 1987, p. 17.

[20] See *Smith v. Daily Mail Publishing Co.*, 443 U.S. 97 (1979), and *Oklahoma Publishing Co. v. District Court in and for Oklahoma County*, 430 U.S. 308 (1977).

[21] Richard B. Herzog Jr., *Bankruptcy: A Concise Guide for Creditors and Debtors* (New York: Arco, 1983), p. 113.

Chapter Nine

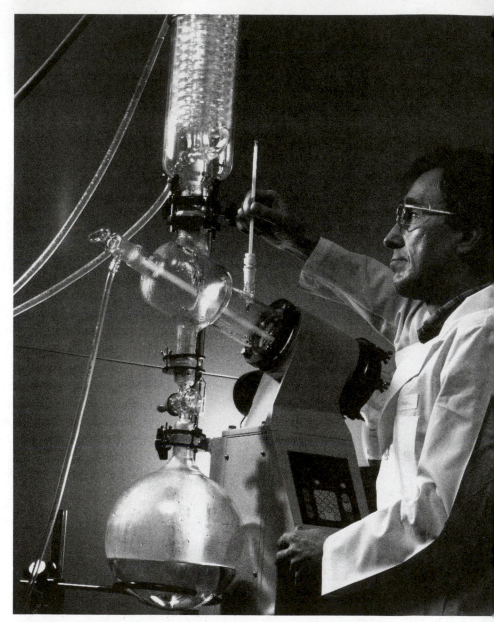

A scientist at work. An increasingly complex society—characterized by increasingly specialized forms of knowledge—presents new challenges to the public affairs reporter. (© Joel Gordon 1987)

Special Beats, New Challenges

General-assignment reporters cover the day's news as it unfolds— from a hail storm in the morning to an American Legion convention that afternoon. They are valued for many reasons, such as the ability to transform a dull press release into a page-one story. Few assignments intimidate or deter competent general-assignment reporters, who can cover a first-grade play and the opening day of the state legislature with comparable verve and results.

General-assignment reporters do important work, but, increasingly, they lack the expertise to cover complex subjects and events. "Good general-assignment reporters—in print and television—are an invaluable asset," says *Time* and *Newsday* veteran reporter Richard Clurman. "But specialists are an imperative." As Clurman correctly notes, "Generalized knowledge or the ability to 'take the information down right' is essential but today it is insufficient. Very few big stories are any longer simple. They are intertwined with economics, law, government, new technology, history, sciences. The essential homework on many an assignment can no longer be done by simply reading the clips."[1]

Journalists in the 21st century can anticipate more significant, rewarding roles in reporting the news. But to remain relevant and meaningful in a rapidly changing, diverse society, reporters should be masters of information and experts on particular subjects and issues. New York University professor Jay Rosen says journalism is becoming even more of a *thinking profession*. According to Rosen, "Reporters will have to be skilled in recognizing patterns, spotting connections, isolating and integrating key facts. The mind of a thinking journalist is an excellent device for reducing information, and this will be a vital service in the years ahead—reducing, rather than providing information."[2]

The journalist's ability to reduce and distill information will be needed for other reasons. Media observer Neil Postman says we kept our eyes warily on 1984, but the Orwellian nightmare of an oppressive, Big Brother–controlled society never materialized. Instead, he says, we should have been heeding the words of Aldous Huxley's *Brave New World.* As Postman sees it, "[George] Orwell feared those who would deprive us of information. Huxley feared those who would give us so much that we would be reduced to passivity and egoism. Orwell feared that the truth would be concealed from us. Huxley feared the truth would be drowned in a sea of irrelevance."[3] If we are closer to Huxley's world than Orwell's, journalists of the 21st century not only must skillfully navigate through a sea of irrelevance; they also have to be on guard for what Stewart Brand calls "toxic information," a by-product of communications technology. Although toxins—disinformation, propaganda and other forms of media manipulation—are nothing new, Brand fears a future of bigger and more dangerous lies and deception. In his view, "Two centuries of lively experience with the practice of free speech and press in America suggests that most information that might be considered toxic can be handled by the public kidneys. Yelling, 'Fire!' in a crowded theater (unless there's a fire) has proven toxicity, however. There's insufficient time to sort out the truth of the matter before serious harm is done; could that happen in the crowded theater of world communication? Inevitably."[4] Besides providing news of importance and usefulness, journalists must do their best to keep information free of contamination. This chapter explores special areas of societal concern and the formidable challenges to news coverage they pose.

MEDICINE AND SCIENCE

Elizabeth Whitney, who retired from the *St. Petersburg Times* in 1990 after a distinguished career of reporting and editing, told her readers about a 15-year-old story she simply could not forget. Her experience began routinely enough, when she read a medical journal report about a remedy for traveler's diarrhea and children's diarrhea that could be made with ingredients found in anyone's kitchen.

Whitney called the chief of intestinal diseases at the Centers for Disease Control in Atlanta—a key source of information for medical reporters—to learn details. The doctor said the remedy was "a medical breakthrough" not then available in the United States. He gave Whitney the formula, which she published. Whitney recalled what happened:

> The day it was published, I was visited by a delegation of grim-faced pediatricians. They said my story omitted a crucial fact—that the formula had to be diluted with water. A child taking large quantities of the formula as given could develop salt poisoning which would cause brain hemorrhage, convulsions and brain damage.
>
> When I called the CDC chief, he said the local doctors were right and he had forgotten to mention the water. The next morning the *Times* published a prominent correction headed "Diarrhea remedy held dangerous."[5]

To her great relief, Whitney never heard about any child becoming ill from taking the formula, but she blamed herself for not knowing to ask whether the formula should be diluted. "Though I covered medicine for two years, I never overcame my discomfort with science. I asked to be taken off the beat."

In covering medicine, science and health, careful, precise reporting is an absolute necessity, not simply an ideal. As Whitney knew, making a mistake covering medicine and science can lead to far more serious consequences than an editor's scolding or a libel suit. People tend to put great faith in news reports about medical cures, wonder drugs, weight-loss programs, surgical procedures, tips for improved health and fitness and warnings about dangerous chemicals or treatments. Reporters who misinform or mislead in their coverage, however unintentionally, can do harm by raising false hopes or passing on bad advice. Worse, lives may be endangered.

Medicine

AIDS continues to dominate medical news. With a few exceptions, the press slowly reacted to AIDS, at first writing it off as an isolated disease of gay men. After 1985, however, coverage quickly expanded and gradually improved. Today, reporters who cover AIDS on a regular basis are familiar with medical terms and sources of reliable information. They know, for example, that the correct name for the AIDS virus is HIV—human immunodeficiency virus—and that testing positive for HIV is not equivalent to having AIDS.

The AIDS crisis demonstrates the need for medical reportage that is clear and straightforward. In the early stages of coverage, newspapers and broadcasters avoided sexual terminology and descriptions pertaining to the transmission of HIV for fear of offending people. Reference was made to "bodily fluids" and "unsafe sex." Finally, news organizations began using graphic explanations, as the *Boston Globe* did in reporting that "no semen, pre-ejaculatory fluid or vaginal secretions should enter anyone's vagina, rectum or mouth."[6] In matters of life and death, delicacy and decorum must yield to the need for reliable facts.

AIDS also illustrates several danger zones in medical reporting— the urgency of research in certain areas of medicine; the pressure on scientists to secure grants and win acclaim; and the tendency of journalists to look for "breakthroughs" and "cures." Obviously, reporters must first get the facts right. It is also vitally important for them to resist the urge—and the efforts of others—to exaggerate the importance of medical developments. In all areas of scientific reporting, reporters must proceed with caution and restraint.

Usually, findings published in a professional publication, such as the *New England Journal of Medicine*, are prescreened by experts who review a submitted article for the soundness of its methodology and conclusions. Not every study of importance, however, is carried by the leading journals. Can reporters judge research or medical reports for themselves? To a degree, yes, but safeguards should be taken. In *News & Numbers*, a guide to coverage of science and medicine, Victor Cohn suggests questions that reporters can ask to gain understanding and to judge the validity of research.[7] If there is a study, Cohn says, obtain a copy. Ask researchers to explain and justify methods and procedures. If the research involves human test subjects, it is important to know the number of subjects and how they were selected and monitored.

As a final prepublication step, reporters should check with the researchers to ensure against errors in describing or assessing the study. If appropriate, reporters should also consult with other experts in the field for reaction and insight. Outside experts may save reporters from a serious blunder or mistake of judgment.

Medical coverage includes examination of the economics and

ethics of care and treatment. The rising costs of hospitalization and medical procedures already is a societal problem of multiple dimensions. Recently, two Stanford University researchers touched off a debate, as they knew they would, by suggesting that the $2.6 billion spent annually on neonatal intensive care in the United States could be better used to address the root causes of prematurity. It may be better to let some extremely small premature babies die, they said, adding that doctors must "confront the inescapable fact that ours is an era of shrinking resources, and ask whether setting limits is not both necessary and inevitable."[8] Tomorrow's reporters can anticipate even more collisions of medicine, money and morals.

Medical reporters are responsible for monitoring a broad range of critical issues and concerns. No single reporter can begin to address them all, which is why most journalists should concentrate on news closest to home. One starting point is to obtain and examine mortality rates of local hospitals. As always, statistics should be approached skeptically. Although a high mortality rate might suggest a hospital is a death trap, other factors, such as the age and socioeconomic status of patients, might explain the figures. The mortality rate might also reveal a problem concentrated in one unit, not the entire hospital.

Another area to explore is the availability and quality of medical services. Some communities, for example, are without obstetric (childbirth) care because high rates for malpractice insurance have forced doctors to limit their practices to general medicine. Not all doctors do right by their patients. Medicine has its share of incompetents, drug users, molesters, charlatans and mercenaries. State agencies and professional boards attempt to police medicine, but some bad doctors go undetected. Reporters on the medical beat must listen to patients, monitor lawsuits against physicians and check records of medical improprieties.

When new drugs, treatments and surgical procedures are announced, medical reporters should get details to the public quickly. With the national emphasis on good health, more people are alert for medical developments that affect them, family members or friends. Often they pass along information gleaned from news reports to doctors—not all of whom read newspapers, much less studies from medical journals. A story about a new method of cancer detection, for example, could save lives. Medical reporters should not assume that "everyone" knows about the latest cancer news simply because the major media, particularly network television, gave it heavy coverage. Important medical stories deserve local coverage with local angles as well.

Science

Science coverage can range from mindboggling theories of cosmic evolution to studies about drought-resistant lawns. Obviously, scientific developments touch our lives in innumerable ways, but for most people, science news becomes a priority when it directly touches their lives. People, for example, want to know if Nutrasweet is a safe substitute for sugar or whether depletion of the ozone layer is as alarming as it sounds. Consequently, a great deal of science reporting focuses on threats to humans and the planet. In covering such stories, reporters must be aware of their potential role in setting off false alarms.

The Alar scare offers an example of how science coverage can unduly heighten fears. Alar is Uniroyal Chemical Co.'s trade name for daminozide, a pesticide used on apples primarily to improve color and prolong shelf life. Studies dating to the early 1970s suggested that large doses of daminozide cause cancer in laboratory animals. Little media attention was given to risks of eating Alar-treated apples until an environmental group called the Natural Resources Defense Council released a report early in 1989. The report predicted that 6,000 preschool children in America today would get cancer solely due to exposure to eight pesticides used on food, and it named Alar as the chief threat. The report received widespread coverage, leading *New York Times* columnist William Safire to question whether journalists overreacted. "We are prone to be terrified of risk, any risk," Safire says, "and malleable media amplify the alarmists' cries." Environmental lobbyists like NRDC, Safire contends, undermine public trust in government scientists. "Government scientists have no monopoly on the truth," he says, "and it's healthy for them to be challenged—provided the alarm's coverage is accompanied by reassuring rebuttals."[9]

Science reporters are under a doubly difficult obligation, says ABC correspondent Jeff Greenfield. "They have to interpret and understand very complicated disputatious material. Not only that, they have to render it in English without leaving the audience in the dark."[10] As Greenfield notes, sources of science information are often trade or industry groups that can be helpful but potentially biased. Turning to opponents, such as environmental groups, for reaction would add balance to coverage but not necessarily shed light. As a consequence, determining who is right and who is wrong—when to worry and when not to—can be difficult if not impossible. A balanced view is important, and a free, 24-hour hotline (800-223-1730) operated by Scientists Institute for Public Information can usually provide journalists with the names of experts on different sides of an issue.

Health

Many people are exceedingly concerned about staying healthy. They read labels and shun products that are fatty or laced with chemical additives. Those who zealously want to be trim and fit are susceptible to dangerous weight-loss treatments or vitamin regimens. Reporters on the health beat must watch for the latest fitness trend and subject it to a thorough critique, not laugh it off as "wacky."

Health, like science and medicine, is another area where there are few unequivocal answers about what is good for us—and what is not. Should people be brooding about their cholesterol count? Does a high-fiber diet reduce the risks of cancer? If we turn to chicken instead of red meats, are we exposing ourselves to serious risk of salmonella poisoning? Studies and claims by experts vary and often contradict one another, leading columnist Russell Baker to say in exasperation: "Almost everything they say is good for you will turn out to be bad for you if you hang around long enough, and almost everything they say is bad for you will turn out not to matter."[11]

If both journalists and the public become exasperated, it stems from trying to keep up with the crush of competing health claims. Take coffee, for example; dozens of studies have examined the effects of coffee and caffeine. No reader or viewer can be expected to mentally log and compare each study. That job should be the reporter's. On any beat where a new study or report joins a growing stack of prior studies and reports, reporters should periodically provide an accompanying chronology, identifying past findings and providing follow-ups on continuing research. Information on coffee, for instance, could be recorded and stored in a computer file maintained by the reporter. Once a chronology is started, it becomes fairly easy to update.

Environment

Medical, science and health reporting overlap at times or intersect with another fast-growing area of coverage—environmental reporting. Much of what is considered environmental reporting focuses on humankind's abuse of nature, which includes pollution of water, land and air. Casey Burko, environmental reporter for the *Chicago Tribune* since 1967, worries that too few reporters at smaller news organizations receive the chance to specialize and learn the environmental beat.

He stresses the need for journalists to understand issues, not merely report the arguments or claims. Burko cites early coverage of nuclear power as an example: "We missed the boat on nuclear power because [we] became cheerleaders for technology. We just swallowed that stuff and didn't look at the downside at all."[12] Environmental reporters not only need to report today's problems and anticipate tomorrow's; they also should be determining whether programs and technologies offered as solutions to environmental problems are working, such as water-treatment plants.

The environmental beat may also include coverage of the use and transportation of chemicals. When mishandled, chemicals can poison water supplies, contaminate soil and cause health problems for humans and animals. Potential stories range from the dangers of lawn-spraying services to regulation of industrial byproducts. A related problem involves disposal and transportation of radioactive materials, such as wastes from a hospital radiology department. Everyday, radioactive materials are shipped through towns by truck or train, which means there is always the potential for a mishap. (Does your community have an emergency plan if toxins are accidentally released into the environment?) Reporters should also be prepared to react to environmental emergencies. A booklet produced by the National Safety Council—*Chemicals, the Press and the Public: A Journalist's Guide to Reporting on Chemicals in the Community*— includes information on coverage of emergencies.[13]

EDUCATION

A typical education reporter can be found at 10 p.m. on a Tuesday night struggling to stay alert as she covers a marathon meeting of the school board. The next day she may be dodging a midmorning rush of university students as she heads to an interview with the school's president.

Education-beat coverage includes a tossed salad of meetings, bond issues, graduation ceremonies, homecomings, budgets, strikes and assorted controversies. It is an expansive beat that may range from preschool to the state capital. Education reporters can expect to encounter an interplay of many forces: unions, legislators, courts, school officials, parents, citizens and state boards of education. But in covering the groups and personalities, they must never lose sight or contact with the main target—students.

Education on the Local Level

Newsday reporter Emily Sachar felt she needed remedial work in education writing, so she went back to school—as an eighth-grade mathematics teacher in Brooklyn. Prior to her journey into the classroom, Sachar had written frequently about the decrepit physical conditions of city schools and the tough job of being a teacher. Despite her past experiences, Sachar quickly discovered she really knew little about her beat. Her work as a teacher turned out to be exhausting, frustrating and disturbing. Particularly disturbing were the school district's lax requirements that allowed students to be promoted out of the eighth grade without having passed mathematics or language arts. "As a reporter, I had suspected that the promotional standards were weak. But, until I worked as a teacher, I had no idea what practical meaning the lack of standards has for kids."[14]

Sachar easily obtained a job because New York so desperately needed teachers. Not all reporters could—or would want to—go so far to learn their beat. But Sachar reinforces the value of direct observation and firsthand experience. Even a one-day visit is useful, says *Lansing State Journal* reporter Lisa Gutierrez: "Education reporters must get into the classrooms. Being there breathes detail and life into education stories. I would never have known a picture of Jesus Christ hangs next to the American flag in an award-winning Michigan teacher's classroom if I hadn't been there."[15] Gutierrez understands that meetings of the school board or interviews with the district superintendent rarely tell the whole story, much less reveal how administrative decisions affect students, teachers and parents. "Meetings reveal what administrators want the public to know," she says, "not necessarily what it should know. Meetings don't tell you that the budget cuts being discussed mean that students will keep using history books written in the 1960s."[16] Gutierrez regularly talks to teachers, students and parents, providing them with her business card and urging them to call with concerns or story ideas.

Education reporters, however, cannot ignore administrators as news sources or skip meetings. The presence of reporters at school meetings is particularly important for the sake of accountability. Unless a controversy over a tax hike or a book ban is brewing, school meetings are lightly attended. As with governmental meetings, reporters are there as the surrogate listeners and observers for the public. State open-meetings laws generally give the press access to school board deliberations, but, at times, access is granted grudgingly and closed-door "executive sessions" are common. In some districts, reporters and school officials perpetually battle over access to meetings and records.

Invariably, a key source on the local education beat is the school superintendent, who is usually accustomed to meeting with reporters. Superintendents, however, face considerable pressure; the more pressure, the less likely they are to be candid and expansive in answering questions. While a powerful superintendent may rule a district with little opposition from the school board, circumstances and personalities might lead to frequent clashes and discord within the education hierarchy, further complicating news coverage. At the top of the hierarchy is the school board (or *board of education*), which is responsible for setting educational policy and making budgetary decisions. School board members are either elected or appointed laypersons who tend to reflect a cross-section of the community population—homemakers, insurance agents, dentists, factory workers. Are they, by education and experience, well suited to oversee the school system? That is something education beat reporters should try to determine. As with coverage of any politicized beat, journalists need to know who wields power and how effectively that power is exercised.

The local education beat encompasses much more than the public schools, grades K through 12. Education begins in homes, where children ideally receive emotional and educational nourishment. Of course, home environments vary dramatically; an infant from the inner city might receive more verbal stimulation than one from a middle-class home, but the odds are against it. Comprehensive education reporting examines social conditions that eventually will be felt in the classroom, such as the alarming increase in teenage pregnancies and cocaine babies.

A community's education "system" also includes an array of private and special schools. Early childhood education is especially prevalent as parents seek places for their preschoolers. In some cases, the need is practical—someone must watch the children while the parents work. In other cases, parents enroll children in preschool programs because they believe it is a prerequisite for the educational and, ultimately, the professional success of their offspring. Private schools and parochial elementary and high schools provide options to public education. They should not be dismissed as havens for the elite or bastions of religious doctrine. In fact, many serve as innovative education models from which to draw lessons and make comparisons.

Non-traditional educational programs warrant regular coverage as well. These include schools for "special" children, whether gifted or mentally disabled. Vocational, trade and technical schools prepare an important segment of the population for the service-related jobs of today and tomorrow, although some trade school programs deserve special scrutiny for fraudulent claims about job-placement rates or dishonest practices, such as signing up "phantom" students for federal grants. Other areas of education include "elderhostel" programs for retirees who enjoy combining travel and study; the home-schooling movement; continuing-education programs for professionals; and adult-education classes.

Reporters who draw the boundaries of the education beat too narrowly will miss important stories.

State and Federal Involvement

Increasingly, educational policies are influenced by forces and factors outside the local community. While property taxes still constitute the major source of funding for local schools, the annual influx of state and federal money is critical for nearly all districts, particularly big-city systems. As government involvement spreads beyond local districts, politics and politicians play an even greater role in education, going well beyond debates on taxes and budgets.

Part of the attention being directed at education by the White House, Congress, governors, state legislators and assorted agencies can be traced to publication in 1983 of *A Nation at Risk,* a report of the National Commission on Excellence in Education. Alarm over declining academic performance of students and teachers prompted politicians to form task forces and commissions, which in turn led to a spate of legislation and programs. In Florida and several other states, for example, legislators tried to curb high dropout rates by denying driver's licenses to anyone quitting school before the age of 18. Teachers and school administrators saw some of these efforts as needless meddling. Politicians justify an active role in school business, arguing that the condition of education is directly related to the social and economic well-being of the entire state.

The state's involvement in local education is substantial largely because of the governance structures and fiscal policies. Most school boards and districts are highly dependent on state funding. A handful of states have comprehensive boards of education that oversee and coordinate all public schools. In most states, however, there are separate boards and agencies for elementary-secondary education and higher education.

State boards, agencies and commissions engage in policymaking and planning, but nearly everything in education boils down to financing. On a national average, about 50 percent of school funding comes from state sources, 44 percent is locally generated principally by property taxes and 6 percent comes from federal programs.[17] State education boards normally recommend how state money should be spent, but ultimately the legislature and governor battle over the education budget. In covering school financing, reporters need both state and local sources. In all cases, reporters covering public education must know and report where the money comes from and *how* and *where* it is being spent. The public is always sensitive about how its taxes are handled, and rightly so.

The symbol of federal involvement is the Department of Education, created in 1980. Although it remains the smallest of the cabinet-level departments in terms of budget, it helps set priorities for education and provides funding for important programs, such as "Chapter 1" of the Education Consolidation and Improvement Act, which aids academically disadvantaged younger students with supplemental work in basic skills. Local schools depend on Chapter 1 funds to help children overcome those disadvantages.

Congress becomes involved by providing funding for the Department of Education. Less obvious is Congress' role in other education-related programs, such as the work of congressional committees and subcommittees. The Senate Agriculture Committee, for example, oversees school food programs that provide hot meals for students.

Higher Education

State involvement is especially apparent in regard to higher education. Public universities and colleges are highly dependent on state subsidies because, with the exception of two-year community colleges, they do not collect property tax money. Appropriation bills for higher education sometimes become political hostages as legislators and the governor battle over budget priorities. Annual funding for higher education may be in doubt up to the final hours of legislative sessions. Critical books, such as 1990's *Killing the Spirit* by Page Smith and 1989's *Profscam* by Charles J. Sykes, have helped make the case that college students are not getting their money's worth. Unfair images persist of overpaid, underworked tenured professors who enjoy sabbaticals and other leisure pursuits. Some politicians find academicians tempting and safe subjects, so they pander to public mistrust of what goes on at colleges and universities.

Regardless of the political unpleasantries involved, covering higher education can be an enjoyable, rewarding assignment. Today's colleges and universities reflect a new diversity in courses and students. With the pool of 18- to 22-year-old students dwindling, higher education is finding renewed life in older students who are returning to school. Some are women who have nurtured families and now seek careers outside the home; others are "lifelong learners"—men and women who enroll to stay intellectually active; and some are people who are making midcareer changes. Colleges and universities have reacted to a shifting clientele by offering a wider range of classes for part-time and evening students.

Thousands of potential human-interest stories are to be found in college classrooms. Other important, appealing stories can be found outside the classroom in faculty offices, research labs, clinics or auditoriums. Reporter John Carlson of the *Des Moines Register* tells about covering the University of Iowa:

> In the past year, I've stood alongside surgeons at University of Iowa Hospitals as they performed a rare 12-hour-long double-lung transplant and watched as physicists received and analyzed data sent back millions of miles from outer space.
>
> I have held the 300,000-year-old jawbone of an extinct ape and sat backstage as the Joffrey Ballet auditioned Iowa children for the company's performance of *The Nutcracker*.

And I didn't come up with these ideas covering a dull faculty meeting or rewriting a press release.[18]

Worthwhile stories are not likely to emerge when a reporter simply drops by the campus for an occasional visit. Too much is happening—some of it out of sight—for part-time coverage to be effective. Moreover, part-timers cannot easily develop a mix of sources or build a reputation for reliability.

What's Wrong with Education—or What's Right?

Crisis seems to be the word most frequently used to characterize American education. In his book, *Among Schoolchildren*, based on a year of observing a fifth-grade class in Holyoke, Mass., journalist Tracy Kidder noted:

> The history of education in America is the history of attempts to reform it. The latest movement deplores high dropout rates and declines in the College Board scores of new teachers. Many tests and surveys show that large percentages of American youth come out of high school and even college incompetent in the three R's and ignorant of basic facts about history, geography, science and literature. The bad news has inspired many commissions and from them many reports that make use of the word "crisis." As in the late 1950s, these reports often invoke an external threat—not Soviet competition now, but Japanese economic power.[19]

Reporters often feel overwhelmed in trying to assess what is right and, more important, what is wrong with education. Is it as bad as it appears? Should we despair? Looking for clearcut answers to such questions might be futile and fruitless. At best, reporters must keep a steady eye on what is happening immediately around them. That means critically examining teacher performance and training, curricula, student-achievement scores, counseling services, financial support and instructional materials and equipment. Something as seemingly inconsequential as classroom design might reflect a significant element of a school district's educational philosophy.

Reporters covering education must be as knowledgeable, well read and alert to developments in their field as counterparts on the legal or medical beats. They must know, for example, how to read and interpret test scores, such as the Scholastic Aptitude Test (SAT), and how to understand budgetary processes and state-funding formulas. They must also be aware of what is happening behind the scenes, such as the debated but widespread use of drugs like Ritalin to control "hyperactive" children. Obviously, a reporter lacking a background in education cannot become an expert overnight. As a starting point, however, a concise overview of the beat and guide to coverage is available from the Education Writers Association in Washington, D.C.[20] The underprepared education reporter is at a distinct disadvantage, consigned largely to reporting the theories, observations, interpretations and explanations of others.

Education reporters who concentrate on the shortcomings and failures of our schools and de-emphasize the success stories can expect criticism. It is a valid criticism, considering the high number of news reports about drug deals, stabbings, rapes, truancy, dropouts and illiteracy. Bad-news reporting is a common criticism of journalism, not one exclusive to the education beat. While the ugly side of education cannot, of course, be sanitized or ignored, reporters must remember that for every negative incident there may be 10 positive ones.

RELIGION

Religion news no longer languishes in journalism's backwaters. Long before the televangelist scandals of the late 1980s, religion offered fertile ground for news coverage. Until recently, however, journalism largely neglected religion, with the exception of covering papal pronouncements or Easter services. For years, many newspapers quarantined religion news on an inside page—the church page—of Saturday editions. Why? Partly because editors feared serious religious news would generate too much controversy and ill feelings among readers. Partly because they saw religion as "soft" news. And partly, perhaps, because a majority of journalists, as surveys indicate, are not active churchgoers.[21]

The Jim Bakker episode demonstrated that religious news, although still controversial, was every bit as "hard" as news from the police beat, state capital or White House. Bakker and his wife, Tammy Faye, had built a fledgling Christian television show into a multimillion-dollar empire when accusations of Bakker's hushed affair with a 21-year-old church secretary and his extravagant misuse of church donations brought Bakker and his PTL ("Praise the Lord" or "People That Love") ministry into disrepute.

When Bakker resigned from PTL in 1987, he blamed the *Charlotte Observer:* "I am not able to muster the resources needed to combat a new wave of attack that I have learned is about to be launched against us by the *Charlotte Observer,* which has attacked us incessantly for the past 12 years."[22] The newspaper won a Pulitzer Prize for its efforts, and its coverage prompted news organizations to investigate the financial affairs of other ministries.

The Bakker investigation reinforced the point that religion stories can belong on front pages and at the top of newscasts. Often, however, it takes a fall from grace, such as the Bakkers', or the saintly deeds of a Mother Teresa to capture substantial coverage. Religious leaders and groups can be found at the forefront of social movements, financial empires, political intrigue and community activism throughout the nation and world. Consider the diverse beliefs and methods of such religious figures as preacher-politician-presidential candidates Jesse Jackson and Pat Robertson; evangelist Jerry Falwell, who founded the now-defunct Moral Majority; Nation of Islam leader Louis Farrakhan; and the Dalai Lama, winner of the Nobel Peace Prize in 1989. Such an array of notable newsmakers alone suggests that media organizations need full-time religion reporters.

There is no formula or traditional pattern for working the religion beat. For one thing, the beat lacks a central spot, like city hall, around which to organize coverage. But like most beats, it cannot be adequately covered by telephone from a newsroom. In fact, to achieve thorough, balanced coverage of religion, reporters need to expand their cultural, moral horizons, quell feelings of cynicism and take an ecumenical view of religion. Religion reporters should look for news in storefront churches as well as cathedrals and synagogues. They should attend tent revivals, bar mitzvahs and Jehovah's Witnesses' services, without passing unfair judgment about what they see or hear. They should recognize that God's work is being done in both cloistered convents and halfway homes for ex-convicts. Occasionally, religion reporters must be prepared to disqualify themselves from stories that deeply touch their own beliefs. A reporter committed to the pro-life movement probably should not cover either an abortion-clinic protest or a pro-choice rally. The same view, of course, applies to a pro-choice activist.

Finally, all reporters, not just those on the religion beat, should neither judge too harshly the failings and flaws of "religious" people—nor accept their words and apparent good deeds uncritically. When it was disclosed during the 1988 presidential campaign that one of Pat Robertson's children was conceived out of wedlock, did some journalists privately gloat? When a cleric is arrested on charges of indecent exposure, is the press overly eager to publicize the offense? On the other hand, when Franciscan priest Bruce Ritter was raising millions of dollars for Covenant House, a shelter for homeless youths, few news organizations questioned his growing power and influence. Until Ritter faced allegations of sexual and financial misconduct, says *Washington Post* columnist Colman McCarthy, the press took most of what Ritter said and did as "gospel." Whether Ritter is guilty as accused, his organization, with its $85 million budget, warranted press scrutiny. "Ritter's operation in 1988 was nearly twice the size of the federal government's funding for runaway-youth programs," McCarthy noted, "except no General Accounting Office was on hand to monitor what happened to the money sent in by some 650,000 donors." McCarthy advises reporters: "It shouldn't be a sacrilege to look at one of the haloed and wonder: If we give him a free ride, will we end up being taken for a ride?"[23]

Despite their small numbers, religion reporters are organized through the Religion Newswriters Association, which, among its activities, issued in 1989 its first "Into the Darkness Award" to recognize the individual or group "that has done the most during the year to stifle the people's right to know." (The award went to the National Conference of Catholic Bishops, which met behind closed doors for an entire afternoon, never revealing what its members discussed.) The RNA can serve as a support group for reporters seeking guidance and ideas for covering religion-related news.[24]

CAMPAIGNS AND ELECTIONS

It seems as though the political beat is the pinnacle of reporting. It certainly has its notables—from Hunter S. Thompson, the iconoclast who reports for *Rolling Stone* and whose books include *Fear and Loathing: On the Campaign Trail '72*, to David Broder, the *Washington Post's* Pulitzer Prize—winning columnist whom a colleague described as "our most respected reporter and commentator on politics." Yet with so many of journalism's stars on the political beat, why is campaign reporting, in particular, so frequently criticized as shallow or trivial, even by those assigned to cover the candidates and elections? There are dozens of explanations, apologies and excuses. Broder, for example, offers one view: "Because as campaign reporters we are very atypical—unlike most of our readers and even many of our newsroom colleagues—much of our output has an insider quality." The insider quality, Broder says, helps explain why reporters sometimes focus on minor incidents and disputes that are tangential to the central issues voters ought to know.[25]

Despite the stellar glow of the political beat, there is no mystery about covering campaigns and politics. Basically, campaign coverage is bread-and-butter reporting with few special requirements beyond a sense of history; a commitment to focus on the meat of issues, not the sizzle; skill at detecting "bull" when it appears, which will be often; and, most of all, a determination to report not tangential insider news, but news central to what voters *ought to know.*

Politicians and the Press

Politicians and journalists enjoy a symbiotic relationship at times. For reporters, the balance in the relationship should fall somewhere between chumminess and cynicism. Getting too close to politicians presents obvious problems of potential favoritism. An unrelenting adversarial relationship poses another set of problems. Reporters on the political beat must constantly suppress personal views—good or ill—of politicians. Covering politics requires that journalists remain true to their principal role of keeping the public informed. As James Deakin, White House correspondent for the *St. Louis Post-Dispatch* from 1955 to 1980, reminds us: "A reporter is a person who tells other people what has happened. He tells them what was said or done and, if possible, why."[26]

The Character of Campaigns

The vernacular of campaigns includes *lugs, roorbacks* and *spin control.* They are unpleasant-sounding words that seem appropriate in the often unpleasant world of politics. Lugs, for example, are "voluntary" contributions government employees in an elected official's office sometimes must make to the boss's re-election fund. Roorbacks are smear charges leveled against a candidate in the final days of a campaign. Spin control, a strategy popularized by Ronald Reagan's White House staff, usually refers to efforts by political aides to contact reporters one-on-one and frame an event, report, speech or other news development within a favorable context. Let's say a gubernatorial candidate issues a 20-page policy statement on tax reform. Spin control might involve the candidate's media adviser "helping" reporters determine which details to emphasize and why. As political reporters learn the latest language and games of politics, they often discover they amount to new terminology for old practices.

While some aspects of politics remain unchanged, technology continues to reshape campaigns and strategies. Television's influence is undeniable. Nearly all candidates for state or federal office make heavy use of 30-second political advertisements to win voters. More recently, campaign strategists have turned to direct-broadcast satellites to help lesser-known candidates gain notice and reach remote audiences. The VCR is also being enlisted as a campaign tool as videotaped messages by candidates are shown at informal home discussions and other political gatherings.[27]

The use of media technology has increased the role of advisers who are skilled at marketing candidates through image making and opinion shaping. Media advisers suggest issues and themes for the campaign, direct political advertising, orchestrate staged news events (particularly photo or video "opportunities"), draft punchy one-liners and sound-bite comments sure to be quoted repeatedly in the news and rehearse candidates for media appearances. At times it seems as though U.S. voters elect the best media adviser instead of the best candidate. Reporters cannot overlook the influence of campaign advisers; indeed, it is often part of coverage to profile the people behind the candidate. The focus, however, should always be on the person running for election, not those running the campaign.

Campaign Financing

The fallout of the Watergate scandal included widespread campaign reform on the federal, state and local levels. Leading the list of reforms were limits and regulations governing campaign contributions by individuals, corporations and organizations and laws requiring candidates to disclose the amounts and sources of campaign funds.

Spending limits vary according to state and federal laws. Typically, individual contributions to a candidate's election are restricted to $1,000 or less; for corporations or groups, the ceiling usually is

$5,000 or less per candidate. But there are few restrictions on how much candidates may spend on campaigns. Political messages, even those that look and sound like product commercials, enjoy First Amendment protection. Moreover, election pragmatics enter into the picture; spending limits generally hurt challengers and help incumbents. A challenger to a well-established congressional incumbent, for example, might be forced to spend in excess of a million dollars simply to gain name recognition, much less get elected.

Money talks in politics as it does in other fields of endeavor. Money buys television advertising, the lifeblood of most campaigns. It also pays for billboards, fliers, office space, pollsters and travel. Without the ability to accumulate a campaign "war chest," few candidates for a contested office stand a chance of election. There are some refreshing exceptions, but they are usually candidates for the local school board, sewer district or city council.

Campaign funds may come from a variety of sources. Some are self-generated by the candidate, who may tap personal wealth, take out loans or accept family gifts. Contributions from individual contributors can add up, particularly when solicited by a large direct-mail effort. Cocktail parties and fund-raising dinners also bring in contributions from individuals, whose chief reward might be a handshake and hastily taken picture with the candidate while passing through a reception line. Loyal, "electable" Democratic or Republican candidates can often expect additional contributions from the party treasury. Finally, some money comes from corporations and organizations, most notably funds dispensed by *political action committees* (PACs).

PACs represent a formidable force in campaigns, particularly on the congressional level. In the 1980s the number of PACs registered with the Federal Election Commission exceeded 5,000, and total outlays by PACs to Senate and House candidates passed the $100 million mark.[28]

PACs represent a range of corporate, trade, labor or special interests. A PAC for automobile dealers, for example, might back candidates who support quotas on the import of foreign automobiles. Most often, PAC money goes to incumbents, especially those who hold leadership positions. Usually PACs support candidates, although occasionally PAC money is spent to defeat a candidate or wage a negative campaign. PACs or equivalent organizations also operate on state and local levels.

While money fuels campaigns, it also tends to leave candidates politically "in debt" and vulnerable to demands for paybacks. After all, those who contribute to candidates usually expect something in return. Part of the watchdog function of the press includes regular inspection of candidates' *financial disclosure statements* to learn who is contributing—and how much. A review of records might yield some surprises, such as a candidate who has received contributions from supporters on both sides of the abortion issue.

Disclosure statements are filed on federal, state or local levels, depending on the office being sought. For a city council candidate, disclosure records might be as close as a two-block walk to the county courthouse. A federal office seeker's file will be kept by the Federal Election Commission in Washington, D.C. Since most of the FEC's records are computerized, they are fairly accessible, but there may be a fee for copying documents. Once a reporter determines where records are kept, obtaining copies generally involves filling out a simple request form. Keep in mind, however, that disclosure records may be neither complete nor truthful. Unscrupulous candidates look for loopholes or employ dishonest reporting practices to withhold information from the public and press.

Election Coverage

Reporters cover campaigns and elections primarily to help people learn enough about candidates and ballot propositions to make intelligent, informed decisions once they enter the voting booth. To do a thorough job, reporters need to dig beneath surface impressions to explore issues, qualifications and motives.

Focus on facts, not on symbols, images and rhetoric, says political scientist James David Barber, who believes reporters too infrequently ask candidates the right questions—or test the candidates' answers to questions. He offers two examples from the 1988 presidential campaign. To ask Jesse Jackson, "Reverend Jackson, what are the three things you're going to do when you get to be president?" invites a long, well-rehearsed discourse that sheds little light on the candidate's record or qualifications. But a specific question ("How did you operate Push/Excel") based on solid research, might, Barber says, "change the nature of a campaign." Barber's second example stresses the need to compare clever comments to past performance. When presidential-debate moderator David Brinkley asked a panel of candidates, "Which of the pictures would you change in the cabinet room after you were president?," Paul Simon won applause and news coverage by saying, "I would take them all down. I would put up a picture of an Iowa housewife and of a coal miner from West Virginia. I would put up a picture of a kid from the Bronx, and so every time the president and his cabinet members came into that room they'd remember whom they were serving." Barber reminds reporters that a candidate's quotable response may not reflect a true devotion to a cause or issue; although Simon in this case may have been quite sincere, check the facts and the record.[29]

There are other distractions that reporters face when trying to stay focused on issues. One is the poll. Political polls are not without value in helping reporters gauge voter attitudes. The danger arises when the press relies too heavily on polls. Polls suggest certainty or exactness because they deal in numbers and statistics. But not all polls are created equal; they can be poorly constructed instruments of opinion measurement or skillfully constructed instruments of opinion manipulation. Reporters who practice "precision journalism" and conduct their own polls are less susceptible to manipulation—but more susceptible to self-deception. Although few political reporters have time to do their own scientific polling, many news organizations now have an outside research firm or in-house research department on call. In any case, reporters must recognize the impact of polls and know how to read them.[30]

Some polls are more credible than others, but in all cases polls tend to reduce campaigns to races, featuring "frontrunners," "long shots" and "dark horses." In covering polls ("Representative Denise Smith has a commanding lead over her opponent, according to a recent poll"), the press ironically may influence the outcome of future polls. As election day draws near, voters may react to poll results, elevating last month's "underdog" to today's "strong contender."

Naturally, journalists and voters are curious about who is going to win an election. But reporting a campaign as a horse race and attempting to predict outcomes put journalists at risk of being misled. Some campaign advisers, for example, believe in intentionally setting lower public expectations of a candidate's performance, saying in a grim voice, "It will be a close vote," when their private polls indicate a win is nearly certain. The rule at work: "Never set—or let the press set—expectations so high that you cannot meet them."[31]

There is also concern that polls and surveys discourage reporters from doing old-fashioned legwork. Polling expert Albert Cantril makes this observation: "A generation ago when a political reporter got to a new state or location, he or she would usually call the local political organizations, labor unions, the chambers of commerce, the political party people, editors of local newspapers, to get some sense of what the texture was of what was going on in that area."[32] Now reporters covering major campaigns rely on poll printouts or turn to the candidates' polling experts for a picture of community attitudes instead of digging for stories and talking to people. Move away from the polls, the candidate and his or her inner circle and get among voters, advises David Broder.[33]

The 1988 presidential campaign also illustrates how pursuit of scandal stories could lure political reporters away from coverage of more substantial questions. The biggest story was the *Miami Herald's* stakeout of a Washington, D.C., townhouse that caught presidential candidate Gary Hart weekending with a young woman. Subsequent coverage, including a photo of Hart nuzzling the woman while aboard a yacht called *Monkey Business*, forced Hart to end his candidacy, although he later re-entered the race before dropping out for good. Evidence of a candidate's womanizing or heavy drinking, for example, is germane to what some call "the character issue." Still, reporters who operate as "morality police" ought to consider whether their time and efforts could be better spent on serious investigation of a candidate's ability and public performance instead of chasing rumors.

Campaign coverage should not end on election day. Although day-to-day responsibility for covering the newly elected official might shift to another reporter, someone—preferably the political writer— needs to provide continuity in coverage to see what happens to the former candidate's campaign pledges.

BUSINESS AND ECONOMIC NEWS

As journalism entered the 1990s, business and economic news remained the profession's Cinderella story. Once given stepchild treatment, the gray, dull business page—often little more than column after column of stock market reports—grew into well-written, well-edited daily sections, brimming with lively profiles, in-depth analysis pieces and attractive graphics.

People who turn to business reports usually are more than news "browsers." Many of them seek information to help make business decisions. And these information-seekers are not strictly male corporate executives. The audience for business news is varied, and generally it is knowledgeable and discerning.

Those who rely on business news expect solid, accurate and responsible reporting; they are among the most careful and critical of news consumers. When a business reporter misreads a company's annual report, people will react, including the chief executive officer, who is not likely to be happy with news coverage in general. Mistakes just confirm his or her impressions that reporters cannot be trusted to report business accurately or fairly.

Business and economic news also touches many other beats—government, law, medicine, to mention a few. When a bank teeters on the brink of collapse after making bad loans, the impact is likely to reach far beyond its employees, stockholders and customers. Business reporters must see economic developments within the broadest contexts.

Challenges to Coverage

On all beats, aggressive coverage is likely to generate occasional tensions between journalists and their news subjects. The business beat is particularly tension-ridden because, as one observer put it, "Businessmen rank journalists with bureaucrats and environmentalists as their most irksome tormentors."[34] The common complaint from the business world is that reporters are ignorant or biased—or both. From the journalist's perspective, top executives can be ruthless, greedy types, driven by a bottom-line mentality. Examples of both biased reporters and ruthless executives can be found, but neither image is fair.

Given the beat's climate of suspicion and hostility, a polite, patient reporter stands a better chance of success than a demanding, combative one. Business reporters, some of whom come from covering public officials, must remember that business executives are under no "right-of-access" obligation to grant interviews, answer questions or open files to the news media. A reporter will not get past the guard at the front gate if the chief executive officer declines to talk.

Complicating the situation is the aggressive stance certain business executives believe is necessary when dealing with the press. A leading proponent of aggressive tactics is Herbert Schmertz, who served as Mobil Oil's vice president for public affairs. In his book *Good-bye to the Low Profile,* Schmertz advocates "creative confrontation," which he defines as the willingness and ability of business people to challenge opponents and critics, among them journalists, head on.[35] As a result, business reporters must be prepared for defensiveness and argumentation. Overcoming an executive's hostility might not be accomplished in the course of a single interview. But competent reporting over a period of time should improve relations. For reporters, there is a simple, initial step toward building rapport with business executives: Do your homework prior to an assignment. At a minimum that means knowing the executive's background, the company's history and the products it makes or services it provides.

Reporters, of course, cannot begin to establish rapport when their requests for an interview are turned down or their phone messages go unanswered. At times, getting to a top executive is an involved, discouraging process of working through—or around—public relations people, whom some business reporters consider intentional obstacles to coverage. But an able, cooperative public relations person can make a business reporter's job easier by providing information and opening closed doors. A realistic view of the PR role is needed; reporters must understand that public relations people owe loyalty to the employer, not the press. Does that make PR people "hired guns" or "hacks"? Let's try to be fair: Few in public relations take company loyalty to the point of lying or cheating, but shaping favorable coverage is part of the job. Realistic reporters—and realistic PR people—quickly reach an understanding about their respective roles.

At the other extreme are reporters who let PR staffers do too much. A recent study found two interesting tendencies of business reporters. First, they refer to documents less frequently than reporters do on other beats, despite the impression that business reporting involves a great deal of time sifting through reports, figures and numbers. Second, they rely heavily on press releases and press conferences.[36] The study offers no explanations for these patterns, but given the complexity of business and economic reporting, it seems reasonable to assume that reporters, especially inexperienced ones, will turn to the predigested information of press releases or the interpretations of public relations people or government officials when at a loss to understand fiscal reports or economic developments. Obviously, reporters without proper preparation or knowledge of the business world lean toward dependency on the very people they are supposed to critically assess and question.

Into the Business World

Business reporters must deal with stock-market trends, government economic indicators, merger proposals, annual reports, takeover bids, trade deficits and corporate bankruptcies. Ideally, business reporters should be educated in law, accounting, business administration, finance and organizational psychology. A section of a textbook cannot adequately prepare a reporter for the business beat, but it can provide an overview and a starting point for coverage.

Most major businesses are organized as corporations, which means they have a board of directors and issue stock. There are two basic types of for-profit corporations—*privately held* (or closely held) and *publicly held.* A privately held corporation does not put its stock out for public sale; usually there is a limited number of stockholders who are under legal restrictions about the sale or transfer of their stock shares. A publicly held company invites outside investment by a large number of shareholders. The crucial difference for reporters is that publicly held corporations must file extensive financial reports with government agencies, particularly the federal Securities and Exchange Commission (SEC); privately held companies face few reporting requirements.

Corporations raise capital by selling *shares* of *stock.* There is *common* stock, which amounts to units of ownership in the corporation. Those holding common stock also gain voting privileges to elect or remove board members and directors or to decide important fiscal matters. Common stockholders also receive a portion of the corporation's profits, called *dividends. Preferred* stock usually is distinguished from common stock by two features: Those holding preferred stock do not hold voting privileges, but they normally receive a higher, fixed and more secure return *(dividends)* on their shares.

Investors make decisions to buy or sell stock in American companies based on a variety of financial information, including advice from stockbrokers, annual reports by corporations and, of course, stock-market performance as listed by the New York Stock Exchange, the American Stock Exchange and the National Market System (NASDAQ). Not all corporations, however, elect to have stock *traded* (or listed) on an exchange. A clearly written guide to the stock market and other financial reports is Gerald Warfield's *How to Read and Understand the Financial News.*[37]

Business reporters are expected to check the financial health of companies and businesses in the community regularly. If publicly held, quarterly and yearly reports of earnings, losses, assets and liabilities are available from government sources. An important document is the 10K report, which businesses must file annually with the SEC; it is a public document. Other sources of information are records of lawsuits involving the company, reports in the trade press and data from investment services, such as Dun & Bradstreet and Moody's, and company-produced annual reports to stockholders.

Some newspapers take out stock in major companies to ensure receipt of both annual reports and notices of stockholder meetings. In addition, says *Los Angeles Times* reporter Chris Welles, former employees are valuable sources as are those who do business with the corporations, such as customers and suppliers. "[Competitors] are especially valuable," says Welles. "Major companies have large and sensitive intelligence networks to keep them informed about what everyone else in their industry is doing. Few outsiders know as much about what is going on at General Motors as the executives at Ford do."[38]

Takeovers and Poison Pills

In the 1980s corporate mergers and takeovers dominated business news. Mergers may be friendly and mutually sought by the two corporations involved. There is a negative connotation, however, to *takeover*, which frequently is preceded by the adjective *hostile*. A hostile takeover is one mounted despite opposition by the takeover target's board of directors and executives. Occasionally, though, a takeover may be in the best interests of the corporation and its stockholders.

A takeover can be accomplished in a number of ways. One is a *leveraged buyout*. The public associates leveraged buyouts with Wall Street raiders who use massive amounts of borrowed money to acquire major companies, such as the $25 billion purchase of RJR Nabisco in 1988, which left the corporation facing $3 billion of annual debt payments. But most leveraged buyouts are quietly engineered, small-scale transactions, sometimes undertaken by employees who secure enough financial backing to purchase the company from its present owner. The buyout movement lost momentum in the 1990s, largely because many leveraged deals put large corporations so deeply in debt that stringent cost-saving measures, including employee layoffs and the sale of subsidiaries, were necessary.

Another form of takeover involves purchase of the majority of a company's stock through a *tender offer,* which is an outside corporation's advertised offer to stockholders to sell stock at a price well above the current market value. Some corporations turn to "poison pills" to thwart takeovers. One type of anti-takeover measure involves creating additional shares, making it more difficult for an "unfriendly" suitor to buy a majority interest. A takeover turns ugly when the cost to gain—or resist—control is so high it threatens the corporation's financial health.

A business reporter's errors or naiveté in covering reports of mergers, takeovers or acquisitions can give devious people the means to profit unfairly and illegally. Bad reporting can also damage the companies involved. Reporters and editors must be alert constantly for news manipulation and guard against careless coverage. The *Star Tribune* in Minneapolis fell victim to a clever hoax by a man who telephoned the newspaper, identifying himself as Richard L. Thomas, president of a Chicago bank. The caller said he wanted to correct a previous *Star Tribune* story that reported his bank was interested in buying a Minneapolis savings and loan. His bank, he said, actually was interested in another Minneapolis financial institution, which he identified. Despite some reservations, the newspaper published the information, and both the stock of the Chicago bank and its alleged takeover target went up in price amid heavy trading. In hindsight, according to business editor Larry Werner, the story should not have been run without full confirmation. In trying to explain what happened, Werner said, "Clearly, . . . people try to manipulate the market to their advantage and I think it's done too many more times than we like to think, but often it's done with anonymous information. I think you don't get caught when they do it that way [as much] as when you have a first name, a last name and a middle initial."[39] Obviously, all anonymous tips must be checked out.

Economic Indicators

Part of the business journalist's job is to report on the condition of the economy. Often the job requires that reporters depend on figures collected and issued by government agencies. One set of figures is called the *Index of Leading Economic Indicators,* published monthly by the U.S. Department of Commerce and available in major libraries. The index is supposed to forecast changes in the economy based on a number of national indicators of economic activity. Among them are new building permits, new orders for consumer goods and new claims for state unemployment insurance. Only a steady, three- or four-month rise or fall in the index percentage rate is considered a significant sign of growth or decline in the economy.

Other signals of economic conditions include the *U.S. Consumer Price Index,* which measures price changes for several hundred goods and services typically affecting consumers, and the *gross national product,* a figure reported by the Commerce Department quarterly that measures the total retail-price value of all goods and services produced by the nation's economy during a specific time period.

Federal and state government reports can help business reporters compare and contrast economic conditions locally, such as the number of new housing starts and the rate of unemployment. Statistics and percentages, however, need to be humanized to show how economic developments affect people. Look for economic stories at distribution centers for free government food or at foreclosure sales on farm property.

Understanding the economy also involves knowing about money supply as determined by federal borrowing and the role of the *Federal Reserve System,* whose board of directors can influence the economy by regulating interest rates it charges when banks borrow money directly from the U.S. central bank. The Federal Reserve Board (also known by the abbreviation of "Fed") often reacts to control both recession and inflation. The board lowers interest rates to stimulate the economy; it raises interest rates to tighten credit when inflation becomes a problem. The money supply process is complex, but serious business journalists make the effort to learn about each twist and turn of the economy.

Labor

Big Labor's day is over. Unions no longer possess the power and energy of the past. Mob corruption, foreign competition and recessionary spirals helped weaken the labor movement. But the demise of union strength and influence should not result in inadequate, stereotypical coverage of labor issues. Labor's image—today and yesterday—cannot be reduced to insatiable wage demands and violent strikes. Younger Americans, including reporters, need to remember what labor has done for them, such as the 40-hour week, sick leave, pensions and paid vacations. Labor still has an agenda that warrants fair, thorough coverage.

A chief item on labor's agenda is safety in the workplace. Old dangers remain, such as those facing coal miners. New dangers involve hazardous wastes from chemical plants, radiation from video-display terminals and carpal tunnel syndrome, a debilitating muscle inflammation caused by repetitive motion at a keyboard or factory assembly line. Journalists who work in pleasant, relatively risk-free environments must remember those who risk injury and long-term health problems each day. Business reporters who go no farther than the corporate offices will miss important stories that can be found only by going into factories and developing sources among workers.

Critic Michael Parenti says the news media in general give labor few opportunities to be heard. In his view, "The network evening news regularly reports the Dow Jones average and other stock market news but offers no weekly tabulations on industrial accidents, housing evictions or environmental violations. The major newspapers and weeklies have no 'labor' section to go along with their 'business' section. The Gross National Product is reported but there is no 'quality-of-life index' to tell us what the GNP takes away or fails to give us."[40] Parenti may overstate the case against the press, but he reminds business reporters that management's perspective sometimes dominates coverage.

MULTICULTURAL PERSPECTIVES

By publishing a photograph of a newlywed couple, the *Everett* (Wash.) *Herald* took a small step in 1990 toward recognizing the diversity of its community. The decision to publish the picture required a period of soul searching, but the *Herald*'s managing editor, Stan Strick, felt it was the right thing to do. Why the soul searching? The photograph was of a lesbian couple, who had exchanged vows in a commitment ceremony before friends and family.

The decision provoked a strong reaction from readers, including several who threatened to cancel subscriptions because the newspaper no longer reflected "family values." As one subscriber put it, "It's not something I want my children to accept as normal life. I

don't want my children to think that's the way God wants us to live."
The pastor of a gay church, however, had this view: "I think it's
healthy for society to see that there are gay people who are willing to
commit to each other in a long-term relationship. For so many years
all you saw was the seamier side. We indeed are a community of
committed people."[41]

The *Herald* joined a growing number of news organizations that
now are trying to achieve *representative* coverage that *recognizes
differences among people.* A responsibility for all journalists—
specialists and general-assignment reporters alike—is to try to maintain a *multicultural perspective.* Although news assignments offer a
smorgasbord of people and places, journalists tend to be a homoge-
neous group with little sustained involvement with the larger world
outside its middle-class environment.[42] Journalists will miss important stories unless they hear the voices and recognize the issues
outside their immediate frames of reference. They must understand,
relate to and accurately represent different generations, different
races, different ethnic groups, different genders and different living
conditions.

To some extent, any group of people—from the homeless of New
York to Miami's Cuban community—develops distinctive values,
styles of communication and patterns of behavior; in effect, despite
obvious shared characteristics, various segments of our larger society therefore possess distinctive "cultures." Here is a sampling of
some distinctions and differences as they relate to journalists. It is
not meant to be an inclusive list; it is meant to awaken and expand
your awareness and sensitivity.

The Homeless and Disadvantaged

The story of homelessness and poverty cannot be covered by 9-to-
5 journalists accustomed to the comfort and security of their offices.
Reporters must go to the source—into the streets—and not rely
strictly on the pronouncements of politicians, government agencies
or special-interest groups.

Advocacy groups, church leaders, politicians and police cannot
agree on the number of homeless people—or why they are homeless.
Reports in the 1980s said that millions of Americans, many of them
middle-class people down on their luck, were living in shelters or on
the streets. More recently, a study put the number of U.S. homeless
at 600,000, noting that most of them had mental, physical or medi-

cal problems that kept them out of the mainstream.[43] It is not easy to count the homeless and the "street people," but they exist in all cities, and their plight warrants coverage.

In covering emotionally loaded issues such as homelessness, balanced treatment is essential. Reporters must be careful not to overreact to staged events, such as celebrities camping out overnight in cardboard boxes, or sensationalize accounts of families living in abandoned cars or elderly men and women subsisting on dog food. Although the public needs to hear stories of people on the streets and in trouble, coverage should be sustained and substantial, not primarily anecdotal and occasional. Journalist Michael Moss says the press is "far better at simply discovering the poor than we are at explaining the causes of poverty and exploring the solutions."[44]

Stories about the homeless and hungry sometimes overshadow a growing substratum of the population—the "underclass." There is no universal definition for the underclass, but the designation suggests a category of people who are even more economically strained than the "lower class." Members of the underclass are often second- or third-generation welfare recipients trapped in a cycle of unemployment, poverty and despair, with little hope or motivation to improve their lives. The problem is compounded when news people begin to see the underclass as trapped in a hopeless state and fail to continue exploring conditions and solutions.

African-Americans

The civil rights movement of the 1960s focused the nation's attention on racism and discrimination, leading to reform and improvement. But many of the most deeply rooted problems were only superficially treated by government programs and money, not cured or eradicated. More than 50 percent of black Americans still live in inner cities, where riots occurred 25 years ago. Not much has changed for the better, including news coverage.

The press long has been criticized for its treatment of black issues; at worst the press has been blamed for perpetuating stereotypes, particularly in regard to crime news. It would help, of course, if more blacks opted for careers in journalism. Indeed, minority recruitment is a top priority for the profession, but blacks often are likely to see media organizations as institutions of racism where chances for advancement are poor.[45] According to one recent study, only 3.7 percent of the nation's 54,700 newsroom professionals are black, and more than 50 percent of the country's 1,650 newspapers do not employ a single minority news professional.[46] Prospects for immediate improvement are not promising.

If reporting black issues remains the responsibility of a largely white, middle-class press corps (whose editors come from the same background), then heightened awareness and education are needed. From a black perspective, too much news focuses on negative images—criminals, welfare cheats, drug dealers. As a result, stereotypes persist and distrust between races remains high. As columnist Clarence Page observes, "Statistics show more whites than blacks live in poverty, use drugs and bear children out of wedlock. Yet stories and special reports on these problems tend to focus on blacks. . . . Is it fair to always cast prosperity as the purview of whites, and poverty and depravity as the purview of blacks?"[47]

A continuing obstacle to improved news coverage is the white journalist's lack of sustained contact with blacks, followed by lack of understanding of black experiences. White reporters rarely drive through black neighborhoods, much less hunt for stories that are behind the closed doors. Is it any wonder that white reporters face difficulties communicating with blacks or identifying with the issues and problems of the African-American community? Occasionally a news report is revealing, such as a *Washington Post* piece about Michael McGee, a black Milwaukee alderman who uses rhetoric and outrageous behavior to draw attention to the problems of the inner city. He has worn a bag over his head to protest racism and has threatened violence against whites unless $100 million is invested in Milwaukee's black community by 1995. It might be easy for some people to dismiss McGee as a crackpot or a racist, but reporter David Maraniss' story showed another side to the man. In one scene McGee is making rounds in the community:

McGee toured four blood plasma centers on North Avenue. At each he encountered dozens of black men waiting to be hooked to machines that extracted plasma in exchange for a $10 payment. The process takes about 40 minutes and leaves many men feeling dizzy. They are supposed to do it only twice a week, but many men roam from center to center, giving plasma several times a day to acquire money for malt liquor and cigarettes.

"They milk these people," McGee said, his voice cracking. "They milk them like cows."[48]

The story captured both McGee's anger—and anguish.

Even the best intentions of white journalists sometimes go astray. Articles about black fashions or black filmmakers blazing "new trails" would be appropriate—once more central stories are told. A step toward better coverage of blacks is to open lines of communication by establishing bureaus or beats within black neighborhoods, not just at the local police precinct. Once into the community, reporters can cultivate a spectrum of reliable sources of information.

Another step toward improved coverage, suggests *Washington Post* reporter Courtland Milloy, is to report news of "the black middle class with the same sensitivity that most white people get." Milloy's comments are directed primarily at the Washington, D.C., media but relate to other cities as well. "Distorted and truly unfair images of the black community not only promote self-hatred," Milloy says, "they help to drive a wedge between the middle class and the poor, to say nothing of black and white. Because black people have been made to look so bad, so hopeless and helpless for so long, I believe that many of them have become just that."[49] Milloy's words offer a guide for future coverage of blacks that is more balanced and sensitive.

Women

In the 1960s and 1970s consciousness raising about the essential equality of the sexes enhanced the rights of women, but in its wake a new set of stereotypes and problems emerged. First came "Super Mom," who excelled at managing both job and family. Then came "Career Woman," who could match any man in terms of drive and savvy. Women rightly seek careers that match their talents, but many women also work because economically they must. These include both married women with children and single parents. News coverage, however, tends to highlight women who are well-educated, well-paid executives in pursuit of self-fulfillment, money and power.[50] Fewer stories examine the concerns of women who are worried, for example, about safe, inexpensive child care or who are returning to school at great sacrifice, perhaps surviving on food stamps.

Journalism remains a male-dominated profession, certainly at the news decision-making levels, and males do not always understand the issues that concern women. Will a male editor, for exam-

ple, take a report about premenstrual syndrome seriously enough—
provided he's aware of the report—to assign a reporter to do a story?
Of course, women editors do not necessarily empathize with the
woman at the checkout counter or the factory; they, too, may require
fuller exposure to the problems of other women.

An enhanced sensitivity to the concerns of women includes
awareness that, despite the feminist era, sexism—some of it unin-
tentional—remains influential. Would either male or female journalists describe a man as *perky* or *svelte*? Would most stories about
men include reference to a wife's job or position? All journalists
must be careful to avoid images and language that diminish the
credibility or seriousness of women.

There is another major shortcoming in the way the press treats—
or fails to treat—women. Too many "authorities" quoted by the press
are men. That fact alone does not mean journalists necessarily devalue women as news sources; sometimes a male is the best or only
source for information or insight. But where there is a choice, how
often do both male and female reporters turn first to a male spokesperson? In 1989 a one-month study of front pages of 10 major U.S.
newspapers found women quoted as sources 11 percent of the time;
the *New York Times*, at 5 percent, was lowest of the group. Commenting on the study, a female reporter noted, "Being consistently left out
of the news reports—where the movers and the shakers of the world
are recognized—reinforces the second-class status of women by reflecting a world where women are not as significant as men."[51] The
simple prescription to improve both the image and coverage of women
is for reporters to decide to seek out women as news sources whenever
possible.

People with Disabilities

America's disabled population is becoming an increasingly vocal
and visible minority. Although some want the media to notice their
problems and agendas, they do not appreciate being portrayed as
extraordinary for doing what they consider the ordinary—succeeding
in a job, raising a family or excelling in athletics. When reporting
about disabled individuals, it is important to think of the *person* first,
not the *disability*.[52] Indeed, reference to a person's disability might
be no more relevant to the story than the person's hair color or shoe
size. When the disability is germane, reporters should view the disability as merely *one* aspect of the story, not *the* story. At all times, avoid

terms or descriptions that might be considered negative or which suggest limitations, such as "wheelchair-bound" or "a victim of cerebral palsy." It is better to say someone "uses a wheelchair" or "has cerebral palsy."

Some people feel uncomfortable in the presence of those who are severely impaired, such as quadriplegics, and, as a result, treat physically disabled individuals as if they also are mentally disabled. An ill-at-ease reporter who acts unnaturally or clumsily when communicating with a disabled person puts an interview at risk. Usually there is no need to treat a disabled person any differently than other news sources. If you cannot understand someone's speech, say so. If you must talk to a hearing-impaired person through an interpreter, remember to speak directly to the person you are interviewing, not the interpreter. Focus on the person, not the wheelchair or the disability.

Disabled Americans are now protected under the Americans with Disabilities Act of 1990, which prohibits housing, employment and other forms of discrimination against people with physical or mental impairments. The law, for example, requires that all public buses, trains and subways and all new restaurants, hotels and stores (or those being renovated) be accessible to disabled persons, including those with emotional illnesses, epilepsy, drug addiction and alcoholism. Journalists can expect to encounter conflicts over implementation of the law's provisions. The Disabilities Act, like earlier civil rights legislation, will not automatically accomplish equality or end discrimination.

Older Citizens

Covering news of older people forces younger reporters to face mortality and to confront such uncomfortable subjects as Alzheimer's disease. With the accelerated "graying" of our population, the issues and problems of age must be squarely addressed, not ignored because they are too disturbing or depressing to investigate.

Besides overcoming a generational reluctance to cover issues of age, journalists must recognize and attempt to dispel the myths of growing old. Some younger Americans, including reporters, resent what they perceive to be their tax "burden" for support of social-service programs. Despite images in recent advertising, many older Americans are not robust, well-to-do and living the good life. When older people bitterly complain about Medicare problems or their own tax burdens, reporters must be the first to take those complaints seriously. In some cases, the problems of the aged are hidden away in rooming houses or nursing homes, where no one is going to be staging a protest or holding a press conference. Journalists should listen for the voices of those who sometimes cannot easily demand audiences for themselves.

When older people do make it into the news, stories that relate the "achievements" of older people often sound sappy or patronizing. They harp on "youthful" activities or images, such as a group of grandmothers "kicking up their heels" at an aerobics class or a "hot-sounding" band of "spry" octogenarians that plays at the nursing home. In one particularly insensitive episode, the *Sacramento Bee* ran the headline "Party Animals" over a picture of a couple at their 74th wedding anniversary; the caption led off, "Are we having fun yet?" The editors involved later apologized.[53]

More serious pursuits—and more serious, significant stories—frequently go untold. As the nation ages, journalists must devote increased coverage to areas such as "eldercare," retirement communities, health care and government services and de-emphasize stereotypical images of "sexy seniors" enjoying the "Golden Years."

Children

Children depend on adults for help. But too many children are being battered and abused, and too many are troubled by drugs, peer pressures and split families. Journalists aggressively pursue such stories—after they surface. But instead of waiting to report the latest child-beating death or teenage suicide, they should be "patrolling" the world of children, alert for signs that society is not doing its job to protect them from danger. The sensational episode, such as a child abduction from a shopping center, can overshadow greater dangers existing in the home or other "safe" places. "Despite all the pictures of missing children on shopping bags and milk cartons, children are more likely to be kidnapped by their own parents than by strangers," say Richard Gelles and Murray Straus, authors of *Intimate Violence.*[54]

The old saying, "Children should be seen but not heard," cannot be a guideline for journalists. Reporters, even ones who are parents themselves, should remain alert to the changing, special problems and concerns of children, which means talking to children and, more important, really listening to them.

In 1990 the leaders of 71 nations adopted a declaration at the first World Summit for Children, pledging to fight hunger, disease and illiteracy affecting children. The summit focused on worldwide conditions, but it also helped illuminate problems in particular countries. According to a news report, one U.S. child in five is poor; one in five lacks health insurance. An estimated 100,000 are homeless. The United States ranked 19th in the world in combatting infant mortality and 39th for success in immunizing children.[55] Clearly, the plight of children is compelling not only in Soweto and Calcutta; it is also compelling in Detroit and El Paso.

Other groups that can be considered significant minority "cultures" in American life include gays, Hispanics and Asian-Americans. They, too, contribute to our mosaic society. Reporters who accept diversity as a healthy societal condition will include the views and concerns of *all* cultural groups in their coverage.

At times journalists lean toward advocacy when reporting about the issues affecting children, disabled Americans or other minorities they see as underrepresented or victimized. That is understandable. Try, however, to stay focused and objective. Reporters should question the motives and arguments of any minority proponent as thoroughly and critically as they would those being espoused by a politician running for office or bureaucrat explaining a controversial policy. In fact, most advocates for causes have learned to *become* politicians.

A multicultural perspective requires that journalists attempt to see the world as others see it. It also requires that journalists constantly recheck their perceptions, recognizing that the world changes. Language, for example, that was once acceptable may now offend because of stereotypes it evokes. It took time, but in the 1960s news organizations replaced *Negro* with *black*. In the 1990s a more appropriate reference may be *African-American*. In other instances, overused terms, such as *Third World*, can acquire pejorative meanings.

Reporters who attempt to broaden their perspectives will be rewarded with eye-opening discoveries. Consider one example. In many black communities, the men, and occasionally the women, "gather under the trees." It is a tradition—an institution—that is rooted in African culture. In some African villages, according to reporter Peggy Peterman, only the elders gather—or those who come to the elders in search of wisdom or solutions to problems. Peterman's story told about the fellowship and goodwill of the tree gatherings in St. Petersburg, where food, conversation and emotional support are shared by all—rich and poor, young and old.[56] To the uninformed, an outdoor gathering of black men could be misunderstood. The reaction might be, "Why are they 'hanging out' like that? Don't they have anything better to do?" Journalists who fail to learn about other cultures are destined to misperceive or misjudge based on what they *think* they are seeing.

A multicultural perspective should be global. The idea of the "shrinking world," although now a cliché, persists; the nations of the world are more interconnected and interdependent than ever before. Information technology is removing the few remaining barriers, making it possible to report about Cairo, Egypt, from Cairo (pronounced "Kay-row"), Ill., and vice versa. If properly tapped, knowledge and technology can expand the journalist's horizons, and the journalist, in turn, can expand the public's horizons. Opportunities abound for journalists to produce a more culturally diverse and representative news product: Take advantage of them.

EXERCISES

1. Attend a service at a church, temple or synagogue to sample the ceremonies and rituals of another religion. Prior to your visit, call the pastor, minister or rabbi to arrange for an interview, possibly after the services. Discuss, among other topics, the role of the press in covering religion and how well that role is being carried out.

2. Educators increasingly are taking steps to identify and help so-called at-risk students. At-risk programs usually focus on the elementary grades. Find out what the local school system is doing—or not doing—to reach dropouts, pregnant teens, suicidal students, homeless children and other young people whose academic futures and personal lives are in jeopardy.

3. Collect oral history by interviewing several older members of your community. You might first call the local newspaper or talk to your professor to gather names of possible interviewees. One might be a former mayor; another, an early principal of the high school. Expect them to provide you with finely detailed, vivid accounts of the past.

NOTES

[1] Richard M. Clurman, *Beyond Malice* (New York: Meridian, 1990), p. 145.

[2] "Six (or Seven) Things Editors Should Think About But Don't" *APME Redbook 1989* (New York: Associated Press Managing Editors, 1989), p. 19.

[3] Neil Postman, *Amusing Ourselves to Death* (New York: Penguin Books, 1985), p. vii.

[4] Stewart Brand, *The Media Lab: Inventing the Future at M.I.T.* (New York: Penguin Books, 1988), pp. 258, 259.

[5] Elizabeth Whitney, "A Look Back," *St. Petersburg Times*, Feb. 25, 1990, pp. 1I, 2I.

[6] See *Covering AIDS: A Handbook for Journalists* (Eugene, Ore.: Pacific Media Center, 1987).

[7] See Victor Cohn, *News & Numbers* (Ames, Iowa: Iowa State University Press, 1989).

[8] Debra Hale, "Let Some Premature Babies Die, Study Says," *St. Petersburg Times*, May 16, 1990, p. 1A.

[9] William Safire, "Fruit, Panic and Public Policy," *St. Petersburg Times*, March 24, 1989, p. 21A.

[10] Jeff Greenfield, "Good Science Reporting Requires More Than a 'Nose for News,' " *ASNE Bulletin*, Oct. 1985, p. 32.

[11] Russell Baker, "Cholesterol Makes the Mind Wonder," *St. Petersburg Times*, Nov. 30, 1989, p. 27A.

[12] Marjorie Mandel Brooks, "Environmental Journalism," *Editor & Publisher*, April 21, 1990, p. 21.

[13] Contact the Environmental Health Center, National Safety Council, 1050 17th St. NW, Suite 770, Washington, D.C. 20036, (202) 293-2270.

[14] Emily Sachar, "Teaching School for a Year Gave Reporter New Insights into Reporting on Education," *ASNE Bulletin*, Jan.–Feb. 1990, p. 23.

[15] Lisa Gutierrez, "Editorially Speaking: Reporting from Classroom Breathes Life and Detail in Education Stories," *Gannetteer*, July–Aug. 1989, p. 4.

[16] Gutierrez, "Editorially Speaking," p. 4.

[17] Lisa Walker and John Rankin, eds., *Covering the Education Beat* (Washington, D.C.: Education Writers Association, 1987), p. 5.

[18] John Carlson, "Editorially Speaking: From Giant Apes to Lung Transplants, the College Beat Can Be Exciting," *Gannetteer*, July–Aug. 1989, p. 5.

[19] Tracy Kidder, *Among Schoolchildren* (Boston: Houghton Mifflin, 1989), p. 301.

[20] *Covering the Education Beat*, Education Writers Association, 1001 Connecticut Ave. NW, Suite 310, Washington, D.C. 20036, (202) 429-9680.

[21] S. Robert Lichter, Stanley Rothman and Linda S. Lichter, *The Media Elite* (Bethesda, Md.: Adler & Adler, 1986), p. 22.

[22] Charles E. Shepard, "Jim Bakker Resigns from PTL; Jerry Falwell Assumes Leadership," *Charlotte Observer*, March 20, 1987, p. 1A.

[23] Colman McCarthy, "The Fall of Father Ritter," *St. Petersburg Times*, March 23, 1990, p. 18A.

[24] Religious Newswriters Association, P.O. Box C 32333, Richmond, Va. 23293, (804) 649-6754.

25 David Broder, *Behind the Front Page* (New York: Touchstone, 1988), p. 241.

26 James Deakin, *Straight Stuff* (New York: William Morrow, 1984), p. 327.

27 See *Covering Campaign '88: The Politics of Character and the Character of Politics* (New York: Gannett Center for Media Studies, 1988).

28 Stephen A. Salmore and Barbara G. Salmore, *Candidates, Parties, and Campaigns* (Washington, D.C.: Congressional Quarterly Press, 1985), pp. 51–52.

29 *Covering Campaign '88*, p. 17.

30 See Herbert Asher, *Polling and the Public: What Every Citizen Should Know* (Washington, D.C.: Congressional Quarterly Press, 1988).

31 Philip Seib, *Who's in Charge? How the Media Shape News and Politicians Win Votes* (Dallas: Taylor, 1987), p. 48.

32 "Polling," in *Problems of Journalism: Proceedings of the ASNE 1981 Convention* (Washington, D.C.: American Society of Newspaper Editors, 1981), p. 94.

33 Broder, *Behind the Front Page*, p. 243.

34 A. Kent MacDougall, *Ninety Seconds to Tell It All: Big Business and the News Media* (Homewood, Ill.: Dow Jones–Irwin, 1981), p. 7.

35 Herb Schmertz with William Novak, *Good-bye to the Low Profile: The Art of Creative Confrontation* (Boston: Little, Brown, 1986).

36 James T. Hamilton and Joseph P. Kalt, *Study of Economic and Business Journalism* (Los Angeles: Foundation for American Communications, 1987), p. 6.

37 See Gerald Warfield, *How to Read and Understand the Financial News* (New York: Harper & Row, 1986).

38 Chris Welles, "For-Profit Corporations," in John Ullmann and Steve Honeyman, *The Reporter's Handbook* (New York: St. Martin's Press, 1983). p. 251.

39 Mark Fitzgerald, "Hoaxed," *Editor & Publisher*, March 3, 1990, p. 16.

40 Michael Parenti, *Inventing Reality* (New York: St. Martin's Press, 1986), p. 78.

41 Ferdinand M. de Leon, "*Herald's* Decision to 'Reflect Diversity' Stirs Controversy," *Seattle Times*, Dec. 7, 1990, Sec. C, p. 1.

42 Lichter, Rothman and Lichter, *The Media Elite*, p. 53.

43 "Shattering Myths About the Homeless," *U.S. News & World Report*, March 20, 1989, pp. 27, 28.

44 Michael Moss, "The Poverty Story," *Columbia Journalism Review*, July–Aug. 1987, p. 43.

45 See Carolyn Martindale, *The White Press and Black America* (New York: Greenwood Press, 1986).

46 *The Next Newspapers: Future of Newspapers Report* (Washington, D.C.: American Society of Newspaper Editors Foundation, 1988), p. 27.

47 Clarence Page, "Blacks Versus Media: Not a Pretty Picture," *St. Louis Post-Dispatch*, July 13, 1990, p. 3C.

48 David Maraniss, "McGee Steers with His Own Code of Ethics," *Milwaukee Journal*, July 22, 1990, sec. J, p. 1.

49 Courtland Milloy, "For the Sake of Fairness, Let's Give the Full Story About Blacks," *Washington Post*, Jan. 18, 1990, p. 1J.

50 *The Next Newspapers*, p. 17.

[51] Diane Mason, "News for the Other Half," *St. Petersburg Times*, April 19, 1989, p. 1D.

[52] *Fit to Print: A Terminology and Reference Guide for the Colorado News Media* (Colorado Developmental Disabilities Council, undated), p. 3.

[53] "They Were Just Funnin,' " *The Quill*, March 1990, p. 11.

[54] Richard J. Gelles and Murray A. Straus, *Intimate Violence* (New York: Simon and Schuster, 1988), p. 18.

[55] Reena Shah, "Leaders Embrace Agenda for Young," *St. Petersburg Times*, Oct. 1, 1990, p. 1A.

[56] Peggy Peterman, "A Community Branches Out," *St. Petersburg Times*, Jan. 15, 1991, p. 1D.

Chapter Ten

A distraught woman is encircled by reporters. (Thierry Orban—Patrick Robert/Sygma)

Lessons in
Law and Ethics

Stephen A. Cousley knows firsthand how litigation can smother aggressive journalism. As editor of the *Alton* (Ill.) *Telegraph*, he fought to prevent a $9.2 million libel award from killing his family-owned newspaper.[1] The *Telegraph* survived, but at a dear price.

The *Telegraph*'s troubles began with a confidential memo written by two of its reporters and sent to investigators for a Justice Department task force on organized crime. The memo outlined the reporters' suspicions about possible financial corruption involving a Chicago "family" of the Cosa Nostra, an Alton savings and loan and James Green, a Granite City, Ill., builder. The reporters were taking the tentative first steps—perhaps fruitless steps, they realized—required in investigative reporting. They still lacked enough verifiable evidence and documentation to print anything, but they hoped their contacts in the Justice Department would exchange information and provide leads. The reporters assumed the memo would be seen only by the investigators; they were wrong. In time, the memo reached the federal agency overseeing savings and loan associations, touching off a probe of the Alton firm and the termination of further loans to Green.

Somehow, Green obtained a copy of the memo, and he and several others implicated in the memo's accusations filed a libel suit in 1975. Few people, least of all Steve Cousley, expected the lawsuit to succeed, but when it went to trial five years later, the *Telegraph* lost decisively. Green's attorney convinced the jury that what the *Telegraph* did to his client was no different than allowing one of its delivery trucks to run over Green, leaving him crippled. While the case was being appealed, the *Telegraph* settled with the plaintiffs in 1982 for $1.4 million. In the meantime, the *Telegraph* already had undergone a personality change. Once aggressive in its news coverage, it had become cautious, even passive.

In a *Wall Street Journal* interview, Cousley said the *Telegraph* was like "a tight end who hears footsteps," meaning that his reporters and editors now anticipated being jarred by a tackler, leaving them reluctant to pursue tough stories.[2] Cousley later told another journalist: "All the ideals and principles in the world don't mean a damn when it comes down to hard economics. I like aggressive journalism. Newspapers have to keep doing their job; it's their constitutional responsibility. But when the trail of the story leads into the counting house and threatens the economic existence of the newspaper, watch out."[3] Eventually, the *Telegraph*'s mounting legal and financial troubles contributed to the sale of the newspaper to a privately owned newspaper chain managed by Ralph M. Ingersoll II. In 1986 Stephen A. Cousley resigned, marking the end of the 125-year association of the *Alton Telegraph* and the Cousley family.

What happened to the *Alton Telegraph* dramatizes the litigious climate of journalism. Its chilling effect is understood more viscerally by those who experience litigation than by those who understand it only in theory. While there may be some glory in carrying the First Amendment banner into battle, litigation (like warfare) usually is painful and costly. The price paid goes beyond lawyers' bills and damage awards. Media defendants also can expect their lives to be disrupted for months or years as they undergo intense scrutiny. In a lawsuit, nearly all aspects of a journalist's professional deportment and reputation are subject to question and attack. It is not an enjoyable experience.

In the 1964 landmark libel case of *New York Times v. Sullivan*, the Supreme Court endorsed a "profound national commitment to the principle that debate on public issues should be uninhibited, robust and wide-open."[4] Today that commitment is being tested as the public, press and courts disagree over just how uninhibited, robust and wide open that debate should be.

Media defendants cannot expect much sympathy or support from those outside the profession. Generally, the public shares the plaintiff's point of view: No matter how important a free press is to society, journalists should be held strictly accountable for what they publish or broadcast. Some people believe a stinging legal blow is needed on occasion to remind all journalists to act responsibly. Such a blow landed in 1990, when the *Philadelphia Inquirer* incurred the largest libel award on record against an American newspaper—$34 million. Plaintiff Richard Sprague, a prominent lawyer and former prosecutor, sued over a series of stories that suggested he had interfered with a 1963 murder investigation. Speaking after the verdict, Sprague said news organizations must be punished for their falsehoods. "That is the message the jury wanted to send," he said. "They wanted to get the attention of the media around the country."[5]

Two areas of press law—libel and privacy—receive special attention in this chapter. But an overarching issue connects libel and privacy: journalist-source relationships. Various dimensions of that issue will be explored as well.

Covering news of public affairs is not a job for timid souls who fail to ask tough questions and shy away from potentially explosive stories. Nor is it a job for gung-ho types who seek news with reckless abandon, hurting people and inviting lawsuits. Reporting public affairs requires aggressiveness and enterprise balanced by compassion, caution and common sense. Journalists of equilibrium possess an admirable sensitivity to the legal and ethical rights and wrongs of reporting of the news.

Unfortunately, there are few certainties or firm rules to follow. Media law is complex; media ethics is more complex. As journalists pursue stories, they often must enter a legal-ethical forest. Those who try hard to understand the law and navigate around hazards stand a better chance of reaching the destination all responsible journalists seek—a truthful story that can be told in good conscience.

LIBEL

For journalists, March 9, 1964, represents Liberation Day. On that date, the Supreme Court announced its *New York Times v. Sullivan* decision. *Times v. Sullivan* invited the press to practice an aggressive form of journalism, particularly in coverage of government and public officials. Errors are "inevitable in free debate," the Court's majority said, and to require that critics of government prove the truthfulness of every utterance leads to self-censorship. For freedom of expression to survive, let alone flourish, the justices concluded that "breathing space"—a tolerance for error—was needed. The Court provided that breathing space through the *actual malice rule* (or *New York Times* Rule), which requires public officials suing for libel to prove that a defamatory statement was published "with knowledge of its falsehood or with reckless disregard of whether it was false or not." The actual malice rule shifted the burden of proof in libel cases to public officials, making it more difficult for them to succeed in a libel suit against the news media, which, indeed, was the Court's intent.

As opinions of the Supreme Court and decisions of lower courts further defined and redefined libel law, the actual malice rule proved to be something less than invincible. Ironically, despite *Times v. Sullivan*'s intent to encourage and protect robust coverage of public affairs, libel litigation increased.[6] Over the years, juries and judges have sided frequently with libel plaintiffs, ranging from entertainer Carol Burnett to factory worker David Rouch.

In Rouch's case, the *Battle Creek* (Mich.) *Enquirer* erroneously reported his arrest for the knifepoint rape of a 17-year-old babysitter; the mistake cost the Gannett-owned newspaper a $1 million libel judgment. In closing arguments to the jury, Rouch's attorney alluded to David v. Goliath. "Big Gannett, $364 million last year [and] David Rouch, $30,000 factory worker, 10 years trying to protect himself."[7] The David v. Goliath analogy touches a sensitive public nerve. "The average citizen and juror views the newspaper, its methods and motives skeptically," says editor Steve Wilson. "We are seen as the plaintiffs want us to be seen—a business with a greater desire to sell papers than to inform the public."[8] Even public figures are often viewed as victims of Big Media.

Statistics support Wilson's assessment. A two-year study of jury awards nationwide, for example, found that in 54 libel or privacy trials, the plaintiff won in 42 of 48 jury trials and in 5 of 6 bench trials.[9] The study also found that most libel judgments were either reduced or overturned by appellate courts, but the promise of an appeals victory offers little consolation to journalists facing a lawsuit.

Elements of Libel

Knowledge of libel begins with an indefinite definition: In its broadest sense, *libel* is any published communication that is injurious to another person's reputation, occupation or social contacts. The meaning and language of libel law, though, vary from year to year and state to state, determined by both statute and court decisions.

Persons suing for libel generally must provide evidence that five elements exist: publication, identification, defamation, falsehood and fault. Each element can be tricky and imprecise for plaintiffs and defendants alike.

Publication. In most libel cases, a copy of the offending article or a video (or audio) tape of a broadcast establishes "publication." But as the *Alton Telegraph* case demonstrates, publication can include any communication for which there is a record, such as a memo, letter or notes, including electronic notes and records stored in a news organization's computer system. Publication occurs when someone other than the writer and the subject—a secretary, for example—sees or reads the communication.

Identification. People are usually identified by name, age, address, occupation and other forms of personal description. Identification, however, also can be established by circumstances or context. A police-beat story, for example, that reports the theft of equipment at a work site might quote the construction foreman as saying, "We think it's an inside job, probably involving a worker on the night shift." As everyone at the construction company knows, three guards regularly are on duty at night. The story casts doubt on the honesty of all three, and, although no names are used, dozens of people know the guards' identities.

Misidentifying someone is always embarrassing; it is legal dynamite when the story involves material harmful to a person's reputation. Crime reports, in particular, pose a constant hazard. A careless reporter covering the arrest of a man named Gregory M. Ingram on armed robbery charges checks the newspaper's library for previously published stories about Ingram, finds reference to a Gregory G.M. Ingram, the owner of a hardware store. Without confirming the identity of the man in custody, the reporter describes the suspect as a local businessman. It does not occur to the reporter that there could be two or more Gregory Ingrams; the similarity of the middle initials seems good enough. Not every case of misidentification leads to a libel suit, but few news organizations will tolerate careless, lackadaisical reporters who fail to check for accuracy.

Defamation. A story is not libelous unless defamation occurs. By most definitions, defamation amounts to a falsehood that causes perceptible injury to a person's reputation, such as being fired, losing clients or being ostracized. Not every falsehood, of course, injures. A story that inaccurately reports a jaywalking violation by Jon R. Chase is not likely to tarnish Chase's reputation. Inaccurately reporting Chase's arrest for driving under the influence of alcohol, though, is defamatory.

Circumstances may also affect defamation. For example, incorrectly reporting Mary Davidson once had an abortion might not be defamatory, particularly if Davidson has made it known that she favors abortion as a matter of choice. But if Davidson is a legislator campaigning for re-election on a pro-life platform, the report will do damage and probably is defamatory.

Above all, defamation is a subjective determination. To say a politician has "failed to look out for the well being of her constituents" might strike some people as harmless; to the thin-skinned, the words could be considered injurious.

Falsehood. The falsehood of defamatory statements used to be assumed. Under the common law of libel, it was up to the *defendant* to prove that the statements were *true*. In 1986 the Supreme Court required evidence of factual falsehood as part of a libel *plaintiff*'s burden of proof. The Court went further to state that when evidence of truth or falsity is uncertain, the balance should tip in favor of true speech. Justice Sandra Day O'Connor wrote: "We recognize that requiring the plaintiff to show falsity will insulate from liability some speech that is false, but unprovably so. Nonetheless, . . . the First Amendment requires that we protect some falsehood in order to protect speech that matters."[10] Justice O'Connor's position is consistent with the *Times v. Sullivan* constitutional requirement that the plaintiff prove that the defendant made a defamatory statement with actual malice or negligence. The Court's ruling has given reporters added protection against libel suits.

Fault. The final element of a plaintiff's burden of proof is establishment of fault. The criteria for fault vary, depending to a large degree on the "status" (or category) of plaintiffs. In libel law, plaintiffs fall under two broad, often fuzzy categories: (1) *public official* or *public figure* and (2) *private individual*. The status of a libel plaintiff is critical because it determines which level of fault is to apply—the stricter standard of *actual malice* or the lesser standard of *negligence*.

Determining Fault: A Tough Call

In most instances, attorneys would prefer to represent a "private individual" plaintiff because of the less demanding burden of proving negligence instead of actual malice. As a result, one of the earliest battles in a libel suit is likely to be over the plaintiff's status. In defining *public official,* the Supreme Court has said that the designation "applies at the very least to those among the hierarchy of government employees who have, or appear to the public to have, substantial responsibility for or control over the conduct of governmental affairs."[11] The definition, however, is ambiguous. Many courts, for example, consider police officers to be public officials, but a handful of courts have held otherwise. Similar ambiguity applies to teachers or other public servants whose "responsibility for or control over" governmental affairs may or may not be "substantial." In short, the designation "public official" may be up for grabs.

The Supreme Court's 1974 decision in *Gertz v. Welch* helped distinguish the difference between a public figure and a private individual. A public figure generally falls under five categories: (1) someone of general fame or notoriety in the community; (2) a person with pervasive involvement in societal affairs and issues; (3) an individual who invites public attention; (4) someone who thrusts himself or herself to the forefront to influence the outcome of issues; and (5) a person who is drawn into a particular public controversy involuntarily, although the Supreme Court has noted that "the instances of truly involuntary public figures must be exceedingly rare."[12]

Gertz by no means ended debate over public and private status. A succession of post-*Gertz* decisions both clarified and confused the issue. In one case, the Supreme Court said mere "media interest" in a person does not convert that person into a public figure, nor do those involved in litigation automatically become public figures.[13] In another case, the justices indicated that with a passage of years, someone who was once a public figure could revert to private-individual status.[14]

Plaintiffs deemed by a court to be either a "public official" or a "public figure" must prove *actual malice,* which has come to mean the defendant published a "calculated falsehood,"[15] proceeded with publication despite entertaining "serious doubts" as to its truthfulness,[16] or engaged in conduct that constituted "an extreme departure from the standards . . . of reporting ordinarily adhered to by responsible publishers."[17]

The Supreme Court has not provided many examples of "extreme departures" from normal standards of journalism, leaving that responsibility to trial courts and juries. Obviously, one person's definition of "extreme departure" is going to be another's definition of "moderate departure." Even within the profession, journalists will disagree about what constitutes reckless disregard for the truth. Libel cases from federal and state courts offer little concrete guidance. For example, the Supreme Court, in one of its rare instances of specificity, said in a 1968 libel case that relying totally on an "unverified anonymous phone call" suggests actual malice. In the same decision, the Court said, "Likewise, recklessness may be found where there are obvious reasons to doubt the veracity of the informant or the accuracy of his information."[18]

Most often, judicial guidance is in the form of what is *not* actual malice. Reckless disregard, for example, is *not automatically established by a reporter's failure* (1) to investigate charges, (2) obtain and present both sides of the controversy or (3) include material contradictory to the damaging statements. Reckless disregard obviously is difficult to establish but not impossible. Journalists who think the actual malice rule protects them from incomplete, sloppy reporting are only deluding themselves. Few juries are going be understanding when journalists fail to do a conscientious job of being fair, truthful and thorough in news coverage.

That message came through in one of the Supreme Court's most recent libel cases, when it affirmed a $200,000 damage award against the *Journal News* of Hamilton, Ohio. The newspaper reported that Daniel Connaughton, a candidate for municipal court judge, offered jobs to a grand jury witness and her sister in appreciation for the sisters' help with an investigation damaging to Connaughton's opponent. In his majority opinion, Justice John Paul Stevens said the key factor was the newspaper's failure to interview the grand juror's sister, whom Stevens called the "most important witness to the bribery charges." Failure to investigate is not in itself evidence of actual malice, Stevens said, but "the purposeful avoidance of the truth is a different category."[19] Since motive bears on a finding of actual malice, the Supreme Court has allowed attorneys for libel plaintiffs to vigorously inquire into the state of mind and decision making of journalists.[20] As a result, libel defendants can anticipate a barrage of dozens of questions from the plaintiff's attorney, such as: "Why did you interview Mr. Bowen, an enemy of the plaintiff, and not Mr. Clark, a friend?" or "Why did you include details about my client's tax problems but not details about his charitable work?"

Libel plaintiffs can more easily establish *negligence*, the standard of proof required of private individuals since the *Gertz* decision, when the Supreme Court decided it was unfair to hold private individuals to the same strict standard of proof that applied to influential, visible and powerful persons.[21] By legal definition, there are various degrees of negligence, some more serious than others. Generally, the definition being applied in libel law is either *failing to exercise a degree of care that a prudent person would exercise under similar circumstances* or *doing something a reasonable person would not do.*

Understandably, the standard of journalistic negligence is even more subjective than that of actual malice. Does failure to investigate defamatory charges establish actual malice? Apparently not. But failure to investigate *does* appear to constitute negligence. For example, a magazine writer was found to be negligent for not verifying information about fire hazards of wood-burning stoves. The court said the writer failed to examine two previously published sources for his article or contact the authors of either source, did not know about another article from a different publication that repudiated his claims, and failed to contact anyone in the stove industry for test results relevant to his article.[22]

Admittedly, the difference between public official–public figure and private individual is critical to the outcome of many libel cases. But media defendants who must pin their hopes on the plaintiff's status probably are fighting an uphill battle from the start. As always, journalists who are meticulously accurate and scrupulously fair in news coverage will not have to pray that the plaintiff is designated a "public figure."

Defenses

The constitutional libel defense provided by *New York Times v. Sullivan* is the journalist's principal protection. However, anyone facing a libel suit would prefer multiple layers of protection that include the defenses of *truth, consent, neutral reportage* and *privileged communications.*

Truth. Truth normally is an absolute defense in libel cases. If truth is on your side, victory and vindication *should* be yours, with an emphasis on *should.* Libel cases are exceedingly unpredictable. Whose version of the "truth" will the judge and jury believe? Despite the plaintiff's burden to prove, among other things, falsity, media defendants should be prepared to face an unofficial burden to prove truthfulness. Stories based on solid documentation notes, tape recordings, records and reliable, named sources are far easier to defend, if it comes to that.

Consent. When people talk to reporters, there is an assumption of implied consent. It is further assumed that news sources are talking freely without conditions, aware that what they say might later be broadcast or published. Dangers arise when a news subject withdraws consent prior to publication or broadcast, denies ever talking to the reporter or claims the reporter concealed his or her intent to publish what was said. A particularly self-damaging statement ought to be recorded verbatim, transcribed and accompanied by the subject's signed consent.

Neutral reportage. The defense of neutral reportage protects journalists who cover accusations and statements involving newsworthy public controversies. Neutral reportage is a promising development in libel law, but questions about its validity will remain until the Supreme Court addresses the issue. The defense, first recognized in 1977 by a U.S. Circuit Court of Appeals, has been endorsed by state courts in Illinois, California and Ohio, for example, but rejected in several other federal and state courts.

Where it is accepted, neutral reportage is a conditional or qualified defense intended to allow news organizations to disseminate the words of prominent, responsible persons or organizations regarding serious charges on an issue of public importance, provided coverage is disinterested and accurate.[23] Those conditions must be met for the defense to apply. It remains a viable defense even when reporters entertain doubts about the truthfulness of the charges.

Privileged communications. A broad category of public meetings, proceedings, pronouncements and records are considered *privileged communications* and immune from a lawsuit. In libel law, a *privilege* is an exemption from liability based on a premise that society's interests in unimpeded communication occasionally outweigh society's concern for an individual's reputation. The privilege is either absolute or conditional. *Absolute privilege* normally covers official acts of public officers and all judicial and legislative proceedings, such as city council meetings and court hearings. Lawmakers, for example, enjoy absolute privilege so they can freely debate and resolve public issues germane to their official duties. *Conditional* (or qualified) *privilege* applies to communication that falls outside of absolute protection but nonetheless is related to important societal interests. Conditional privilege, for example, might protect a citizen who errs in identifying a holdup suspect in a good-faith attempt to assist police.

For the most part, the press enjoys a conditional privilege to report official meetings and communications with immunity, as long as coverage is accurate and free of any "extraneous" (outside) libelous material. Unfortunately, it is hard to know from state to state or jurisdiction to jurisdiction what is a privileged communication or situation and what is not. As a rule, information and statements emerging from open court proceedings and legislative sessions are privileged. Generally, so are public reports issued by governmental officials or offices. But more gray exists than black and white.

A few examples underscore the problem:

Is an arrest report an official government document? In some jurisdictions, courts have ruled it is; in others, it takes issuance of a warrant before information of an arrest becomes privileged communication.

Is a complaint or petition that initiates litigation a privileged communication? In a majority of states that have ruled on the question, privilege does not automatically commence with the initial filing; there must be either action by the court or a formal response by the other side before privilege clearly applies. One reason for such a policy is to protect people from damage done by a frivolous, unwarranted lawsuit.

Is fair, accurate reportage of a legislator's attacks on another person privileged? This, too, is a hazy area. In most instances, the legislator's words must directly relate to official business, or, as the Supreme Court has said, to the "deliberative process" of the legislative body. Lawmakers do not enjoy absolute privilege every time they speak, so reporters may not be free of liability, for example, when they publish or broadcast a legislator's comments made during a corridor news conference or on a television talk show.

Obviously, reporters cannot always predetermine privileged communication. The safest course is never to spread any damaging accusation or comment without a serious effort to verify the charges and present the other side's story. When phone calls or messages fail to elicit a response, some news organizations will send certified letters to establish that the news source knew that his or her comments were sought.

PRIVATE LIVES VS. THE PUBLIC'S BUSINESS

Reporters can invade someone's privacy by word, deed or both. By definition, libel centers on publication. Privacy poses a double danger. Publishing embarrassing details about someone's life might constitute one type of privacy action; a second privacy action might be based on the alleged deception a reporter used to obtain information.

Privacy actions fall under four categories:

- embarrassing facts—publicly disclosing private facts, such as someone's confidential medical records

- intrusion—violating someone's solitude by trespass, harassment, surveillance or other intrusive means

- false light—misrepresenting someone's views or characteristics in the public eye

- appropriation—using someone's name or likeness for financial gain, which usually arises from advertising or promotion of products and services

Three of the four privacy actions—intrusion, embarrassing facts and false light—apply most directly to reporters. Each contributed to a prison guard's lawsuit against the *Dallas Times Herald*. The guard was one of 12 taken hostage and tortured during a 1980 riot at a New Mexico state penitentiary. According to the lawsuit, the reporter accompanied a visitor to the guard's hospital room. What happened in the hospital room is disputed. The guard claims the reporter eavesdropped on a private conversation, later producing a story that disclosed embarrassing facts about how he had been sodomized with an ax handle and placed him in a false light by referring to his "near-poverty" wages. A federal court jury awarded the guard $200,000 in damages.[24]

Privacy clashes are complicated because two constitutional interests are at stake—the public's right to know versus the individual's right to be left alone. Privacy is cherished, especially in an Information Age when so little about our lives is hidden or protected. Yet the Supreme Court, employing much the same reasoning it applied to libel law, has given the press considerable freedom to report and publish, even when reporters go where they are unwelcome and report on matters people dearly want to keep private. The Supreme Court's leading privacy case, *Time, Inc. v. Hill*, decided three years after *Times v. Sullivan*, stressed the importance of debate on all matters of public interest.[25] In subsequent cases, the court expanded rights to report about the private affairs of public officials and public figures. More recently, the Court rulings have given journalists the right to publish identities and details about society's most heinous assault on personal privacy—rape.[26]

While, indeed, there is considerable freedom to gather and report news, there are also limits, and when reporters exceed those limits, they can expect public scorn and dire legal consequences. Problems invariably arise when reporters expose private details in a manner and to a degree most people would find offensive.

Intrusion

Several privacy cases serve as warnings for journalists. One is *Dietemann v. Time*. In that case, a photographer and reporter for *Life* magazine posed as patients to secretly photograph and record what happened inside the home office of a man suspected of practicing medicine without a license. He was found guilty, but even guilty people have rights. Upholding a $1,000 award in the plaintiff's favor, the court said the First Amendment was not "a license to trespass, to steal or to intrude by electronic means into the precincts of another's home or office."[27]

Does *Dietemann* place reporters in jeopardy of litigation whenever they masquerade, conceal their identities, use hidden tape recorders or employ high-tech equipment to intercept private communication? No, partly because *Dietemann* represents the views of a single court. Additionally, federal law and statutes in some states require one-party consent (the journalist's) to electronically record conversations in person by use of an inexpensive suction-cup device that allows taping of telephone calls. But reporters who engage in trickery or subterfuge to enter private property or acquire confidential information ask for trouble, as *Dietemann* demonstrates.

A profession that resorts to lies and deception risks loss of public respect, trust and cooperation. Do not, for example, expect Patricia

Martin, her family or friends to place much trust in the press. Martin, widow of a South Dakota state official, accused a local journalist of pretending to be an "old dear friend" of her husband, who said he wanted to express condolences. Only later did she realize she had been tricked into revealing her feelings about a painful situation that became known after her husband's death—he secretly had a second wife and separate family in another South Dakota city.[28] Few stories are so big or significant that they justify deceit and lies. Journalism is best served by honest, up-front reporting methods.

Galella v. Onassis sounds another alarm: Reporters who engage in aggressive tactics may cross the indistinct line that separates legitimate newsgathering from intrusion. Despite her public stature as a former first lady, Jacqueline Kennedy Onassis obtained an injunction that ordered freelance photographer Ron Galella to keep a distance from her and her children. In issuing the injunction, the court commented: "There is no general constitutional right to assault, harass, or unceasingly shadow or distress public figures."[29] When does reporting amount to harassment or cause distress? A reporter seeking information relevant to a legitimate news story is right to pursue a public official by telephone or other means, like camping outside the official's office. A reporter who calls at 3 a.m., when his questions can wait until a reasonable hour, hassles the official's spouse or children or engages in threatening tactics no longer is enterprising or determined. Such a reporter is abusive.

Intrusion can occur in public or semi-public places as well as private ones. Depending on the circumstances, people are entitled to a personal *zone of privacy* that invisibly encircles them. Courts have ruled that a privacy zone applies, for example, to a patient recuperating in a hospital room or an executive conducting private business in a public facility, such as a transaction at a bank. Reporters are not legally free to wander into any room or peer over shoulders, even when their snooping occurs in places generally accessible to the public. Nor are they free to use electronic devices (telephone bugs, hidden tape recorders) or high-powered lenses to intercept private communications or spy from afar.

In most cases, private places are strictly off limits to reporters; no matter how important the story, no matter how newsworthy the individual, trespassing or eavesdropping on private property constitutes intrusion. An apparent exception is coverage of a disaster, such as a fire, tornado or plane crash, particularly if law enforcement personnel grant reporters permission to enter private property.

An invitation by public officials is not, however, an unconditional passport to all news scenes. Reporters who accompanied authorities on a midnight raid of a private school for troubled youths learned that lesson when the Florida Supreme Court said, "In this jurisdiction, a law enforcement officer is not endowed with the right or authority to invite people of his choosing to invade private property."[30] Even when covering emergencies, reporters should show respect for the property and privacy of others and seek permission if the owner is present.

Embarrassing Facts

A critical point to remember about publication of embarrassing facts is that *truth offers no protection against litigation.* Some facts are simply too private, too intimate or too hurtful to be disclosed. There is no inclusive list of embarrassing facts, but many people, including journalists, would say at minimum the list includes details about an individual's sexual life, family relationships and physical or mental health. Nonetheless, reporters still may be ethically correct and legally safe to report, for example, that a candidate for judge takes an anti-depressant drug or that an ex-Marine who saved the president from a would-be assassin's bullet is gay. Privacy rights can be overcome by a nebulous, highly subjective, catchall defense called *newsworthiness.*

What, then, is newsworthy? There is no telling how a particular judge or jury is going to determine which published or broadcast stories are "newsworthy" and which are not, but the standard applied by various courts focuses on information of legitimate "public interest" or "public concern." In applying that loose standard, courts frequently have looked to the tastes and mores of the mythical "reasonable person." As one court put it, "The line is to be drawn when the publicity ceases to be giving of information of which the public is entitled and becomes a morbid and sensational prying into private lives for its own sake, with which a reasonable member of the public, with decent standards, would say that he had no concern."[31] Style or intent appears to be a factor. A breathless, *National Enquirer*–type presentation may suggest a "sensational prying into private lives."

A reasonable person probably would find much of the daily stream of information about public affairs—crime, accidents and litigation—"newsworthy." Less clear is how a reasonable person would categorize details about life's misfortunes, curiosities or oddities, such as the birth of Siamese twins. Most journalists would say, "That's news." But laypeople might respond, "Let the family decide whether it is news or not."

The question of newsworthiness is undoubtedly related to an individual's position or status in life. For celebrities and public officials, little is private and outside the realm of public interest or concern. The question of newsworthiness is less settled when a child or spouse of a public person becomes an object of media attention. The mayor's treatment for drug dependency is newsworthy. But what if the mayor's 24-year-old son is being treated privately? Is that newsworthy? Perhaps, depending on the circumstances. Are the son's problems preoccupying the mayor's thoughts, taking him away from city hall for long stretches of time and adversely affecting important city business? The mayor's absences and lack of attention must be explained, which invariably would mean reference to his son, but the focus should, it seems, remain on the public person—the mayor—and not the son.

Reporters need to be especially sensitive to the privacy of children, even children involved in stories with tempting human-interest appeal. For the most part, courts are protective about minors, particularly those who are considered "special" because of physical, mental or psychological needs. A reporter may feel proud after doing a story on an experimental program that has accomplished wonders for a group of fourth-graders with learning disabilities. But what if several sets of parents, while immensely gratified over their child's progress, have kept the learning disability a private matter? Even the neighbors do not know. Reporters are advised to proceed carefully with stories about children and, in most cases, to talk to the parents to discover whether they object to coverage. The parents may have compelling reasons for privacy that never occurred to the reporter.

Privacy rights generally yield when the information comes from public records. In several cases, the Supreme Court has upheld the press in privacy actions, holding in one of those cases, which involved publication of a rape victim's name, that the First Amendment "protects the publication of truthful information contained in official court records open to public inspection."[32] The public-records defense, however, is slippery because not all records held by government agencies and departments are open and accessible to the public. In fact, in many states, scores of records, such as identities of people receiving public aid, are exempt from disclosure for privacy considerations. Check with officials to ensure that the records in question are, indeed, "public."

Reporters should never, however, use availability of private information in public records as an *excuse* or *rationalization* to disclose embarrassing facts. Of special concern are rape victims. Although police records, available to reporters, might reveal names, nearly all news organizations voluntarily withhold the identity of rape victims to protect them from additional emotional trauma. Only the most reckless or thoughtless reporter would identify a rape victim when her assailant is at large. Nonetheless, that has happened in several instances, subjecting the victims to threatening telephone calls and other forms of harassment.

A handful of legitimate exceptions to the general policy of non-disclosure in rape cases allow the prominence of the victim and the circumstances surrounding the case to outweigh the individual's privacy rights. Still, the press goes to great lengths to protect identities. In 1989, a gang of youths brutally beat and raped a young investment banker who was jogging through New York City's Central Park. As *Newsweek* noted, "We've followed her remarkable recovery, from a shattered and comatose shell . . . to a walking miracle who returned to work. We seem to know everything except her name." For once, writer David Kaplan noted, the press "applauded itself for not doing its job" to report.[33]

At times, journalists' access to public records allows them to disclose facts that do more than embarrass, as the ordeal of Texas pediatrician Robert J. Huse illustrates. After Huse tested positive for the AIDS antibody, his former roommate began telling people the doctor had AIDS. Fearing the parents of his patients would react with needless alarm, Huse sought a restraining order to attempt to silence the former roommate, and Huse filed the petition under his actual name, not as "John Doe." By doing so, Huse made his medical condition a matter of public record, and before long several newspapers, including both Dallas dailies, had reported Huse's exposure to the AIDS virus.

Admittedly, there are no sure, easy answers to guide the press in handling stories like Huse's, partly because there are no sure, easy answers to AIDS. The fact remained that Dr. Huse did not have AIDS, and, as one newspaper reported, a "person with the AIDS virus has no more than a 30 percent chance of contracting the disease over the next five years."[34] Nonetheless, if the doctor felt there was no need to inform patients of his condition, did it fall to the press to do so? Many editors—and laypeople—would say, "yes." What about alternatives? Would withholding the doctor's name and using a reference such as a "local pediatrician" be an acceptable option? Perhaps not, because then all pediatricians in town would be suspect.

Normally, journalists strive to be precise and complete in covering stories and naming names. Should AIDS carriers be an exception? The publicity cost Dr. Huse his career in medicine. Do not look for easy answers. Ethical reporters, though, consider the range of consequences whenever a story poses the possibility of harming others. In the end, you may be faced with the painful task of determining where the *greatest* potential harm resides. In the aftermath of the Huse case, reports from Florida established that a dentist with AIDS had infected at least three patients. The deadly consequences of AIDS pressure journalists to inform the public of potential risks.

False Light

False light resembles libel. In privacy law, however, a false light often pertains to non-defamatory falsehoods—ones that may not necessarily damage reputation but cause embarrassment or distress. In one case, a man photographed standing in a line at a state unemployment office unsuccessfully sued for false light. It turned out that the man was not there to receive jobless benefits but to serve as a translator for a friend who did not speak English.[35]

For a plaintiff who is either a public figure or public official, the burden of proof in false light cases is identical to the libel plaintiff's—the actual malice standard. What is not clear is whether the actual malice standard applies to *all* false light plaintiffs, including private individuals. In libel law, the Supreme Court has declared that private individuals need only prove negligence to collect all but punitive damages. The Court has not, as yet, made a similar distinction in false light cases, although several state courts have applied the negligence standard in the false light suits of private individuals, further clouding the waters.

False light actions involving news reporters usually fall under one of two categories—fictionalization or distortion. With fictionalization, a reporter remakes a real-life person to sharpen features, invent dialogue or create scenes through a blending of fact and fiction. Fictionalization is most likely to occur when a reporter draws on the techniques of creative writing, such as characterization, scene-setting and internal dialogue, to produce a detailed profile or narrative. Reporters are right to borrow the style and devices of fiction to energize their writing as long as they remain true to journalism's tenets of accuracy and fairness. Occasionally, a reporter will go too far, swept away by unbridled imagination or ambition. Good stories, however, do not require fictionalized treatment. In the hands of a skilled, sensitive and honest writer, a mother's struggle to support seven children after her husband's death in a bridge collapse remains compelling without a need for embellishment.

False light by distortion most often occurs when a reporter quotes someone out of context or omits crucial facts or details. Because journalists often make hundreds of judgments as they decide how to best report and write a story, the possibility of distortion is high. Of thousands of words spoken in an interview or the hundreds of facts and details collected during newsgathering only a fraction usually end up in a story. Journalism inherently is a process of selectivity; reporters must remember that as they *choose* and, particularly, as they *discard* story material. Distortion can be accidental or calculated. Neither type of distortion is excusable, but intentionally misrepresenting someone's views or characteristics is a serious offense in journalism and evidence of actual malice in privacy law.

On being sued

Journalists might mistakenly assume the law is firmly on their side, as libel or invasion of privacy plaintiffs struggle to meet a heavy burden of proof. In the courtroom, though, lofty legal principles of free expression often get swept aside. When journalists face the opposing side's attorneys, a lawsuit can degenerate to a dogfight. Remember the statistics of libel and privacy trials; they suggest that the plaintiff's burden of proof can be met to the satisfaction of a majority of trial judges and juries. Journalists who fail to vigorously defend their actions increase the odds that already are heavily against them.

The fact is, any journalist sued for libel or invasion of privacy must be prepared to *prove* his or her innocence. If you face a deposition hearing or cross-examination on the witness stand, expect to be challenged and questioned by a skilled interrogator intent on making you look inept, reckless, malicious or all three. Explanations of newsroom practices can be made to sound absurd or laughable: "Let me get this straight, Mr. Jackson. So you tried only two times to call Mr. Jones about a story that has wrecked his career? And that's what is considered responsible journalism in your newsroom?" The journalist's credentials will be fair game. "Ms. Evans, when's the last time you had a course on libel law? 'Not since journalism school?' That was 15 years ago, wasn't it Ms. Evans? Was it a full course on libel— or a unit or just a week?" Your attorney might shout objections, and the jurors might be told by the judge to "disregard" the opposing attorney's remarks. By then, though, it might be too late. You have been portrayed as an ill-prepared, sloppy journalist.

PRIVACY AND LIBEL DANGER ZONES

Journalists seldom anticipate the mistakes that lead to libel or privacy lawsuits. One of the main danger zones in libel and privacy centers on *expunged* (erased) *records.* Most states, depending on the circumstances, permit courts to remove or expunge arrest records, particularly if charges have been dropped. Occasionally, even records of convictions are expunged. When that happens, it is as if the records never existed. As a result, a libel defendant cannot easily cite "truth" or "privileged communication" as defenses when the records to establish those defenses do not officially exist. Similarly, a privacy defendant may find newsworthiness no protection because expungement, after all, is meant to guard against disclosure.

Another set of legal problems arises when journalists routinely include arrest and conviction information lifted from previously published stories or obtained through unofficial sources. Journalists must consider the possibility that the court documents no longer are part of the public record. Suppose a reporter doing a routine check on a finalist for police chief calls the candidate's hometown newspaper for background information and learns that six years ago, the chief pled "no contest" to charges that he beat a girlfriend in a quarrel. Rather than settle for secondhand information, the reporter calls the court clerk's office to confirm details and obtain, if possible, a photocopy of records. (Failing to obtain confirmation from an official source is sloppy work and potentially reckless reporting, regardless of whether the records have been expunged.) A clerk tells the reporter there is no record of the case. Obviously, the reporter has encountered an obstacle, but it does not mean the story of the police chief's past problems must be killed. Considering the chief's stature and the importance of his position in the community, the odds of a successful suit are slim. Some stories are not risk-free. In this scenario, however, the reporter and his editors were able to anticipate the risks and figure the odds.

With both libel and privacy cases, passage of time diminishes the legal and ethical justification for the press to resurrect facts and information that continue to harm a person's reputation or feelings. In the opinion of some courts, public persons who purposefully shun publicity eventually revert to private-individual status. That is even truer of private persons who voluntarily or involuntarily became public figures for a short time—perhaps a five-minute act of heroism in a plane crash. How long must they be expected to pay the price of once being a news subject? Reporters cannot be oblivious to this problem or assume that the individual will not mind having his or her story retold.

Journalists should be particularly sensitive when reporting about people who occupied news for their misdeeds but now, after being punished, are trying to rebuild their lives. As one court explained, "One of the premises of the rehabilitative process is that the offender can rejoin that great bulk of the community from which he has been ostracized. . . . In return for becoming a new man, he is allowed to melt into the shadows of obscurity."[36] Remember, too, that no matter how well intended a story might be, it still may cause pain or troubles for the people it affects.

Computer-smart reporters face a newly emerging category of dangers when they search for electronic records, even public ones, without authorization. Today, anyone who illegally extracts information from private or public data bases may face criminal charges for electronic trespassing. Certainly those who break into computer files face civil action if the material they obtain discloses private facts or falsely injures a reputation. Medical records are a special problem. When policyholders routinely sign consent forms that give the insurance company access to medical records, those records may be stored in information clearinghouses, such as the Medical Information Bureau in Boston, that share records with other insurance companies. Records that once were difficult or impossible to obtain now are readily available.[37] Reporters with the means to obtain computerized records must never forget the power they possess. Extraordinary circumstances are necessary to justify disclosure of medical records or other private, potentially harmful details that are meant to be confidential under the law and public policy. Moreover, any record, especially those stored in huge electronic depositories, can be misfiled or contain incorrect information, adding further meaning to the computer-age expression of "garbage in, garbage out."

For reasons that go far beyond fear of litigation, journalists must always be vigilant for errors. Writer Martha Hume survived a libel suit but the experience taught her a lesson. "Being sued . . . made me hypersensitive about every little fact," she said. "[I now] double-check and triple-check every last detail." Hume wrote about the dangers of fitness tests conducted by health clubs. Wired to a heart monitor, she took a test and reported that her pulse rate reached 178 beats a minute, what she described as a dangerously high rate without a doctor or emergency equipment standing by. Her notes included hundreds of details but no reference to the figure "178." It could have been, she said, an expensive omission if the plaintiff's attorney made it an issue.[38]

Precise, legible notes, tape-recorded interviews and thorough, careful, eyes-on examination of all documents and records help ensure against mistakes that lead to lawsuits. Never let deadline pressure force you to skim documents or take reporting shortcuts.

JOURNALISTS AND THEIR SOURCES

Several years ago, a student interning at a small daily newspaper came by her journalism teacher's office to share some exciting news. "I'm going to get a byline on a story I did on some teenagers who break into homes." The teacher listened intently and then said, "Bonnie, are you prepared to go to jail over this story?" He never meant to shock her, but he did. Quickly, he explained what might happen if she refused a judge's orders to reveal the names of the youths. It turned out that a junior editor planned to use the story in a weekend edition, but he had not cleared the story with superiors. In the end, the newspaper's editor decided the story was not worth the grief it might cause for the intern. The intern and her teacher agreed.

Journalists who build stories on unnamed, confidential sources ought to understand the consequences. Among the legal entanglements are contempt citations, libel suits and reporter-source contractual disputes. The ethical problems include what columnist James Kilpatrick derisively calls "trust-me" journalism.[39]

Another set of reporter-source problems arises when reporters abuse, mistreat or deceive people in pursuit of the news.

Granting Anonymity: Risks and Rewards

Reporters need confidential sources; they provide tips, information and insights that lead to important stories. The classic confidential source is Watergate's "Deep Throat," the shadowy figure who helped Carl Bernstein and Bob Woodward investigate the Nixon administration. Over the years, reporters have courageously or stubbornly refused to reveal the identity of their confidential sources, enduring jail, fines and ostracism, even from colleagues.

At issue is a controversial legal concept called *journalists' privilege*. A privilege, in this context, is an exception to the law. Journalists have long argued that they are entitled to the same testimonial privilege traditionally reserved for lawyer-client, doctor-patient, priest-penitent and husband-wife. The argument is based on a reasonable premise: Forcing reporters to reveal confidences would dry up a major tributary of news, depriving people of their right to know about important issues. Journalists' privilege, however, clashes with another reasonable premise: For the courts (or other judicial bodies) to administer justice and seek the truth, they must be as unrestricted as possible to compel testimony and produce evidence.

The Supreme Court addressed the question of journalists' privilege just once, in the 1972 decision of *Branzburg v. Hayes*.[40] Although the Court's majority declined to recognize a constitution-based journalists' privilege, the decision did not, as it might have done, strip the press of protection against forced disclosure of confidential sources. *Branzburg* proved to be a flexible opinion, offering courts room to maneuver. As lower courts attempted to resolve journalists' privilege disputes case by case, a number adopted a three-part standard urged by Justice Potter Stewart in his *Branzburg* dissent. Stewart said those seeking confidential information from journalists should (1) establish the relevancy of the information sought to the legal question at hand; (2) demonstrate that the information sought cannot be obtained by alternative means or from other sources; and (3) show a compelling and overriding governmental interest in the information.

There are no guarantees when a journalist decides to protect a confidential source; some courts are more sensitive to the demands of newsgathering and the importance of anonymity than others. But certain situations leave reporters with little hope for protection. For example, a reporter who witnesses a serious crime or whose testimony can lead to an arrest can expect to be subpoenaed and ordered to disclose information. A similar fate probably awaits a reporter who possesses information crucial to determining guilt or innocence in a criminal trial or that goes to the "heart of the matter" in a civil case.

When a story based on anonymous sources results in a libel or privacy suit, one of the first steps the plaintiff's attorneys will take is to ask the reporter to name names. If the court agrees that the identity of the sources is central to the plaintiff's ability to establish fault, the reporter can further anticipate an order to disclose identities. Refusal may result in a contempt citation and possibly jail. Another possibility is that the judge will instruct the jury to assume that the anonymous sources do not exist.

In 26 states, reporters are protected to varying degrees by statutes commonly known as "shield laws." Many of those laws, however, include exceptions to a general policy of non-disclosure of confidential sources and information. In other words, there may be ways for those determined to force disclosure of sources to circumvent a shield law.

Until recently, journalists who revealed the names of confidential sources risked only professional ostracism. Now, however, they may be liable for breach of contract. In 1988 a Minnesota jury awarded $700,000 in damages to Dan Cohen, who had been identified in a *St. Paul Pioneer Press* story despite reporters' promises that his name would not be used. Six days before an election, Cohen, a spokesperson for a political candidate, gave reporters documents showing that a rival candidate had admitted to shoplifting $6 worth of merchandise in an incident dating back 12 years. Over objections of their reporters, editors at the newspaper decided Cohen needed to be identified to give readers the fullest information about the campaign.[41]

The Minnesota Supreme Court overturned the damage award, arguing that enforcing a contract agreement would violate the defendants' First Amendment rights. In 1990 the case went to the U.S. Supreme Court.[42] No matter what the outcome, newsgathering is likely to suffer. If the Supreme Court upholds the contract argument, then reporters can expect news sources to demand legal safeguards before revealing sensitive information. If the Court supports the First Amendment argument, then many news sources, concluding that a reporter's promise of confidentiality is meaningless, will remain silent.

The *Cohen* case also demonstrates another important point

about confidential sources: The decision to pledge anonymity to a news source is not the reporter's alone, and editors and reporters do not always share the same views. A reporter who disobeys an editor's order to reveal a source might retain his or her principles but lose the news organization's legal backing in the process.

Journalists are especially wary about confidential sources as a result of the Janet Cooke affair. Cooke, a *Washington Post* reporter, won a Pulitzer Prize in 1981 for her moving story of an 8-year-old heroin addict named Jimmy. The story was based on anonymous sources; no real names or addresses were used. The *Post's* editors did require Cooke to reveal her sources. It turned out the story was fiction, and Cooke was stripped of her Pulitzer Prize. No wonder many editors and news directors now insist on knowing the names of reporters' confidential sources.

A subpoena can be the ultimate test of a journalist's commitment to sources and the First Amendment. The experience of William Farr is an example. In 1970 Farr, covering the murder trial of Charles Manson, obtained a sworn deposition in which one of Manson's followers described how Manson planned to butcher several Hollywood stars. Farr's newspaper, the *Los Angeles Herald-Examiner*, published details in the deposition despite the objections of the trial judge, who earlier had ordered participants not to make any out-of-court statements. Apparently, either a defense or prosecution attorney leaked the deposition to Farr. Over the next 11 years, the case bounced from court to court—federal and state—with Farr either under threat of confinement or embroiled in court hearings and motions. Farr eventually spent 46 days in jail for refusing to identify the source of the deposition. Later, several attorneys connected to the Manson case sued Farr for libel, seeking to clear themselves of suspicion; they, too, wanted to know which attorney on the case violated the judge's order. Although, in a sense, Farr prevailed, the case left him financially and emotionally drained.

Journalists' privilege involves more than complications over subpoenas, contempt citations and contract suits; it can also lead to a malady known as "sourcery." Some reporters, say critics, too quickly and too often grant anonymity. As a consequence, confidential sources are handed the means to spread accusations and plant information without accountability. The ultimate loser is the public, which is denied the opportunity to judge the credibility of these nameless, faceless "authorities."

Sourcery's roots are in Washington, D.C., where story after story cites "high-ranking officials" or "sources close to the White House." But sourcery has spread from big-city dailies to small-town weeklies, with rookie reporters and school board members engaging in the D.C. jargon of "deep backgrounders," "off the record" and "not for attribution."

Actually, few stories require pledges of confidentiality. Reporters should first determine whether there is a genuine need for anonymity. Is the information so sensitive that exposing its source is dangerous? In many cases, there is no danger, only a reluctance to be identified as the source. Sometimes, with additional digging and legwork, the information can be obtained in other ways or from other sources willing to go on record. Indeed, many reluctant sources, if approached properly and persistently, ultimately will speak without conditions.

In those handful of cases where reasons for confidentiality appear strong and the story is important, the next step is to assess the reliability and motives of the source. Seek documentation and corroboration, especially if the sources are government officials, who may be using the press to plant a bogus story about an issue to test public reaction. Never agree to grant anonymity to someone whose intent is to launch a personal attack on a rival.

When reporters and editors agree that confidentiality is justified, the story should explain the reasons for not naming a source. Try to identify unnamed sources as precisely as possible, using a title or a job description. Finally, reporters should determine whether they and their sources speak the same language. To a reporter, "off the record" may mean, "Not to be used in any way." To a news source it may mean, "Quote my words, but don't attribute them to *me* in any way."

Reporting Rumors

Rumors ought to carry a warning sign: "Handle with Great Care." Many rumors that become news stories deal with what might be considered "scandalous" or "shocking" details of public figures and public officials, such as extramarital affairs, drug use, alcoholism and mental illness.

Asking a news source to confront a rumor in a public forum, such as a press conference, often does more harm than good. In 1986 on the *Today* show, an NBC reporter asked Rep. Jack Kemp if he ever had a homosexual encounter. A *Today* official said the question enabled Kemp to put the rumor to rest. It did not. Other news outlets, including the *New York Times* and *Washington Post*, repeated the NBC reporter's question and Kemp's response, further spreading the rumor.[43] Prior to any thought of broadcast or publication, reporters should confirm significant rumors, learn who is spreading them and determine why they are being spread. Rumors tend to dry up when rumor-spreaders are pressed for details or asked to go on record.

Obviously, some rumors must be addressed by the press, but the objective should be a good-faith, non-judgmental attempt to either verify or dispel rumors, not spread or profit from them. Today's coverage of rumors calls for some introspection: Do reporters too eagerly snap at the bait of gossip, forgetting that many rumors are spread out of ill will? And is the press too moralistic about the personal behavior of public persons? A *Newsweek* article made a point all journalists ought to ponder. By scrutinizing moral minutiae, such as ascertaining whether a congressional candidate ever smoked marijuana, the press may be overlooking issues or questions of far greater importance.[44] Moreover, coverage of rumors may unfairly put public persons on trial for an isolated indiscretion or mistake. Fair, serious journalism calls for a thorough examination of all available evidence and consideration of the individual's full record. Rushing into print or onto the air with a snippet of gossip might undermine or even destroy an entire career of good deeds.

Dealing with Sources

Janet Malcolm's book *The Journalist and the Murderer* explores the relationships between journalists and news sources.[45] Malcolm focused on the battle between writer Joe McGinniss, author of *Fatal Vision*, and his subject, Jeffrey MacDonald, the ex–Green Beret doctor who was convicted of murdering his wife and two daughters. But her commentary applies to everyone whose job is to draw stories and information out of others for publication or broadcast. Malcolm's stinging attack on journalists, first published in *New Yorker* magazine, is quoted in Chapter 2. Her words, however, bear repeating in a context of law and ethics: "Every journalist who is not too stupid or full of himself to notice what is going on knows that what he does is morally indefensible. He is a kind of confidence man, preying on people's vanity, ignorance, loneliness, gaining their trust and betraying them without remorse."[46] Critics accused Malcolm of exaggeration, yet her attack helped draw attention to what she called a "messy drawer" of legal and ethical issues.[47]

McGinniss spent a year cultivating a close relationship with Mac-Donald, presumably preparing to vindicate his friend in a forthcoming book. But when *Fatal Vision* was published in 1983, it portrayed MacDonald as a psychopathic killer. Feeling used and betrayed, MacDonald sued McGinniss for distorting the "essential integrity of his life story." MacDonald's lawyer framed the case as an issue of a "false friend" journalist who violated the trust of his interview subject by lying and deceit. McGinniss' lawyer argued that the case placed all journalists at risk of being sued "for writing truthful but unflattering articles should they ever have acted in a fashion that indicated a sympathetic attitude toward their interview subject."[48]

Although MacDonald and McGinniss settled out of court, the issues raised by the case remain disturbingly unsettled. As Martin Garbus, an attorney who handles press law issues, explains: "Taking Malcolm's argument at its extreme that nearly all journalists manipulate, seduce and even lie to get a story the question remains: Do we balance that ethical breach against the need to get out the truth, or do we 'forget the story'?"[49] Is the story—the Truth—of paramount importance? As Garbus correctly notes, "For those of us who hold both First Amendment values and honesty dear, there is a conflict." Of course, honesty and First Amendment values do not inherently conflict each time a reporter pursues a story. Conflicts are most likely to arise with stories of great significance. A few stories must be told, even if it takes lies and deception to do so. Nonetheless, once an ethical line is crossed, where is it to be drawn the next time and by whom? Moreover, what happens to a profession that tolerates and even encourages manipulation and lies in the name of truth seeking? In the long run, will manipulation and lies only encourage manipulation and lies in return?

Journalists rarely will feel compelled to hide, misrepresent or lie about their conclusions during an interview if they genuinely delay the mental process of "concluding"—which is what they should do—until it is time to write the story. Reporters who approach people with an open mind can expect to improve possibilities of openness from others.

Quoting Sources

With the McGinniss-MacDonald questions still reverberating within the journalism community, Malcolm ignited another debate within the profession. It stemmed from a libel suit brought against

Malcolm by psychoanalyst Jeffrey Masson, central figure of another article she wrote for *New Yorker* magazine and later published as a book, *In the Freud Archives*. Masson accused Malcolm of putting words in his mouth, particularly when she quoted Masson as describing himself as an "intellectual gigolo." But the U.S. Circuit Court of Appeals in California dismissed Masson's libel suit. In a 2-to-1 vote, the judges said even fabricated quotations were permissible as long as they were either a "rational interpretation of ambiguous" comments or did not "alter the substantive content" of the speaker's words.[50] The serious issues at stake brought the case to the U.S. Supreme Court in 1990.[51]

The Malcolm-Masson dispute opened a second messy drawer: Is it right for journalists to alter or invent direct quotations? Malcolm, in a defense that is almost convincing, argues that journalists not only are correct to modify direct quotations, it is their duty to do so: "When a journalist undertakes to quote a subject he has interviewed on tape, he owes it to the subject, no less than to the reader, to translate his speech into prose. Only the most uncharitable (or inept) journalists will hold a subject to his literal utterances and fail to perform the sort of editing and rewriting that, in life, our ear automatically and instantaneously performs."[52]

Once again, Malcolm brought a set of longstanding assumptions into question, leaving reporters even more unsure of what is right and wrong conduct in the use of direct quotes. Most news sources and journalists would say that direct quotations are "untouchables." Veteran AP editor Rene Cappon speaks for the majority of the profession when he says, "Once words are enclosed by quotation marks, they must be what the source said. Attempts to 'improve' that by reshuffling or even changing words are high crimes and misdemeanors. The furthest you can go is to fix minor grammatical errors and omit pure padding or meaningless repetition."[53]

The Masson-Malcolm libel suit challenges that rule. The appellate court hearing Malcolm's case ruled that tampering with direct quotations did not constitute actual malice unless the reporter altered the substance of the speaker's remarks. Few journalists celebrated the *Masson* case as a First Amendment victory, but, in the context of *New York Times v. Sullivan*, the ruling appears legally correct and sensible. Holding journalists liable for the strict accuracy of direct quotations would chill coverage. Although strict accuracy should always be the goal, in practice, reporters often fail to quote news subjects verbatim. That is especially true of reporters who rely on handwritten notes instead of tape recorders. Reporters will make human mistakes as they gather and report the words of others, but relaxing standards of factuality, even if the courts give journalists additional breathing space, is dangerous.

As any examination of press law and ethics shows, the public's apparent predisposition against Big Journalism is reason enough for reporters to take every precaution in news coverage. Above all, however, common decency requires journalists to treat others as they themselves would want to be treated. Sometimes the profession is its own worst enemy, becoming excessively defensive when attacked for its behavior. At times, journalists must suppress the urge to be self-righteous, admit they have erred and say, "We're sorry." That may be all a victim of media malpractice requires to feel vindicated. Certainly, such a demonstration of humility would go far to restore goodwill between the press and the public.

EXERCISES

1. Check with a managing editor or news director to learn the company policy on use of confidential sources. In particular, find out how far the news organization will go to legally support a reporter who has been ordered to reveal a confidential source. Remember that court appeals are expensive.

2. Some public university officials have cited a federal law known as the Buckley Amendment, which ensures the privacy of student records, to deny reporters access to campus police reports. Find out the policy at your university or another public school nearby and discuss the policy with university officials.

3. Receive four issues of the *News Media & the Law* by making a $20 contribution to the Reporters Committee for Freedom of the Press (Room 300, 800 18th St. NW, Washington, D.C. 20006). The magazine provides an overview of recent media law issues and court decisions. Your donation supports both the magazine and the organization's 24-hour advice hotline for legal emergencies.

NOTES

[1] See Thomas B. Littlewood, *Coals of Fire: The* Alton Telegraph *Libel Case* (Carbondale, Ill.: Southern Illinois University Press, 1988).

[2] John Curley, "How Libel Suit Sapped the Crusading Spirit of a Small Newspaper," *Wall Street Journal,* Sept. 29, 1983, p. 1.

[3] Littlewood, *Coals of Fire,* p. 190.

[4] *New York Times v. Sullivan*, 376 U.S. 254 (1964).

[5] "Libel Settlement a Record $34 Million," *St. Petersburg Times*, May 4, 1990, p. 11A.

[6] See Rodney A. Smolla, *Suing the Press* (New York: Oxford Press, 1986).

[7] "Michigan Daily Appeals $1 Million Libel Verdict," *Editor & Publisher*, Aug. 26, 1989, p. 26.

[8] Steve Wilson, "How I Spent My Summer Vacation," *ASNE Bulletin*, Nov. 1983, p. 36.

[9] "Few Libel Damage Awards Are Sustained on Appeal," *Editor & Publisher*, Sept. 4, 1982, p. 16.

[10] *Philadelphia Newspapers, Inc. v. Hepps*, 475 U.S. 767 (1986).

[11] *Rosenblatt v. Baer*, 383 U.S. 75 (1966).

[12] *Gertz v. Robert Welch, Inc.*, 418 U.S. 323 (1974).

[13] *Time, Inc. v. Firestone*, 424 U.S. 448 (1976).

[14] *Wolston v. Reader's Digest Association*, 443 U.S. 157 (1979).

[15] *Garrison v. State of Louisiana*, 379 U.S. 64 (1964).

[16] *St. Amant v. Thompson*, 390 U.S. 727 (1968).

[17] *Curtis Publishing Co. v. Butts*, 388 U.S. 130 (1967).

[18] *St. Amant v. Thompson*, 390 U.S. 727 (1968).

[19] *Harte-Hanks Communication, Inc. v. Connaughton*, 491 U.S. 657 (1989).

[20] *Herbert v. Lando*, 441 U.S. 153 (1979).

[21] *Gertz v. Robert Welch, Inc.*, 418 U.S. 323 (1974).

[22] *General Products v. Meredith*, 526 F. Supp. 546 (D.C. Va. 1981).

[23] *Edwards v. National Audubon Society*, 556 F.2d 113 (2d Cir. 1977).

[24] "Dallas Times Herald Loses $200,000 Suit," *Editor & Publisher*, Oct. 16, 1982, p. 57.

[25] *Time, Inc. v. Hill*, 385 U.S. 374 (1967).

[26] *Florida Star v. B.J.F.*, 491 U.S. 524 (1989).

[27] *Dietemann v. Time, Inc.*, 284 F. Supp. 925 (C.D. Calif. 1968), 449 F.2d 245 (9th Cir. 1971).

[28] "Widow of Man with 2 Wives Sues," *St. Louis Globe-Democrat*, Dec. 23, 1976, p. 10.

[29] *Galella v. Onassis*, 487 F.2d 986 (2d Cir. 1973).

[30] *Green Valley School v. Cowles Florida Broadcasting*, 327 So. 2d 810 (Fla. App. 1976).

[31] *Virgil v. Time, Inc.*, 527 F.2d 1122 (9th Cir. 1975).

[32] *Cox Broadcasting Corp. v. Cohn*, 420 U.S. 469 (1975).

[33] "Should We Reveal Her Name?," *Newsweek*, April 2, 1990, p. 48.

[34] Deni Elliot, "Identifying AIDS Victims," *Washington Journalism Review*, Oct. 1988, pp. 26–29.

[35] *Cefalu v. Globe Newspaper Co.*, 391 N.E. 2d 935 (Mass. App. 1979).

[36] *Norris v. King*, 355 So. 2d 21 (1978).

[37] See Clark Norton, "Threats to Privacy: Is There No Confidentiality?," *Current*, Jan. 1990, pp. 14–18.

[38] Quoted in Barbara Dill, *The Journalist's Handbook on Libel and Privacy* (New York: Free Press, 1986), pp. 76, 77.

[39] James J. Kilpatrick. " 'Trust-Me' Journalism," *Washington Journalism Review*, Jan.–Feb. 1988, p. 45.

[40] *Branzburg v. Hayes*, 409 U.S. 665 (1972).

[41] Dan Oberdorfer, "Cohen Awarded $700,000 in Newspaper Suit," *Minneapolis Star Tribune*, July 23, 1988, p. 1A.

[42] Linda Greenhouse, "Justices to Hear a Case on Newspapers' Ethics," *New York Times*, Dec. 11, 1990, p. A14.

[43] William Boot, "The Gossip Mill," *Ethics: Easier Said Than Done*, Jan. 1989, p. 52.

[44] "Trial by the Ethics Squad," *Newsweek*, Dec. 26, 1988, p. 25.

[45] See Janet Malcolm, *The Journalist and the Murderer* (New York: Knopf, 1990).

[46] Janet Malcolm, "The Journalist and the Murderer: I—the Journalist," *New Yorker*, March 13, 1989, p. 38.

[47] Janet Malcolm, "The Morality of Journalism," *New York Review of Books*, March 1, 1990, p. 20.

[48] Malcolm, "The Journalist and the Murderer: I—the Journalist," p. 39.

[49] Martin Garbus, "McGinniss: A Travesty of Libel," *Publishers Weekly*, April 21, 1989, p. 69.

[50] M.L. Stein, "9th Circuit: It's OK to Make Up Quotes," *Editor & Publisher*, Aug. 12, 1989, p. 16.

[51] Linda Greenhouse, "High Court to Rule on Libel Suit over Quotations," *New York Times*, Oct. 2, 1990, p. A1.

[52] Malcolm, "The Morality of Journalism," p. 20.

[53] Rene J. Cappon, *The Word: An Associated Press Guide to Good News Writing* (New York: Associated Press, 1982), p. 71.

Selected Readings

Chapter 1

Russell Baker, *The Good Times* (New York: Arbor House, 1989).

Herbert Gans, *Deciding What's News* (New York: Vintage, 1980).

Robert Karl Manoff and Michael Schudson, eds., *Reading the News* (New York: Pantheon, 1987).

John Naisbitt and Patricia Aburdene, *Megatrends 2000* (New York: Morrow, 1989).

Deborah Tannen, *You Just Don't Understand* (New York: Morrow, 1990).

Chapter 2

David Broder, *Behind the Front Page: A Candid Look at How the News Is Made* (New York: Simon & Schuster, 1987).

David P. Demers and Suzanne Nichols, *Precision Journalism: A Practical Guide* (Newbury Park, Calif.: Sage, 1987).

Lauren Kessler and Duncan McDonald, *Uncovering the News: A Journalist's Search for Information* (Belmont, Calif.: Wadsworth, 1987).

George M. Killenberg and Rob Anderson, *Before the Story: Interviewing and Communication Skills for Journalists* (New York: St. Martin's, 1989).

John Ullmann and Jan Colbert, eds., *The Reporter's Handbook: An Investigator's Guide to Documents and Techniques* (New York: St. Martin's, 1991).

Chapter 3

Gary Atkins and William Rivers, *Reporting with Understanding* (Ames, Iowa: Iowa State University Press, 1987).

Daniel Boorstin, *The Image: A Guide to Pseudo-Events in America* (New York: Atheneum, 1971).

Victor Cohn, *News & Numbers* (Ames, Iowa: Iowa State University Press, 1989).

Herbert Strentz, *News Reporters and News Sources: Accomplices in Shaping and Mis-Shaping the News* (Ames, Iowa: Iowa State University Press, 1989).

Jim Willis, *The Shadow World: Life Between the News Media and Reality* (New York, Praeger, 1991).

Chapter 4

Elie Abel, *Leaking: Who Does It? Who Benefits? At What Cost?* (New York: Priority Press, 1987).

James R. Bennett, *Control of Information in the United States: An Annotated Bibliography* (Westport, Conn.: Meckler Corp., 1987).

Richard O. Curry, ed., *Freedom at Risk: Secrecy, Censorship and Repression in the 1980s* (Philadelphia: Temple University Press, 1988).

Donna A. Demac, *Liberty Denied: The Current Rise of Censorship in America* (New Brunswick, N.J.: Rutgers University Press, 1990).

Government-in-the-Sunshine Manual (Tallahassee, Fla.: First Amendment Foundation, 1990).

Chapter 5

John C. Bollens, *The Metropolis,* 4th ed. (New York: Harper & Row, 1982).

Timothy E. Cook, *Making Laws and Making News* (Washington, D.C.: Brookings Institute, 1989).

Barbara Ferman, *Governing the Ungovernable City* (Philadelphia: Temple University Press, 1985).

Edward I. Koch, *All the Best: Letters from a Feisty Mayor* (New York: Simon & Schuster, 1990).

Paul E. Peterson, *City Limits* (Chicago: University of Chicago Press, 1981).

Chapter 6

Mark Baker, *Cops: Their Lives in Their Own Words* (New York: Simon & Schuster, 1985).

Edna Buchanan, *The Corpse Had a Familiar Face* (New York: Random House, 1987).

Andrew Karmen, *Crime Victims: An Introduction to Victimology* (Pacific Grove, Calif.: Brooks/Cole, 1984).

Patricia A. Kelly, *Police and the Media: Bridging Troubled Waters* (Springfield, Ill.: Charles C. Thomas, 1987).

Samuel Walker, *Sense and Nonsense about Crime,* 2d ed. (Pacific Grove, Calif.: Brooks/Cole, 1989).

Chapter 7

Robert E. Drechsel, *News Making in the Trial Courts* (New York: Longman, 1983).

Ellis Rubin and Dary Matera, *"Get Me Ellis Rubin!" The Life, Times and Cases of a Maverick Lawyer* (New York: St. Martin's, 1990).

Robert Satter, *Doing Justice: A Trial Judge at Work* (New York: Simon & Schuster, 1990).

Paul B. Wice, *Chaos in the Courthouse* (New York: Praeger, 1985).

Bruce Wright, *Black Robes, White Justice* (Secaucus, N.J.: Lyle Stuart, 1987).

Chapter 8

Renata Adler, *Reckless Disregard: Westmoreland v. CBS et al., Sharon v. Time* (New York: Knopf, 1986).

Alan M. Dershowitz, *Reversal of Fortune: Inside the Von Bulow Case* (New York: Random House, 1986).

William H. Rehnquist, *The Supreme Court: How It Was, How It Is* (New York: Morrow, 1987).

Sol Stein, *A Feast for Lawyers, Inside Chapter 11: An Expose* (New York: Evans, 1989).

Bob Woodward and Scott Armstrong, *The Brethren: Inside the Supreme Court* (New York: Simon & Schuster, 1979).

Chapter 9

Donald W. Blohowiak, *No Comment! An Executive's Essential Guide to the News Media* (New York: Praeger, 1987).

Bryan Burrough and John Helyar, *Barbarians at the Gate* (New York: HarperCollins, 1989).

Timothy Crouse, *The Boys on the Bus* (New York: Random House, 1973).

Tracy Kidder, *Among Schoolchildren* (Boston: Houghton Mifflin, 1989).

Nicholas Lemann, *The Promised Land* (New York: Knopf, 1991).

Chapter 10

Richard M. Clurman, *Beyond Malice: The Media's Years of Reckoning* (New York: Meridian, 1990).

Lois G. Forer, *A Chilling Effect* (New York: Norton, 1987).

Tom Goldstein, *The News at Any Cost* (New York: Simon & Schuster, 1985).

Thomas B. Littlewood, *Coals of Fire: The Alton Telegraph Libel Case* (Carbondale, Ill.: Southern Illinois University Press, 1988).

Rodney A. Smolla, *Suing the Press* (New York: Oxford University Press, 1986).

Index